EVOLVE

STUDENT'S BOOK

Leslie Anne Hendra, Mark Ibbotson,
and Kathryn O'Dell

5

CAMBRIDGE
UNIVERSITY PRESS

CAMBRIDGE
UNIVERSITY PRESS

University Printing House, Cambridge CB2 8BS, United Kingdom

One Liberty Plaza, 20th Floor, New York, NY 10006, USA

477 Williamstown Road, Port Melbourne, VIC 3207, Australia

314–321, 3rd Floor, Plot 3, Splendor Forum, Jasola District Centre, New Delhi – 110025, India

79 Anson Road, #06–04/06, Singapore 079906

Cambridge University Press is part of the University of Cambridge.

It furthers the University's mission by disseminating knowledge in the pursuit of education, learning and research at the highest international levels of excellence.

www.cambridge.org
Information on this title: www.cambridge.org/9781108414500

First published 2020

20 19 18 17 16 15 14 13 12 11 10 9 8 7 6 5 4 3 2 1

Printed in the United Kingdom by Latimer Trend

A catalogue record for this publication is available from the British Library

ISBN 978-1-108-40533-1 Student's Book
ISBN 978-1-108-40511-9 Student's Book A
ISBN 978-1-108-40926-1 Student's Book B
ISBN 978-1-108-40534-8 Student's Book with Practice Extra
ISBN 978-1-108-40513-3 Student's Book with Practice Extra A
ISBN 978-1-108-40927-8 Student's Book with Practice Extra B
ISBN 978-1-108-40907-0 Workbook with Audio
ISBN 978-1-108-40881-3 Workbook with Audio A
ISBN 978-1-108-41195-0 Workbook with Audio B
ISBN 978-1-108-40519-5 Teacher's Edition with Test Generator
ISBN 978-1-108-41074-8 Presentation Plus
ISBN 978-1-108-41205-6 Class Audio CDs
ISBN 978-1-108-40800-4 Video Resource Book with DVD
ISBN 978-1-108-41450-0 Full Contact with DVD
ISBN 978-1-108-41156-1 Full Contact with DVD A
ISBN 978-1-108-41421-0 Full Contact with DVD B

Additional resources for this publication at www.cambridge.org/evolve

ACKNOWLEDGMENTS

The *Evolve* publishers would like to thank the following individuals and institutions who have contributed their time and insights into the development of the course:

Asli Derin Anaç, **Istanbul Bilgi University**, Turkey; Claudia Piccoli Díaz, **Harmon Hall**, Mexico; Daniel Martin, **CELLEP**, Brazil; Daniel Nowatnick, USA; Devon Derksen, **Myongji University**, South Korea; Diego Ribeiro Santos, **Universidade Anhembri Morumbi**, São Paulo, Brazil; Esther Carolina Euceda Garcia, **UNITEC (Universidad Tecnologica Centroamericana)**, Honduras; Gloria González Meza, **Instituto Politecnico Nacional, ESCA (University)**, Mexico; Heidi Vande Voort Nam, **Chongshin University**, South Korea; Isabela Villas Boas, **Casa Thomas Jefferson**, Brasilia, Brazil; Ivanova Monteros, **Universidad Tecnológica Equinoccial**, Ecuador; Lenise Butler, **Laureate Languages**, Mexico; Luz Libia Rey G, **Centro Colombo Americano Bogotá**, Colombia; Maria Araceli Hernández Tovar, **Instituto Tecnológico Superior de San Luis Potosí**, Capital, Mexico; Monica Frenzel, **Universidad Andres Bello**, Chile; Ray Purdey, **ELS Educational Services**, USA; Roberta Freitas, **IBEU**, Rio de Janeiro, Brazil; Rosario Aste Rentería, **Instituto De Emprendedores USIL**, Peru; Verónica Nolivos Arellano, **Centro Ecuatoriano Norteamericano**, Quito, Equador.

To our speaking competition winners, who have contributed their ideas:

Alejandra Manriquez Chavez, Mexico; Bianca Kinoshita Arai Kurtz, Brazil; Gabriel Santos Hernández, Mexico; Gerardo Torres, Mexico; Giulia Gamba, Brazil; Hector Enrique Cruz Mejia, Honduras; Jorge, Honduras; Ruben, Honduras; Stephany Ramírez Ortiz, Mexico; Veronica, Ecuador.

To our expert speakers, who have contributed their time:

Bojan Andric, Carolina Hakopian, Jacqueline Castañeda Nuñez, Lucia D'Anna, Odil Odilov, Wendy Sanchez-Vaynshteyn.

And special thanks to Wayne Rimmer for writing the Pronunciation sections, and to Laura Patsko for her expert input.

Authors' Acknowledgments
The authors would like to extend their warmest thanks to the team at Cambridge University Press. They'd particularly like to thank Gillian Lowe and Nino Chelidze for their kind, thorough, and encouraging support.

Leslie Anne Hendra would like to thank Michael Stuart Clark, as always.

Mark Ibbotson would like to thank Nathalie, Aimy, and Tom.

Kathryn O'Dell would like to thank Kevin Hurdman for his support throughout the project and for his contribution to this level.

The authors and publishers acknowledge the following sources of copyright material and are grateful for the permissions granted. While every effort has been made, it has not always been possible to identify the sources of all the material used, or to trace all copyright holders. If any omissions are brought to our notice, we will be happy to include the appropriate acknowledgements on reprinting and in the next update to the digital edition, as applicable.

Key: REV = Review, U = Unit.

Text

U1: Text from 'The Maker Movement Taking Over America. Here's How.' by Zara Stone, 11.12.2015. Copyright © Zara Stone. Reproduced with permission; U3: Adapted text from 'Quiet Revolution'. Copyright © Susan Cain. Reproduced with permission; U5: Wareable Ltd. for the adapted text from 'I tried VR therapy to cure my fear of flying' by Luke Johnson. Copyright © Wareable Ltd. Reproduced with kind permission; U6: The Moth for the text from 'Storytelling Tips & Tricks'. Copyright © The Moth. Reproduced with kind permission; MailOnline for the adapted text from 'Man trades up from a paperclip to a house', *MailOnline*, 11.07.2006. Copyright © MailOnline. Reproduced with permission; U7: Interview text of 'Sofian and Nathalie'. Copyright © Nathalie Grandjean and Sofian Rahmani. Reproduced with kind permission of Mark Ibbotson; TalentSmart Inc. for the text from 'Why You Should Spend Your Money on Experiences, Not Things' by Travis Bradberry, Ph.D. Copyright © TalentSmart and Dr. Travis Bradberry. Reproduced with kind permission; U8: The Guardian for the adapted text from 'How to complain effectively' by Anna Tims, *The Guardian*, 18.02.2010. Copyright Guardian News & Media Ltd 2018. Reproduced with permission; U9: The Art of Manliness for the text from 'How to Make Small Talk with Strangers: My 21-Day Happiness Experiment' by John Corcoran, https://smartbusinessrevolution.com/. Copyright © Art of Manliness. Reproduced with kind permission;

U10: Telegraph Media Group Limited and Michal Ben-Josef Hirsch for text 'Can you find your doppelganger in a day?' by Maxine Frith. Copyright © Telegraph Media Group Limited 2015 and Michal Ben-Josef Hirsch. Reprinted by permission of Telegraph Media Group Limited and Michal Ben-Josef Hirsch. All rights reserved; Monster Worldwide for the text from '8 ways to make your social media profile an employer magnet' by Mack Gelber. Copyright 2018 - Monster Worldwide, Inc. All Rights Reserved. U11: SiteSell Inc. for the text from 'Fake Reviews: Spot 'em and Stop 'em!' by Ken Envoy. Copyright © Ken Evoy, Founder & CEO of SiteSell. Reproduced with kind permission; U12: Interview text of 'Kevin Hurdman'. Copyright © Kathryn O'Dell with Kevin Hurdman. Reproduced with kind permission.

Photography
The following photographs are sourced from Getty Images.

U1–U12: Tom Merton/Caiaimage; U1: Alex Trautwig/Major League Baseball; xavierarnau/E+; Mathisa_s/iStock/Getty Images Plus; MajchrzakMorel/DigitalVision; Spin12/iStock/Getty Images Plus; Steven Puetzer/Corbis/Getty Images Plus; RyanJLane/E+; stocksnapper/iStock/Getty Images Plus; Halfdark; Morsa Images/ DigitalVision; Emma Farrer/Moment; TommL/E+; Hero Images; Pacific Press/ LightRocket; JGI/Jamie Grill; alexsl/E+; Pekic/E+; Halfdark; kozak_kadr/iStock/Getty Images Plus; Images Of Our Lives/Archive Photos/Getty Images Plus; TonyBaggett/ iStock/Getty Images Plus; SuperStock/Getty Images Plus; Michelle Bennett/ Lonely Planet Images/Getty Images Plus; RyanJLane/E+; George Marks/Retrofile RF; U2: Tunatura/iStock/Getty Images Plus; frentusha/iStock/Getty Images Plus; Science Photo Library - NASA/ESA/STSCI/J.HESTER & A.LOLL, ASU/Brand X Pictures; Rodolfo Parulan Jr/Moment; Martín Damian Monterisi/iStock/Getty Images Plus; Jonathan Therrien/500px Prime; robas/iStock/Getty Images Plus; PeopleImages/ E+; damircudic/E+; Emilija Manevska/Moment; AFP/Stringer; Wolfgang Kaehler/ LightRocket; Wildroze/E+; THEPALMER/iStock/Getty Images Plus; tdub_video/E+; swissmediavision/E+; U3: andresr/E+; Roger Hunt/500px; Lisa Barber/Photolibrary/ Getty Images Plus; sergoua/iStock/Getty Images Plus; Ekaterina Gorskikh/EyeEm; Franziska Uhlmann/EyeEm; Svetlana Zhukova/Moment; Sisoje/E+; Noah Clayton; Tara Moore/Taxi/Getty Images Plus; Ronnie Kaufman/DigitalVision; Martin Beck/ arabianEye; Anthony Charles/Cultura; Jon Feingersh Photography Inc/DigitalVision; Jose Luis Pelaez Inc/DigitalVision; Francesco Carta fotografo/Moment; Seth Joel/ The Image Bank/Getty Images Plus; Blair_witch/iStock/Getty Images Plus; Reinhardt Dallgass/EyeEm; kali9/E+; Patrick Frischknecht/robertharding/Getty Images Plus; H. Armstrong Roberts/ClassicStock/Archive Photos/Getty Images Plus; FG Trade/ E+; Cris Cantón Photography/Moment; Ippei Naoi/Moment; Mawardi Bahar/ EyeEm; Emmanuel Nalli/iStock/Getty Images Plus; Putra Kurniawan/EyeEm; Angela Bax/EyeEm; ajr_images/iStock/Getty Images Plus; Delmaine Donson/E+; REV1: fotoVoyager/iStock Unreleased; U4: Graiki/Moment Unreleased; GeorgePeters/ E+; Pete Saloutos/Image Source; Klaus Vedfelt/DigitalVision; Vesnaandjic/E+; Emilija Manevska/Moment; PeopleImages/E+; Sean Gladwell/Moment; Hinterhaus Productions/DigitalVision; South_agency/E+; Michel Dória/Moment; Caiaimage/Chris Ryan; U5: Visual China Group; Ariel Skelley/DigitalVision; real444/E+; Luis Alvarez/ DigitalVision; Asia-Pacific Images Studio/E+; FREDERIC J. BROWN/AFP; SOPA Images/ LightRocket; Brent Olson/Moment; John Lamb/The Image Bank/Getty Images Plus; pbombaert/Moment; 10'000 Hours/DigitalVision; SolStock/E+; Django/E+; Hero Images; U6: SAFIN HAMED/AFP; Michel PONOMAREFF/PONOPRESSE/Gamma-Rapho; Idaho Statesman/Tribune News Service; Bryn Hughes Photography/DigitalVision; 5m3photos/Moment; Caiaimage/Chris Ryan/OJO+; Daniele Carotenuto Photography/ Moment; kozmoat98/iStock/Getty Images Plus; Chayapon Bootboonneam/EyeEm; by wildestanimal/Moment Open; ADRIAN DENNIS/AFP; Caiaimage/Sam Edwards; Butsaya/iStock/Getty Images Plus; WHL; ilbusca/E+; Hiroshi Watanabe/Stone/Getty Images Plus; Chris Tobin/DigitalVision; Simon Winnall/Stone/Getty Images Plus; Martin Barraud/The Image Bank/Getty Images Plus; REV2: selimaksan/E+; U7: Barcroft Media; Flying Colours Ltd/DigitalVision; Ariel Skelley/Photodisc; Nancy Honey/Cultura; Sophie Powell/EyeEm; wanderluster/iStock/Getty Images Plus; kolderal/Moment; Bread and Butter/DigitalVision; Erik Isakson; Franz Pritz/Picture Press/Getty Images Plus; Elizabeth Beard/Moment; maurizio siani/Moment; maurizio siani/Moment; Barry Winiker/Stockbyte; U8: 10'000 Hours/DigitalVision; momentimages; Louis Turner; Alexander Walter/DigitalVision; Abraham/Moment; Mikael Dubois/Publisher Mix; Igor Golovniov/EyeEm; aluxum/iStock/Getty Images Plus; PhotoAlto/Frederic Cirou; 3alexd/iStock/Getty Images Plus; TokioMarineLife/iStock/Getty Images Plus; PhonlamaiPhoto/iStock/Getty Images Plus; RapidEye/E+; Suparat Malipoom/EyeEm; frema/iStock/Getty Images Plus; monkeybusinessimages/iStock/Getty Images Plus; U9: Boston Globe; Andrew Brookes/Cultura; 10'000 Hours/DigitalVision; Rubberball/ Mike Kemp; Michael Blann/DigitalVision; Dan Dalton/Caiaimage; GoodLifeStudio/ DigitalVision Vectors; Fentino/E+; The AGE/Fairfax Media; miodrag ignjatovic/E+; fstop123/E+; REV3: Sky Noir Photography by Bill Dickinson/Moment; U10: Trevor Williams/DigitalVision; Juanmonino/E+; Fuse/Corbis; Ken Reid/The Image Bank/Getty Images Plus; xavierarnau/E+; maxicake/iStock/Getty Images Plus; Junior Gonzalez; YinYang/E+; kupicoo/E+; Jose Luis Pelaez/Photodisc; Maskot; sturti/E+; twomeows/ Moment; U11:

VCG/Visual China Group; TANG CHHIN SOTHY/AFP; PHILIPPE LOPEZ/AFP; anilakkus/ iStock/Getty Images Plus; Donald Bowers/Stringer/Getty Images Entertainment; NASA/Handout/Getty Images News; SeppFriedhuber/E+; JohnnyGreig/E+; Stephen Marks/The Image Bank/Getty Images Plus; cglade/iStock/Getty Images Plus; KatarzynaBialasiewicz/iStock/Getty Images Plus; Nataba/iStock/Getty Images Plus; AndreyPopov/iStock/Getty Images Plus; U12: ANDY BUCHANAN/AFP; Devon Strong/ The Image Bank/Getty Images Plus; Roberto Ricciuti/GettyImages Entertainment; FabianCode/DigitalVision Vectors; mrPliskin/iStock/Getty Images Plus; sal73it/iStock/ Getty Images Plus; Tetra Images; Carlos Alvarez/Stringer/Getty Images Entertainment; DenKuvaiev/iStock/Getty Images Plus; Nick Dolding/DigitalVision; Westend61; Indeed; Flashpop/DigitalVision; trinetuzun/iStock/Getty Images Plus; REV4: Stephan Zirwes; gawrav/E+.

The following photographs are source from other libraries/sources.

U1: Copyright © Hailey Dawson. Reproduced with kind permission of Yong Dawson; U6: Dinodia Photos/Alamy Stock Photo; Copyright © Kyle MacDonald. Reproduced with kind permission; U10: Copyright © Telegraph Media Group Limited 2015; U12: Copyright © JD Dworkow.

Front cover photography by Bernhard Lang/Stone/Getty Images Plus/Getty Images.

Illustrations
U1, U3: Alessandra Ceriani (Sylvie Poggio Artists Agency); U4: Denis Cristo (Sylvie Poggio Artists Agency); U9: Ana Djordjevic (Astound US); U12: Lyn Dylan (Sylvie Poggio Artists Agency).

Audio production by CityVox, New York.

EVOLVE

SPEAKING MATTERS

EVOLVE is a six-level American English course for adults and young adults, taking students from beginner to advanced levels (CEFR A1 to C1).

Drawing on insights from language teaching experts and real students, EVOLVE is a general English course that gets students speaking with confidence.

This student-centered course covers all skills and focuses on the most effective and efficient ways to make progress in English.

Confidence in teaching.
Joy in learning.

Better Learning WITH EVOLVE

Better Learning is our simple approach where insights we've gained from research have helped shape content that drives results. Language evolves, and so does the way we learn. This course takes a flexible, student-centered approach to English language teaching.

EVOLVE

STUDENT'S BOOK

Leslie Anne Hendra, Mark Ibbotson, and Kathryn O'Dell

5

Experience Better Learning

Meet our expert speakers

Our expert speakers are highly proficient non-native speakers of English living and working in the New York City area.

Videos and ideas from our expert speakers feature throughout the Student's Book for you to respond and react to.

Scan the QR codes below to listen to their stories.

Wendy Sanchez-Vaynshteyn
from Bolivia
Data scientist

Bojan Andric
from Serbia
Interpreter

Carolina Hakopian
from Brazil
Dentist

Jacqueline Castañeda Nuñez
from Mexico
Urbanist

Lucia D'Anna
from Italy
Lead Promotion Specialist

Odil Odilov
from Tajikistan
Finance Assistant

INSIGHT
Research shows that achievable speaking role models can be a powerful motivator.

CONTENT
Bite-sized videos feature expert speakers talking about topics in the Student's Book.

RESULT
Students are motivated to speak and share their ideas.

Student-generated content

EVOLVE is the first course of its kind to feature real student-generated content. We spoke to over 2,000 students from all over the world about the topics they would like to discuss in English and in what situations they would like to be able to speak more confidently. Their ideas are included throughout the Student's Book.

"It's important to provide learners with interesting or stimulating topics."

Teacher, Mexico (Global Teacher Survey, 2017)

8.3 THE LITTLE TOUCHES

LESSON OBJECTIVE
- suggest and show interest in ideas

1 LISTENING

A ◀)) 2.13 **PAIR WORK** Look at the pictures. What kind of event do you think the items in picture A would be good for? What can you see in picture B? Are you sure? Then listen to a podcast about event planning and check your answers.

B ◀)) 2.13 **RECOGNIZE EMPHASIS** Listen again. The speakers emphasize the following words. Does the emphasis for each word (a) show a contrasting idea or (b) mean *very*?

1 and small ___
2 awesome ___
3 complex ___
4 the birthday girl ___
5 such ___
6 really ___

C ◀)) 2.13 **PAIR WORK** **THINK CRITICALLY** Listen again. What ideas do the speakers have for "little touches"? Do you like the ideas? What kind of things, do you think, make events special and memorable? What kind of things are not worth the trouble? Why?

2 PRONUNCIATION: Listening for emphasis

A ◀)) 2.14 Listen to the emphasis on the underlined words.
Plan all types of events – big and small   That's an awesome idea.   Or it can be a complex theme like travel.

B ◀)) 2.15 Listen and underline the words that are emphasized.
1 Well, the birthday girl loved it, but not everyone likes strawberries.
2 That's such a terrific idea.
3 And it really is the little things they remember.

C Circle the correct options to complete the sentences.
When we want to show emphasis, we put the main stress on the word we want to emphasize. We usually do this by using a *higher / lower* pitch on this word. The main stress *can / cannot* include functional words like determiners.

80

3 SPEAKING SKILLS

A ◀)) 2.13 Complete the expressions from the conversation in exercise 1B on page 80. Then decide if they are used to suggest an idea or to show interest in an idea. Write *S* (suggest) or *Sh* (show). Listen to the podcast again to check.

Suggest and show interest in ideas

1 One/Another ___ you/we can do is … ___
2 That's ___ a terrific / an awesome idea. ___
3 What a ___ idea! ___
4 … always goes ___ well. ___
5 I ___ everyone loved / will love that! ___
6 It never ___ to … ___
7 That's always ___ considering. ___
8 … is a good ___ to approach it. ___

B **PAIR WORK** You're planning a small summer party for your classmates. Complete the conversation with your own ideas. Then compare with another pair. Which of their ideas would you like to use?
A Do you have any ideas for the party?
B Well, I think ¹___ is a good way to approach it. Actually, ²___ always goes over well.
A That's ³___ idea. Also, it never hurts to ⁴___ .
B True, and another thing we can do is ⁵___ .
A Yeah, that's always worth considering. And how about ⁶___ ?

4 PRONUNCIATION: Saying words that show a contrast

A ◀)) 2.16 Listen to the recording. Can you hear the pitch change on one key word in each sentence? Underline these words.
1 I bet everyone loved that!
2 Well, most people did.
3 Her birthday's not in March, it's in April.

B ◀)) 2.17 Underline the words that show a contrast. Listen and check your work. Then repeat the sentences.
1 It wasn't her birthday, it was his.
2 I don't have any ideas, but Diego does.
3 Shall we get a present or give her some money?
4 He didn't just like it, he loved it!

C **PAIR WORK** One student says a sentence. The other replies with a contrast.
1 Let's drive to the party.   No, we'll walk.
2 We'll celebrate at home.
3 Tom will be late.
4 Wasn't she wearing the red dress?
5 The party finishes at ten.

5 SPEAKING

A **GROUP WORK** You are planning an event together. Choose an idea in the box. Talk about the theme, music, decorations, and food you'll have. Include little touches to make the event special. You can check online for ideas.

a birthday party for a child   a company dinner
a family reunion   a graduation party

B Describe your plan to the class. Which is the most entertaining?

OK, let's plan a company dinner. I think choosing an interesting theme is a good way to approach it.

OK, well, a beach theme always goes over well. One thing we can do is give everyone sunglasses to wear.

81

Find it

FIND IT

INSIGHT
Research with hundreds of teachers and students across the globe revealed a desire to expand the classroom and bring the real world in.

CONTENT
Find it are smartphone activities that allow students to bring live content into the class and personalize the learning experience with research and group activities.

RESULT
Students engage in the lesson because it is meaningful to them.

Designed for success

Pronunciation

INSIGHT
Research shows that only certain aspects of pronunciation actually affect comprehensibility and inhibit communication.

CONTENT
EVOLVE focuses on the aspects of pronunciation that most affect communication.

RESULT
Students understand more when listening and can be clearly understood when they speak.

8.1 ANNOYING LITTLE THINGS

LESSON OBJECTIVE
- talk about neatness and messiness

1 LANGUAGE IN CONTEXT

A **PAIR WORK** Think about the best thing about growing up in your family home. Tell your partner what your family does that you love and appreciate. What little things do they do that annoy you?

B 🔊 2.10 In an episode of a TV show called *You Should Talk!*, family members talk about living with each other. Read and listen. What annoying habits do Nicole and Paul have?

🔊 2.10 Audio script

Host So, Nicole and Paul, who's more **disorganized**?

Paul Definitely Nicole. Like, the other night, we were supposed to meet some friends at seven, and Nicole was going to drive us. We were about to leave the house, but she couldn't find her keys – as *usual*. We normally **hang them up** on the wall by the front door.

Nicole Yeah, Paul likes to **line up** all the keys from the biggest to the smallest. He also **puts his books in alphabetical order**, and his desk is always **organized** with all his office stuff …

Paul OK, OK, but we're talking about you right now. Her keys were bound to be in the house somewhere, so we were forced to go room by room looking for them. Eventually she found them. They **were tangled up** with some earphones in the pocket of some jeans. Unbelievable!

Nicole You should talk! At least my jeans were in the closet – unlike your shoes!

Host Wait. A minute ago, you were saying how Paul **arranges keys and books neatly**. And now I'm hearing he **leaves his shoes all over the place**?

Nicole Yes! I mean, they're not all **jumbled up**. They're sure to be neatly placed side by side on the floor, but they're everywhere!

Paul At least I don't **throw** my clothes **on** the floor, like some people I know. I **fold them** neatly and **put them in a pile** on the chair by my bed.

Nicole Yeah. Even when he doesn't **put things away**, he does it neatly!

C 🔊 2.10 **PAIR WORK** **THINK CRITICALLY** Read and listen again. Who would you find more annoying to live with? Why do you think people get annoyed over small, silly things? What compromises do we need to make when living with other people?

INSIDER ENGLISH
Say *You should talk* to mean "You are guilty of the same behavior you have just criticized."

2 VOCABULARY: Describing neatness and messiness

A 🔊 2.11 Look at the expressions in **bold** in the text. Which do we use to talk about things that are neat, messy, or both? Copy the chart and complete it. Then listen and check your work.

Neat	Me…

B ▶ Now go to page 147. Do the vocab…

C **PAIR WORK** What expressions from th… describe the person or people you live…

76

INSIDER ENGLISH
Say *You should talk* to mean "You are guilty of the same behavior you have just criticized."

Insider English

INSIGHT
Even in a short exchange, idiomatic language can inhibit understanding.

CONTENT
Insider English focuses on the informal language and colloquial expressions frequently found in everyday situations.

RESULT
Students are confident in the real world.

8.4 A SMILE GOES A LONG WAY

LESSON OBJECTIVE
■ write a complaint letter

1 READING

A Have you ever made a formal complaint? What was the problem? Was your complaint effective?

B **IDENTIFY WRITER'S PURPOSE** Read the article. What's its purpose? What specific examples of customer problems does the writer mention? Which are valid reasons for complaints?

Do you have a problem with a product, service, or company? It might be time to make a formal complaint. Anna Tims, a writer who focuses on consumer affairs, offers a list of tips for successful complaining. The secret is getting a lot of small things right.

HOW TO COMPLAIN EFFECTIVELY

Most large companies get hundreds of complaints – some silly and some serious. No matter how important your complaint is to you, it will just be added to a pile of complaints that a stressed-out customer service worker needs to read. So to be sure it makes the biggest impact, you must know how to state your complaint effectively. Follow these steps, and you're bound to get your problems solved.

☑ MAKE SURE YOUR COMPLAINT IS VALID
Your concern needs to be realistic. For example, if fees for ending a cell phone service contract early stop you from going to a cheaper cell phone service provider, that's too bad. You should have understood the contract. If, however, you have received poor service, you have the right to end your contract early. Or if you dropped your product and then stepped on it accidentally, it's your fault. But if a product breaks when you set it down gently, it's sure to be faulty.

☑ FIGURE OUT WHAT YOU WANT TO ACHIEVE
Do you want a refund, a replacement, or simply an apology? If you want a refund, you have to act quickly or you might lose your right to one. If you complain by phone, make a note of who you spoke to and when, and follow up the call with a letter restating your complaint and the response you got on the phone. Do the same if you sent the complaint through the company's website, so you have a record of it.

☑ ALWAYS ADDRESS A LETTER TO A SPECIFIC PERSON
It is best to start with the customer service manager. (If you aim too high – for example, the company president – you will be waiting while your letter is passed around until it reaches the right person.) Find out the manager's name and use their full title – Dr., Mrs., or Ms. A little thing like using someone's name can make a big impression.

☑ INCLUDE YOUR DETAILS
Remember to include your full name, address, and any order or reference numbers near the top of the letter. If a company can't easily find you in their system, they may not respond.

Adapted from an article by Anna Tims in The Guardian

☑ KEEP COPIES
Make copies of all relevant documents – such as receipts, bank statements, order forms, and advertisements – and include them to support your complaint. If you want a new but stained couch replaced, include a photo of the damage.

☑ CHECK YOUR SPELLING
Carelessly written letters suggest you are as sloppy as the company you are complaining about.

☑ BE POLITE AND REASONABLE
Whether you are writing or calling, stay calm. Anger will give companies an excuse to refuse to deal with you.

☑ NAME NAMES
If you mention the unhelpful attitude of, for example, a store manager or customer service representative, try to include their names.

☑ SET A DEADLINE
Give the company a deadline for sending a useful response – 14 days is fair. Make a note of the date so you can increase the pressure if it is missed.

☑ MAKE SURE YOUR COMPLAINT ARRIVES
Send all letters by certified mail or special delivery so the company can't deny receiving them. If you use email, ask the person to confirm once they get it.

GLOSSARY
consumer affairs (n) a system related to protecting people who buy products and services
faulty (adj) not perfectly made or does not work correctly
sloppy (adj) not being careful or making an effort

C Read the article again. Which points apply to (1) both a complaint letter and a phone call and (2) only a complaint letter?

D **PAIR WORK** **THINK CRITICALLY** Which three points in the article do you think would be the most effective? Why? Are there any points that won't have an effect? Why not?

82

2 WRITING

A Read Karen's letter to the customer service manager of Markus Appliances. What's the problem? Why is she not happy with the sales manager's response? What does she want?

To: Mr. Edwards
From: Karen Rebecca Mason
Subject: RE: Faulty SUPERWASH Washing Machine, model number RCM205

Dear Mr. Edwards,

I am writing to complain about the above washing machine, which I bought during your Summer Sale on July 15. I purchased it for $175.99 at the Main Street branch of Markus Appliances and include a copy of the receipt as proof of purchase.

After the machine was delivered, I tried to use it, but it wouldn't turn on. I checked the connection, which was fine, but the machine had no power. I immediately returned to the store and explained the problem to the sales manager, Rob Clark. At first, he suggested there was something wrong with the power in my house. When I insisted that the machine was faulty, he said, "Sorry, but you bought it during the half-price sale. We don't accept the return of sale items."

I find this unacceptable. First, the item is obviously faulty. Second, your company advertisement (copy included) states that you accept all returns without question. I believe that includes sale items. Third, I feel Mr. Clark should be friendlier. It's a small thing, but a smile goes a long way.

I would like your company to pick up the washing machine from my house and send me a refund of $175.99. I look forward to hearing from you within the next ten days.

Sincerely,

Karen Rebecca Mason

REGISTER CHECK

In formal written complaints, we often use expressions like *I find, I feel, I believe,* or *I think* to make statements less direct and more polite.

Direct
This is unacceptable.
Mr. Clark should be friendlier.

Less direct
I find this unacceptable.
I feel Mr. Clark should be friendlier.

B **PAIR WORK** **THINK CRITICALLY** Which of the tips in the article in exercise 1A on page 82 did Karen follow?

C **AVOID RUN-ON SENTENCES AND SENTENCE FRAGMENTS** Read about two kinds of sentences to avoid in more formal writing. Look at the examples below. How could the sentences be improved? Then find good versions of each in Karen's letter in exercise 2A.
Run-on sentences (They go on and on.)
1 I am writing to complain about the above washing machine, which I bought during your Summer Sale on July 15 for $175.99 at the Main Street branch of Markus Appliances and for which I include a copy of the receipt as proof of purchase.
Sentence fragments (Incomplete sentences)
2 Went back to the store. Explained problem to sales manager Rob Clark.
3 Unacceptable. First, obviously faulty.

🖉 **WRITE IT**

D **PLAN** You're going to write a complaint letter. Choose an idea in the box or something you experienced yourself. With a partner, describe the problem and how you want the company to solve it. Then look at the letter in exercise 2A. What type of information should each paragraph contain in a complaint letter? How will you start and end the letter?

a bad restaurant meal	a broken or faulty item or package
poor customer service	an item that's different from the advertisement

E Write your complaint letter.

83

Register check

INSIGHT
Teachers report that their students often struggle to master the differences between written and spoken English.

CONTENT
Register check draws on research into the Cambridge English Corpus and highlights potential problem areas for learners.

RESULT
Students transition confidently between written and spoken English and recognize different levels of formality as well as when to use them appropriately.

REGISTER CHECK

In formal written complaints, we often use expressions like *I find, I feel, I believe,* or *I think* to make statements less direct and more polite.

Direct
This is unacceptable.
Mr. Clark should be friendlier.

Less direct
I find this unacceptable.
I feel Mr. Clark should be friendlier.

> "The presentation is very clear, and there are plenty of opportunities for student practice and production."

Jason Williams, Teacher, Notre Dame Seishin University, Japan

Accuracy check

ACCURACY CHECK

Use the future continuous, not the present continuous, for an action in progress in the future.

In a couple of years, I'm looking for a job. ✗
In a couple of years, I'll be looking for a job. ✓

INSIGHT

Some common errors can become fossilized if not addressed early on in the learning process.

CONTENT

Accuracy check highlights common learner errors (based on unique research into the Cambridge Learner Corpus) and can be used for self-editing.

RESULT

Students avoid common errors in their written and spoken English.

You spoke. We listened.

Students told us that speaking is the most important skill for them to master, while teachers told us that finding speaking activities which engage their students and work in the classroom can be challenging.

That's why EVOLVE has a whole lesson dedicated to speaking: Lesson 5, *Time to speak*.

Time to speak

INSIGHT

Speaking ability is how students most commonly measure their own progress, but is also the area where they feel most insecure. To be able to fully exploit speaking opportunities in the classroom, students need a safe speaking environment where they can feel confident, supported, and able to experiment with language.

CONTENT

Time to speak is a unique lesson dedicated to developing speaking skills and is based around immersive tasks which involve information sharing and decision making.

RESULT

Time to speak lessons create a buzz in the classroom where speaking can really thrive, evolve, and take off, resulting in more confident speakers of English.

8.5 TIME TO SPEAK
The key to less stress

LESSON OBJECTIVE
- make a podcast on ways to reduce stress

NOT STRESSED AT ALL ← → VERY STRESSED

A **DISCUSS** How stressed are you? Where would you put yourself on the scale above? Would you say most of your stress is caused by one or two big things or a number of small things? In pairs, discuss examples of big and small things that can make you feel stressed. For ideas look at the pictures. Add four ideas of your own.

B Compare your ideas with other pairs. Find out common causes of stress.

C **DECIDE** Which of the causes of stress from part B can be reduced by taking simple actions? What actions can be taken? With your partner from part A, discuss the ideas in the box and your own ideas. Then choose your top three effective and simple actions.

> **SIMPLE ACTIONS TO REDUCE STRESS:**
> Delete it.   Don't read it.   Don't reply.
> Make "to-do" lists.   Do it right away.   Get up earlier.
> Go to bed later.   Say "No!"   Discuss the problem.

D **PREPARE** You're going to present your actions in a short podcast. Plan: (1) the introduction, (2) your actions and the reasons why you think they're simple and effective (give some examples), and (3) the conclusion. You can take notes.

E **PRESENT** Present your podcast to the class. Answer any questions about it.

F **AGREE** The class compares the podcasts and chooses two that have the best ideas and are well presented.

» To check your progress, go to page 155. »

USEFUL PHRASES

DECIDE
One/Another thing you could do is …
It never hurts to …
… is always worth considering.
… is a good way to approach it.

PREPARE
If you do this, you're bound to / sure to …
You're going to …
You might …
You'll be + verb + *-ing* …

84

Experience Better Learning with EVOLVE: a course that helps both teachers and students on every step of the language learning journey.

Speaking matters. Find out more about creating safe speaking environments in the classroom.

x

EVOLVE unit structure

Unit opening page

Each unit opening page activates prior knowledge and vocabulary and immediately gets students speaking.

Lessons 1 and 2

These lessons present and practice the unit vocabulary and grammar in context, helping students discover language rules for themselves. Students then have the opportunity to use this language in well-scaffolded, personalized speaking tasks.

Lesson 3

This lesson is built around an off-the-page dialogue that practices listening skills. It also models and contextualizes useful speaking skills. The final speaking task draws on the language and strategies from the lesson.

Lesson 4

This is a skills lesson based around an engaging reading text. Each lesson asks students to think critically and ends with a practical writing task.

Lesson 5

Time to speak is an entire lesson dedicated to developing speaking skills. Students work on collaborative, immersive tasks which involve information sharing and decision making.

CONTENTS

Listening	Speaking skills	Reading	Writing	Speaking
Upgrade ■ A conversation between two coworkers	■ Discuss issues and agree strongly	**Back to basics** ■ An article about the Maker Movement	**An opinion essay** ■ Organize information	■ Talk about your attitude toward change ■ Talk about things from when you were younger that aren't around anymore ■ Compare things in your past and present life ■ Talk about the Maker Movement **Time to speak** ■ Talk about what life was like in a past decade
Finding out ■ A conversation between a guide and a tourist	■ Exchange information	**Extreme living** ■ An interview about living in Antarctica	**A description of an area** ■ Use numerical words and phrases	■ Talk about the most important areas of research and exploration ■ Talk about life forms in difficult environments ■ Give advice on doing a free-time activity you enjoy ■ Talk about living in an extreme environment **Time to speak** ■ Plan an outdoor vacation
Asking for favors ■ Conversations between an intern, an employee, and their bosses	■ Make and respond to requests	**The right job for me** ■ An advertisement for jobs in a zoo	**A personal statement** ■ Compose and evaluate a personal statement	■ Talk about introverts and extroverts ■ Talk about how different things or experiences make you feel ■ Make and respond to requests ■ Talk about a job you would like to do and a job you would be best at **Time to speak** ■ Interview a job candidate
Two people, one job ■ A counseling session on job sharing	■ Discuss advantages and disadvantages	**The me team** ■ An article about disadvantages of teamwork	**Summary of an article** ■ Summarize main points	■ Talk about an experience of coordinating a group of people ■ Talk about making group decisions ■ Discuss advantages and disadvantages of job sharing ■ Talk about your attitude toward teamwork **Time to speak** ■ Discuss organizing a fund-raising event
Stop blaming gaming ■ A TV debate about video games	■ Consider and contrast ideas	**What language barrier?** ■ An article about translation apps	**Online comments** ■ State opinion and give examples	■ Discuss how VR programs can help people in different areas of life ■ Discuss how the development of technology can affect the way we communicate with different people ■ Discuss benefits of video games ■ Discuss translation apps **Time to speak** ■ Plan a community improvement campaign
Something in the water ■ An interview with a couple who thought they saw a shark	■ Make, contradict, and clarify assumptions	**Getting it wrong** ■ Posts about being in the wrong place at the wrong time	**A story** ■ Make a story interesting	■ Tell a story about someone who went viral ■ Talk about managing expectations ■ Describe an interesting experience ■ Talk about unexpected situations resulting from small mistakes **Time to speak** ■ Tell a story for a contest

	Learning objectives	Grammar	Vocabulary	Pronunciation
Unit 7 **Priorities**	■ Discuss worthwhile experiences ■ Talk about purchases ■ Bargain for a purchase ■ Write a for-and-against essay ■ Negotiate a boat trip	■ Gerunds and infinitives after adjectives, nouns, and pronouns ■ Infinitives after verbs with and without objects	■ Positive experiences ■ Making purchases	■ Listening for vowel linking between words ■ Saying /ŋ/
Unit 8 **Small things matter**	■ Talk about neatness and messiness ■ Talk about side projects ■ Suggest and show interest in ideas ■ Write a complaint letter ■ Make a podcast on ways to reduce stress	■ Modal-like expressions with *be* ■ Future forms	■ Describing neatness and messiness ■ Talking about progress	■ Listening for emphasis ■ Saying words that show a contrast
Unit 9 **Things happen**	■ Talk about how your life might be different ■ Talk about mistakes ■ Reassure someone about a problem ■ Write an article giving tips ■ Talk about key events in your life	■ Unreal conditionals ■ Wishes and regrets	■ Luck and choice ■ Commenting on mistakes	■ Listening for different word groups ■ Using intonation in conditional sentences
	Review 3 (Review of Units 7–9)			
Unit 10 **People, profiles**	■ Talk about people's characteristics ■ Talk about customer research ■ Give your impressions ■ Write a professional profile ■ Develop a plan to improve a company website	■ Gerunds after prepositions ■ Causative verbs	■ Describing characteristics ■ Describing research	■ Quoting from a text ■ Recognizing /eɪ/, /aɪ/, and /ɔɪ/
Unit 11 **Really?**	■ Talk fake goods ■ Talk about untrue information ■ Express belief and disbelief ■ Write a persuasive essay ■ Share tips on solutions	■ Passive forms ■ Passives with modals and modal-like expressions; passive infinitives	■ Describing consumer goods ■ Degrees of truth	■ Listening for intonation on exclamations and imperatives ■ Saying /oʊ/ and /aʊ/
Unit 12 **Got what it takes?**	■ Talk about talent ■ Discuss how to make life better ■ Describe your ambitions ■ Write a review of a performance ■ Give a presentation about yourself	■ Adverbs with adjectives and adverbs ■ Making non-count nouns countable	■ Skill and performance ■ Describing emotional impact	■ Listening for sounds that change ■ Using syllable stress in words
	Review 4 (Review of Units 10–12)			
	Grammar charts and practice, pages 129–140 Vocabulary exercises, pages 141–152			

UNIT OBJECTIVES

- talk about how we deal with change
- talk about past difficulties
- discuss issues and agree strongly
- write an opinion essay
- talk about daily life in the past

STEP FORWARD

1

START SPEAKING

A   Describe what you see in this picture. What do you think is special about the girl's right hand? Read the caption and check.

B   In what ways can 3D-printed objects improve our lives? How might a 3D-printed object cause us problems?

C   Talk about something you often use or do that has improved your life. This could be an app, a gadget, or something else.

D   With a partner, list some other helpful inventions. How can they help us? For ideas, watch Jacqueline's video.

EXPERT SPEAKER

What do you think of Jacqueline's example?

1.1 LIFE CHANGES

LESSON OBJECTIVE
- talk about how we deal with change

1 LANGUAGE IN CONTEXT

A **What are some of the biggest changes that people experience in life? Are they positive or negative?**

B 🔊 **1.02** **Read and listen to an episode from Christa Garcia's podcast "No Fear." What life changes does she mention?**

> 🔊 1.02 Audio script
>
> Ten months ago, as regular listeners will know, I made two big life changes: I moved to a new city, and I changed jobs. My work situation wasn't great: I'd just lost a job, and I couldn't find a single engineering position anywhere in Florida. Then this job in Chicago came up. It was perfect and too good to refuse. But … but … but … .
>
> I'd lived in Florida all my life. My family was here, and my friends. And I **was frightened of tackling** a new job. Plus, it's really cold in Chicago, and this girl is 100% Florida. You know what I mean?
>
> I said to my brother, "I **can't take** all this change!" He just said, "**Get a grip**, Christa. You**'re** perfectly **capable of** handling all this."
>
> After I stopped being mad at him for not being more understanding, I realized that I'm always looking for an excuse to avoid change, and I'll do anything to keep my life simple. And I'm not alone. We often talk negatively about the future, don't we? We tend to fear change. And when we're feeling scared, we **underestimate** our ability to **cope with** things. But actually, we **adapt** to new situations extremely well. Think about huge changes like starting college, getting your first job, having a baby – people **get through** challenges like this all the time. We should **accept** that we're terrific at **surviving**, and instead of **resisting** change, we should **welcome** it. That's what I did, and now life is good, and that**'s a** real **step forward**!

C 🔊 **1.02** **Read and listen again. What did Christa realize about people's ability to change? How did her own attitude change?**

2 VOCABULARY: Facing challenges

FIND IT

A 🔊 **1.03** | PAIR WORK | **Look at the expressions in the box. Look at how they're used in the podcast and describe each one using other words. Use a dictionary or your phone to help you. Then listen and check.**

accept	adapt	be a step forward	be capable of	be frightened of
can't take	cope with	get a grip	get through	resist
survive	tackle	underestimate	welcome	

B ▶ **Now go to page 141. Do the vocabulary exercises for 1.1.**

C | PAIR WORK | **Do you agree with Christa's thoughts about our ability to change? Tell your partner, and use examples if you can. Use the words in exercise 2A.**

3 GRAMMAR: Present habits

A Read the sentences in the grammar box. Circle the correct options to complete the rules.

> **Present habits**
>
> I**'m always looking for** an excuse to avoid change, and I**'ll do** anything to keep my life simple.
>
> We **often talk** negatively about the future, don't we?
>
> We **tend to fear** change.
>
> When we**'re feeling** scared, we underestimate our ability to cope with things.

1 For a habit that is more noticeable or frequent than usual, you can use *always* or *constantly* with the **simple present / present continuous**.

2 You can use the modal *will* for **present / past** habits.

3 You can use the verb **tend to / keep** + a verb to talk about present habits.

4 You can use the **simple present / present continuous** for a continuing activity that happens at the same time as another habit.

B ▶ **Now go to page 129. Look at the grammar chart and do the grammar exercise for 1.1.**

C PAIR WORK Think of something you do regularly, such as going to the gym, meeting friends, studying, or working. Describe your present habits using the prompts below. Then compare your sentences with a partner. How different or similar are your regular habits?

1 I tend to …

2 My friends and I often …

3 When I'm feeling …

4 I'm always …

5 When I'm tired, I'll …

D Think of one thing you'd like to change about your life. What habits do you have that prevent you from moving forward? How can you tackle these habits?

4 SPEAKING

A GROUP WORK THINK CRITICALLY Do you welcome change, or do you prefer to stick to your habits? Explain your answers. Is it easier to adapt to changes that you decide to make or ones that are outside your control? Think of some examples.

> I **tend to worry** about big changes. I**'ll follow** the same routine every day and be perfectly happy about it. I think things outside our control, like losing your job or your best friend moving away, are harder to **cope** with because you can't plan and prepare for them.

MEMORY LANE

1 LANGUAGE IN CONTEXT

A   PAIR WORK   Look at the pictures. When were the items popular? When did people stop using these items? Why?

B   Read Amy's blog post. What time period does she describe? How old do you think she was then? How old is she now?

banana seat bike

The TIME MACHINE
in my living room

TV with no remote control

Do you ever binge-watch TV shows and feel like you've taken a time machine to a different place and time? I just watched *Stranger Things*, which takes place in the 1980s. It was like going back in time to my childhood.

Remember those bikes with banana-shaped seats? One of the boys in the series rides one, just like the one I used to ride to school every day. I wouldn't even lock it – I'd just leave it outside all day. In many ways, life was simple then. But some things were **frustrating** …

When you're on the phone, do you move around a lot, like me? Well, in the 1980s, we could only walk as far as the cord reached. And with only one phone in the house, we didn't use to have any privacy. I'd **drive** my brother **crazy** because I talked to my friends for hours. Making calls away from home was **tricky**, too. Have you ever used a pay phone? I never used to have enough coins with me – it was **infuriating**! And how about sharing music? You probably use a music app, right? My older sister used to make me mixtapes with different songs she liked. I realize now how **complex** and **time-consuming** it was. Even watching TV was more difficult then. It **got on my nerves** to have to get up and change the channel all the time because there was no such thing as a remote control. Now I just push the "off" button from the couch to travel back to the present and take a break from binge-watching!

wall phone with a cord

C60

cassette tape

GLOSSARY
binge-watch (*v*) to watch many or all episodes of a TV show in one session

2 VOCABULARY: Describing annoying things

A   Cover the blog post. Can you remember which seven words and phrases from the box below Amy uses? What does she describe with the words?

awkward	be a waste of time	be hard to operate	clumsy
complex	drive sb crazy	frustrating	get on sb's nerves
infuriating	lose patience	time-consuming	tricky

!   *sb* = somebody

FIND IT

B   🔊 1.04 Look at the words in the box again. Which ones are adjectives, and which ones are verb phrases? Use a dictionary or your phone to help you. Then listen and check. Which words mean *annoying*? Which mean *difficult, uncomfortable, takes a lot of or too much time*?

C   ▶ Now go to page 141. Do the vocabulary exercises for 1.2.

D   PAIR WORK   THINK CRITICALLY   Describe some present-day everyday objects using words from exercise 2A. Which of them do you think will still be used in ten years' time? How might they change?

3 GRAMMAR: Past habits

A   Read the sentences in the grammar box. Circle the correct options to complete the rules. Can you find more examples in the text in exercise 1B on page 4?

> **Past habits**
>
> We **didn't use to have** any privacy.   **I never used to have** enough coins.
> I'**d drive** my brother crazy.
> It **got** on my nerves to have to get up and change the channel all the time.

> **!** Use the simple past for single completed past actions:
> *I just **watched** the last episode of Stranger Things.*

1   *Used to*, *didn't use to*, and *never used to* can show past habits, **single / repeated** past actions, and past states.

2   *Would* (*not*) can mean the same thing as (*not*) *used to* / *could* (*not*) for past habits and repeated actions. Do not use *would* (*not*) for past states.

3   You **can / can't** use the simple past for past habits, repeated past actions, and past states.

B   ➤ **Now go to page 129. Look at the grammar chart and do the grammar exercise for 1.2.**

C   Change the sentences so they're true for you. Use (*not/never*) *used to* or *would* (*not*). Then check your accuracy. Compare your statements with a partner.

> ✔ **ACCURACY** CHECK
>
> Do **not** use *be* before *used to* when talking about past habits.
> *I ~~am~~ used to cycle to school.* ✗
> *I used to cycle to school.* ✔

1   When I was a child, I rode my bike without a helmet.

2   My parents cooked with a microwave.

3   I didn't stream music in the 1990s.

4   When I was a kid, I texted my friends every day.

5   Before cell phones, I had to memorize my friends' phone numbers.

4 SPEAKING

A   **PAIR WORK**   Think of objects from when you were younger that aren't around anymore. Why aren't they around anymore? Do you miss those objects? Why or why not? For ideas, watch Jacqueline's video.

> I **used to have** this game console that fit in my pocket. It only had one game, but I'**d carry** it around everywhere and play the game all the time. It was really **frustrating** if I forgot to bring it with me. Now I simply play games on my phone …

EXPERT SPEAKER

How similar are Jacqueline's memories to yours?

1 LISTENING

A **PAIR WORK** In what situations do you send or receive emails? Do you think it's an effective way to communicate? Why or why not?

B 🔊 **1.05** Listen to coworkers Shawn and Lorena talk about problems with email. What other ways of communication do they mention?

C 🔊 **1.05** **LISTEN FOR OPINIONS** Listen again. What does Lorena think the problems with email are? Do you agree with her? What does Shawn think about the alternative that Lorena mentions? Do you agree with him?

D **PAIR WORK** **THINK CRITICALLY** Compare different ways of communication, such as face-to-face conversations, texts, IMs, video calls, etc. What are their advantages and disadvantages? Which ways of communication do you find most effective in which situations?

Shawn Harvey
Managing Director

Lorena Cook
Team Leader

2 PRONUNCIATION: Listening for main stress

A 🔊 **1.06** Listen. What do you notice about the underlined words?

1 … I can get some <u>real</u> work done.
2 … people usually choose the <u>easy</u> option.
3 All this technology was supposed to help us be more <u>efficient</u> …

B 🔊 **1.07** <u>Underline</u> the word in each item that you think has the main stress. Listen and check.

1 When it comes to technology, …
2 … waiting to use the single fax machine we had in our office.
3 And don't forget about all that paper!

C Circle the correct words to complete the sentences.

One word / Several words in each word group will have the main stress. Words with the main stress are usually near the *beginning / end* of the word group, and they give information that is *new (and important) / old (and not so important)* to listeners.

> **INSIDER** ENGLISH
>
> When something used to connect to the internet isn't working, it's "down."
>
> *It looks like the server is **down**.*
>
> *My Wi-Fi is **down** again!*

3 SPEAKING SKILLS

A 🔊 **1.05** Look at the sentences from the conversation in exercise 1B on page 6. Are the speakers discussing issues (D) or agreeing strongly (A)? Write *D* or *A*. Where, do you think, is the main stress in each sentence? Listen to the conversation again to check.

> ### Discuss issues and agree strongly
>
> 1 **When it comes to** technology, you can rely on the server to be unreliable. ___
>
> 2 **That's so true!** ___
>
> 3 **You can say that again.** ___
>
> 4 **I couldn't agree more.** ___
>
> 5 **Looking at the big picture**, I think email isn't that bad. ___
>
> 6 **Overall**, if I had to choose … ___
>
> 7 **Have it your way!** ___

B **PAIR WORK** With your partner, take turns making and responding to statements using the prompts below and **bold** expressions from exercise 3A.

1 writing / easier / laptop / tablet

2 texting / the best way to communicate with …

3 video calls / for work / personal communication

4 face-to-face / most important for …

C **PAIR WORK** **Student A: Go to page 157. Student B: Go to page 159. Follow the instructions.**

4 PRONUNCIATION: Saying /tʃ/

A 🔊 **1.08** Listen to the /tʃ/ sound in these words and then repeat the words.

> pic<u>t</u>ure   <u>ch</u>eap   sugges<u>t</u>ion   a<u>ch</u>ieve   tou<u>ch</u>   ques<u>t</u>ion

B <u>Underline</u> the /tʃ/ sound in each pair of words.

status   statue   stomach   watch   actual   action   nature   major

🔊 **1.09** Listen and check. Then repeat the words with the /tʃ/ sound.

C <u>Underline</u> the /tʃ/ sounds in the conversation below. Then take turns practicing the conversation with a partner.

A Looking at the bigger picture, we've got more of a chance now.

B Actually, I don't think we're going to achieve very much. We need to make some big changes.

5 SPEAKING

A **GROUP WORK** Compare something from your past with something in your present life. Look at the ideas below. Discuss your views on the issues.

> last job / current job   high school / college
> last home / current home   old device / current device

Generally speaking, I think the atmosphere in college is more relaxed than in high school.

I couldn't agree more.

*So, **overall**, do you think college is easier?*

BACK TO BASICS

1 READING

A **IDENTIFY MAIN IDEAS** What skills or knowledge have your grandparents and parents passed on to you? Can you tell your partner something that you do or make that they taught you? Read the article and say what Barbara's grandparents passed on to her. What is the Maker Movement?

COMING AROUND AGAIN

When I was a kid, I used to spend weekdays with my grandpa and grandma while my mom was at work. I'd sometimes help my grandma make her special oatmeal cookies. To be honest, I used to be better at eating them than I was at baking them. They were so good! But in those days, more often than not, I'd watch my grandfather in his workshop – actually their garage – where he spent most mornings. He was an amateur inventor, and he would take old pieces of metal or wood and make something new and practical that he or my grandmother could use around the house. He once gave me a wallet to hold dollar bills that he had made out of flat cardboard, leather, and elastic. It was a magic wallet – you opened the wallet, placed the bill on top of the elastic inside, closed the wallet, opened it again from the other side and – lo and behold – the bills were behind the elastic and held securely. He had put a ten dollar bill in there, "just in case you need it." Every time I use it I think of my grandfather, and I know it's the only wallet in the world like it.

Fast forward to earlier this year. I went to a Maker Faire with my friend. "What's a Maker Faire?" I hear you ask. Well, first I need to tell you about the Maker Movement. This was founded way back in 2005 as a way to encourage DIY through art, electronics, and craft projects. Since then, it's gone from strength to strength around the world. There are about 135 million makers in the U.S. alone – that's over half the population. Maker Faires are basically festivals which celebrate and promote these skills. The 2015 Maker Faire had over 1.1 million visitors – the same audience size as Taylor Swift's *1989 World Tour*.

So, how is the Maker Movement different to what my grandpa was doing in his workshop all those years ago? It's hard to define, but a lot of it is about individuals using new technologies – technologies that are accessible to you and me, like 3D printers – so that they can create unique items and projects that have a use beyond their original intention. A maker is anyone who is creating, and if you're building or adapting something or trying to make something new, that means you.

The future could be pretty exciting for all makers out there. Dale Dougherty, founder of Maker Media which published *Maker: Magazine* back in 2005, and that kicked off the movement, believes the future of makers depends on education. He says young people need help to develop their creative and technical abilities. "When kids play *Minecraft* they expect not just to play, but also to evolve," Dougherty said. It's fun, and everyone tackles projects and learns skills together.

My grandparents are gone now, but I'd love to think that if they were around today they would be makers, too. I've inherited my grandfather's love of finding out how things work, and I've just sold my first handmade lamp that I made from recycled glass and other materials. By using the creative skills they passed down to me, in my own way I've joined the maker movement.

By Barbara Cohen

GLOSSARY
amateur (*adj*) doing something as a hobby
craft (*n*) an activity in which you make something using a lot of skill, especially with your hands
DIY (do-it-yourself) (*n*) repairing and making things yourself instead of paying someone to do it

B **IDENTIFY SPECIFIC INFORMATION** Read the article. What's the significance of these numbers?

a 2005   **b** 135,000,000   **c** 2015   **d** 1,100,000

C **THINK CRITICALLY** Why do you think the Maker Movement has become so popular around the world? What do you think of this movement? Would you be interested in becoming a maker?

2 WRITING

A   Read Carmen's essay about forgotten skills. Which ones does she mention? What was good about them?

Reviving forgotten skills

Recently, there has been some discussion about reviving skills from the past, such as repairing mechanical items like watches and raising animals. These skills are good for the environment, save money, and can be extremely enjoyable. I think this is an excellent trend and would like to share two almost-forgotten skills that my grandmother used to have.

The first is sewing. Most of us buy our clothes at the store, and we throw them away when they're worn. My grandmother, however, used to make clothes for my father, and later in life for my sisters and me. She would fix holes and small tears in our clothes, too, so they would last until we grew out of them.

The second skill is preserving food. My grandmother used to preserve all kinds of fruit and vegetables in the fall and store them in jars. Then, in the middle of the winter, she'd bring out a jar of raspberries or cucumbers, and it would immediately bring back a wonderful feeling of summer. It also cost less than buying them in the store.

I think bringing back skills like these is a fantastic idea. In fact, I'm planning to research how to raise chickens so I can have fresh eggs.

GLOSSARY
revive (v) to make something from the past exist again
preserve (v) to treat food in a particular way so it can be kept for a long time

B   **ORGANIZE INFORMATION** Read about organizing an opinion essay. Then check if Carmen's essay has all these features.

1st paragraph: Introduce the topic and state your opinion.

2nd paragraph: Use a topic sentence to introduce your example and give the main idea of the paragraph; describe the example.

3rd paragraph: (same as second paragraph)

4th paragraph: Restate your opinion but with different words than before.

WRITE IT

FIND IT

C   **PLAN** You're going to write a formal opinion essay about skills from the past. With your partner, discuss two or three forgotten skills and what you would like to say about them. Choose from the skills in the pictures below or use your phone to find other ideas. Then think how you will organize your essay, using the structure described in exercise 2B. What points are you going to include in each paragraph?

D   Write your opinion essay. You can write a similar introduction and conclusion to Carmen's.

knitting

baking

beekeeping

making pottery

E   **PAIR WORK** Read your partner's essay. What do you think of the skills he or she describes?

TIME TO SPEAK
Blast from the past

| 1910 | 1920 | 1930 | 1940 | 1950 | 1960 | 1970 | 1980 | 1990 |

A   **PREPARE**   Look at the pictures. In pairs, discuss which decade you think each picture is from. Then work with another pair and discuss your ideas. How else was life different in each time period?

B   **DECIDE**   Imagine you are on a reality TV show where you have to live for a week the way people did in the past. In groups, say which decade you want to live in, from 1910 to 1990, and why. Then decide on one decade together.

C   **RESEARCH**   In your group, answer the questions about what life was like in the decade you chose. You can go online to research ideas.

FIND IT

1   How did people use to do everyday chores?
2   What transportation did they use?
3   What styles of clothes did they wear?
4   What tech items did they have?
5   How did they entertain themselves?

D   Imagine you just finished your week on the TV show. In your group, talk about your imagined experiences. How does living in that decade compare to life today? What was better? Worse? What did you enjoy about the experience? What difficulties did you have?

E   **DISCUSS**   You are going to debate whether it's better to live now or in the decade you discussed. Make two teams within your group. Team A: Think of reasons why life was better then. Team B: Brainstorm the reasons why it's better to live in the present day. Each team has two minutes to present their points to the other team.

F   Report the results of your debate to the class. Would most people prefer to live in the past or now?

To check your progress, go to page 153.

USEFUL PHRASES

PREPARE

It was very awkward.
It was hard to operate.
It used to drive … crazy
It was really tricky.

DISCUSS

It was a step forward from …
We shouldn't underestimate …
It helped to cope with …
It was a waste of time.
It used to be so time-consuming.

Generally speaking, …
Looking at the big picture …
Overall …
When it came to …

UNIT OBJECTIVES

- talk about exploration and research
- talk about life forms in different environments
- exchange important information
- write a description of an area
- plan an outdoor experience

START SPEAKING

A What can you see in the picture? What effect do you think it has on the fish and other wildlife in the ocean?

B In what other ways does human activity affect wildlife? Can you think of examples from your area or country?

C What are the benefits and drawbacks of human activity you discussed in exercise B? Do you think the activity is justified? For ideas, watch Odil's video.

EXPERT SPEAKER

What do you think of Odil's ideas?

DEEP OCEAN OR DEEP SPACE?

1 VOCABULARY: Space and ocean exploration

A Look at the pictures. Which one is in space? Which is in the ocean? Which do you think most people would want to learn about?

A An amoeba

FIND IT

B 🔊 **1.10** **PAIR WORK** Look at the words and phrases in the box and discuss their meanings. Use a dictionary or your phone to help you. Then listen and check your work. Which words and phrases could you use to talk about space, which about the ocean, and which about both?

atmosphere	come across	exploration	investigation
launch	monitor	observe	preserve
resources	satellite	species	surface
use up			

B A supernova

C Now go to page 142. Do the vocabulary exercises for 2.1.

D **PAIR WORK** **THINK CRITICALLY** Why do we explore space and the ocean? What effect can it have on our daily lives? Are there other issues we should be using our resources on instead?

2 LANGUAGE IN CONTEXT

A 🔊 **1.11** **PAIR WORK** Read and listen to the podcast. What are the advantages and disadvantages of space and ocean exploration according to the speakers? Which speaker do you agree with more. Why?

🔊 1.11 Audio script

Host Today's guests on *Discovery Now*, Ronnie Jones and Johanna Flores, are here to discuss the question: Which is more important, space or ocean **exploration**? Ronnie?

Ronnie I would definitely prefer to explore space rather than study the ocean. There's so much mystery beyond Earth's **atmosphere**. And we can learn more from research into space than most people realize. Without it we would probably never have inventions like phone cameras, ear thermometers, wireless headsets, and even clean energy technology.

Johanna I disagree. How about the benefits of underwater research for industry, for medicine, for technology? And it's much less expensive and a lot safer than space travel. Space exploration just isn't useful enough to justify the cost.

Host Good point. Can you justify the cost, Ronnie?

Ronnie Of course. The earth is getting overcrowded, and it won't be long before we'll need other places to live. Solving future problems on Earth is worth any price.

Johanna It's less important to fix future problems than to fix current ones. People depend on the ocean for jobs, food, and even breathing! Ocean plants produce about 70 percent of Earth's oxygen. Maybe we should find ways to **preserve** our oceans' **resources** instead of **using** them **up** – which is a lot easier than trying to live in space.

Ronnie But what about life in space? On Mars, for example, there's water, and where there's water, there could be life!

Johanna But we don't know for sure if any other planets support life. However, there's definitely life below the **surface** of the ocean we still know almost nothing about. We keep discovering amazing **species** deep under the water. Only about five to ten percent of the deep ocean has been explored. Overall, it is obvious to me that there are fewer benefits to space exploration.

3 GRAMMAR: Comparative structures

A Read the sentences in the grammar box. (Circle) the correct options to complete the rules.

> **Comparative structures**
>
> I would definitely prefer to explore space **rather than study** the ocean.
>
> We can **learn more** from research into space **than** most people realize.
>
> Space exploration just **isn't useful enough** to justify the cost.
>
> It's **less important to fix** future problems **than** (it is) **to fix** current ones.
>
> There are **fewer benefits** to space exploration.

1 When comparing, put the thing you like less after **prefer** / **rather than**. To compare actions, use a gerund or the **base form of the verb** / **past participle** after *rather than*.

2 When using *more* or *less* as a pronoun, put it **after** / **before** a verb.

3 Use **a gerund** / **an infinitive** after an adjective + *enough*.

4 Use *less* with **count** / **non-count** nouns. Use *fewer* with **count** / **non-count** nouns.

5 You **always have to** / **don't always have to** repeat the first subject + verb in comparative structures.

B Now go to page 130. Look at the grammar chart and do the grammar exercise for 2.1.

C Complete the sentences with your own ideas using the constructions in parentheses. Then check your accuracy. Compare ideas with a partner.

1 Ocean exploration is … (adjective + *enough* + infinitive)

Ocean exploration is not important enough to justify the risks.

2 Space travel is … (adjective + *enough* + infinitive)

3 Space exploration is … (comparative adjective + *than*)

4 I prefer … (verb/gerund + *rather than* + verb/gerund)

5 We can learn … (*more* or *less* as a pronoun)

6 It's less important … (infinitive *than* infinitive)

> ✔ **ACCURACY** CHECK
>
> Use *than*, **not** *then*, with comparative structures.
>
> *There is less oxygen on Mars ~~then~~ on Earth.* ✗
>
> *There is less oxygen on Mars than on Earth.* ✓

4 SPEAKING

A **THINK CRITICALLY** What environments do people explore? What do you think are the top areas of research and exploration that can help us and the planet? Why? For ideas, watch Odil's video.

> People explore the natural world around them and also their own biology. It may be **easier to solve** our most urgent issues by **observing** the results of human activity or studying our DNA, **rather than trying** to **investigate** …

> **EXPERT SPEAKER**
>
> *Do you think Odil's suggestions are good? Why or why not?*

2.2 EXTREME LIFE

- talk about life forms in different environments

1 LANGUAGE IN CONTEXT

A **PAIR WORK** Make a list of ten wild animals in your country. Where can you usually find them? Does your country have an official national animal?

B Read the article about four unusual animals. What are they? Where do they live?

NATURE'S "TOUGH COOKIES"

We often discuss how to preserve **endangered** species of wildlife but rarely talk about the opposite side of nature: **creatures** that can survive in extremely difficult **environments**. So here are four examples of nature's "tough cookies."

Nicaragua's Masaya Volcano is one of the most active **volcanoes** in Central America. **Poisonous** gas rises from the volcano. It's an absolutely awful place to live. Yet hundreds of small, green parrots have made it their home. Experts aren't sure how they survive in a **habitat** that would kill other **forms of life**, but somehow they've managed to adapt to it.

In Alaska, where temperatures remain below zero for several months, wood frogs survive by freezing. Almost two-thirds of their body water turns to ice. They become very hard and appear to be dead. But in the spring, they thaw out and head straight for the nearest **pond**.

Super-hot water and poisonous gases boil up from holes in the ocean floor off the coast of Ecuador. This is surely the least suitable environment for anything to live. Yet in and around these holes, various forms of **sea life** exist. The tiniest and most common are microbes called "extremophiles." Their existence may help explain the **origins** of life on earth.

The final "tough cookie" has few limits to its **territory**. Rats are the most **adaptable** mammal that we know of. They live almost everywhere and recover fast from whatever we do to them. They won't win a popularity contest, but they definitely get the first prize for being super **survivors**.

GLOSSARY
head (straight) for (v) go toward something
microbe (n) a very small living thing that can only be seen with a microscope
mammal (n) an animal that feeds its babies milk

C Read the article again. What makes each living thing a "tough cookie"? Which one do you think is the toughest? Why?

INSIDER ENGLISH

Someone is a *tough cookie* if they are not easily hurt emotionally or physically.

You don't need to worry about Rachel. She is a really tough cookie.

2 VOCABULARY: The natural world

A 🔊 **1.12** Look at the words in the box. Which two are not in the article? Which ones are nouns or noun phrases, and which are adjectives? Listen and check your work.

adaptable	animal life	creature	endangered	environment
form of life	habitat	origin	plant life	poisonous
pond	sea life	survivor	territory	volcano

B ▶ Now go to page 142. Do the vocabulary exercises for 2.2.

C **THINK CRITICALLY** What are some endangered animals that you know of? What do you think can be done to protect them?

3 GRAMMAR: Superlative structures; ungradable adjectives

A Read the sentences in the grammar boxes. Circle the correct options to complete the rules.

> **Superlative structures**
>
> Nicaragua's Masaya Volcano is **one of the most active** volcanoes in Central America.
>
> Yet in and around these holes, various forms of sea life exist. **The tiniest and most common** are microbes.
>
> Rats are **the most adaptable** mammal (that) we know of.

> **Ungradable adjectives**
>
> It's an **absolutely awful** place to live.
>
> They become very hard and appear to be **dead**.
>
> The **final** "tough cookie" has few limits to its territory.

1 After *one of the most* + adjective, use a **singular / plural** noun.

2 Nouns are not always repeated after superlative adjectives. After "the tiniest and most common," the missing words are *holes / forms of sea life*.

3 For superlative structures with *that* clauses, *that* is **always / not always** needed.

4 You **can / can't** use ungradable adjectives with *absolutely* and *completely*.

B ▶ Now go to page 130. Look at the grammar chart and do the grammar exercises for 2.2.

C Complete the sentences about the natural world. Compare with a partner. Answers are at the bottom of the page.

1 The black mamba is one of the most poisonous _____ .

2 The dwarf lantern shark is one of the _____ animals in the ocean.

3 Out of all the planets in the solar system, Neptune and Uranus are the _____ .

4 The water in the geysers can be very hot or even absolutely _____ .

4 SPEAKING

A PAIR WORK Choose one of the topics below. Where can these life forms be found? How difficult is life for them? You can check online if you want. Then tell another pair about the topic you chose.

- wild animals that have adapted to life in your city
- the rarest animals, birds, or plants in your country / the world
- the most beautiful or the most dangerous forms of life you know of

> One of the most common wild animals in our city is the raccoon. A common **habitat** of urban raccoons are people's sheds and attics. Raccoons come out into the streets to find food, but city life is **extremely dangerous** for them ...

FIND IT

Answers: 1 snakes 2 smallest 3 coldest or farthest from the sun 4 boiling

15

FINDING OUT

1 LISTENING

A **PAIR WORK** Do you think hiking is a fun activity? Why or why not? Tina is preparing to go hiking in the mountains of Peru. She calls her guide to ask about things she needs to take with her. Imagine you're Tina. Think of some important questions to ask.

B 🔊 **1.13** Listen. What are the four different problems with water and sweat that the guide discusses?

C 🔊 **1.13** **LISTEN FOR DETAILS** Listen again. Complete the information that the guide provides.

1 Type of coat to bring: _____
2 Type of T-shirt <u>not</u> to bring: _____
3 Minimum size of backpack: _____ liters
4 Weight of backpack without water: _____ kilos
5 Weight of water: _____ kilos

D In your opinion, which of the water problems described by the guide is the most dangerous? Explain why.

2 PRONUNCIATION: Listening for weak forms and rhythm

A 🔊 **1.14** Listen to the phrase *a couple of questions*. What pattern does it have?

1 a couple of questions
2 a couple of questions
3 a couple of questions

B 🔊 **1.15** Put the phrases into the columns. Then listen and check your answers.

at least 50 liters   what sort of coat   a risk of snow
prepare for the worst   I'm sure you know   a good waterproof coat

Pattern 1 | **Pattern 2** | **Pattern 3**

C Are these statements true or false?

1 Phrases usually have a rhythm where there is a combination of stressed and unstressed words.
2 Words that carry the main meaning, like nouns and verbs, are usually stressed.
3 Functional words, like prepositions and articles, are also usually stressed.

3 SPEAKING SKILLS

A 🔊 **1.13** Look at these sentences from the conversation in exercise 1B on page 16. Find two expressions that indicate danger (D), and two expressions that indicate essential information (E). Write *D* or *E*. Which words in these sentences are unstressed? Listen again to check.

Asking for information

Is there any danger of really bad weather? ____

What exactly do you mean by "the worst"? ____

Is there a risk of snow? ____

What sort of coat **would you recommend** taking? ____

Providing information

The most important thing to consider is that mountain weather is unpredictable. ____

First and foremost, you need a good waterproof coat. ____

One thing to keep in mind is that you don't want a thick coat. ____

Another thing to consider is the kind of T-shirt you wear. ____

B ▶ PAIR WORK **Student A: Go to page 157. Student B: Go to page 159. Follow the instructions.**

C Imagine you are going hiking somewhere in the mountains. What two pieces of information would you like to ask for? What information would you give someone going hiking somewhere near you? Use expressions from exercise 3A.

4 PRONUNCIATION: Saying /w/ and /v/

A 🔊 **1.16** Listen to the /w/ sound in these words and then repeat the words.

weather	wear	waterproof	worst	would
quick	quite	swim	language	

B 🔊 **1.17** Listen and circle the word you hear twice. Then check and repeat the words.

1 wet   vet   3 worse   verse

2 vine   wine   4 vest   west

C Underline the /w/ and /v/ sounds in the questions below. Then work in pairs and ask one another the questions.

1 What's the worst weather you've experienced?

2 What would you wear if you were going hiking in winter?

3 Have you ever been worried about your safety?

4 What makes people do very dangerous or weird sports?

5 SPEAKING

A Think of a free-time activity you enjoy. Imagine you're going to give some advice to someone who'd like to take up the activity. What important information could you provide?

B PAIR WORK Give the advice to a partner. Answer your partner's questions. Then change roles.

> What sort of equipment **would you recommend** buying?

> Well, **first and foremost**, you need …

EXTREME LIVING

1 READING

A Look at the picture. What do you think would be the most difficult thing about living in this place? Read the article. Did Noah Harris mention your idea?

❄ COLDER THAN COLD
by Piper Reid

Noah Harris is usually behind the camera, filming documentaries in unusual places. But last month, he took some time out to talk about his most recent – and most extreme – trip. He spent a month at a research center in one of the coldest places on Earth, Antarctica.

First and foremost, I have to ask the question everyone wants to know. How cold was it?

It was absolutely freezing! Where I was, the average temperature was –5°C in January, the warmest month, and –28°C in August, one of the coldest months. I was there in October, and it was about –15°C during the day.

How about the climate in general? What was the weather like, besides cold?

They say Antarctica is the driest, windiest, and brightest continent. It's dry because it's a desert, and surprisingly, it doesn't snow a lot. The area only gets 60 to 80 millimeters of snow a year, but the wind blows up to 185 kilometers per hour. It's full of snow and ice, and everything turns white. But many days there are blue skies and sunshine. It can actually be more difficult to see when the sun is bright.

I am also wondering about the temperature indoors. Where does everyone stay? Is it warm?

I stayed at one of New Zealand's research centers, and all of the buildings are heated. It's one of the 37 centers in Antarctica open all year. In fact, 4,000 people live in Antarctica in the summer months, but only about 1,000 stay for the winter. Where I visited, up to 85 people are at the research center in the warmer months. Fewer people are there when it's colder – about 25. When it's less crowded, everyone has their own bedroom, but when more people are there, it's four to a room.

I am curious about living so close to the same few people in such limited space. What is it like? Does everyone get along?

I was only there for a month – imagine a year of living and working with the same 20 people every single minute of every single day! But everyone really got along well, and they all seem very happy. They have to have good attitudes to survive, but they also love what they do. They're doing some of the most incredible land and ocean exploration in the world.

How was the food? Always an important question!

Eating was the least difficult part of my stay. The chef was totally amazing. People often wanted her to cook meals from New Zealand rather than having international dishes. When you live in an extreme environment, it's nice to have the comforts of home sometimes.

You didn't mention eating local food. What about the fish?

It's against the law to kill any animals in Antarctica. It's also illegal to bring plant life there, so they don't grow food at the research center. All of the food comes by boat or plane. You can't "eat local" in Antarctica!

Final question: What is the most extreme part of living in Antarctica, the biggest challenge?

The scientists often go on trips far from the center to study plant and animal life. Sometimes they camp for up to 100 days! I went on a three-day research trip with a team. After staying in a tent and having no running water or indoor bathroom, the research center seemed like a five-star hotel when I got back!

B **PAIR WORK** What are Noah's main points about the weather in Antarctica? The people? The food? What do you think about his experience? Could you live there for a month?

C UNDERSTAND NUMERICAL WORDS AND PHRASES Look at the meanings of some expressions with numbers. Find examples in the article. Then think of other things to describe with the expressions.

about = approximately, could be a few more or a few less

average = usual

to = shows a range, the number can fall anywhere in that range

up to = no more than

D THINK CRITICALLY In what kind of text would you expect to see a lot of numbers? What kind of information do they provide?

2 WRITING

A Read the description of a town in Canada. What are the town's attractions?

●●● < >

Drumheller in Alberta, Canada

Drumheller is a town of about 8,000 people in southern Alberta. It's 138 kilometers northeast of Calgary and is located in a desert-like environment. The highest rainfall it gets is about 60 millimeters in June. Temperatures can be extreme. The record highest was 40.6°C, and the lowest was –43.9°C, but the normal range is –18° to 26°C.

Drumheller seems like the least likely place to visit, but almost 500,000 tourists arrive every year. This is because it's the Dinosaur Capital of the World. The Royal Tyrrell Museum has one of the world's largest collections of dinosaur fossils, including more than 200 complete skeletons.

For nature lovers, however, the landscape is even more attractive than the dinosaurs. Parts of it look as strange and dry as the moon's surface, but many species of wildlife live there. The hoodoos are the most fascinating things to see. They're natural towers of rock, up to 6 meters high, with "caps" on the top. People love taking selfies with them.

GLOSSARY
fossil (*n*) part of an animal or plant from thousands of year ago, preserved in rock

B USE NUMERICAL WORDS AND PHRASES Complete the phrases with numbers from the description in exercise 2A. Which ones are about distance (*D*), height (*H*), quantities (*Q*), or temperatures (*T*)?

1 a town of about _____ people

2 _____ kilometers northeast of Calgary

3 the record highest temperature was _____

4 the normal temperature range is _____ to _____

5 almost _____ tourists

6 more than _____ complete skeletons

7 up to _____ meters high

WRITE IT

C PLAN You are going to write a description of an area. With your partner, talk about an area with an interesting environment or features you know. Describe what makes it interesting. You can check online for ideas. Then look at the description in exercise 2A. Do you need to divide your description into paragraphs? What kind of information could you start and end your description with?

D Write your description of the area you discussed in exercise 2C. Use comparative and superlative structures and numerical words and phrases.

E PAIR WORK Read your partner's description. Have you visited the area? Would you like to?

FIND IT

REGISTER CHECK

Make an adjective with a noun + -*like* to show that something is similar to something else.

*It's 138 kilometers northeast of Calgary and is located in a **desert-like** environment.*

*The ground is very dry and **rock-like**.*

This is more common in less formal texts, like personal writing, magazines, and web pages.

TIME TO SPEAK
Going wild

A **PREPARE** With a partner, talk about natural places you've been to and any outdoor activities you've done. Discuss how they made you feel.

B Imagine you and your partner work for the Wild Ideas travel agency. You're planning a vacation for your class. What kinds of outdoor vacations might they like? Come up with several different ideas and compare them. Use the questions below to help you.

| Home | News | About | Contact Us | 🔍 |

Questions we ask

Where do you want to go? Mountains? Ocean? …

What do you want to see? Landscapes? Wildlife? …

What do you want to do? Hiking? Biking? Kayaking? …

Where do you want to sleep? In a hotel? In a tent? …

How long do you want to stay? A day? A week? …

For many people, outdoor vacations are way too wild. They're too tough, too long, and too far away. At **Wild Ideas**, we're changing that by listening to our customers. They tell us how wild they want to go, and we design a suitable experience for them.

C Work with another pair and share your ideas. Ask for and give each other advice on how to improve your ideas, and note down any useful advice.

D **DECIDE** With your partner, use the advice from part C to help you choose your best idea and improve it. Include interesting facts with numbers. You can look online if you want.

FIND IT

E **PRESENT** Tell the class about your plan. Use superlatives to make it sound attractive. The class compares plans, considers the points below, and votes for the best one. Why is it the best plan?

| has most interesting facts | sounds like the most fun | is not too wild or difficult |
| is something all would enjoy | your own ideas | |

» To check your progress, go to page 153. »

USEFUL PHRASES

PREPARE

I've been to …

I've been … before.

I've gone … in the past.

I went … once.

It felt absolutely …

It made me feel extremely …

It was the … of my life.

The environment was …

PRESENT

One of the most exciting ideas was …

Another great option was …

But that's not all!

Overall, …

■ talk about personality types
■ talk about things you love or hate
■ make and respond to requests
■ write a personal statement for a job application
■ interview for a full-time position

THE WAY I AM

3

START SPEAKING

A Imagine you were on this ride. Which person's expression would yours be most like? What would you say when you got off the ride?

B What does this picture tell us about the personalities of the people? Do you think their faces reveal their true feelings?

C What situations can you think of that reveal what people are really like? For ideas, watch Wendy's video.

EXPERT SPEAKER

Do you agree with Wendy's ideas?

POWER IN QUIET

1 LANGUAGE IN CONTEXT

A PAIR WORK **Look at the picture. Which person are you most like? Would you describe yourself as an outgoing person? Why or why not?**

B 🔊 1.18 **Read and listen to part of a radio show. What are the three personality types mentioned?**

🔊 1.18 Audio script

Welcome to *Book Ends*. It's Saturday morning, when we discuss my choice of the week. Today, it's Susan Cain's book titled *Quiet: The Power of Introverts in a World That Can't Stop Talking*, as well as ideas on her website called Quiet Revolution. Cain, whose work explores the character of introverts, feels that American society often prefers extroverts. Her goal is to show that there is power in quiet. She says, "I prefer listening to talking, reading to **socializing**, and cozy chats to group settings. I like to think before I **speak (softly)**." She feels you don't have to **be an extrovert** to be heard.

We often talk about extroverts and introverts, but what do we really mean by these words? An extrovert is someone who easily **attracts attention**, **enjoys the company of** others, and can **be the life of the party**. Some think that extroverts like to **show off**, whereas an introvert is someone who **is reserved**, may find it difficult to **speak up** and express opinions, and often **feels left out** in social situations. These are the two stereotypes accepted by most people, but there's a third personality type, which Quiet Revolution explores: an ambivert. This is a person who sometimes needs quiet and gets energy from it and at other times works best **interacting with people**. I'd never heard of an ambivert before but immediately realized I am one! Which means part of me **is an introvert**. And suddenly, the book got a whole lot more interesting.

GLOSSARY

stereotype (*n*) a set idea that people have about what someone or something is like

C 🔊 1.18 THINK CRITICALLY **Listen and read again. What is the aim of Susan Cain's work? Why do you think she started this project? Do you think it will be helpful to people?**

2 VOCABULARY: Describing personality

FIND IT

A 🔊 1.19 **Look at the expressions in bold in the script in exercise 1B. Which describe introvert behavior? Which describe extrovert behavior? Can any of the expressions describe both? Define each expression using other words. Use a dictionary or your phone to help you. Listen and check your work.**

B Now go to page 142. Do the vocabulary exercises for 3.1.

C PAIR WORK THINK CRITICALLY **In what jobs or other areas of life do you think it's helpful to be an introvert? An extrovert? Explain why.**

3 GRAMMAR: Relative pronouns; reduced relative clauses

A Read the sentences in the grammar box. Circle the correct options to complete the rules.

> ### Relative clauses
>
> It's Saturday morning, **when we discuss my choice of the week**.
>
> Cain, **whose work explores the character of introverts**, feels that American society often prefers extroverts.
>
> An extrovert is someone **who easily attracts attention**.
>
> These are the two stereotypes **accepted by most people.** (= that are accepted).

> **!** Use *which* with times, dates, and days when the word defined by the relative clause is a subject or object, **not** a time adverbial.
>
> *She loves **Fridays, which** is the worst day of the week for me.*

1 The relative pronoun can be **the subject** / **the subject or the object** of a relative clause.

2 Use *when* / *which* to add information about particular times, dates, and days.

3 In relative clauses, *who* / *whose* shows possession.

4 Reduced relative clauses **include** / **don't include** the relative pronoun and the verb *be*.

B ▶ **Now go to page 131. Look at the grammar chart and do the grammar exercise for 3.1.**

C Make true sentences about yourself using relative clauses and the prompts below. Check your accuracy. Then share with a partner. Were any of your ideas similar?

1 going to parties with a lot of people
2 the kind of people you like to be friends with
3 something you like to do in a certain type of weather
4 something you read recently
5 something to describe one of the jobs you've had

> **✓ ACCURACY** CHECK
>
> Use an article or possessive pronoun with a singular noun followed by reduced relative clauses with *-ed*.
>
> *Cain wrote about young introverts in~~ book~~ called* Quiet Power. ✗
> *Cain wrote about young introverts in a/ the/her book called* Quiet Power. ✓

4 SPEAKING

A **PAIR WORK** **THINK CRITICALLY** Student A: Talk about advantages of being an introvert. Student B: Talk about advantages of being an extrovert. Then try to convince your partner that you're right. Change roles and repeat. Then say which you agree with more.

> People **who are introverts** often make good choices. They think about things carefully, **which helps them** make good decisions.

> People **that are extroverts** often **speak up** at meetings and **attract** the boss's attention. In the office where I work, people **whose voices are heard** are promoted faster.

23

THINGS AND EMOTIONS

1 LANGUAGE IN CONTEXT

A **Look at the pictures and identify the objects in them. What do you think of when you see these things? Then read the posts. What is each post about?**

Comments

Profile   Sign Out

@dougj: I'm just sitting here, thinking about the strange things I love and hate. For example, most people think crows are **creepy**, but I think they're **impressive**. A crow flying slowly across the sky looks **stunning**. Some people like to stand on beaches, watching sunsets. But I watch big black birds flying by. What about you?

@dannys22: I find mushrooms **disgusting**. Not the taste. It's because they feel like rubber in my mouth. Gross!

@asans5: I love opening a jar of peanut butter and hearing that popping sound! It's more enjoyable than *eating* the peanut butter.

@davidortiz: Popping bubble wrap. It's *so* **satisfying**.

@happyjia: I can't stand touching wool. I find the feel of it really **irritating**. Just looking at it makes me feel **uneasy** and **tense**.

@mandymandy: This might be **bizarre**, but I think the smell of subway stations is **fabulous**. I hardly ever go on the subway these days, but as a child living in New York City, I took it a lot with my mom. Now, that smell reminds me of my childhood.

@greatj: The smell of a swimming pool reminds me of my childhood. I just love it!

@msalex5: I kind of like the smell of gasoline. It reminds me of trips with my family. Maybe we're all a little **weird**!

> ### INSIDER ENGLISH
>
> *gross* = something extremely unpleasant
> *Gross!*   *That's **gross**!*
> *Mushrooms are **gross**.*

B **Read the posts again. What does each person like or dislike?**

C GROUP WORK **What little things in life do you love and hate?**

2 VOCABULARY: Strong feelings

A 🔊 **1.20** Look at the words in the box. Cover the posts in exercise 1A on page 24 and look at the pictures. Can you remember which words were used to describe them? Which ones are used to talk about things that are good, bad, or unusual? Listen and check your work.

bizarre	creepy	disgusting	fabulous	impressive	irritating
satisfying	stunning	tense	uneasy	weird	

B ▶ **Now go to page 143. Do the vocabulary exercises for 3.2.**

C **PAIR WORK** Describe something that gives you one of the feelings in exercise 2A. Your partner guesses the feeling. Take turns. For ideas, watch Wendy's video.

EXPERT SPEAKER

Do the things that Wendy talks about make you feel the same way? Talk about other things that give you those feelings.

3 GRAMMAR: Present participles

A Read the sentences in the grammar box. Complete the rules.

> **Present participles**
>
> I'm just sitting here, **thinking** about the strange things I love and hate.
> A crow **flying** slowly across the sky looks stunning.
> Some people like to stand on beaches, **watching** sunsets.
> … as a child **living** in New York City, I took it a lot with my mom.

1 To describe two events happening at **the same time** / **different times**, put the verb that describes the second event after a comma, and use the *-ing* form of the verb.

2 To add more information about a **noun** / **verb**, use the *-ing* form of the verb.

B ▶ **Now go to page 132. Look at the grammar chart and do the grammar exercise for 3.2.**

C Look at the present participles in the grammar box in exercise 3A. Make new sentences true for you, using the participles to describe two events happening at the same time or to give more information about a noun.

4 SPEAKING

A **PAIR WORK** Look at the pictures. How do you feel about these things? Think what you might be doing, seeing, or experiencing when you see these things.

> I think freshly ground coffee smells fabulous. It's so nice to smell it, relaxing on the balcony every morning.

3.3 ASKING FOR FAVORS

1 LISTENING

A How do you react when your boss or teacher asks you to do something you're not confident about?

B 🔊 **1.21** Listen to the conversation. Kelly is an intern at the International Student Services office of a college. What is she asked to do? What is she worried about? What does her boss, Sandra, suggest?

> **GLOSSARY**
> **intern** (*n*) a student, or someone who has recently finished their studies, who works for a company for a short time, sometimes without being paid, in order to get work experience

C 🔊 **1.22** Listen to Mateo and his boss, David. What is Mateo asked to do? What excuses does he make? What happens in the end?

> **GLOSSARY**
> **deadline** (*n*) a time or day by which something must be done

D 🔊 **1.21 and 22** **LISTEN FOR INFERENCE** Listen to both conversations again. What does Kelly say to show that she's not comfortable talking about the program? What does Mateo say to show he's not happy about giving a presentation?

E **PAIR WORK** **THINK CRITICALLY** We can often guess how people feel, even if they don't say it directly. Discuss the speakers' situations and complete the sentences together. What clues or knowledge do you use to guess how people feel?

1 Sandra probably understands that Kelly is uneasy because _____ .

2 Hwan is probably happy to help because _____ .

3 David wants Mateo to say yes. Therefore, David _____ .

4 Mateo probably feels uncomfortable saying no to David because _____ .

F Do you think Mateo acts professionally with his boss? Why or why not?

2 PRONUNCIATION: Listening for /t/ at the ends of words

A 🔊 **1.23** Listen to the /t/ sounds in this sentence. Which ones are pronounced differently?

I just want the rest of the team to get a general sense of the project.

B 🔊 **1.24** Underline the /t/ sounds in the conversation. Which ones could be pronounced differently? Listen and check.

A That's OK. I just want the rest of the team to get a general sense of the project.

B Um … Sorry, but I wouldn't be comfortable speaking in front of the whole team. My English isn't very good for that kind of thing.

A Your English is fine. Don't worry about it. So, will you do it?

B Yes, I can probably manage that.

C Circle the correct options to complete the sentences.

When /t/ is at the *beginning / end* of a word and the sound before it is /n/ or *a vowel / another consonant*, then the /t/ may be pronounced silently. But if that /t/ is also followed by a *vowel / consonant* sound, it might be pronounced more like /d/.

3 SPEAKING SKILLS

A Look at the expressions from the conversations in exercises 1B and 1C on page 26. Write *M* (making a request), *A* (accepting a request), or *R* (refusing a request) next to each one.

> ### Make and respond to requests
>
> 1 Is there any chance you could … ?   _____
> 2 I don't mean to be rude, but …   _____
> 3 Would you be willing to … ?   _____
> 4 I'd be happy to help out.   _____
>
> 5 Do you think it would be possible (for you) to … ?   _____
> 6 I don't know how much I'd be able to …   _____
> 7 Sorry, but I wouldn't be comfortable [*-ing* verb] …   _____
> 8 Yes, I can probably manage that.   _____

B **PAIR WORK** With your partner, take turns making and responding to requests in the two situations below. Use expressions from exercise 3A.

1 You need help with an essay.

2 You would like your partner to work next weekend.

C **PAIR WORK** Student A: Go to page 157. Student B: Go to page 159. Follow the instructions.

4 PRONUNCIATION: Using polite intonation for requests

A 🔊 **1.25** Listen to each request said twice. Which version sounds more polite to you – the first or the second?

1 Is there any chance you could finish the presentation today?

2 Do you think it would be possible to help me right now?

B 🔊 **1.26** Listen and circle the ending of the request that you think sounds more polite. Then repeat the polite requests.

1 Could you please *think about it? / wait for me outside?*

2 Do you think it would be possible for you *to call me back later? / to be a little quieter?*

3 Is there any chance you could *speak to her yourself? / spell that for me?*

4 Would you be willing to *give the presentation? / check my presentation?*

C **PAIR WORK** Take turns saying these requests to each other politely and agreeing to help. If you think the request is not said politely, try to explain why you feel this way. Then give your partner the chance to try again.

Would you be willing to work on Saturday?

Do you think it would be possible to do that again?

Is there any chance you could come ten minutes earlier?

Would you be willing to share with Alex?

Do you think it would be possible to translate it into English?

5 SPEAKING

A **PAIR WORK** Role play one of the situations. Decide who makes the request and who responds. The person making the request tries to convince the other to say yes. Then change roles, choose another situation, and repeat.

1 Student A: You want help painting your apartment because you're having a party.
   Student B: You don't like painting.

2 Student A: You need someone to take care of your dog for a week because you're going on vacation.
   Student B: You don't like dogs.

3 Student A: You need someone to give English lessons to your child.
   Student B: You've never worked with children before.

> Is there any chance you could take care of my dog for a week, starting this Friday?

> Your dog? Um … I don't mean to be rude, but I'm kind of uncomfortable with dogs.

I O U :)

3.4 THE RIGHT JOB FOR ME

LESSON OBJECTIVE
■ write a personal statement for a job application

1 READING

A **Would you like to work with animals? What kind of work would you like to do? What kinds of zoo jobs do you think involve working with animals? Which don't involve working with animals? Read the text. Were any of the jobs you thought of mentioned?**

www.wellsbrookzoo/jobs.mzorg

WELLS BROOK **ZOO**   Job Search • <u>View All Jobs</u> • Internships • Volunteer Opportunities

Are you good with people and penguins? Then the Wells Brook Zoo needs you.

CURRENT JOB OPENINGS

JOB TITLE: Sales Assistant

Position Summary: Sales assistants work in the Wells Brook Zoo gift shop, called Zoovenirs, helping customers with sales.

Responsibilities: You will greet customers as they enter Zoovenirs and answer any questions they may have about the products. You will arrange merchandise, maintaining an organized appearance in the store. You will also be expected to handle cash and credit card sales.

Skills Needed: Experience with customer service and handling cash is preferred. You must have good communication skills and be able to work independently.

JOB TITLE: Face Painter

Position Summary: Face painters work in areas throughout the zoo, painting animal designs on customers.

Responsibilities: You will paint animals on customers' faces and hands, using a variety of Wells Brook Zoo's preset designs. You will greet customers as they walk by and will take cash and make change if required.

Skills Needed: You must be patient and be able to interact well with children. Previous art training is required, and face painting experience is preferred. You must be comfortable working outside.

JOB TITLE: Zookeeper Assistant

Position Summary: Zookeeper assistants help the zookeepers take care of the animals.

Responsibilities: You will feed a variety of animals, including penguins, birds, and turtles, and will keep animal areas clean and safe. You will enter information into a database about animal behavior and health.

You will also give tours and educational information to school groups visiting the zoo.

Skills Needed: Experience working with animals and speaking in front of people is preferred.

JOB TITLE: Assistant Cook

Position Summary: Assistant cooks work in the Wells Brook Zoo cafeteria, helping the cook prepare food.

Responsibilities: You will follow instructions from the head cook as you prepare and cook preset menu items. You will clean kitchen equipment and cookware. You may sometimes have to cook and serve food at food stands located throughout the zoo.

Skills Needed: You must be able to follow instructions but also work independently when necessary. Food service experience is strongly preferred.

Email a personal statement and résumé to wellsbrookzoo.job@mz.org.

GLOSSARY
database (n) information stored in a computer system in an organized way so that it can be searched in different ways
cookware (n) items such as pans, bowls, knives, spoons, etc., used in cooking

B PAIR WORK | IDENTIFY AUDIENCE Read again. Who is the audience for the text? What do you think are the most important responsibilities and skills they need to do and have for each job?

C GROUP WORK Which job would you like to have the most? Which job would you be the best at? Give reasons.

D THINK CRITICALLY Which aspects of each job are good for introverts? Extroverts? Ambiverts?

2 WRITING

A Read Jonathan's personal statement for the zookeeper assistant job at the Wells Brook Zoo. What are his (1) qualifications, (2) experience, and (3) goals? How good of a candidate do you think he is?

REGISTER CHECK

In order to is often used in more formal writing. *To* is often used in less formal writing.

Formal

*My goal is to expand my experience **in order to** become a zookeeper.*

Less formal

*My goal is to get more experience **to** become a zookeeper.*

Jonathan Mendoza | 123 Park Road, Langley, VA 22101 •
575-555-6201 • jmendoza1992@xyz.com

Personal Statement

I am a recent college graduate with a BS in Animal Science and Management, I have a lifelong interest in animals and birds. Summer jobs as an assistant animal keeper at Rosco Wildlife Center gave me practical experience in observing animals for signs of bad health, preparing their food and sleeping areas, cleaning and repairing their living areas, and educating the public about the inhabitants of the zoo. Interacting with children visiting the zoo was particularly rewarding. I am able to work year-round and on weekends and am excited about helping maintain the excellent standards of animal care at the Wells Brook Zoo. My goals are to expand my knowledge and experience in order to become a full-time zookeeper and to provide the animals with the best environment so that they can enjoy their life in the zoo.

FIND IT

B PAIR WORK These are useful words for personal statements: *lifelong interest, expand, maintain, standards*. Find them in the text and discuss what they mean. You can look online for help.

C COMPOSE AND EVALUATE A PERSONAL STATEMENT Read the guide to writing and evaluating personal statements. How well does Jonathan's statement follow this advice?

IS YOUR PERSONAL STATEMENT …

CONCISE? Keep it short. Avoid unnecessary words that add no meaning. Avoid overusing the word "I." Vary the sentence structure. Put the information in one paragraph.

RELEVANT? Write about who you are and what you can do. Emphasize only skills and talents relevant to the job. Avoid common expressions such as "good at working on a team" or "a dedicated and enthusiastic worker." Say how you can contribute to the organization. Briefly mention your career goals.

ACCURATE? Check your punctuation (avoid exclamation points), spelling, and grammar.

WRITE IT

D PLAN You are going to write a personal statement. Work with a partner. Choose one of the other job listings from exercise 1A on page 28. Discuss the skills, experience, qualifications, and goals to include and things to avoid. Then, looking at Jonathan's statement, say how you are going to structure yours.

E Write your personal statement. Then look at the guide in exercise 2C. Have you followed all the tips? Make any changes if necessary.

F PAIR WORK | THINK CRITICALLY Read your partner's personal statement. Which job did they apply for? What are the strongest points in their statement?

TIME TO SPEAK
Getting the job

A **DISCUSS** In many jobs, it's helpful to be good at the things below. In your opinion, what personal qualities do you need in order to do each of them well?

meet deadlines   work on a team   make decisions   give your opinion at meetings

B Work with a partner. Read the text from a company's website. Then imagine you work for this company in human resources. It's your job to interview interns who may have the qualities to become full-time employees. Decide together what to ask in the interviews. Design two or three questions to find out about the things in part A. See the examples below.

MEET DEADLINES
What's the main reason for missing deadlines, and how would you avoid it?

WORK ON A TEAM
How would you handle working with a person you didn't like?

MAKE DECISIONS
What steps would you take before making an important decision?

GIVE YOUR OPINION AT MEETINGS
If you disagreed with everyone else in a meeting, would you speak up?

Our company has a high percentage of "home-grown" employees. These are people who joined us as interns, showed that they were valuable to the company, and were hired for full-time positions.

C **PREPARE** Work with a different partner. Test your questions from part B. Imagine your partner is an intern and interview them. Change roles and repeat. How well did your questions reveal whether you and your partner have the qualities to work at the company? If necessary, revise your questions to improve them.

D **PRESENT** Tell the class about your questions and why you chose them. The class compares all the questions and chooses the best four. What were the best answers you heard to the four questions?

To check your progress, go to page 153.

USEFUL PHRASES

PREPARE

This question revealed that …

Our question about … shows someone who … would be a good employee.

We thought this question would … , but it didn't.

We could improve this question by …

REVIEW 1 (UNITS 1–3)

1 VOCABULARY

A Complete the paragraph with the correct words.

accept	adapt	company	complex	cope	extrovert
frightened	left	resist	socialize	time-consuming	waste

My family moved to Tokyo, Japan, when I was 17 because of my father's job. I couldn't speak any Japanese, so I was
[1] _____ at first. And Tokyo was so huge and crowded. I had no idea how to [2] _____ with so many
changes. I felt [3] _____ out of everything, even though I'm a(n) [4] _____ . But then I made some friends
and started to [5] _____ again. I also started learning Japanese, which was [6] _____ and [7] _____ ,
but learning a language is never a(n) [8] _____ of time. Anyway, the whole experience taught me that if we don't
[9] _____ change, but instead [10] _____ and welcome it, we'll probably [11] _____ to new situations
much better. And for those who enjoy the [12] _____ of people, it helps to try to make friends right away.

B **PAIR WORK** Imagine a friend is moving to a different country and is nervous about it. Give them some advice.
Complete the sentences with your own ideas.

1 It's important to tackle _____ .

2 Don't underestimate your ability to _____ .

3 Try not to be irritated when _____ .

4 Remember: It's never a waste of time to _____ .

5 It's tricky to _____ , but I'm sure you'll be fine.

2 GRAMMAR

A Complete the conversation with the correct form of the verbs in parentheses ( ). Use comparative and
superlative forms when necessary. Use *would* and *used to* when possible. Sometimes there is more than one
correct answer.

A When I was a kid, I [1] _____ (hate) vegetables. I [2] _____ (not, eat) them but [3] _____ (push)
them to the side of my plate. I [4] _____ (always, cause) trouble at meal times.

B Well, luckily our tastes in things [5] _____ (tend, change) as we get older. In school, I [6] _____ (play)
soccer and basketball, but I [7] _____ (never, play) any sports now. My friends say I'm [8] _____ (less,
active) person they know!

A I'm the opposite. I'm [9] _____ (athletic) now than I was before. And what about spending habits? As a child,
I [10] _____ (spend) all my money on comics and candy. Now, two of my [11] _____ (big) expenses are
electronics and my car.

B For me, a car [12] _____ (not, useful, enough, spend) money on. It's
[13] _____ (important, see) friends than [14] _____ (drive) a car.

B **PAIR WORK** Discuss how your tastes and habits have changed since you were a child.

3 VOCABULARY

A **Circle the correct options.**

Some people believe that instead of exploring space or the ocean, we should explore our own backyards. By "backyards," they mean our own local area. They say there are many interesting ¹*species / animal life* in our local ²*surface / environment*, including rare, ³*endangered / adaptable* ones, that we can discover. So in your area, there might be a field, a park, a ⁴*sea life / pond*, or a forest where you can ⁵*launch / come across* various birds, insects, and small animals. It's fascinating to ⁶*explore / observe* these creatures in their natural ⁷*satellite / habitat*. Backyard ⁸*exploration / origin* can also help teach children why it's important to ⁹*preserve / use up* animal and plant ¹⁰*life / creature*. It creates a healthy and more pleasant environment for us all. We must learn to live with the other ¹¹*resources / forms of life* around us. The ¹²*investigation / resources* of our own backyards makes us appreciate our world.

B **PAIR WORK** **Complete the statements with your own ideas. Then compare ideas with another pair.**

1 I think the idea of exploring our own backyards _____ because
_____ .

2 I find zoos _____ because the habitat in many of them is
_____ .

3 It's _____ to monitor animal and plant species because
_____ .

4 Learning about Earth's resources and forms of life is _____ than learning about space because _____ .

5 The most important thing we can do in our lives is _____ . The reason is
_____ .

4 GRAMMAR

A **Complete the sentences with the correct words.**

considered	found	living	selling	that/which
when	where	which	who	whose

1 In your city, are there any activities _____ encourage people to explore their environment?

2 Describe the area _____ you live.

3 As a person _____ in an urban environment, how do you keep in touch with nature?

4 Do you know any people _____ jobs involve working in nature or with animals?

5 Name someone _____ has helped protect or preserve animal life or natural areas.

6 Name three places _____ to be the most natural and untouched areas in your country.

7 Describe a time _____ you celebrated an occasion outdoors.

8 What are some ways in _____ we can bring nature into our homes?

9 Of all the natural resources _____ in your country, which are the most valuable?

10 Are there any stores _____ green, nature-friendly products near you?

B **PAIR WORK** **Take turns responding to the sentences in exercise 4A. Give as much information as you can.**

UNIT OBJECTIVES
- talk about your support team in life
- make decisions
- discuss advantages and disadvantages
- write a summary
- plan a fund-raising event

COMBINED EFFORT

4

START SPEAKING

A What are the people doing? Have you or someone you know had a similar experience?

B What are the benefits of teamwork in this situation? What impact is it having on what the people are doing and how they're feeling?

C In your opinion, what are the biggest advantages or challenges of teamwork? Discuss your views. For ideas, watch Lucia's video.

EXPERT SPEAKER

Are any of Lucia's ideas different from yours? Do you agree with them?

IT TAKES A TEAM

1 LANGUAGE IN CONTEXT

A **PAIR WORK** Think of people who are important to you. What roles do they have in your life? Then read about eight important kinds of people in our lives. According to the article, which one knows the most about you?

A TEAM FOR LIFE

We all need help sometimes. Most of us have developed a network of "helpers" who play such important roles in our lives that it would be hard to manage without them. Do you recognize any of these people in your life?

The Listener
quietly **keeps an eye on** you and is willing to listen whenever you want to talk.

The Fixer
demonstrates an amazing ability to solve problems. They can suggest practical and creative solutions to problems with technology, the home, your studies, and even relationships.

The Organizer
knows your schedule, wants to **oversee** arrangements, and **acts as** a kind of boss. This helpful person enjoys planning trips, making reservations, buying tickets, and much more.

The Reporter
photographs everything your group does and posts it online. This person helps **build a** good **relationship** in the group by sharing whatever you do together.

The Memorizer
is good at remembering important information. They **take on** the responsibility of reminding you of everything, including what you said and did in the past!

The Teacher
is the one you **turn to** for help, who **assists** you by giving advice about big life decisions. Because of their experience, they can even **steer you away from** trouble.

The Long-Timer
has known you for so long that you've **built** total **trust**. This person knows about your background, experiences, and views. They only need to look at you to know what you're thinking.

The Joker
is always cheerful and makes you laugh. This person **enables you to** see the funny side of life and **contributes** a lot to your happiness.

B Read again. Summarize the main way in which each person is helpful.

2 VOCABULARY: Professional relationships

A 🔊 **1.27** Look at the words from the article in exercise 1A in the box. Then describe each one using other words. Use a dictionary or your phone to help you. Listen and check your work.

FIND IT

act as	assist	build a relationship	build trust
contribute	demonstrate	enable (sb) to	keep an eye on
oversee	steer (sb) away from	take on	turn to

B ▶ **Now go to page 143. Do the vocabulary exercises for 4.1.**

C **PAIR WORK** **THINK CRITICALLY** Think of a situation for each of the personality types described in the article in exercise 1A in which they would be most helpful. Can you think of any situations where they would do more harm than good? Explain your answers.

3 GRAMMAR: Adding emphasis: *so … that, such … that, even, only*

A Read the sentences in the grammar box. Complete the rules with the words in the box.

> **Adding emphasis:** *so … that, such … that, even, only*
>
> … who play **such important roles** in our lives **that** it would be hard to manage without them.
>
> They can **even** steer you away from trouble.
>
> The Long Timer has known you for **so long that** you've built total trust.
>
> They **only** need to look at you to know what you're thinking.

even	only	so	such

1 You can use *so* (*that*) and *such* (*that*) to emphasize the result of something. Use _____ + adjective or adverb (*that*). Use _____ (*an/an*) + (adjective) noun (*that*).

2 _____ can add emphasis or signal that something is surprising. _____ means "no one else" or "nothing else."

B Now go to page 132. Look at the grammar chart and do the grammar exercise for 4.1.

C Complete the sentences with *so, such, even,* or *only* and your own ideas. Sometimes more than one answer is possible. Then check your accuracy.

1 Some people have _____ busy lives that …

2 _____ quiet people sometimes want …

3 It's not good to take on _____ much responsibility that …

4 _____ people who know a lot need …

5 Friendship is _____ important that …

D GROUP WORK Compare your sentences from exercise 3C. Whose ideas do you agree with the most?

> ✔ **ACCURACY** CHECK
>
> Remember to use a pronoun or a noun after *so* + adjective + *that*.
>
> *He's so funny ~~that makes~~ everyone laugh.* ✗
>
> *He's so funny that he makes everyone laugh.* ✓

4 SPEAKING

A PAIR WORK Have you ever had to coordinate a group of people? Discuss what the situation was and how it went. How did you feel about being the decision-maker? For ideas, watch Lucia's video.

EXPERT SPEAKER

Was your experience similar to Lucia's?

> I once had to **act as** a guide to a big group of friends who wanted to see my town. It proved to be **such a difficult** task to keep everyone happy **that** I'd think twice before doing it again! I did enjoy being the person they **turned to** for help, though.

DESTRUCTIVE TEAMS

1 LANGUAGE IN CONTEXT

A   How do you feel when someone criticizes your ideas? Do you think negative comments are useful?

B   🔊 **1.28** Read and listen to an interview with management consultant Zack Sanchez from a podcast called *Better Teamwork*. What are red teams? Sum them up in one sentence.

The red team

🔊 1.28 Audio script

Host	Every business school graduate knows that good teams are **constructive**, right? Well, Zack Sanchez is here to present another idea: a *destructive* team, or a red team. Zack, welcome to the show.
Zack	Thanks for having me.
Host	So, a red team. What is that exactly?
Zack	Well, first, imagine you're part of a group that's starting a big project. Everyone's excited and congratulating themselves on how great it's going to be. Well, that kind of enthusiasm can actually be dangerous. When everyone is super positive, they often can't see the negative **aspects** of a plan.
Host	I see. So that's why you need a red team?
Zack	Exactly. A red team is two or three people from the group whose job is to play the bad guy – look for **weaknesses** and **draw attention to** possible negative **consequences**. A red team doesn't **weigh the pros and cons**, balancing **strengths** and weaknesses. That's a job for others to do. A red team honestly **assesses** a project and **points out** problem areas.
Host	And teams are open to this? I mean, teams are used to supporting one another, not criticizing each other. I've been on a red team myself, and it wasn't much fun.
Zack	That's why a red team's criticisms should not be **unreasonable**. You've seen for yourself that they need to be **valid** points that have been **thought through** carefully. The other team can't do that by itself.
Host	And that's when destructive becomes constructive.

C   🔊 **1.28** Read and listen again. What does it mean to "play the bad guy"? How does this relate to red teams?

2 VOCABULARY: Assessing ideas

A   🔊 **1.29** Look at the words from the podcast in the box. Which are verbs / verb phrases? Which are adjectives? Which are nouns? Listen and check your work.

aspect	assess	consequence	constructive	destructive
draw attention to	point out	strength	think through	unreasonable
valid	weakness	weigh the pros and cons		

B   ▶ **Now go to page 144. Do the vocabulary exercises for 4.2.**

C   PAIR WORK | THINK CRITICALLY   Discuss the pros and cons of red teams. Overall, do you think they're a good idea? Would you be a good red team member? Why or why not?

3 GRAMMAR: Reflexive pronouns; pronouns with *other/another*

A   Read the sentences in the grammar boxes. Circle the correct options to complete the rules.

> ### Reflexive pronouns
>
> Everyone's excited and congratulating **themselves** on how great it's going to be.
> I've been on a red team **myself**, and it wasn't much fun.
> You've seen for **yourself** that they need to be valid points.
> The other team can't do that **by itself**.

1   You can use reflexive pronouns when the subject and object of a sentence are **different / the same**.
2   You **can / can't** use reflexive pronouns to emphasize that an action is performed by the subject.
3   *By* + a reflexive pronoun means **alone, without help / with other people**.

> ### Pronouns with *other/another*
>
> Zack Sanchez is here to present **another** idea.   **The other** team can't do that by itself.
> That's a job for **others** to do.
> Teams are used to supporting **one another**, not criticizing **each other**.

4   *Another / The other* is the second half of a pair. *Another / The other* means "one more."
5   *Others* shows there **is one more / are several more** of something.
6   The meaning of *each other* and *one another* is **the same / different**.

B   ▶ **Now go to page 133. Look at the grammar chart and do the grammar exercise for 4.2.**

C   Complete the questions with words from the grammar boxes in exercise 3A. Then ask and answer them with a partner.
1   What sports can people play by _____ ? Do you play any sports by _____ ?
2   What do you and your friends do to enjoy _____ ?
3   Who in your family helps you the most? How do the _____ help you?
4   How can neighbors help each _____ ? In what ways can they annoy one _____ ?

D   PAIR WORK   Talk about an experience working on a team. What did the team members do together, and what did they do by themselves? How did they help each other?

4 SPEAKING

A   PAIR WORK   THINK CRITICALLY   How do people make group decisions? How effective is this process? What are the challenges?

> In project groups, I find some people want to **draw attention to themselves** and don't listen to others.

> And some people just **point out** the **weaknesses** of other people's ideas but don't have any ideas **themselves**.

4.3 TWO PEOPLE, ONE JOB

1 LISTENING

A What do you think job sharing is? Have you, or has anyone you know, experienced it?

B 🔊 **1.30** Listen to Rafael and Shelby talk with Heather, their college professor. What advantages and disadvantages of job sharing do they mention?

C 🔊 **1.30** **LISTEN FOR ATTITUDE** Listen again. Which attitude does each speaker have? Circle one answer for each speaker.

Rafael:	**a**	positive	**b**	negative	**c**	curious
Shelby:	**a**	kind	**b**	sensible	**c**	unreasonable
Heather:	**a**	helpful	**b**	jealous	**c**	unpleasant

D **PAIR WORK** **THINK CRITICALLY** Do you think job sharing is a good idea for employees, bosses, and companies? Why or why not?

> **INSIDER** ENGLISH
>
> *be/get stuck with* = be left to deal with something you don't want

2 PRONUNCIATION: Listening for consonant–vowel linking between words

A 🔊 **1.31** Listen to this word group. Which words are linked together, and why?

It's an interesting idea worth considering.

B 🔊 **1.32** Listen. Underline the examples of consonant–vowel linking from exercise 1B.

1 So you're interested in job sharing?

2 I'm interested in finding out more about it.

3 … the advantage of doing the parts of a job you're best at …

4 … that's what I read in an article …

C Circle the correct options to complete the sentence.

When one word finishes in a consonant sound and the next word starts with a *consonant / vowel* sound, the two words are usually linked together when they are in *the same word group / different word groups*.

3 SPEAKING SKILLS

A 🔊 **1.30** Look at the expressions from the conversation in exercise 1B on page 38. Are they used to discuss advantages (A) or to discuss disadvantages (D)? Write *A* or *D*. Which words, do you think, might have linked sounds in these sentences? Listen to the conversation again to check.

> ### Discuss advantages and disadvantages
>
> 1 The main benefit is (that) … ____
> 2 A/Another plus is (that) … ____
> 3 The downside is (that) … ____
> 4 One/The tricky issue is (that) … ____
> 5 It gives the company/us/you/me the advantage of [-*ing* verb] … ____
> 6 I'd be / I'm concerned (that) … ____
> 7 The upside is (that) … ____
> 8 One/Another potential problem is (that) … ____

B ▶ | PAIR WORK | **Student A: Go to page 157. Student B: Go to page 159. Follow the instructions.**

4 PRONUNCIATION: Using stress in compounds

A 🔊 **1.33** Look at these pairs of words. Which word in each pair is stressed? Why?

college student   young children

B 🔊 **1.34** Draw the stress pattern at the top of each column. Then listen and add the phrases to the correct columns.

noun + noun	adjective + noun
college student	young children

C | PAIR WORK | Think of some more examples of compounds like these, and use them to make a short story. Give your story to another pair to read out loud. Listen and give them feedback on how they pronounce the compounds.

5 SPEAKING

A | PAIR WORK | THINK CRITICALLY Choose a job below or your own idea. Discuss the advantages and disadvantages of job sharing for that job. One person points out the advantages and the other the disadvantages. Then choose another job, change roles, and repeat.

> accountant   chef   dentist
> graphic designer mechanic   receptionist
> teacher   truck driver

> It's a good idea for chefs to job share. **The main benefit is** having more personal time for creative projects. And **a plus is** that there are two people to think of ideas for the menu.

> I don't know. **One potential problem is** that it can be difficult to agree on the ideas.

THE ME TEAM

1 READING

A **PAIR WORK** Do you prefer working alone or as part of a team? Why?

B **UNDERSTAND AUTHOR'S ATTITUDE** Read the article. Then circle the word in each pair that describes the author's writing.

1 **a** curious **b** critical

2 **a** objective **b** subjective

3 **a** optimistic **b** pessimistic

HOME   NEWS   **BLOG**   SIGN IN

Teamwork makes the dream work?

I'm not so sure.

Bev Shannon
The work-at-home office blogger

We all enjoy being part of a group – there's no better work than teamwork, right? Actually, I disagree. Teamwork can be tough. In fact, it was so difficult that I left my office job and started working from home on my own. It's a much better fit for me, and it has made me think about why teamwork can make our jobs harder rather than easier.

Personalities can make teamwork difficult. There's a famous saying, *There's no "I" in TEAM*, meaning I have to do what's best for the team, not what's best for me. But there's often someone on the team that puts their needs first: "**I** want to do it this way. **My** way is best." The team often goes along with this person, whose ideas might not be the best, just the loudest. Teamwork can be difficult for an introvert, like me. It's hard to speak up if there's a dominant voice in the group. And then there's that team member who likes to argue – and not in a constructive way – who just wants to say "no" because the others said "yes." And, my least favorite, the people pleaser – someone who is such a nice person that they feel they can't be honest. They don't want to hurt anyone's feelings, so they say "yes" to every idea. Just one difficult personality can make teamwork tough. Combine several challenging personality types, and it's even tougher.

Lack of time together can also make teamwork challenging. For example, I was once on a team where we never had enough time to meet as a group. Team member A was at a conference, B had to meet with a customer, C had an important phone call to make, and so on. To successfully work as a team, you need time together – and lots of it.

A final reason teamwork is difficult is because there's often no training on how to work on a team. You can't just put people in a room and expect them to work well with each other. You need to build trust with your team members. Think of football players: They aren't just given a ball and told to play. They practice, and they train. They also have different positions, know who does what, and how they affect one another. It helps to have clear roles on company teams, too, with the right people in them. It's not such a good idea to give the role of a leader to the ME, ME, ME person.

Teams can be tough, but working alone has its challenges, too. When my computer doesn't work, I don't have an IT person to turn to. When I have a great idea, I don't have anyone to share it with to see if it *really is a great idea*. Don't get me wrong – I still like my team of one and enjoy making all of the important decisions myself. But now I realize what was wrong with the teamwork I did in the past and how good teamwork could be if done correctly. And that's useful information – because one day I might want to turn my ME TEAM into a WE TEAM.

C Read again. What three main reasons does the author give to support her opinion about teamwork? What's her last thought about teamwork?

D **PAIR WORK** What examples does the author give to support each of her three main reasons? Which do you think are the strongest?

E **GROUP WORK** **THINK CRITICALLY** Think about your answer to exercise C on page 33. Has your opinion changed at all after reading this text? If so, how? Why? What's your attitude toward teamwork?

2 WRITING

A   Read the summary of an article called "The Power of the Team." Based on the summary, what is the main argument of the article?

> In his article "The Power of the Team," Max Jackson states that no one can achieve as much alone as they can on a team. Teamwork is essential to success in personal, educational, and professional situations. The most basic team is the family, which assists and cares for each member in order to make sure the entire family is secure. At school or college, teachers encourage their students to work together in order to produce superior projects or presentations. At work, teamwork is so important that without it, any company would fail. Even healthy competition between teams can build trust and improve relationships within the company. The secret of good teamwork is that each member should contribute their individual skills, talents, and ideas, but never forget that they are working as part of a team toward a common goal.

B   **SUMMARIZE MAIN POINTS** A summary is a short version of a longer text. Read about how to write a summary. Then answer these questions about the summary in exercise 2A.

1   What three situations does the writer mention?

2   What are the main points for each situation?

3   Does the last sentence sum up the main points?

REGISTER CHECK

The verb *state* is often used in more formal writing. *Say* is often used in less formal writing.

Summary writing

■   Keep your summary short (about ¼ of a page in length). Use one paragraph.

■   Use your own words. Don't rewrite the original text.

■   Mention the title and author of the text. State the main topic.

■   Briefly describe the author's main points.

■   After each main point, include the most relevant details or examples.

■   Don't add your own opinions. The summary should be based on information from the article.

WRITE IT

C   **PLAN** You're going to write a summary of the article "Teamwork makes the dream work? I'm not so sure." in exercise 1A on page 40. With your partner, look again at the main points and reasons you discussed in exercises 1B and 1C on page 40. Try summarizing them briefly in your own words. Then look at the summary writing tips in exercise 2B and plan the structure of your summary.

D   Write your summary of the article.

E   **PAIR WORK** **THINK CRITICALLY** Read each other's summaries. What are the strong points of your partner's summary? How do you think you could improve your own summary?

4.5 TIME TO SPEAK
The big event

LESSON OBJECTIVE
- plan a fund-raising event

A **AGREE** Imagine you want to organize a local event to raise money for a cause in your community. Work in a group and choose one of the causes below or think of one of your own.

research at a local hospital   an after-school youth program   improvements to the fire station
new equipment and uniforms for a local sports team   a music program for the local high school

B **DISCUSS** In your group, look at the events below for raising money for the cause you chose in part A. Think of more events. Discuss the advantages and disadvantages of each event. Consider the type of people who would support the cause you chose.

an art show   a barbecue   a concert   a fancy dress party   a marathon   a sports event

C **DECIDE** Choose an event or a combination of events. To help you decide, consider any skills, experience, equipment, or contacts you have that could be useful.

D Think about the jobs your team will need to do before, during, and after the event. Agree on who will be responsible for each job.

E **PRESENT** Tell the class about your event. Explain why it will be popular and why the people on your team have the ability to make it successful. The class chooses the best event.

To check your progress, go to page 154.

USEFUL PHRASES

AGREE
We could try …
Why don't we … ?
That might (not) be the best option …
That could work.

DISCUSS
The main benefit is …
Another plus / potential problem is …
The downside/upside is …
I'd be concerned that …

UNIT OBJECTIVES
- discuss how new technology can help people
- discuss the future of communication
- consider and contrast ideas
- write an online comment with examples
- plan a community improvement project

THE HUMAN FACTOR

5

START SPEAKING

A   What is happening in the picture? Do you think robots could be better at this activity than humans? Explain your answer.

B   Discuss some examples of tasks and situations that a robot might handle better than a human. Say why.

C   In your opinion, what things will always be done by humans and never by robots? Why? Discuss some examples. For ideas, watch Carolina's video.

EXPERT SPEAKER

Do you agree with Carolina's predictions?

5.1 IMITATING REALITY

1 LANGUAGE IN CONTEXT

A Look at the picture. How does the man feel? How do you feel about flying?

B Read the article about a man's experience with virtual reality. How many times did he use VR therapy? How successful was his experience in the end?

CAN VR THERAPY CURE ME?

I'm scared of flying. Not just a little. Whenever I get on a plane, I**'m scared to death**. I've cried on planes. As an adult. More than once. The fear **isn't rational**, but it is not something I**'m in control of** either. I read about a virtual reality treatment that has helped people like me, so I decided to try it.

STEP 1: GET A REAL THERAPIST
If you want to **try this therapy**, you'll need a therapist. That part's real, not virtual! During my sessions, however, we spent a lot of the time in the virtual world. And even then, the therapist was always in control of the software.

STEP 2: PANIC
The first time I put on a VR headset, I was surprised by my body's reaction. When you're in a VR environment, your mind can't tell what's real or not real. Within minutes, I **was panicking**. The therapist taught me how to **regain control** by using **a breathing technique**.

STEP 3: REPEAT
At my first session, my **anxiety level** was extremely high. There was still a lot of fear the second time, but now I **was more conscious of** what was happening. With careful breathing, I **calmed down**. By my third session, I felt almost relaxed.

STEP 4: FLY
Engine noise rising, speed increasing, ground disappearing – and all without the usual fear. I still felt nervous – a real plane is definitely more intense than a VR plane, but I really **had overcome my fear**. VR therapy had worked! I may even take flying lessons if the therapy continues to work so well. Nah!

Adapted from an article by Luke Johnson on the Wareable website

C Read again. What feelings did the man experience before, during, and after the therapy?

2 VOCABULARY: Dealing with emotions

A Look at the expressions in the box. Then describe each one using other words. Use a dictionary or your phone to help you. Then look at how they are used in the article in exercise 1B.

anxiety level	be conscious of	be in control of	**!** *sth* = something
be rational	be scared to death	breathing technique	
calm down	cure (an illness)	overcome my fear	
panic (about sth)	regain control	try a therapy	

FIND IT

B 🔊 **1.35** Look at the expressions in the box again. Which are verb phrases? Which are noun phrases? Listen and check your work.

C ▶ Now go to page 144. Do the vocabulary exercises for 5.1.

D PAIR WORK | THINK CRITICALLY What other strong fears do people have? What advice would you give on how to overcome these fears? Say why.

3 GRAMMAR: Real conditionals

A Read the sentences in the grammar box. Which rule is about the *if* clause? Which is about the main clause? Complete the rules.

> **Real conditionals**
>
> **Whenever** I **get** on a plane, I**'m** scared to death.
>
> **When** you**'re** in a VR environment, your mind **can't tell** what's real or not real.
>
> I **may** even **take** flying lessons **if** the therapy **continues** to work so well.

1 When something is a general fact or a routine, you can replace *if* with *when* and *whenever* in the _____ .

2 You can use modals to describe possible future situations and their results in the _____ .

B **Now go to page 133. Look at the grammar chart and do the grammar exercise for 5.1.**

C Write sentences with real conditionals from exercise 3A using the ideas below. Check your accuracy. Then compare with a partner. How similar are your ideas? Ask questions to find out more.

> ask for help   decide to try something new   feel uneasy
> see a spider   want to attract attention

✓ **ACCURACY** CHECK

Whenever is one word.

I feel scared when ever I'm in a tall building. ✗

I feel scared whenever I'm in a tall building. ✓

4 SPEAKING

A GROUP WORK THINK CRITICALLY How can VR be useful in medicine? In sports? For shopping? In training/education? Discuss in your group. For ideas, watch Carolina's video.

> If someone **wants** to learn how to drive, they **can try** a VR training program first.

> Yeah, I think their anxiety level **won't be** so high **if** they **practice** with an app.

EXPERT SPEAKER

How similar are Carolina's views to yours?

45

5.2 THE END OF THE OFFICE?

1 LANGUAGE IN CONTEXT

A **PAIR WORK** In your lifetime, what have been the biggest changes in how we communicate?

B 🔊 **1.36** Read and listen to Ramon and Jack discussing communication in a college debate. Do they change their attitudes in the end?

🔊 1.36 Audio script

Helena	The topic for this month's debate is the office of the future. We've asked millennials Ramon and Jack if they'd rent traditional office space for a future company or go virtual.
Ramon	Right. Well, millennials will soon be the largest group of workers. We communicate virtually day and night and **have no desire to** work in an office 9 to 5. Millennials will **be eager to** work for a virtual company as long as the technology is good.
Jack	OK, that may be true, but only if we're talking about future workers. Many current employees, older than us, **aren't prepared to** work like that. Even if the tech is amazing, face time is important.
Ramon	But how important? Companies can save hundreds of thousands of dollars a year in rent if they go virtual.
Jack	Well, I'**m not against** saving money, and I'**d be more than happy to** use videoconferencing for most meetings. But if you'**re passionate about** an idea and **are dying to** share it, you want to do it in person. You can't really connect with your team unless you're all in a room together.
Ramon	*All* communication will be virtual eventually, so we shouldn't **be reluctant to** lead the way. It could be the next big thing, providing companies invest more in technology.

> **GLOSSARY**
> **millennial** (*n*) a person who was born in the 1980s, 1990s, or early 2000s
> **face time** (*n*) time spent talking to people directly, not virtually

C 🔊 **1.36** Read and listen again. What does Ramon think about the office of the future? What does Jack think? What reasons do they give? Who do you agree with?

2 VOCABULARY: Willingness and unwillingness

FIND IT

A 🔊 **1.37** Look at the expressions in the box. Which ones were used in the script in exercise 1B? Use your phone to find examples online of the expressions that are not in the script, or make your own sentences. Which expressions mean you want to do something, and which mean you don't want to do something? Listen and check your work.

be against	be anxious to	be dying to	be eager to
be more than happy to	be passionate about	be prepared to	be reluctant to
be unwilling to	have no desire to	have no intention of	hesitate to

B ▶ Now go to page 145. Do the vocabulary exercises for 5.2.

C **PAIR WORK** Discuss how your friends and family communicate in different situations. When are they eager to talk face-to-face? What ways of communication are they reluctant to use?

3 GRAMMAR: Conditionals: alternatives to *if*

A Read the sentences in the grammar box. Circle the correct options to complete the rules.

Conditionals: alternatives to *if*

Millennials will be eager to work for a virtual company **as long as** the technology is good.

That may be true, but **only if** we're talking about future workers.

It could be the next big thing, **providing** companies invest more in technology.

Even if the tech is amazing, face time is important.

You can't really connect with your team **unless** you're all in a room together.

> **!** *Providing* and *as long as* are more common in writing.

1 Use *as/so long as*, *only if*, and *providing/provided* to show that the result **will / won't** happen when a specific condition becomes true.

2 Use *even if* when you believe the result **will / won't** change. *Even if* means "whether or not."

3 Use *unless* to describe a possible **positive / negative** condition in the present or future. It has a similar meaning to "except if" or "if … not."

B Now go to page 134. Look at the grammar chart and do the grammar exercise for 5.2.

C **PAIR WORK** Complete the sentences with your own ideas. Then compare and discuss your ideas with a partner.

1 Even if virtual reality improves a lot, _____ .

2 I wouldn't want to _____ unless I was paid a lot of money.

3 I'm prepared to work long hours, providing that _____ .

4 As long as _____ , I feel comfortable with people.

5 I'm more than happy to work in an office, but only if _____ .

4 SPEAKING

A **GROUP WORK** **THINK CRITICALLY** How, and under what conditions, can changes in technology affect the way we communicate with these people?

> bank staff   coaches / gym staff   doctors/therapists   government employees   teachers

> I think we'll have more doctor's appointments by video call, **providing** our privacy is protected.

> Yeah, but **only if** people are prepared to accept that. Some people **are unwilling to** share private information virtually.

STOP BLAMING GAMING

1 LISTENING

A 🔊 **1.38** **Talk about some good and bad things people say about video games. Then listen to a TV debate about video gaming. How many of your ideas do the speakers mention?**

B 🔊 **1.38** **Listen again. What does Parker think is a problem? Why does Nadia think gaming is a social activity?**

C 🔊 **1.38** **LISTEN FOR SPEAKER'S DEGREE OF CERTAINTY** **Listen again. Is the speaker certain or uncertain about their ideas? Listen to the language around these ideas and check (✓) the ones that sound confident.**

1 ☐ **Parker:** If you can't control your gaming, it's a problem.
2 ☐ **Host:** Young people spend 20 hours a week gaming.
3 ☐ **Parker:** A lot of people spend too many hours gaming.
4 ☐ **Nadia:** We would hear about major problems with gaming if there were any.
5 ☐ **Nadia:** Gaming doesn't cause isolation. It's a social activity.

D **PAIR WORK** **THINK CRITICALLY** **Whose views on video games seem the most believable? Why? Which view do you agree with?**

2 PRONUNCIATION: Listening for lower pitch information

A 🔊 **1.39** **Listen to this sentence. How are the underlined phrases connected to the noun phrases before them? What do you notice about how they are pronounced?**

With me to discuss this is Nadia Rivera, <u>a video game developer</u>, and Parker Wendell, <u>from the group Game On – Game Off</u>, which offers advice about gaming.

B 🔊 **1.40** **Listen to the sentence and then to a version of it with extra information added in parentheses. Repeat the original sentence and then the new version.**

And it's fantastic for the brain. It improves thinking speed, the ability to concentrate, and problem-solving skills.

And it's fantastic for the brain. It improves thinking speed (information processing), the ability to concentrate (how long we can concentrate for), and problem-solving skills (like critical thinking).

C (Circle) **the correct options to complete the sentence.**

When extra information is added next to a noun phrase, for example to define, explain, or give more details about the noun phrase, this extra information is usually pronounced *as part of the same / with a different* tone in a *lower / higher* key.

3 SPEAKING SKILLS

A Look at the expressions from the TV program in exercise 1A on page 48. Which ones show the speaker is certain, uncertain, or giving a contrasting idea? Complete the chart.

> At the same time, …
> It's a well-known fact (that) …
> Who knows …
>
> I don't have a clue …
> On the contrary, …
> You can bet (that) …
>
> I guarantee (that) …
> That said, …

Certain	Uncertain	Giving a contrasting idea

B Find the best place in the sentences below to add one of the expressions from exercise 3A. Use a different expression in each sentence. Then tell a partner if you agree with the statements. Say why or why not.

1 Most children like playing video games.

2 Video games are not relaxing. They're stressful.

3 VR games are the future, but there will soon be something even better.

4 … what crazy video games creators will come up with ten years from now.

5 Many games help develop useful skills and should be encouraged. We have to be careful about the time we spend playing them.

C ▶ PAIR WORK Student A: Go to page 157. Student B: Go to page 160. Follow the instructions.

4 PRONUNCIATION: Saying front vowels /ɪ/, /e/, and /æ/

A ◀)) 1.41 Listen. Then repeat the words and focus on the underlined vowels.

/ɪ/	video	figures	listen	industry	billion
/e/	ten	pleasure	bet	said	friends
/æ/	average	ask	fantastic	exact	actually

B Circle the correct options to complete the sentences.

The tip of the tongue is nearer to the *front / back* of the mouth for these vowels. The jaw moves *down / up* as you go from /ɪ/ to /e/ to /æ/.

C ◀)) 1.42 Listen and circle the words you hear.

1 bit bet bat   4 sit set sat
2 slipped slept slapped   5 rip rep wrap
3 tin ten tan   6 hid head had

D PAIR WORK Take turns saying one of the words from exercise 4C. Your partner should repeat the word you said.

5 SPEAKING

A PAIR WORK THINK CRITICALLY What are the different ways that video games can benefit people of all ages?

> It's a well-known fact that some video games can improve concentration and reaction speed. At the same time, we have to be conscious of the amount of time spent gaming …

WHAT LANGUAGE BARRIER?

1 READING

A **Have you ever used a translation app? Did you find it useful? Read the article. According to Lance, how can people be helped by translation apps? What can't they do?**

Sign up   Log in

🚲 THE TRAVELER'S TAKE

By Lance Levine

Do translation apps break down barriers or put up new ones?

A few years ago, while I was on a cycling trip in Brazil, I fell off my bike. I was a little banged up, but the front wheel of my bike was damaged badly. It looked like I was in for a difficult day. I needed tools to fix the bike, and I only had an air pump and some glue. I had seen a house a few minutes before, so I picked up my bike and started walking.

My Portuguese consisted of "please" and "thank you," so the language barrier was an issue. I had no idea how to explain what happened or ask for help or a ride to town. Then I remembered my translation app! What a relief. I spent about 20 minutes on the side of the road tapping out the story and creating requests for different things. I knew it wouldn't be perfect, but at least it would tell people the basics. I approached the house, app in hand, and knocked on the door.

Before I could press PLAY on my carefully constructed greeting, the elderly woman who answered the door was on the job. One look at me, my damaged bicycle, my dirty knees and torn shirt, and that translation app was about as useful as air conditioning on a motorcycle.

In five minutes' time, I was sitting on the patio with my leg on a stool, clean and bandaged. Maria (the elderly woman), her husband Gustavo, two of their kids, seven of their grandchildren, and a constantly changing group of neighbors had appeared from nowhere, and my tragedy was quickly becoming a party. Gustavo and

a neighbor were enjoying a heated debate about the best way to repair the wheel on my bicycle. The kids were exploring the contents of my backpack piece by piece and finding each hilariously funny. And the smell of food started to fill the air. A bike accident is usually a bad thing. But by the time Maria and her son João left me at my hotel that night, with a full stomach and a shiny, clean, fully repaired bicycle, I felt like the luckiest man in the world.

We're so independent these days. The internet and smartphones make information and services so easy to access. Translation apps, too, have their place and are very useful. I think from now on, though, I'm going to use that app for work or maybe in stores when I travel and need something specific. When it comes to people, I'll take the risk.

I won't catch story details, and I'll misunderstand instructions now and again. I'll definitely have trouble with jokes, but humor usually doesn't translate, even if your app gives you all the right words. I'll get surprises, maybe some bad ones but mostly good ones. I'll get to act things out and look ridiculous doing it, and I'll get to solve the puzzle of what someone else is trying to tell me. I'll get gestures, laughter, attention, and the kindness of strangers.

Language barrier? What language barrier?

> #### GLOSSARY
> **barrier** (*n*) something that prevents communication, action, or progress
> **gesture** (*n*) a movement you make with your hand, arm, or head to express your meaning

B **UNDERSTAND PROBLEMS AND SOLUTIONS** **Read again. After his crash, what problems did Lance expect to have? What happened instead?**

C **What's Lance's opinion of translation apps?**

D **PAIR WORK** **THINK CRITICALLY** **What's your opinion of translation apps? Do they make it harder to show our feelings, or do they enable us to have conversations we never thought possible?**

> **INSIDER** ENGLISH
>
> *Be in for* means *be about to experience something unpleasant.*

2 WRITING

A Read Julieta's comment in response to Lance's article in exercise 1A on page 50. What's her opinion of translation apps? How many situations does she describe to support her opinion?

COMMENTS

Julieta M.
New York

I think translation apps are great, but I use them more for writing than speaking. My company does business with an Italian company. We usually communicate in English, but sometimes they send me information in Italian. My app translates them just fine. I also exchange emails with a Chilean friend. Her English is only beginner level, so I use my app to send her messages in Spanish and to translate her messages. OK, we could try English, but I think she'd gradually stop writing. As long as I use my app, everything's fine.

As for speaking, when I was in Tokyo once, I got lost on my way to a meeting. I just stood there on the street, helpless. Finally, I stopped a man and used my app to ask, "Excuse me. Where's the Panorama Building?" He looked surprised, so I played it again. Then he laughed and pointed at the building right behind me. Well, at least I didn't have far to walk! So yes, I'm a big fan of these apps.

⌕ 2   ♡ 7   ⇆ 1

REGISTER CHECK

We use different organizing and connecting expressions in informal and formal texts. Look at these formal examples. Find informal examples in Julieta's comment.

Formal

That said, we could try English.

With regards to speaking, when I was in Tokyo once …

Therefore, I'm a big fan of these apps.

B **STATE OPINION AND GIVE EXAMPLES** Read about one way to organize an opinion comment. Then check Julieta's comment in exercise 2A. Does it have all these features?

1 **Make an opening statement.** Give your opinion of translation apps: for, against, or mixed feelings.

2 **Support your opinion with examples.** For each example, …

- **give some background.** Give a short explanation about the situation at the beginning.
- **describe what happened.** You can include direct speech if you want.
- **add a comment.** You can comment after each example, e.g., *My app translates them just fine*.

3 **Make a closing statement.** Give your opinion again but in different words.

WRITE IT

C **PLAN** You are going to write a comment in response to Lance's article. With a partner, discuss your opinion and give examples. The examples can be about your own or other's experiences. Then plan your opening statement, background information, description of what happened, and your closing statement.

D Write your comment.

E **PAIR WORK** Exchange your comments with a different partner. Do you have the same opinion about translation apps? What do you think about the examples your partner gave?

TIME TO SPEAK
Community improvement campaign

LESSON OBJECTIVE
■ plan a community improvement project

FIND IT

A Talk about a community project or event you know about. What was its purpose? Did it involve working with technology? How successful was it? Tell a partner. You can look online for ideas if you need to.

B **DECIDE** Work with a group and choose something to improve in your community. Use one of the ideas below or your own idea. Discuss how people will benefit from the project.

clean up and improve a public space

plan social events or activities for elderly people

create after-school programs for teens

start a community garden

C **DISCUSS** With your group, talk about the resources you'll need. How can you use technology in your project? What other materials or tools will you need? What roles will people have? Think of ways to do the project as cheaply as possible and how to encourage others to help.

D **PREPARE** Come up with a plan for your project. Decide how you'll get the resources you talked about in part C.

E **PRESENT** Present your plan to the class. Agree on which plan will benefit the community the most. Which project, other than your own, would you most like to work on?

To check your progress, go to page 154.

USEFUL PHRASES

DECIDE

Now that's a good idea.

On second thought, …

That said, …

Good point.

I see what you mean.

DISCUSS

It's a well-known fact that …

At the same time, we need …

You can bet that …

As long as … , we can …

That will work providing (that) …

If … , we'll …

Who will be in control of …

UNIT OBJECTIVES

- describe unexpected fame
- talk about unexpected situations
- make assumptions
- write an interesting story
- tell a story

EXPECT THE UNEXPECTED

6

START SPEAKING

A What is the situation in the picture? Do you think the people expected this situation? How are they reacting? How would you react?

B Think of some unexpected situations, like winning a lottery or meeting a well-known person. Discuss how you would react in these situations.

C Describe a time when something totally unexpected happened to you or someone you know. How did you, or the person you know, react? For ideas, watch Bojan's video.

EXPERT SPEAKER

How would you handle the situation Bojan describes?

GOING VIRAL

Kyle MacDonald

1 LANGUAGE IN CONTEXT

A Look at these pictures. What are they? How do you think they are connected to Kyle MacDonald? Then read the article and check your guesses.

FROM PAPERCLIP TO A HOUSE

What **makes a story entertaining** enough to go viral? In Kyle MacDonald's case, it was a simple red paperclip. He exchanged it online, and then kept trading for better things until he reached his final goal – his own house.

The 26-year-old from Vancouver had been trading things online for a year before he finally got offered a two-story, three-bedroom, 1920s farmhouse in Kipling, Canada, and **made the headlines**. The 14 trades that he made included a fish pen; a stove; an "instant party kit"; a snowmobile; a vacation to Yahk; a moving van; a recording contract; a year's free rent in Phoenix, Arizona; and a part in the movie *Donna on Demand*.

When Kyle was growing up in the suburbs of Vancouver, he watched children go door to door trying to trade their toys for something more valuable. He was sure as long as he tried hard enough, he would get what he wanted. And sure enough, an opportunity presented itself.

Not many people **had heard of** the small town of Kipling before the story **caught people's attention**. The mayor, Pat Jackson, was trying to promote tourism and decided to make the offer of the house to **get publicity** and **raise awareness of** the town as a friendly, welcoming place. His offer included not just the house, but the key to the town and the opportunity to be mayor for one day.

Since the trade Mr. MacDonald has **made an appearance** on a TV show, given interviews to newspapers, and set up a popular website. The red paperclip was definitely his ticket to fame.

Adapted from an article on the Mail Online website

GLOSSARY
trade (*n/v*) exchange one thing for another

B Read again. How did Kyle achieve his goal? Who is the other person in the story? What role did he play?

C **PAIR WORK** Can you think of another example when an ordinary person became accidentally famous? Tell your partner. You can check online if you need to.

FIND IT

2 VOCABULARY: Talking about fame

A 🔊 1.43 **PAIR WORK** Look at the expressions in the box and discuss their meaning. Then listen and check the definitions. Which of them were used in the article? Can you use any of the expressions to talk about the story you told in exercise 1C?

catch sb's attention	do a/the broadcast	get hits	get publicity
have a good/bad reputation	have (never) heard of sth	make an appearance	make sth entertaining
make headlines	praise sb	raise awareness (of sth)	seek fame

B Now go to page 145. Do the vocabulary exercises for 6.1.

C **PAIR WORK** Why do people seek fame? What are the pros and cons?

D **PAIR WORK** Imagine that your name appeared in the news headlines. What would your reaction be? Tell your partner. For ideas, watch Bojan's video.

EXPERT SPEAKER
Is Bojan's reaction similar to yours?

3 GRAMMAR: Narrative tenses

A Read the sentences in the grammar box. Complete the rules with the correct tenses below.

> ### Narrative tenses
>
> The 26-year-old from Vancouver **had been trading** things online for a year before he finally **got offered** a two-story, three-bedroom, 1920s farmhouse.
>
> Not many people **had heard** of the small town of Kipling before the story **caught** people's attention.
>
> The mayor, Pat Jackson, **was trying** to promote tourism and **decided** to make the offer of the house.

> past continuous
> past perfect (*had* + past participle)
> past perfect continuous (*had* + *been* + verb + *-ing*)
> simple past

1 Use the _____ for an ongoing action or situation that continued up to an event or situation in the past.

2 Use the _____ to describe a completed event that happened before another event in the past.

3 Use the _____ for the main completed events or situations in a story. Use the _____ for background activities happening at the same time as the main event.

B ▶ Now go to page 134. Look at the grammar chart and do the grammar exercise for 6.1.

C PAIR WORK Read the beginning and end of a story. With a partner, take turns making sentences to complete the story. Use a variety of narrative tenses.

Matt wanted his marriage proposal to be special, but he never expected it to make headlines …

… This was a truly happy ending.

> Matt wanted his marriage proposal to be special, but he never expected it to **make headlines**. He **had been planning** the speech for months …

> … and **chose** what he thought was the perfect ring …

4 SPEAKING

A ▶ PAIR WORK Student A: Go to page 158. Student B: Go to page 160. Follow the instructions.

NOT AGAIN!

1 LANGUAGE IN CONTEXT

A GROUP WORK Think of a time when something did not go according to plan for you. What happened? Were you disappointed? Why? What would have made the situation better?

B 🔊 **1.44** Read and listen to the podcast. What was disappointing about each situation? What do you understand by "managing expectations"?

🔊 **1.44 Audio script**

Mike	Accidents happen. Things outside our control can go wrong. So how can we make sure we keep our promises?
Tessa	And keep people around us happy?
Mike	Exactly. Managing expectations might be the key. It may be that explaining things clearly, promising less, and delivering more is all it takes. Let me give you an example of when that didn't happen for me. I was waiting for a flight. The airline **confirmed** that it was on time. A few minutes later, they said it was late. No surprises there. They **estimated** it would be delayed by about 30 minutes. Then they **announced** there could be an even longer wait. And on it went. Each time, they said we wouldn't have to wait much longer … Four hours later we took off. Unbelievably frustrating.
Tessa	Yeah, I totally get it. I have this friend who's always late. She'll **swear** she'll be there at a certain time, and she'll always keep me waiting for ages and doesn't even call or anything. The last time we had plans, I told her I **had doubts about** her being there. She **denied** she'd ever been late and **insisted** she could make it. But guess what! No show. I wish she'd said she might be late and **proposed** a less ambitious time. I would have been so happy to see her waiting for me for a change.

C 🔊 **1.44** THINK CRITICALLY Read and listen again. For each situation, how could the speakers' expectations have been managed better? In general, what different steps can you take to manage people's expectations?

2 VOCABULARY: Reporting verbs

A 🔊 **1.45** Look at the words and phrases in the box. How many can you find in the podcast? Which ones can you use to complete: (a) Both sentences below? (b) Only sentence 1? (c) Only sentence 2? Which verb doesn't work in either sentence? Listen and check your work. In what situations would you use each of these verbs?

announce	argue	boast	claim	confirm	deny
estimate	have doubts about	hope to	insist	propose	swear

1 He … that the plan would work.   **2** He … the plan.

B Now go to page 146. Do the vocabulary exercises for 6.2.

C PAIR WORK Have you been in a situation similar to the ones described in the podcast in exercise 1B? Tell your partner what happened. Use the words in the box above.

3 GRAMMAR: Reported speech with modal verbs

A **Read the sentences in the grammar box. Complete the rules.**

Reported speech with modal verbs

Direct speech	Reported speech
"It **will be** delayed by about 30 minutes."	They **estimated** (that) it **would be** delayed by about 30 minutes.
"There **could be** an even longer wait."	They **announced** (that) there **could be** an even longer wait.
"You **won't have** to wait much longer."	They **said** (that) we **wouldn't have** to wait much longer.
"I **can make** it."	She … **insisted** she **could make** it.
"I **might be** late."	I wish she'd **said** (that) she **might be** late.

In reported speech, change *will* to _____ . Change *can* to _____ and *may* to _____ .
Other modals like *might*, *should*, and *could* don't change.

B ▶ **Now go to page 135. Look at the grammar chart and do the grammar exercise for 6.2.**

C ◀)) **1.46** PAIR WORK **Listen to the messages and announcements and make notes. Take turns reporting them to each other. Then check your accuracy. When was the last time you heard similar messages? Do you remember what they said?**

✓ **ACCURACY** CHECK

Unlike most other verbs, use an object after *tell* in reported speech.
He ~~told~~ that it wouldn't rain in June. ✗
He told me that it wouldn't rain in June. ✓
He said/swore/insisted that it wouldn't rain in June. ✓

4 SPEAKING

A PAIR WORK **Imagine you've heard some news items and you need to report them to someone who'll be affected by them. How will you deliver the news? Use the situations below and your own ideas.**

- City authority announcement: The new highway won't be ready for another two years because of costs, so your friend who commutes to work could be asked to use the longer route into the city.

- Soccer club newsletter: The star player of your friend's favorite soccer team has been injured, and the management may not be able to find a replacement in time for an important game.

- Real estate agent announcement: The construction of the apartment building where your friend bought an apartment has been delayed, they guess by about three years because the builders have discovered archaeological items on the site.

B PAIR WORK THINK CRITICALLY **Think about the news items from exercise 4A. How can officials in charge manage people's expectations in these situations using strategies you discussed in exercise 1C on page 56?**

SOMETHING IN THE WATER

1 LISTENING

A Look at the picture. What do you think it is?

B 🔊 **1.47** Listen to a TV reporter interviewing a couple on the beach. What did they see? How did they react?

C 🔊 **1.47** Listen again. What do Brice and Cynthia remember differently?

D 🔊 **1.48** What do you think happened in the end? Listen to the rest of the report and check. Was your prediction correct?

E 🔊 **1.49** **UNDERSTAND MEANING FROM CONTEXT** Listen to the entire report. What do *fin*, *shaken*, and *narrow escape* mean? What other words helped you figure out the meaning?

F **PAIR WORK** **THINK CRITICALLY** Compare the reporter's assumptions about what happened with Brice's and Cynthia's stories. Which assumptions were totally correct, partly correct, or incorrect?

2 PRONUNCIATION: Listening for complex verb phrases

A 🔊 **1.50** Listen and complete the sentences. Compare with a partner. Which of the missing words are stressed, and which are not stressed?

1 You _____ _____ _____ terrified.

2 I _____ _____ pretty fast myself.

3 And if you _____ never _____ an ocean sunfish …

B 🔊 **1.51** <u>Underline</u> the verb phrases. Read them aloud. Then listen to how they are pronounced on the recording.

I've never seen Brice swim so fast.

It must have been like a scene from *Jaws*.

There may have been some screaming.

It would've been cool to tell people we'd had a narrow escape.

C Circle the correct options to complete the sentence.

When there is a complex verb phrase, the auxiliary verbs are usually *stressed / unstressed* and *contractions / full forms* are often used.

3 SPEAKING SKILLS

A Look at the expressions in the chart. Which ones mean "That's partly true"? Which ones mean "That's not true"? Which two words could be changed to *guess*?

Making assumptions	Contradicting assumptions	Clarifying assumptions
You/It must have been …	Not at all.	Up to a point.
I suppose …	Not in the least.	To an extent.
I assume …	Absolutely not.	In a way.

B PAIR WORK Imagine your partner was in the water when the sunfish appeared. You're a reporter. Interview your partner, making assumptions about how they felt. Your partner reacts. Use the expressions in exercise 3A. Take turns.

4 PRONUNCIATION: Saying short and long vowels

A 🔊 1.52 Listen to the recording. Can you hear the difference between the first and second word? Repeat the words and focus on the underlined vowels.

/ɪ/ l<u>i</u>st   /i/ l<u>ea</u>st

/ʊ/ f<u>u</u>ll   /u/ f<u>oo</u>l

B 🔊 1.53 Listen and circle the first kind of vowels and underline the second kind of vowels.

Sue could see a shark in the sea, so the first thing she did, after screaming, was to reach for her new phone to film it. Sue's phone was deep in her beach bag, and by the time she had found it, sadly, the shark had swum farther away.

C Practice saying the sentences in exercise 4B, paying attention to the short and long vowels.

5 SPEAKING

A PAIR WORK Choose a situation in the box or your own idea. Student A starts by saying one sentence about the event. Student B asks questions, making assumptions about how Student A felt. Student A reacts. Then Student B chooses a different event, and Student A asks questions.

| bus broke down | saw an unusual animal | got lost on a hike or in a city | went to an interesting party |

A few weeks ago, I went to an underwater wedding.

I assume you were wearing a diving suit.

B GROUP WORK Tell your group what your partner in exercise 5A said about the event. Whose story was the most interesting?

YOU MAY EXCHANGE RINGS

59

GETTING IT WRONG

1 READING

A **PAIR WORK** Have you ever made an embarrassing mistake? What happened?

B Read the posts. Which one is about the wrong gift? The wrong place? The wrong time? Summarize what went wrong in each story in one sentence.

> **INSIDER ENGLISH**
>
> *it hit* + object pronoun = just realized something
> Then *it hit me*.
> Suddenly, *it hit her*.

1 Serena B
102 posts

My dumbest mistake was just recently. My best friend's wedding was in Salt Lake City. My husband and I, who live in Los Angeles, decided to make a long weekend of it. I planned it all out very carefully: Drive to Las Vegas on Friday (six hours) and then drive to Salt Lake City (four hours) the next morning. We'd drive the whole ten hours back on Sunday. And the plan worked! We got to Vegas right on schedule, had a great night out, and were on the road by 10:30 the next morning. The wedding wasn't until 4:00, so we took our time and enjoyed the landscape, which is so beautiful. At 3:40 p.m. we pulled into the (very full) parking lot and went inside to get seats. The place was packed, but no one was seated, which was weird. Then, even weirder, we saw the bride and groom standing around chatting with people. I told my husband I hadn't expected to see them until after the ceremony. Then it hit me. Salt Lake City is an hour ahead of Las Vegas. It wasn't 3:45. It was 4:45, and the wedding was over. What a great job I did of planning that weekend!

👍 Like   💬 Comment

2 Vicky S
83 posts

My grandmother lived with us when I was a kid, but sometimes she'd go stay with my uncle, who lived about four hours away. They'd all meet at a McDonald's about halfway between them, and grandma would go home with my uncle. The summer I got my license, I decided I'd be grandma's driver. Mom didn't like the idea but finally agreed. She kept repeating the directions and wanted me to write them down, but I reminded her that I could use the GPS. Nothing could possibly go wrong! That was true for about 90 minutes. There was a big detour through a strange town because of road work, but we finally got back on the highway and eventually arrived at McDonald's. When we went inside, there was no sign of my uncle, so we waited. And waited. After a while we called my uncle to check what was taking him so long, and he said he'd been waiting for us for half an hour! Guess what! The GPS had taken us to the wrong McDonald's. Grandma had commented on the different layout, but we just assumed they'd redecorated. All these restaurants and parking lots look so similar. Needless to say, that was the last time I drove grandma anywhere.

👍 Like   💬 Comment

3 Ivan P
147 posts

I hadn't been living in Marshall long when I met my new friend Jim and his wife Dana. Since I was new in town, I was really happy when Dana invited me to Jim's birthday party. I thought it would be a good way to meet new people. She said that there would be food and even a band. She insisted that I shouldn't bring anything. But I wanted to make a good impression with a nice gift for Jim. I didn't know him well, but I remembered he said he loved baseball. So I got him a Detroit Tigers T-shirt. I thought he probably wore a large. When I got there, I saw animal decorations and realized the party was for *little Jim*, Dana and Jim's one-year-old son. I suppose little Jim liked his new large T-shirt as much as I liked listening to *The Happy Journey* kids' band all day.

👍 Like   💬 Comment

C **UNDERSTAND IRONY** How did the people realize they had made a mistake? Which sentences in the posts are ironic (the opposite of what the person means)?

D Who do you think got the biggest shock? Why?

E **GROUP WORK** **THINK CRITICALLY** What do you think the following people said and did in each story: (post 1) the people getting married, (post 2) the uncle, (post 3) Jim and Dana? Why?

2 WRITING

A **MAKE A STORY INTERESTING** One way to make a story interesting is to mix longer and shorter sentences. Look at how sentences of different length are used in the two extracts from the posts in exercise 1B on page 60.

> I planned it all out very carefully: Drive to Las Vegas on Friday (six hours) and then drive to Salt Lake City (four hours) the next morning. We'd drive the whole ten hours back on Sunday. And the plan worked!

> The place was packed, but no one was seated, which was weird. Then, even weirder, we saw the bride and groom standing around chatting with people. I told my husband I hadn't expected to see them until after the ceremony. Then it hit me.

B You can also follow these points to make a story interesting. Find an example of each point in the posts in exercise 1B on page 60.

1 Use a variety of narrative verb tenses in the past.

2 Use different linking and organizing expressions: *and, but, so, then, later, a few years ago*, etc.

3 Use different kinds of sentences: conditionals (*if*), relative clauses (*who, which*), time clauses (*when, after*), *There was/were*, reported and direct speech, etc.

C PAIR WORK **Improve the sentences to make the story more interesting. Use the information in parentheses ( ) and your own ideas.**

My friend rented a red car from Cars-For-U. She called me. She said she would meet me on Thursday at the mall. She said I should find the red car and wait for her. (time clauses, linking expressions, direct speech)

I went to the mall and found a red car with a Cars-For-U sign on it. I stood next to it. I waited for a very long time. Then my friend found me. (variety of verb tenses, time clauses)

She asked what I was doing by that car. She said it was the wrong one. She pointed to another red car. It was closer to the mall. Sometimes I have the best luck! (relative clauses, direct speech)

WRITE IT

D PLAN You're going to write a story about something unexpected that happened or about someone who made a mistake. Discuss some ideas with a partner. You can use the ideas in the box or your own ideas. The story can be true, or you can make it up. Then think about how you are going to set the scene, what dramatic effects you'll use, and what comments you'll make.

> getting on the wrong bus or train   going to the wrong event   getting caught in bad weather

E Write your story. Make sure you use a mix of longer and shorter sentences and a variety of narrative tenses, linking expressions, and grammatical constructions described in exercise 2B.

F PAIR WORK Exchange stories. What are the most interesting things about your partner's story?

REGISTER CHECK

In more specific, official contexts, use other reporting verbs, rather than *say* or *tell*.
*The couple **announced** their engagement on Thursday.*
*She **promised** she would meet me in the evening.*

TIME TO SPEAK
StorySLAM

A **DISCUSS** Read the rules to a storytelling contest with the theme "The Unexpected." Then look at the pictures. How do they relate to the theme? Discuss with a group.

STORY SLAM

RULES

TELLING A STORY TONIGHT?

- It must be ON THEME.
  The story you've prepared should be related to the theme.
- It should have a strong PLOT.
  How are the characters affected?
  What do they want?
  What happens in the end?
- It must be ON TIME.
  SLAM stories should be five minutes long.

Now think of stories for each of the pictures with your group.

B **PREPARE** You're going to tell a story for the StorySLAM with the theme "The Unexpected." It can be about yourself, someone you know, or someone you've heard about. Share a few ideas with a partner. Help each other choose the best story to develop. You can use one of the ideas from part A or your own idea.

FIND IT

C **RESEARCH** How can you make a story interesting and lively? With your partner from part B, think of ways for the categories below. You can look online for help. You may want to watch some videos of storytellers. Then choose one or two of your ideas and use them to make your story more interesting.

details   language   tone of voice   gestures

D **DECIDE** Tell your story to a group. The group considers these questions and chooses the best story: Did the storyteller follow the rules? Which story was the most interesting? Which storyteller was the liveliest?

E **PRESENT** The winners from part D tell their stories to the class. The class chooses the best story.

To check your progress, go to page 154.

USEFUL PHRASES

DISCUSS

Looking at the picture, I'd say …

It could be a story about …

Maybe what happened was …

RESEARCH

You can catch the listeners' attention by …

I suppose you can …

It's entertaining to …

This website said that …

Another website claimed that …

REVIEW 2 (UNITS 4–6)

1 VOCABULARY

A **Complete the conversation with the correct expressions. There is one expression you won't use.**

acts as	constructive	contributes	draws attention to	keep an eye on
panic	point out	regain control	steer me away from	strengths
think through	turn to	weaknesses		

A Who's the most important person in your life?

B There are so many important people in my life, for example, my parents. They
¹_____ me and always ²_____ making
bad decisions. That's important. But then there's my older sister. When I do make a mistake, she's
the first to ³_____ what I did wrong. It makes me mad, but then she
encourages me to ⁴_____ the situation and learn from it. And she gives me
⁵_____ advice.

A That seems rational.

B Yeah. When I have a problem, I tend to ⁶_____ . She helps me calm down and
⁷_____ .

A It sounds like she ⁸_____ your therapist!

B Yes, I guess she does in a way. Oh, and I can't forget my friend Dave. He ⁹_____ to
my overall happiness. He always ¹⁰_____ my ¹¹_____ ,
which makes me feel good. I can always ¹²_____ him to make me feel better.

B **PAIR WORK** **Who in your life is similar to the people described in exercise 1A? What other people are important in your life? Why?**

2 GRAMMAR

A **Circle the correct options.**

HOME   ABOUT   NEWS   BLOG   CONTACT US

Have you ever heard the expression "claim to fame"? It's that thing that makes
someone famous or interesting. For truly famous people, it usually involves talent.
For example, Shakira's claim to fame isn't ¹*only / even* her voice. People think
of her voice *and* her dance moves ²*unless / whenever* they hear her name. For
³*others / one another*, it's often something silly or unusual. My brother's claim to
fame is doing magic tricks. He would practice in his room ⁴*by himself / by herself*
for hours as a child before he showed the family. ⁵*Providing / Even if* he's in a good
mood, he still likes to show off his tricks today. He does this ⁶*such / so* often that
everyone expects it now. And he does the tricks ⁷*only if / even if* he knows we've
all seen them before. I think it's annoying, but the two of us always annoy
⁸*each other / the others*.

Q 2   ♡ 7   ⇄ 11

B **PAIR WORK** **Answer the questions. Give details.**

1 Providing you're in a good mood, what's something you often do?

2 Do you have a claim to fame? Is it something you do by yourself or with others?

3 Is there something you do even if you know people don't like it?

3 VOCABULARY

A **There is one error in each sentence. Find and replace the errors with the words in the box.**

> argue   claims   happy   have   headlines   make   passionate   praises

1 I'm more than unwilling to help my friends when they need it because it makes me feel good.
2 I am no desire to try extreme sports. They scare me to death.
3 I'm not interested in celebrities who always want to be in the publicity.
4 I don't enjoy being around people who propose.
5 I don't believe it when an ad denies their product is the best. That's why I read the reviews.
6 I'm reluctant about traveling to other countries. I love experiencing other cultures.
7 One of my dreams is to do an appearance on a TV talk show or game show.
8 When someone boasts me, I feel pleased but also a little embarrassed.

B **PAIR WORK** **Do you agree with the sentences in exercise 3A? Why or why not?**

4 GRAMMAR

A **Circle the correct options.**

If you want to go on a cheap vacation, you ¹*should try / won't try* a virtual trip. There are many websites that offer virtual vacations you can take from your couch. For some of them, all you need is a computer and some time. One website ²*denied / boasted* that you ³*would feel / are feeling* like you were there – without ever leaving the house. Even if it's not as good as a real vacation, a virtual vacation ⁴*could make / can't make* you feel relaxed. One VR travel company ⁵*hopes to / claims that* you ⁶*enjoyed / might enjoy* a VR vacation more than a real trip because you don't have to deal with travel. If you take a lot of virtual trips, you ⁷*shouldn't learn / may learn* about amazing places around the world. But some people ⁸*told / argue* that a VR trip ⁹*would be / wouldn't be* the same as going to a new place.

B **PAIR WORK** **Would you try a virtual trip? Why or why not? What are the advantages and disadvantages? Discuss the questions with a partner. Then work with another pair and say how your partner answered the questions.**

UNIT OBJECTIVES
- discuss worthwhile experiences
- talk about purchases
- bargain for a purchase
- write a for-and-against essay
- negotiate a boat trip

PRIORITIES

7

START SPEAKING

A   Where do you think these children are going? What are the risks? Is it worth it?

B   In your opinion, what kind of things are worth taking risks for? Why?

C   How do you define "worth"? Who, or what, do you value most in the world? Why? For ideas, watch Odil's video.

EXPERT SPEAKER

Are the types of things that Odil values, and his reasons for valuing them, similar to your ideas?

WORTHY HELPERS

LESSON OBJECTIVE
■ discuss worthwhile experiences

1 LANGUAGE IN CONTEXT

A **GROUP WORK** **THINK CRITICALLY** What do you understand by the term "emergency services"? What type of jobs do they include? What qualities do people need to do these jobs? Why do you think they choose to do them?

B 🔊 **2.02** Read and listen to Sofian and Nathalie talking about their jobs. What do they do? When did they choose their future careers? Does their work make them happy?

🔊 **2.02 Audio script**

Sofian It's common to dream about driving a fire truck when you're a kid. But I didn't think about being a firefighter until I was 14. I was in a traffic accident, and my foot was broken. It was a horrible situation to be in. But then the firefighters arrived, and suddenly I had people to help me and calm voices to **reassure me**. It was incredible having such an amazing team around me. At that moment, I decided I wanted to **devote my life to** that profession. And today, it's my job. Actually, it's more than just a job. I believe I'm doing something that **is worthwhile** – **I'm a good influence on** others, like those firefighters were on me. It**'s an honor** to be **making a contribution** like that. Plus, driving a fire truck is a seriously cool thing to do!

Nathalie For me, it's important to have contact with people and especially to be helpful. I don't just mean helping medically. I **take pleasure in** that side of the job, but I think I **get more satisfaction out of** the interpersonal side. It can be scary being in the hospital, and some patients have trouble coping. It's really **beneficial** if they have someone to talk to. So for me, it's rewarding to spend time **reassuring patients**. When I decided as a teenager to become a nurse, I guess it was the medical side that interested me. But now I find it's the human side that I **value** the most. That's where I feel I can really **be of use** and **make a difference**.

C 🔊 **2.02** Read and listen again. What aspects of their work do Sofian and Nathalie enjoy? What would and wouldn't you like about doing the two jobs?

2 VOCABULARY: Positive experiences

FIND IT

A 🔊 **2.03** Look at the expressions in the box. Can you guess their meaning from the way they are used in the texts in exercise 1B on page 66? Describe each one using other words. Use a dictionary or your phone to help you. Then listen and check your work.

be a good influence on	be an honor	be beneficial	be of use
be worthwhile	devote my life to	get satisfaction out of	make a contribution
make a difference	reassure sb	take pleasure in	value sth

B ▶ **Now go to page 146. Do the vocabulary exercises for 7.1.**

C PAIR WORK Have you ever been in a situation where you were helped by someone in a caring profession? Describe the situation. How did you feel? For ideas, watch Odil's video.

EXPERT SPEAKER

Was your experience similar to Odil's?

3 GRAMMAR: Gerunds and infinitives after adjectives, nouns, and pronouns

A Read the sentences in the grammar box. Complete the rules with words in the box.

Gerunds and infinitives after adjectives, nouns, and pronouns

It's **common to dream** about driving a fire truck.

I had **people to help** me.

They have **someone to talk to**.

It can be **scary being** in the hospital.

It's rewarding to **spend time reassuring** patients.

---

gerunds	infinitives	gerunds or infinitives

1 You can use _____ after adjectives.

2 After nouns or pronouns, use _____ to show purpose.

3 It's common to use _____ after expressions like *spend / waste time* and *have (no) fun*.

B ▶ **Now go to page 135. Look at the grammar chart and do the grammar exercise for 7.1.**

C Circle the correct options and complete the sentences with your own ideas. Then compare your sentences with a group. Whose ideas were the most unusual?

1 It's unusual *to see / seeing* …

2 I often waste time *to do / doing* …

3 … is an interesting subject *to study / studying*.

4 I need someone *to give / giving* me advice about …

5 I usually feel nervous *to wait / waiting* to …

4 SPEAKING

A PAIR WORK Talk about your job or a job you'd like to have. Explain what satisfaction you (would) get out of it. Compare your thoughts with your partner's.

> As a hairdresser, I get a chance to meet a lot of people. I feel that I can make a difference for my customers. It's not always easy to get things just right, but when you succeed, it's really rewarding.

7.2 BUYER'S REGRET

LESSON OBJECTIVE
- talk about purchases

1 LANGUAGE IN CONTEXT

A PAIR WORK THINK CRITICALLY Do you read product reviews when you're deciding to buy an item online? Do they influence your purchase? What other factors influence your purchase?

B Read the reviews. What did each person buy, and why? Why were the people dissatisfied? What do you think Dan did next?

HOME • ABOUT • NEWS • **BLOG** • CONTACT   SIGN IN

Grrrrreviews | The funniest bad reviews on the internet!

Brandon S

★★★★★ **An accident**

My friend **encouraged me** to buy this expensive treadmill. He **convinced me** that it **made financial sense** because it was cheaper than paying gym fees for years. So I decided to get it. After about a month, something went wrong with the speed settings. It suddenly started going too fast, and I flew off the back of it and broke my ankle. You can imagine how much I **regret the purchase**.

👍 Like   💬 Comment

Julie R

★★★★★ **What a waste!**

I **purchased** this bed for my cat because it's so cute. My husband said it **was not worth the money** and **urged me** not to buy it. He thought I was **being foolish** because we have a closet full of things for the cat that she doesn't use. I really thought it **had potential**, but the cat sleeps everywhere *near* the bed – even in the box it came in – but never *in* the bed! Does anyone want to buy it? The bed is great – it's my cat that's the problem.

👍 Like   💬 Comment

Dan G

★★★★★ **A professional look?**

I bought this small electric shaver and planned to use it for business trips. It seemed like it would **be** very **practical**. I first used it at a hotel a few minutes before an important meeting. I decided to shave off my mustache and beard to look more professional. I got about half way done, and the shaver completely stopped working. I **looked ridiculous**!

👍 Like   💬 Comment

C PAIR WORK THINK CRITICALLY Read again. Which of these reviews would you have found most helpful? Why? In general, which are more helpful: good or bad product reviews? What kind of information do you find most useful?

2 VOCABULARY: Making purchases

FIND IT

A 🔊 **2.04** Look at the expressions in the box. What items are they associated with in the product reviews? Which one is not in the text? What do the expressions mean? Use a dictionary or your phone to help you. Then listen and check the definitions.

be foolish	be practical	convince sb (to do sth)	encourage sb (to do sth)
have appeal	have potential	look ridiculous	make financial sense
not be worth the money	purchase sth	regret a/the purchase	urge sb (to do sth)

B ▶ **Now go to page 147. Do the vocabulary exercises for 7.2.**

C GROUP WORK Talk about a bad purchase you've made. What was it? Why do you regret buying it?

68

3 GRAMMAR: Infinitives after verbs with and without objects

A Read the sentences in the grammar box. Circle the correct option to answer the question.

> ### Infinitives after verbs with and without objects
>
> My friend **encouraged me to buy** this expensive treadmill.
>
> My husband … **urged me not to buy** it.
>
> Does anyone **want to buy** it?
>
> I … **planned to use** it for business trips.

When is the subject of the main verb and the subject of the infinitive different?

a With verbs followed directly by an infinitive, without an object

b When there's an object between the main verb and the infinitive

B Now go to page 135. Look at the grammar chart and do the grammar exercise for 7.2.

C Change the sentences below so that they are true for you. Add one more sentence to each statement using the words in parentheses or your own ideas. Use infinitives in each sentence. Check your accuracy. Then share your sentences with a partner. Did you have similar ideas?

1 My friends often offer to lend me some money. (like)

My parents often offer to lend me some money, but I don't like to borrow from them.

2 I'd like my brother to help me choose a new phone. (advise)

3 My mother expects me to help her with her shopping. (persuade)

4 My manager agreed not to give me so much work. (promise)

5 I hate ads that encourage you to lose weight. (tell)

> ✓ **ACCURACY** CHECK
>
> Remember to use an object or object pronoun after verbs like *encourage*, *persuade*, and *urge*.
>
> The ad ~~encouraged to buy~~ new sunglasses. ✗
>
> The ad encouraged me to buy new sunglasses. ✓

4 SPEAKING

A PAIR WORK Tell your partner about things you've bought for each of these categories. Why did you buy them? Were they worthwhile purchases? Use verbs + infinitives.

| clothing | furniture | sports gear | technology | transportation |

> My friend **persuaded me to buy** a scooter because it **made financial sense** at the time.

B PAIR WORK Choose an item you talked about in exercise 4A and write a short review. Exchange your reviews with a partner. Do you want to buy the product? Why or why not?

A GOOD BARGAIN

1 LISTENING

A Is bargaining (= trying to get a lower price) common in your culture? What kinds of things do people bargain for?

B 🔊 **2.05** Listen. Sergio is studying abroad for a year and wants to buy a desk at a street market for his room. What price does the seller want at first? What is their final agreement?

C 🔊 **2.05** UNDERSTAND PERSUASIVE TECHNIQUES
Listen again. Check (✓) the techniques Sergio and Megan use to get the best deal.

1 Sergio:
- ☐ points out some problems with the desk
- ☐ is prepared to walk away
- ☐ refuses to buy the desk without the chair
- ☐ pretends he doesn't have a way to get it home

2 Megan:
- ☐ says the desk was never used
- ☐ says she'll give Sergio the chair for free
- ☐ says the desk is not too old
- ☐ says she'll deliver the desk for free

INSIDER ENGLISH

you bet = certainly, I'd be happy to

D GROUP WORK THINK CRITICALLY Can you add any more techniques to the list above? In your country, what do buyers and sellers do to get the best price when bargaining? Discuss and then describe a bargaining experience you or someone you know had. How successful was it?

2 PRONUNCIATION: Listening for vowel linking between words

A 🔊 **2.06** Listen to how the underlined words link.

It's only a few years old.   Can you go any lower?

B 🔊 **2.07** Underline the linked words in the sentences below and write whether there is a sound like /j/ or /w/ between them.

How much are you asking?   Would you be willing to accept $125?

How about $120?   I'll walk around and see if …

C Circle the correct option to complete the sentences.

When a word ends with a /uː/ or /iː/ and the next word begins with a *consonant / vowel*, there is usually linking. If the first word ends in /iː/, /eɪ/, /aɪ/, or /ɔɪ/, there is a linking sound like /j/. If the first word ends in /uː/, /oʊ/, or /aʊ/, there is a linking sound like /w/.

3 SPEAKING SKILLS

A 🔊 **2.05** PAIR WORK Look at these expressions from the conversation in exercise 1B on page 70. Which ones are used for (a) accepting an offer, (b) bargaining, or (c) rejecting an offer? Write *a*, *b*, or *c* next to each one. Then say which expressions can be used by the buyer, the seller, or both. Where do you think vowel linking occurs in these expressions? Listen to the conversation again to check.

Negotiate a price

1 So, how much are you asking for … ? ____
2 That's a little on the high side. Can you go any lower? ____
3 I'm sorry, but I can't accept that. ____
4 Would you be willing to accept … ? ____
5 Sorry, but no deal. ____
6 $… is the best I can do. ____
7 Sorry, but I don't think it's worth that much. ____
8 I'll throw … in for free. ____
9 That's my final offer. ____
10 That sounds fair enough. ____
11 I think I can accept that. ____
12 You've got a deal. ____

B PAIR WORK Choose the role of a buyer or a seller. Role play a conversation using the prompts below and expressions from exercise 3A.

Buyer You are interested in a product. Ask the price.
Seller Suggest a price and praise the product.
Buyer Say the price is too high and point out a fault.
Seller Reject the offer.
Buyer Offer an alternative price.
Seller Accept the offer.

4 PRONUNCIATION: Saying /ŋ/

A 🔊 **2.08** Listen and underline the /ŋ/ sounds.

1 Is this the computer you're selling?
2 Would you be willing to accept less?
3 My uncle was angry because I went shopping.
4 There's always a danger of paying too much for something.

B 🔊 **2.09** Write the word with /ŋ/ next to the definition. Then listen to check your work and repeat the words with /ŋ/.

1 _____ – the muscle in your mouth
2 _____ – fast walking
3 _____ – it connects your foot and leg
4 _____ – the opposite of "answering"
5 _____ – your mother's brother
6 _____ – the sound babies make when they are uncomfortable or unhappy

C GROUP WORK Make your own quiz as in exercise 4B, where all the answers are words with /ŋ/. Then groups exchange quizzes and say the words, focusing on the pronunciation of /ŋ/.

5 SPEAKING

A PAIR WORK Student A: Go to page 158. Student B: Go to page 160. Follow the instructions.

MONEY'S WORTH

LESSON OBJECTIVE
■ write a for-and-against essay

1 READING

A **PAIR WORK** What kind of things do you enjoy spending money on? Why?

B **IDENTIFY MAIN POINTS** Read the article. What are the main ideas of the sections "The Problem with Possessions" and "The Power of Experiences"?

Why you should spend your money on experiences, not things

When you work hard every single day and there's only so much money left after your regular expenses, you have to make sure you spend it well. So spend it on what science says will make you happy.

The problem with possessions

A 20-year study by Dr. Thomas Gilovich, a psychology professor at Cornell University, reached a powerful conclusion: Don't spend your money on things. The trouble with things is that the happiness they provide goes away quickly. There are three important reasons for this:

❯ What seemed unusual and exciting at first quickly becomes normal.

❯ As soon as we get used to a new possession, we look for an even better one.

❯ We buy something and are thrilled with it until a friend buys a better one – and there's always someone with a better one.

The power of experiences

Gilovich and other researchers have found that experiences – as short as they may be – bring happiness that lasts longer than things. Here's why:

1 Experiences become a part of our identity. We are not our possessions, but we *are* the combination of everything we've seen, the things we've done, and the places we've been. Buying the newest phone isn't going to change who you are, but hiking across a mountain range from start to finish definitely will.

2 Anticipation is important. Gilovich also studied anticipation and found that anticipation of an experience causes excitement and enjoyment, while anticipation of getting a possession causes impatience. Experiences are enjoyable from the very first moments of planning all the way through to the memories you appreciate forever.

3 Experiences don't last (which is a good thing). Have you ever bought something that wasn't as beneficial as you thought it would be? Once you buy it, it's right there in your face, reminding you of your disappointment. And even if an item does meet your expectations, it's common to regret the purchase: "Sure, it's cool, but it probably wasn't worth the money." We don't do that with experiences. The fact that they last for only a short time is part of what makes them worthwhile, and that value tends to increase as time passes.

Adapted from an article by Travis Bradberry, PhD, on the Talentsmart website.

GLOSSARY
anticipation (*n*) a feeling of excitement about something that is going to happen

C **IDENTIFY SUPPORTING DETAILS** Write the number of the section from the article (1–3) for each supporting detail. If the supporting detail is not in the article, write *X*.

Experiences …

a help us gain confidence and overcome problems. ___
b aren't compared as often as things. ___
c define and change who we are. ___
d cause more excitement than possessions. ___
e can be more expensive than possessions. ___
f add value to our lives that can last a lifetime. ___

D **GROUP WORK** **THINK CRITICALLY** Think of more ideas <u>in favor of</u> buying experiences instead of things. Then think of ideas <u>against</u> buying experiences. Which do you agree with more?

WRITING

A Read part of an essay on the value of possessions. What two arguments are given? What's the author's opinion?

How Valuable Are Our Possessions?

Recently, there have been a number of articles about the value of experiences in comparison with possessions. The writers have described various ways in which experiences are more beneficial and … . Others, however, disagree and … .

Let us consider some arguments in favor of possessions. To begin with, we can keep our possessions, unlike experiences, which only last a short time. We can share … . Valuable possessions can give us a sense of … For example, … . Another advantage is that possessions can have a sentimental value. For instance, … .

On the other hand, there are a number of arguments that challenge the value of possessions. First, although some possessions contribute to our comfort, many are unnecessary and take up a lot of space. Yet we often find it hard to part with them. A lot of people … . Another disadvantage is possessions make us competitive. For example, … . In addition, … .

Overall, I believe that possessions make a great contribution to our lives. Even though there are problems associated with them, they make our day-to-day life more enjoyable and represent a part of who we are.

B **ORGANIZE AN ESSAY** Read about how to write a for-and-against essay. Match the paragraph types in the box with their descriptions.

> **REGISTER** CHECK
>
> *Let us* is often used in formal writing. *Let's* is used in less formal writing or when speaking.

| Against | Conclusion | For | Introduction |

A for-and-against essay is a formal piece of writing in which you write about a topic from opposite points of view. It often has four paragraphs:

1 _____ : Present the topic but don't give your opinion about it.
2 _____ : Give two or three arguments in favor of the topic with examples or reasons.
3 _____ : Give two or three arguments against the topic with examples or reasons.
4 _____ : Give your opinion. Say why you find one side more convincing than the other.

C **PAIR WORK** Which useful expressions below does the author use in the essay in exercise 2A? With a partner think of ideas that could complete the essay.

Useful expressions

Listing: First, To begin with, Second, Finally, One/Another advantage/disadvantage is
Adding: In addition, Furthermore, as well as
Contrasting: On the other hand, However, Nevertheless, Nonetheless, Even though
Giving examples: For example, For instance, such as
Concluding: In conclusion, To sum up, Overall (*followed by* it is my opinion that), I think/believe that

WRITE IT

D **PLAN** You're going to write a for-and-against essay. Choose one of the following subjects:
a How Valuable Are Experiences?
b How Valuable Are Our Possessions?

With a partner, brainstorm some ideas for the essay. Then decide what you'll include in each paragraph from exercise 2B.

E Write your essay. Make sure you use some of the useful expressions from exercise 2C.

F **PAIR WORK** Exchange essays with a partner. Did you choose the same subject? Are your conclusions the same?

TIME TO SPEAK
Bargain boat trip

A Look at the pictures. Which boat trip would you prefer to go on? Who would you go with? Discuss your reasons with a partner.

B **DISCUSS** You and a group of friends won a boat trip and beach party. The trip and activities are free, but you have to pay for extras. In pairs, look at the information from the boat company. Discuss which activities and which extras you want in order to make the day worthwhile. How much will the extras cost?

C **DECIDE** Your group's budget is $500. Compare it with the cost of the extras from part B. Decide what you need to do to stay within your budget. You can remove or add extras. Also, plan how to bargain with the boat company. Which prices do you think are too expensive or unfair and can be negotiated?

D **PREPARE** Talk with your partner about how you could negotiate a better deal. Explain why you believe your strategy could be successful.

E **AGREE** Work with another pair. One pair is the friends and the other is the boat company. Negotiate a deal. Then change roles and repeat.

F **PRESENT** Tell the class which activities you're going to do and which extras you agreed on. The class chooses the best trip.

Beach cruise

River cruise

City cruise

PRICE LIST

Cost for a 2-hour boat tour for 25 people + 3-hour beach stop

Beach activities (choose two):
- beach volleyball
- parasailing
- dance party with a DJ
- live concert
- surfing lessons
- snorkeling

Extras (cost for entire group)
+ sodas on the boat	$50
+ cold food on the boat	$100
+ sodas on the beach	$100
+ cold food on the beach	$200
or barbecued food on the beach	$300
+ beach chairs	$100
+ beach umbrellas	$100
+ cancellation insurance (for bad weather)	$50

To check your progress, go to page 155.

USEFUL PHRASES

DISCUSS

It looks like … is a really good value …

If I have to choose between … and … ,

I'd rather … than …

Having … would make a real difference.

PREPARE

We could ask them to combine … and …

We should pay for … and see if they'll throw in … for free.

Let's see if they'd be willing to accept $… for …

That might work because …

They can't say no to …

- talk about neatness and messiness
- talk about side projects
- suggest and show interest in ideas
- write a complaint letter
- make a podcast on ways to reduce stress

SMALL THINGS MATTER

8

START SPEAKING

A   What can you tell about the person who works here? What objects were used to make the work area more practical and personalized?

B   How do you make your work area more practical? How do you personalize it?

C   In what other areas of your life can you use small things to make them more pleasant or personal (e.g., wallpaper on your phone)? How do these items make a difference? How do they make you feel? Tell your partner. For ideas, watch Jacqueline's video.

EXPERT SPEAKER

Are any of Jacqueline's examples similar to yours?

ANNOYING LITTLE THINGS

1 LANGUAGE IN CONTEXT

A PAIR WORK Think about the best thing about growing up in your family home. Tell your partner what your family does that you love and appreciate. What little things do they do that annoy you?

B 🔊 2.10 In an episode of a TV show called *You Should Talk!*, family members talk about living with each other. Read and listen. What annoying habits do Nicole and Paul have?

> 🔊 **2.10 Audio script**
>
> **Host** So, Nicole and Paul, who's more **disorganized**?
>
> **Paul** Definitely Nicole. Like, the other night, we were supposed to meet some friends at seven, and Nicole was going to drive us. We were about to leave the house, but she couldn't find her keys – as *usual*. We normally **hang them up** on the wall by the front door.
>
> **Nicole** Yeah, Paul likes to **line up** all the keys from the biggest to the smallest. He also **puts his books in alphabetical order**, and his desk **is** always **organized** with all his office stuff …
>
> **Paul** OK, OK, but we're talking about you right now. Her keys were bound to be in the house somewhere, so we were forced to go room by room looking for them. Eventually she found them. They **were tangled up** with some earphones in the pocket of some jeans. Unbelievable!
>
> **Nicole** You should talk! At least my jeans were in the closet – unlike your shoes!
>
> **Host** Wait. A minute ago, you were saying how Paul **arranges keys and books neatly**. And now I'm hearing he **leaves his shoes all over the place**?
>
> **Nicole** Yes! I mean, they're not all **jumbled up**. They're sure to be neatly placed side by side on the floor, but they're everywhere!
>
> **Paul** At least I don't **throw** my clothes **on** the floor, like some people I know. I **fold them** neatly and **put them in a pile** on the chair by my bed.
>
> **Nicole** Yeah. Even when he doesn't **put things away**, he does it neatly!

C 🔊 2.10 PAIR WORK THINK CRITICALLY Read and listen again. Who would you find more annoying to live with? Why do you think people get annoyed over small, silly things? What compromises do we need to make when living with other people?

INSIDER ENGLISH

Say *You should talk* to mean "You are guilty of the same behavior you have just criticized."

2 VOCABULARY: Describing neatness and messiness

A 🔊 2.11 Look at the expressions in **bold** in the text. Which do we use to talk about things that are neat, messy, or both? Copy the chart and complete it. Then listen and check your work.

Neat	Messy	Both

B ▶ Now go to page 147. Do the vocabulary exercises for 8.1.

C PAIR WORK What expressions from the box can you use to describe yourself? Which ones can you use to describe the person or people you live with? Can you give some example situations to illustrate?

3 GRAMMAR: Modal-like expressions with *be*

A Read the sentences in the grammar box. Match the expressions (1–4) to the descriptions (a–d).

> **Modal-like expressions with *be***
>
> We **were supposed to** meet some friends at seven.
>
> We **were about to** leave the house, but she couldn't find her keys.
>
> Her keys **were bound to** be in the house somewhere.
>
> We **were forced to** go room by room looking for them.
>
> They**'re sure to** be neatly placed side by side on the floor.

1	be supposed to ___		**a**	be made to do something we don't want to
2	be about to ___		**b**	be certain to do something or to happen
3	be bound to / be sure to ___		**c**	be expected to happen because it was arranged
4	be forced to ___		**d**	be going to do something very soon

B ▶ **Now go to page 136. Look at the grammar chart and do the grammar exercise for 8.1.**

C Imagine you have a terrible roommate who is messy and disorganized. Make a list of complaints about him or her using modal-like expressions with *be,* the prompts, and some ideas of your own. Then compare with a partner. Whose roommate is more annoying?

1 not wiping feet when it rains

He's sure to walk in without wiping his feet, so I'm forced to clean up the muddy floor.

2 putting away clean dishes

3 cleaning up after a party

4 throwing towels on the floor

5 losing keys to the apartment

4 SPEAKING

A PAIR WORK   Imagine the terrible roommate you described in exercise 3C is gone, and you are looking for a new one. With a partner, try to agree on some house rules for your future roommate.

> *OK, first, pay your rent on time. Second, hang up your clothes. Don't leave them all over the place.*

> *Yeah, and don't just throw the dishes in the sink. Wash them right away, or they're bound to smell bad.*

8.2 SIDE PROJECTS

1 LANGUAGE IN CONTEXT

A Look at the title of Max's blog. What do you think it means? Then read the blog. What's (1) a side project, (2) Kyle's side project, (3) Max's side project?

HOME   ABOUT   BLOG   CONTACT US

LIVING YOUR DREAMS
(On the side)
by FilmGuyMax

My friend Kyle

Do you have a side project? You know, the thing you do that isn't your real job but you do it because you love it? Side projects are often creative, but they're more than a hobby. My friend Kyle, for example, is a mechanic, and in his free time he repairs old bikes for a kids' charity. It's work, but not work. He does it because he **thoroughly** enjoys it. And that's the great thing about a side project. It *won't* cause you stress but *will* give you a real sense of satisfaction. And unlike a job, you can usually do things **at your own pace** and **on your own time**.

I'm a film studies student, and my side project is making a documentary about college. I'm filming it **little by little**, and eventually I'm going to edit it into an hour-long show. It'll be a surprise for my friends because I'm not showing it to them until it's done. But this side project has another purpose. In a couple of years, I'll be looking for a job, and this video is going to be a useful example of my skills as a filmmaker. If things go **smoothly**, I might start my own video production business one day. So, as I work on my video, I'll also be moving **steadily** toward that goal. But if things don't go **as expected**, at least I'll have a nice souvenir of my college years.

B Read the blog again. What are the benefits of a side project? How will Max's side project be useful to him?

C PAIR WORK What side projects do you or the people you know have? Do you think they will help you to achieve your dreams?

2 VOCABULARY: Talking about progress

A 2.12 PAIR WORK Look at the expressions in the box. What do they mean? Use a dictionary, your phone, or the context in the blog to help you. Which were used in the blog post? Which ones have a similar meaning? Then listen to the definitions and check your work.

as expected	at my own pace	effectively	efficiently
little by little	on my own time	smoothly	steadily
successfully	thoroughly	with difficulty	with ease

B ▶ Now go to page 148. Do the vocabulary exercises for 8.2.

C PAIR WORK THINK CRITICALLY Compare main occupations with side projects. What are their pros and cons? What are the differences in (a) how we work on them and (b) how we feel about them?

FIND IT

78

3 GRAMMAR: Future forms

A   Read the sentences in the grammar box. Circle the correct options to complete the rules.

> **Future forms**
>
> It **won't cause** you stress but **will give** you a real sense of satisfaction.
>
> Eventually I**'m going to edit** it.
>
> I**'m not showing** it to them until it's done.
>
> In a couple of years, I**'ll be looking for** a job.
>
> This video **is going to be** a useful example of my skills as a filmmaker.
>
> If things go smoothly, I **might start** my own video production business one day.

1   Use *be going to*, *will*, or **don't / won't** for predictions, expectations, or guesses about the future.

2   Use *be going to* or the **present continuous / simple present** for future plans and intentions.

3   Use *will + be +* verb *+ -ing* for **an action in progress / a finished action** at a time in the future.

4   Use *might*, *may*, or *could* when you're **certain / uncertain** about the future.

B   ▶ **Now go to page 136. Look at the grammar chart and do the grammar exercise for 8.2.**

C   Write six sentences on plans and predictions about your work, studies, or side projects. Use a different future form from exercise 3A in each sentence. Check your accuracy. Then compare with a partner. Are any of your predictions similar?

> ✔ **ACCURACY** CHECK
>
> Use the future continuous, not the present continuous, for an action in progress in the future.
>
> *In a couple of years, I'm looking for a job.* ✗
> *In a couple of years, I'll be looking for a job.* ✔

4 SPEAKING

A   PAIR WORK   Choose a side project from the list below or your own idea. Think about how it will fit with your short-term and long-term plans, ambitions, or goals. Is it linked to your career in any way? Then tell each other about your side project. Ask questions to find out more. For ideas, watch Jacqueline's video.

create an app	do a podcast	grow plants
improve your cooking skills	make jewelry or furniture	play in a band
start an English speaking group	write a blog	write a children's book

> I'm studying to become a teacher, but my side project is learning to play the guitar. Right now, I'm practicing the basics little by little, but in several months, I'll be successfully playing songs. Maybe I could even be a guitar teacher someday. It's going to be fun!

EXPERT SPEAKER

Is Jacqueline's side project something you'd ever do? Why or why not?

THE LITTLE TOUCHES

1 LISTENING

A 🔊 **2.13** **PAIR WORK** Look at the pictures. What kind of event do you think the items in picture A would be good for? What can you see in picture B? Are you sure? Then listen to a podcast about event planning and check your answers.

B 🔊 **2.13** **RECOGNIZE EMPHASIS** Listen again. The speakers emphasize the following words. Does the emphasis for each word (a) show a contrasting idea or (b) mean *very*?

1	and small ____	3	complex ____	5	such ____
2	awesome ____	4	the birthday girl ____	6	really ____

C 🔊 **2.13** **PAIR WORK** **THINK CRITICALLY** Listen again. What ideas do the speakers have for "little touches"? Do you like the ideas? What kind of things, do you think, make events special and memorable? What kind of things are not worth the trouble? Why?

2 PRONUNCIATION: Listening for emphasis

A 🔊 **2.14** Listen to the emphasis on the underlined words.

Plan all types of events – big <u>and</u> small   That's an <u>awesome</u> idea.   Or it can be a <u>complex</u> theme like travel.

B 🔊 **2.15** Listen and <u>underline</u> the words that are emphasized.

1 Well, the birthday girl loved it, but not everyone likes strawberries.

2 That's such a terrific idea.

3 And it really is the little things they remember.

C ⊙Circle⊙ the correct options to complete the sentences.

When we want to show emphasis, we put the main stress on the word we want to emphasize. We usually do this by using a *higher* / *lower* pitch on this word. The main stress *can* / *cannot* include functional words like determiners.

3 SPEAKING SKILLS

A 🔊 **2.13** **Complete the expressions from the conversation in exercise 1B on page 80. Then decide if they are used to suggest an idea or to show interest in an idea. Write *S* (suggest) or *Sh* (show). Listen to the podcast again to check.**

Suggest and show interest in ideas

1 One/Another _____ you/we can do is …	5 I _____ everyone loved / will love that! __
2 That's _____ a terrific / an awesome idea. __	6 It never _____ to … __
3 What a _____ idea! __	7 That's always _____ considering. __
4 … always goes _____ well. __	8 … is a good _____ to approach it. __

B **PAIR WORK** **You're planning a small summer party for your classmates. Complete the conversation with your own ideas. Then compare with another pair. Which of their ideas would you like to use?**

A Do you have any ideas for the party?

B Well, I think ¹_____ is a good way to approach it. Actually, ²_____ always goes over well.

A That's ³_____ idea. Also, it never hurts to ⁴_____.

B True, and another thing we can do is ⁵_____.

A Yeah, that's always worth considering. And how about ⁶_____?

4 PRONUNCIATION: Saying words that show a contrast

A 🔊 **2.16** **Listen to the recording. Can you hear the pitch change on one key word in each sentence? <u>Underline</u> these words.**

1 I bet everyone loved that!

2 Well, most people did.

3 Her birthday's not in March, it's in April.

B 🔊 **2.17** **<u>Underline</u> the words that show a contrast. Listen and check your work. Then repeat the sentences.**

1 It wasn't her birthday, it was his.

2 I don't have any ideas, but Diego does.

3 Shall we get a present or give her some money?

4 He didn't just like it, he loved it!

C **PAIR WORK** **One student says a sentence. The other replies with a contrast.**

1 Let's drive to the party.
   No, we'll walk.

2 We'll celebrate at home.

3 Tom will be late.

4 Wasn't she wearing the red dress?

5 The party finishes at ten.

5 SPEAKING

A **GROUP WORK** **You are planning an event together. Choose an idea in the box. Talk about the theme, music, decorations, and food you'll have. Include little touches to make the event special. You can check online for ideas.**

a birthday party for a child	a company dinner
a family reunion	a graduation party

B **Describe your plan to the class. Which is the most entertaining?**

> OK, let's plan a company dinner. I think choosing an interesting theme is a good way to approach it.

> OK, well, a beach theme always goes over well. One thing we can do is give everyone sunglasses to wear.

FIND IT

8.4 A SMILE GOES A LONG WAY

1 READING

A Have you ever made a formal complaint? What was the problem? Was your complaint effective?

B **IDENTIFY WRITER'S PURPOSE** Read the article. What's its purpose? What specific examples of customer problems does the writer mention? Which are valid reasons for complaints?

Do you have a problem with a product, service, or company? It might be time to make a formal complaint. Anna Tims, a writer who focuses on consumer affairs, offers a list of tips for successful complaining. The secret is getting a lot of small things right.

HOW TO COMPLAIN EFFECTIVELY

Most large companies get hundreds of complaints – some silly and some serious. No matter how important your complaint is to you, it will just be added to a pile of complaints that a stressed-out customer service worker needs to read. So to be sure it makes the biggest impact, you must know how to state your complaint effectively. Follow these steps, and you're bound to get your problems solved.

✅ MAKE SURE YOUR COMPLAINT IS VALID
Your concern needs to be realistic. For example, if fees for ending a cell phone service contract early stop you from going to a cheaper cell phone service provider, that's too bad. You should have understood the contract. If, however, you have received poor service, you have the right to end your contract early. Or if you dropped your product and then stepped on it accidentally, it's your fault. But if a product breaks when you set it down gently, it's sure to be faulty.

✅ FIGURE OUT WHAT YOU WANT TO ACHIEVE
Do you want a refund, a replacement, or simply an apology? If you want a refund, you have to act quickly or you might lose your right to one. If you complain by phone, make a note of who you spoke to and when, and follow up the call with a letter restating your complaint and the response you got on the phone. Do the same if you sent the complaint through the company's website, so you have a record of it.

✅ ALWAYS ADDRESS A LETTER TO A SPECIFIC PERSON
It is best to start with the customer service manager. (If you aim too high – for example, the company president – you will be waiting while your letter is passed around until it reaches the right person.) Find out the manager's name and use their full title – Dr., Mr., Mrs., or Ms. A little thing like using someone's name can make a big impression.

✅ INCLUDE YOUR DETAILS
Remember to include your full name, address, and any order or reference numbers near the top of the letter. If a company can't easily find you in their system, they may not respond.

✅ KEEP COPIES
Make copies of all relevant documents – such as receipts, bank statements, order forms, and advertisements – and include them to support your complaint. If you want a new but stained couch replaced, include a photo of the damage.

✅ CHECK YOUR SPELLING
Carelessly written letters suggest you are as sloppy as the company you are complaining about.

✅ BE POLITE AND REASONABLE
Whether you are writing or calling, stay calm. Anger will give companies an excuse to refuse to deal with you.

✅ NAME NAMES
If you mention the unhelpful attitude of, for example, a store manager or customer service representative, try to include their names.

✅ SET A DEADLINE
Give the company a deadline for sending a useful response – 14 days is fair. Make a note of the date so you can increase the pressure if it is missed.

✅ MAKE SURE YOUR COMPLAINT ARRIVES
Send all letters by certified mail or special delivery so the company can't deny receiving them. If you use email, ask the person to confirm once they get it.

Adapted from an article by Anna Tims in The Guardian

GLOSSARY
consumer affairs (*n*) a system related to protecting people who buy products and services
faulty (*adj*) not perfectly made or does not work correctly
sloppy (*adj*) not being careful or making an effort

C Read the article again. Which points apply to (1) both a complaint letter and a phone call and (2) only a complaint letter?

D **PAIR WORK** **THINK CRITICALLY** Which three points in the article do you think would be the most effective? Why? Are there any points that won't have an effect? Why not?

2 WRITING

A   Read Karen's letter to the customer service manager of Markus Appliances. What's the problem? Why is she not happy with the sales manager's response? What does she want?

To: Mr. Edwards
From: Karen Rebecca Mason
Subject: RE: Faulty SUPERWASH Washing Machine, model number RGM205

Reply   Forward

Dear Mr. Edwards,

I am writing to complain about the above washing machine, which I bought during your Summer Sale on July 15. I purchased it for $175.99 at the Main Street branch of Markus Appliances and include a copy of the receipt as proof of purchase.

After the machine was delivered, I tried to use it, but it wouldn't turn on. I checked the connection, which was fine, but the machine had no power. I immediately returned to the store and explained the problem to the sales manager, Rob Clark. At first, he suggested there was something wrong with the power in my house. When I insisted that the machine was faulty, he said, "Sorry, but you bought it during the half-price sale. We don't accept the return of sale items."

I find this unacceptable. First, the item is obviously faulty. Second, your company advertisement (copy included) states that you accept all returns without question. I believe that includes sale items. Third, I feel Mr. Clark should be friendlier. It's a small thing, but a smile goes a long way.

I would like your company to pick up the washing machine from my house and send me a refund of $175.99. I look forward to hearing from you within the next ten days.

Sincerely,

Karen Rebecca Mason

REGISTER CHECK

In formal written complaints, we often use expressions like *I find, I feel, I believe,* or *I think* to make statements less direct and more polite.

Direct

This is unacceptable.
Mr. Clark should be friendlier.

Less direct

I find this unacceptable.
I feel Mr. Clark should be friendlier.

B   **PAIR WORK**   **THINK CRITICALLY**   Which of the tips in the article in exercise 1A on page 82 did Karen follow?

C   **AVOID RUN-ON SENTENCES AND SENTENCE FRAGMENTS**   Read about two kinds of sentences to avoid in more formal writing. Look at the examples below. How could the sentences be improved? Then find good versions of each in Karen's letter in exercise 2A.

Run-on sentences (They go on and on.)

1   I am writing to complain about the above washing machine, which I bought during your Summer Sale on July 15 for $175.99 at the Main Street branch of Markus Appliances and for which I include a copy of the receipt as proof of purchase.

Sentence fragments (Incomplete sentences)

2   Went back to the store. Explained problem to sales manager Rob Clark.

3   Unacceptable. First, obviously faulty.

WRITE IT

D   **PLAN**   You're going to write a complaint letter. Choose an idea in the box or something you experienced yourself. With a partner, describe the problem and how you want the company to solve it. Then look at the letter in exercise 2A. What type of information should each paragraph contain in a complaint letter? How will you start and end the letter?

a bad restaurant meal	a broken or faulty item or package
poor customer service	an item that's different from the advertisement

E   Write your complaint letter.

F   **PAIR WORK**   Exchange your letters of complaint. How effective is your partner's letter?

TIME TO SPEAK
The key to less stress

LESSON OBJECTIVE
■ make a podcast on ways to reduce stress

NOT STRESSED AT ALL

VERY STRESSED

A   **DISCUSS**   How stressed are you? Where would you put yourself on the scale above? Would you say most of your stress is caused by one or two big things or a number of small things? In pairs, discuss examples of big and small things that can make you feel stressed. For ideas look at the pictures. Add four ideas of your own.

B   Compare your ideas with other pairs. Find out common causes of stress.

C   **DECIDE**   Which of the causes of stress from part B can be reduced by taking simple actions? What actions can be taken? With your partner from part A, discuss the ideas in the box and your own ideas. Then choose your top three effective and simple actions.

> **SIMPLE ACTIONS TO REDUCE STRESS:**
>
> | | | |
> |---|---|---|
> | Delete it. | Don't read it. | Don't reply. |
> | Make "to-do" lists. | Do it right away. | Get up earlier. |
> | Go to bed later. | Say "No!" | Discuss the problem. |

D   **PREPARE**   You're going to present your actions in a short podcast. Plan: (1) the introduction, (2) your actions and the reasons why you think they're simple and effective (give some examples), and (3) the conclusion. You can take notes.

E   **PRESENT**   Present your podcast to the class. Answer any questions about it.

F   **AGREE**   The class compares the podcasts and chooses two that have the best ideas and are well presented.

To check your progress, go to page 155.

USEFUL PHRASES

DECIDE

One/Another thing you could do is …

It never hurts to …

… is always worth considering.

… is a good way to approach it.

PREPARE

If you do this, you're bound to / sure to …

You're going to …

You might …

You'll be + verb + -ing …

UNIT OBJECTIVES
- talk about how your life might be different
- talk about mistakes
- reassure someone about a problem
- write an article giving tips
- talk about key events in your life

THINGS HAPPEN

9

START SPEAKING

A   Look at the picture. What do you think the man expected to be doing that day? What happened instead? How could this situation develop?

B   Think of a situation when something very unexpected completely changed your plans. What happened? Was the change for the better or worse?

C   Do you believe in chance? Or are the best things that happen to us always planned? Discuss some examples. For ideas, watch Carolina's video.

EXPERT SPEAKER

Have you ever had an experience similar to Carolina's?

TURNING POINTS

1 LANGUAGE IN CONTEXT

A   PAIR WORK   **What is fate? Do you believe in it?**

B   **Read the online posts. What is each person's opinion about luck?**

X-ray technician

Comments   Account 👤   Sign out 🔄

Lara_Park   *posted 2 days ago*
Do you believe in **fate**? My brother says there's no such thing. But I think everything happens for a reason, and there are no **coincidences**. When you look back on your life, you can see the **path** that has led to your life today. For example, I was studying finance and wanted to go into banking. Then my brother accidentally slammed the car door on my finger – ouch! The doctor sent me for an X-ray, which was SO COOL! I could see my own bones on the screen, and the X-ray tech explained everything and answered all my questions. Totally fascinating! If I could find her, I'd thank her because that was a **life-changing experience**. I dropped finance and enrolled in a radiology course. Now, I say that was fate. I mean, if my brother hadn't broken my finger, I wouldn't be an X-ray technician today. But he says it was just a **lucky break**! (Ha! That's a good one.)
👍 Like   💬 Comment

PracticalGal   *posted 2 days ago*
I agree with your brother. People make **deliberate decisions** based on current circumstances, even if that's just a **chance encounter**. If you hadn't met that X-ray tech, you might have learned about radiology some other way. But you weren't unhappy in finance, so even if you were a banker now, you'd still be happy.
👍 Like   💬 Comment

Jace_the_Ace   *posted 2 days ago*
I think life is a combination of luck and **determination**. Sometimes, like Lara, you**'re in the right place at the right time**, but it takes hard work and skill to turn luck into a real opportunity.
👍 Like   💬 Comment

C   **Read the posts again. What events led to Lara's job?**

D   GROUP WORK   THINK CRITICALLY   **Say whose opinion you agree with the most. Then talk about someone who played a part in any of your life-changing experiences.**

2 VOCABULARY: Luck and choice

A   🔊 2.18   **Which expressions in the box are about luck, choice, or either luck or choice? Fill in the chart. Then listen and check your work. Which of the expressions are nouns or noun phrases? Which are verb phrases? Which three were not used in the posts in exercise 1A?**

be fortunate	be in the right place at the right time	chance encounter
coincidence	deliberate decision	determination
fate	life-changing experience	lucky break
(not) believe my luck	path	wind up

About luck	About choice	About luck and choice

B   ▶ **Now go to page 148. Do the vocabulary exercises for 9.1.**

C   **Describe a time when you had good luck. What happened? What choices did you make in that situation?**

3 GRAMMAR: Unreal conditionals

A   Read the sentences in the grammar box. Which rules are about the *if* clause? Which are about the result clause?

> **Unreal conditionals**
>
> **If** I **could find** her, I**'d thank** her. (I'd = I would)
>
> **If** you **hadn't met** that X-ray tech, you **might have learned** about radiology some other way.
>
> **If** my brother **hadn't broken** my finger, I **wouldn't be** an X-ray technician today.

1   Present and future unreal conditionals:

Use the past continuous, simple past, or *could* in the _____ clause.

Use *would*, *could*, or *might* + base form in the _____ clause.

2   Past unreal conditionals:

Use the past perfect in the _____ clause.

Use *would*, *could*, *may*, or *might* with *have* + past participle in the _____ clause.

3   Past unreal conditionals can also have an imaginary present result:

Use *would* + base form of a verb in the _____ clause.

B   **Now go to page 137. Look at the grammar chart and do the grammar exercise for 9.1.**

C   Complete the sentences and check your accuracy. Then share your ideas with a partner. Ask questions to find out more.

1   If I had more time, I _____ .

2   If I could work anywhere, I _____ .

3   I _____ if I didn't

_____ .

4   If I hadn't _____ , I wouldn't

_____ .

5   If I hadn't _____ , I might have

_____ .

6   I couldn't have _____ if I hadn't _____ .

> ✔ **ACCURACY** CHECK
>
> In past unreal conditionals, the auxiliary *have* goes in the result clause only, not in the *if* clause.
>
> *If I hadn't ~~have~~ met the doctor, I might not have become an X-ray technician.* ✗
>
> *If I hadn't met the doctor, I might not have become an X-ray technician.* ✔

4 SPEAKING

A   GROUP WORK   Think about how your life might be different now in the following situations.

> you were born in another country
> you hadn't met someone you know
> you didn't have your present job
>
> you had gone to another school
> you could learn without studying
> you had fewer/more siblings

> If I **hadn't convinced** my boss to enter the design competition, we **wouldn't have won** first prize – this amazing project that I am now leading. I'm also really **fortunate** that I have such great coworkers. I **might not enjoy** my job so much if I **weren't working** with such fantastic people.

WHY DID I DO IT?

1   LANGUAGE IN CONTEXT

A   🔊 **2.19**   Look at the picture. What do you think the man regrets? What other kinds of small things do people often regret? Read and listen to a group of friends talking about small regrets. How many regrets do they talk about?

🔊 **2.19 Audio script**

Anne	I was just wondering what kind of things you regret doing. Not big things, like, "I wish I wasn't studying psychology. I wish I could study art instead!" Just little, silly things.
Ruby	Oh, I have a good one! Someone once told me that it's better to wash your hair with regular soap, rather than shampoo. So I tried that …
Sonia	Uh-oh, that **was a bad move**.
Ruby	I know! If only you'd been there to stop me. I couldn't get the flakes out of my hair whatever I did. And of course I had an interview to go to that day. It **was such a silly mistake**.
Sonia	That **was unfortunate**. Well, I **found myself in an awkward situation** the other day: I was on a date – a first date – and I was trying so hard to be interesting that I was talking and talking and **not watching what I was doing**. I went to take a bite of my spaghetti and spilled it all down my white top. Ordering spaghetti with tomato sauce **was such a dumb thing to do**!
David	Well, sometimes you have to **learn things the hard way**. I recently washed my new sweater in hot water, and now it's way too small. It **was completely my own fault**: The label said to use cold. **I was in too much of a hurry**, as usual. If only I had a three-year-old brother, it would fit him perfectly!
Paulo	I once ripped my pants on a dance floor!
Anne	Awkward!
Paulo	Yeah, I was on the floor, doing a breakdance move, when *rip*! But I **saw the funny side of it**. And so did everyone else!
Anne	I bet they did!
Paulo	I'm **totally incompetent at** dancing. I don't even have a sense of rhythm. I don't know what I was thinking. I could have **kicked myself**.
Anne	Well, you could have, but you might have ripped your pants even more.

B   🔊 **2.19**   Read and listen again. What were the friends' regrets? Who do you think made the biggest mistake?

C   PAIR WORK   THINK CRITICALLY   Discuss the best way to deal with small regrets: laugh, forget them, try again, etc.

INSIDER ENGLISH

Use *I bet* to express agreement and show interest in what someone says.

A   *I was really scared.*
B   *I bet!* OR *I bet you were!*
A   *She's so happy.*
B   *I bet!* OR *I bet she is!*

2 VOCABULARY: Commenting on mistakes

A 🔊 **2.20** Look at the expressions from the text in exercise 1A on page 88 in the box. Discuss what each one means. Use a dictionary or your phone to help you. Then listen and check your work.

FIND IT

be a bad move	be a dumb thing to do	be a silly mistake
be incompetent (at)	be in too much of a hurry	be unfortunate
be your own fault	find yourself in an awkward situation	kick yourself
learn sth the hard way	not watch what you're doing	see the funny side of sth

B ▶ **Now go to page 149. Do the vocabulary exercises for 9.2.**

C **PAIR WORK** Describe and comment on mistakes people often make involving these things.

cleaning	clothes	computers/phones	cooking	reservations/tickets	work

3 GRAMMAR: Wishes and regrets

A Read the sentences in the grammar box. Circle the correct options to complete the rules.

> **Wishes and regrets**
>
> **I wish (that) I wasn't** studying psychology. **I wish I could** study art instead.
> **If only** you**'d been** there to stop me! **If only I had** a three-year-old brother.

1 *I wish (that)* and *if only* have **a different / the same** meaning.

2 For wishes and regrets about the present, use *I wish (that)* or *if only* followed by the simple past, **can / could**, or the past continuous.

3 For wishes and regrets about the past, use *I wish (that)* or *if only* followed by a verb in the **present perfect / past perfect**.

B ▶ **Now go to page 137. Look at the grammar chart and do the grammar exercise for 9.2.**

C Use *if only* to describe regrets about the problems below. Then tell a partner about similar experiences of your own using *I wish (that)*.

1 I broke it.
  If only I hadn't broken it. I wish I hadn't broken my favorite mug last week.

2 I can't find it.

3 I forgot to do it.

4 I have to go there.

5 I don't have time to do it.

6 I didn't answer it.

4 SPEAKING

A **PAIR WORK** Are there any little things you've done, or haven't done, in the last few days that you regret (e.g., when shopping for clothes or groceries, decorating your home, going on vacation)? For ideas, watch Carolina's video.

> Some things you **learn the hard way**. The other day I bought lots of groceries, but what I hadn't noticed was that the bag had a hole in it. If only I'd **checked** it more carefully …

EXPERT SPEAKER

Are your regrets similar to Carolina's?

MY MISTAKE

1 LISTENING

A 🔊 **2.21** **Look at the picture. What do you think the woman just did? Then listen to a call-in radio show, where she asks for advice. What did she do? How many people call in to give her advice?**

B 🔊 **2.21** **Listen again. What are the main pieces of advice the callers give to Sandy?**

C 🔊 **2.21** **IDENTIFY FEELINGS** **Listen again. Circle the word that best describes each person's feeling.**

		a		**b**		**c**	
1	Host	a	neutral	b	confused	c	annoyed
2	Marta	a	sad	b	bored	c	amused
3	Jon	a	angry	b	annoyed	c	surprised
4	Ramon	a	bored	b	sad	c	positive
5	Amanda	a	amused	b	calm	c	annoyed

D **PAIR WORK** **What advice would you give to Sandy, and why? How have you handled an awkward situation in the past?**

2 PRONUNCIATION: Listening for different word groups

A 🔊 **2.22** **Listen to how this is divided into word groups.**

Think before you write something // think again before you send it // and check who it's going to // before pushing "Send."

B 🔊 **2.23** **Listen and separate the word groups with //.**

1 Last week I wrote a personal email to a friend a very personal email but by accident I sent it to a senior manager at my company.

2 It happened to me too but with a friend not a coworker I just pretended my brother had gotten into my email and sent it as a joke.

3 That's digital communication we write and send stuff quickly and then we can't "unsend" it so we have to live with our mistakes.

C **Which statement is true about word groups?**

1 A word group has two main stresses, and there is no pause before the next word group.

2 A word group has one main stress, and it is often separated by a small pause from the next word group.

SPEAKING SKILLS

A 🔊 **2.21** **Match the sentence halves to make expressions of reassurance from the radio show in exercise 1A on page 90. Listen to the radio show again to check.**

Give reassurance

1	You're not the only one ___	a	it goes.
2	We all make ___	b	that bad.
3	That's the way ___	c	turn out all right.
4	What are you ___	d	who's done that.
5	It's no use ___	e	is perfect.
6	It's not ___	f	mistakes.
7	It could have ___	g	worrying about?
8	It'll ___	h	been worse.
9	No one ___	i	crying over spilled milk.

B **PAIR WORK** | **THINK CRITICALLY** **Which expressions in exercise 3A are not appropriate for more formal relationships? Why? Are there any expressions in your own language like the ones in exercise 3A?**

C ▶ **Student A: Go to page 158. Student B: Go to page 160. Follow the instructions.**

4 PRONUNCIATION: Using intonation in conditional sentences

A 🔊 **2.24** **Circle the intonation pattern in this conditional sentence.**

If you'd sent the email, it could have been worse.

a If you'd sent the email ↗ // it could have been worse ↘

b If you'd sent the email ↘ // it could have been worse ↘

c If you'd sent the email ↘ // it could have been worse ↗

B 🔊 **2.25** **Underline the word group that has a falling intonation in the conditional sentences below. Listen and check, and repeat the sentences. Then finish the sentences in a different way and read them out to a partner, focusing on the intonation.**

1	If she'd listened to me	this would never have happened // we'd be in a better situation now
2	If I had thought about it more	I might have said no // I may have agreed
3	If you hadn't helped me	no one would have // I would've failed
4	If they'd told me yesterday	things might be better // I could have gotten ready

5 SPEAKING

A **PAIR WORK** | **Think of a problem someone might have. Imagine you're going to talk to that person. Plan what you'll say to reassure them. Then plan how to act out your conversation.**

B **GROUP WORK** | **Act out your situation for another pair. Afterward, say if you agree with the advice given. Were the expressions of reassurance appropriate?**

> I need your advice. I borrowed a suit from my friend for a party, but I lost the jacket somewhere. I don't know what to say to him – or what to do. It was an expensive suit.

> What are you worrying about? We all make mistakes. Just tell him the truth, give the pants back, and offer to help him buy a new jacket.

GOOD CONVERSATIONS

1 READING

A | PAIR WORK | MAKE PREDICTIONS | Read the title of the article. Why do you think the writer calls it a "happiness experiment"? Then read the article. Was your prediction correct? Was he happy at the end?

"HOW TO MAKE SMALL TALK WITH STRANGERS: MY 21-DAY HAPPINESS EXPERIMENT

By John Corcoran

Recently I read that people who talk to strangers are happier than those who keep quiet. I decided to test that theory with an experiment. The rules were simple: For 21 days, I would look for opportunities to talk to strangers. Here are some experiences I had.

FRIDAY, MAY 9

While visiting my hometown for a wedding, I had a chance encounter with a man in the hotel café. We started talking, and I found he had just moved there from Chicago. I told him about the community, the schools, and neighborhoods where he was thinking of buying a home.

How I Felt: The conversation made me feel useful and valuable. The man's daughter was about to enter my old high school, and he seemed relieved to hear it was a good school.

MONDAY, MAY 12

While driving home, I stopped for lunch. A man was wearing a T-shirt that said "Coastal Maine Botanical Gardens." I considered commenting on it, as we have vacationed in coastal Maine, but I didn't say anything.

How I Felt: I regret that I didn't speak up. I am curious if the gardens are close to our summer vacation spot. Sure, I can Google it, but I would have liked to chat with him about the area.

TUESDAY, MAY 20

Three men were at our house to cut our trees. I watched as they climbed the trees like monkeys and went straight to the top. I asked one of them if they fall out of trees frequently. He said, "Almost never." One said, "I've been climbing trees for 27 years," and said he fell out of a tree once and broke his knee.

How I Felt: It's not every day I talk to someone whose job is climbing trees, and it was interesting learning about how they do it.

THURSDAY, MAY 29

Today, I had to take the ferry to my office. I decided to try talking with other commuters and sat at a table. Although I exchanged a few comments, I had no meaningful conversations. At one point, I chatted with a woman, but eventually the conversation died, and she returned to reading her book.

How I Felt: I wish I'd had more conversations, but digital devices often got in the way. The important lesson I learned is to begin a conversation before people put on headphones or start reading.

FRIDAY, MAY 30

I went to a neighborhood party with my wife and our baby. The baby was a great conversation starter.

How I Felt: It's almost too easy to start talking with people when you have a baby because strangers come up and chat. I enjoyed the opportunity to meet more people.

Overall, I felt great about most of my interactions with strangers. Almost every one left me feeling a little happier. However, I will report a few disappointments: I am pretty outgoing, but I often missed an opportunity to talk because I was unsure of what to say. Second, sometimes I wanted to chat, but nearly everyone was on a digital device. I felt like speaking to them would have been interrupting. Third, I would love to report that I made new lifelong friends and found new clients. Unfortunately, that didn't happen.

MY FINAL ADVICE Just go out and try talking with strangers. It is likely that you will improve your own day and make the person you talk to happier as well. "

Adapted from an article by John Corcoran on the Art of Manliness website

B Read again. Which experiences was the writer happy about? What regrets does he have? Would you try the same experiment? Why or why not?

C | IDENTIFY IMPLICATIONS | Match the main things the writer learned from the experiences he had (1–5) with the correct dates (a–e).

1 Talk about things you have in common. ____
2 Start conversations right away. ____
3 Share useful information. ____
4 Have something with you that attracts attention. ____
5 Talk to people who are different from you. ____

a Thursday, May 29
b Friday, May 30
c Friday, May 9
d Monday, May 12
e Tuesday, May 20

D | PAIR WORK | THINK CRITICALLY | What is "small talk"? What are good topics for "small talk" with strangers? Are there any topics it's best to avoid? Why?

2 WRITING

A Read the article about small talk. Summarize the tips it gives. Can you think of more tips on how to be a good listener?

SMALL TALK: HOW TO BE A GOOD LISTENER 🎧

DON'T INTERRUPT

When someone else is talking, don't interrupt them. It's sometimes OK to ask a question in the middle of someone's point, for example, if you don't understand what they mean. But in general, it's best to let someone finish their point before making a comment or asking a question.

SHOW INTEREST

While you're listening to someone else, don't think about what you'll say next. Instead, show interest in their points by asking questions about the topic they're talking about. Don't change the topic or start talking about yourself.

LISTEN WITH YOUR EYES

Watch a speaker's body language, such as eye contact, hand gestures, and posture. Do they seem excited, angry, or worried? This can help you understand their feelings. Then you can ask questions, make a comment, or give advice in an appropriate way.

THINK BEFORE YOU RESPOND

Think about what you're going to say before you speak. Sometimes your opinion is helpful. Other times, it's best just to tell someone you understand or reassure them instead of telling them what you think.

REGISTER CHECK

Describe the situation using *when* or *while* before the imperative to soften the advice you give. Compare:

Strong, direct

Don't interrupt when someone else is talking.

Softer, less direct

When someone else is talking, don't interrupt them.

B **PARALLEL STRUCTURES** When listing items, try to use parallel structures. This means the items have the same grammatical pattern. Look at the sentences. Why are the underlined parts not parallel? Correct them with words from the article in exercise 2A.

1 **Adjectives:**   Do they seem excited, angry, or are worried?

2 **Noun phrases:**   Watch a speaker's body language, such as eye movement, hand gestures, and how they stand.

3 **Verb phrases:**   Then you can ask questions, make a comment, or you should give advice in an appropriate way.

🧭 WRITE IT

C **PLAN** Think of tips for an article entitled "Small Talk: How to Be a Good Talker." Discuss the categories in the box. You can check online for more ideas. Then think about the title and structure of your article. Which tips will you include? What headings will you use for each tip? What advice/explanations will you include under each heading?

FIND IT

audience (who is listening)	body language (eye contact, hand gestures, posture)
content (topic)	delivery (how you speak: attitude, volume)
language (words you use)	

D Write the article you planned. Remember to use parallel structures in lists.

E **PAIR WORK** **THINK CRITICALLY** Exchange your articles. What's the best tip in your partner's article?

93

TIME TO SPEAK
Class reunion

Gaby Arnold
School of Management
BS Finance

Mark Bevilaqua
School of Nursing
BS Nursing

Mia Asner
Arts & Sciences
BA Sociology

Rodney Dacosta
Arts & Sciences
BS Mathematics

A Would you like to go to a class reunion at a school you went to years ago? How would you feel about meeting people you haven't seen for a long time? What would you talk about? Discuss with a partner.

B **PREPARE** Imagine you're going to a class reunion. Work alone to plan what you're going to talk about. Use the topics in the box. Think of important and interesting things you've done or experienced since you were a child.

education	free time	homes	regrets
relationships	sports	travel	work

C **DISCUSS** Share your news and memories with at least three people in the class and listen to what they say. As you listen, make positive comments about good things you hear and reassuring comments about not-so-good things. Encourage people to tell you more about surprising things they did.

D **PRESENT** Tell the class about the most interesting or surprising thing you heard from someone. Each time, the class asks that person to say more about it.

E **DECIDE** The class chooses the most interesting things people did or experienced.

To check your progress, go to page 155.

USEFUL PHRASES

DISCUSS

You were really fortunate!

It sounds like you were in the right place at the right time.

You're not the only one who …

That's the way it goes.

Was it luck or a deliberate decision?

PRESENT

You'll never guess what …

Not only that, but …

Apparently, …

Isn't that amazing?

Are you ready for this?

REVIEW 3 (UNITS 7–9)

1 VOCABULARY

A Complete the product review with the correct forms of the expressions in the box.

arrange	bad move	be jumbled up	be organized
be practical	be worth the money	convince	learn the hard way
purchase	regret	throw in	urge

HOME   ABOUT   NEWS   BLOG   CONTACT US

I needed to ¹_____ a new backpack before I started college. I didn't want something with just a single space inside it because I don't think bags like that ²_____ when you have a lot of different things to carry. You ³_____ your stuff and close the zipper, and then when you open it, everything ⁴_____ inside, and it takes ages to find things. I hate that. I like my stuff to ⁵_____ . So when I saw this model, it looked perfect. The many different pockets inside immediately ⁶_____ me that it was ideal. I figured I could ⁷_____ my stuff neatly in them. So I bought the backpack and did just that. Unfortunately, it was a ⁸_____ because it turned out there's no way to close the pockets. So the first day I used my new backpack, I ⁹_____ that stuff falls out of the pockets and ends up in the bottom of the bag. I paid extra for the bag with pockets, expecting it to ¹⁰_____ . It wasn't. Needless to say, I now ¹¹_____ the purchase. I ¹²_____ you not to buy this backpack.

💬 5   ♡ 12   ⇄ 3

B **PAIR WORK** Tell a partner about something you bought that you were disappointed with. Use some of the phrases from exercise 1A to describe your experience.

2 GRAMMAR

A Use the correct forms of the verbs (*to* + verb or verb + *-ing*) in parentheses ( ) to complete the sentences.

1 I think it's a fascinating subject _____ (read) about.
2 A lot of people don't think it's possible _____ (do) that, but I do.
3 I was dying to have something _____ (eat).
4 It's so easy to waste a lot of time _____ (do) that.
5 Because of the problem, I was forced _____ (start) the whole thing again.
6 I knew I was bound _____ (have) problems with it.
7 That's where I planned _____ (go), but in the end, it wasn't possible.
8 I get bored quickly _____ (play) that game.
9 I have trouble _____ (understand) that subject.
10 If you ask me, it's sure _____ (happen) soon.

B **PAIR WORK** Think of examples of your own opinions and experiences that match the sentences in exercise 2A. Tell a partner about them.

3 VOCABULARY

A   Complete the sentences with the words in the box.

break	difference	ease	encounter	expected
lesson	life	life-changing	pleasure	time

1   To be successful, you need a lucky _____ .

2   Generally speaking, if you take _____ in doing something, you'll do it well.

3   Mistakes are the best way to learn because they always teach you a(n) _____ you won't forget.

4   It's often the small things, not the big things, that make a(n) _____ .

5   If you want to learn a new skill, you should do it on your own _____ .

6   You can expect to change careers at some point – not to devote your _____ to one occupation.

7   Planning things in detail isn't very helpful, since things hardly ever go as _____ .

8   If someone is doing something with _____ , it usually means they're good at it.

9   Learning to speak a second language is a(n) _____ experience for several reasons.

10   The best way to meet your future husband or wife is through a chance _____ .

B   **PAIR WORK**   Say whether you agree, partly agree, or disagree with the sentences in exercise 3A. Say why and give examples to help explain your views.

4 GRAMMAR

A   Circle the correct options.

1   One day, I'm *learning / going to learn* to ride a motorcycle.

2   I'm sure next week *might be / will be* fairly relaxing.

3   According to my schedule, *I'm having / I'd have* my next English lesson tomorrow.

4   Tonight, I *might / would* do some work at home or maybe just get some rest.

5   This time next year, *I'll study / I'll be studying* in college.

6   If I *moved / would move* to Europe, I would live in Spain.

7   If I *could / would* have a free plane ticket to anywhere in the world, I'd go to South Korea.

8   Out of all foreign languages, I wish I *can / could* speak Korean.

B   **PAIR WORK**   Say which sentences from exercise 4A are true for you, or change them so they are true for you.

WEST
SAN BERNARDINO
66
COUNTY

START SPEAKING

A   When you look at the picture, what do you think of the person? Would it be a good choice for a profile picture? What kind of profile would it be appropriate for?

B   Talk about a profile picture you have for social media, work/college, or on an ID card. What impression does it give about the kind of person you are? Is it a true impression?

C   What kind of things do people change about their appearance when they want to make a specific impression in these situations: an extended family gathering, going on a date, a job interview, making new friends? For ideas, watch Lucia's video.

EXPERT SPEAKER

Do you agree with Lucia? Can you think of more examples?

ARE WE UNIQUE?

1 LANGUAGE IN CONTEXT

A   **PAIR WORK**   Look at the picture. How do you think the people are connected?

B   Read the article. How did the author try to find her doppelgänger? Would you want to meet your doppelgänger?

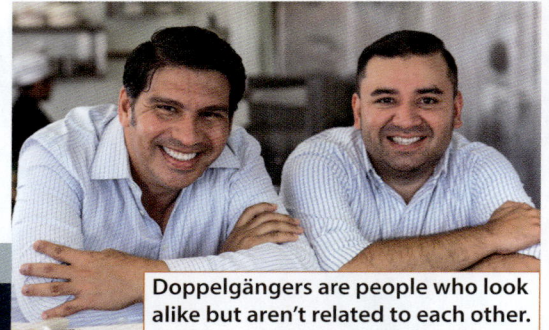

Doppelgängers are people who look alike but aren't related to each other.

⊗ ▭ ⊖

| Home | About | Blog | Contact Us |

Can you find your doppelgänger in a day?
by Maxine Frith

Maxine Frith

Doppelgänger means "double walker," that is, someone walking around this planet that looks just like you. It is said that we are each likely to have at least seven **look-alikes** somewhere in the world. I wondered about the possibility of discovering a few of mine.

I posted a message and picture on Facebook, Twitter, and Instagram, but it didn't result in finding anyone with my **likeness**. Next, I used the "I Look Like You" website, which uses facial recognition software to compare your image with millions of others. The site matched me with a **female** named Kathryn Laskaris. She wasn't a perfect **match**, but we have a similar **look**.

Next, I tried some doppelgänger-matching apps. I was matched with a 20-something **male** and a

baby. Finally, I uploaded my photo into a Google Images search and then clicked to search for something "visually similar." Within seconds, my doppelgänger appeared: Michal Ben-Josef Hirsch. I stared at her, noticing our **similarities** – she has the same **features** as me, the same hair, and the same smile. She's also smart and successful – everything I could hope for in a twin stranger.

I was really interested in learning more. Psychologist Amima Memon explains, "It may seem bizarre that people become obsessed with finding strangers who look exactly like them, but … research shows that … we like people who look like us … ."

I haven't succeeded in learning more about Michal. I suppose I'll just have to be happy with me.

Adapted from an article by Maxine Frith in The Telegraph

C   Read the article again. What matches did the author get? How were they similar to her?

D   **GROUP WORK**   **THINK CRITICALLY**   How would you feel about your doppelgänger contacting you?

2 VOCABULARY: Describing characteristics

A   🔊 **2.26**   What do the nouns in the box mean? Use a dictionary or your phone to help you. Then listen and check. Can you remember which eight were used in the text? Which three words can also be adjectives?

| build | characteristic | feature | female | gender | individual |
| likeness | look | look-alike | male | match | similarity |

B   ▶ Now go to page 149. Do the vocabulary exercises for 10.1.

C   **PAIR WORK**   Describe yourself and some of your typical characteristics using the words in exercise 2A.

3 GRAMMAR: Gerunds after prepositions

A   Read the sentences in the grammar box. Circle the correct options to complete the rules.

> **Gerunds after prepositions**
>
> I wondered about **the possibility of discovering** a few of mine.
>
> I **was** really **interested in learning** more.
>
> I haven't **succeeded in learning** more about Michal.

1   You can use a gerund (verb + *-ing*) **before** / **after** some phrases with a noun + *of*.

2   You can use the verb *be* / *have* + an adjective + a preposition + a gerund.

3   You can use a gerund as **an object** / **a subject** after a verb + preposition.

B   ▶ Now go to page 138. Look at the grammar chart and do the grammar exercise for 10.1.

C   PAIR WORK   What are different ways of meeting new people? Make questions with a gerund and your own ideas. Use the prompts below to help you. Check your accuracy. Then ask another pair the questions.

1   places for / ways of meeting new people

Have you ever thought of meeting people online?

2   things you would most care about / be interested in

3   things you could plan on doing

4   things you might be concerned about / risks

> ✓ **ACCURACY** CHECK
>
> Be sure to use the correct form after a verb + preposition.
>
> *It didn't result in ~~find~~ anyone with my likeness.* ✗
>
> *It didn't result in ~~to find~~ anyone with my likeness.* ✗
>
> *It didn't result in finding anyone with my likeness.* ✓

4 SPEAKING

A   GROUP WORK   Do you like to be similar to your friends or different? Discuss using the topics below and your own ideas. Do most people in your group like to be similar or different?

clothes	education	experiences	goals	hairstyle
hobbies/interests	humor	music	personality	

*I often wear trendy clothes. I like the **idea of looking** like my favorite celebrities.*

*I **wouldn't dream of dressing** like other people. I like to be an **individual** and have my own **look**.*

10.2 YOU, THE CUSTOMER

LESSON OBJECTIVE
- talk about customer research

1 LANGUAGE IN CONTEXT

A 🔊 **2.27** What kinds of information do you think companies collect about their customers, and why? Discuss with a partner. Then read and listen to a radio interview with Lina, a marketing executive. Were your ideas correct?

🔊 **2.27 Audio script**

Host We all know that companies collect a lot of information about us as customers. Why do they do it?

Lina Well, basically it allows them to **identify** your needs and understand what kinds of things you might want to buy.

Host So, what kind of information do they collect?

Lina Well, it can be things like gender, family situation, age, profession, um … financial situation, interests. It could also include likes, goals, … fears. This is the kind of information companies can get from social media, **surveys**, and from past purchases you made.

Host OK. And how is this information used?

Lina Well, let's say a store is **analyzing** a list of customers' purchases for a month. This list lets the store **calculate** how much the customer spent. And the store can also **examine** the types of purchases to see what they reveal. So let's say this person spent $280 on lipstick, expensive sunglasses, baby clothes, two different products to prevent insects from biting, a video game, two tablet cases, and three books: about leadership, negotiating, and Italian cooking. Now, what does an **analysis** of that information **demonstrate**? It allows the store to figure out a lot about this person and helps the store *guess* other things. And that **assessment** enables the store to predict how much this person might spend per month and what other products they might want to buy.

B 🔊 **2.27** Read and listen again. How do companies get information about their customers? Why is it useful?

C PAIR WORK How do you feel about companies collecting different kinds of information about you? For ideas, watch Lucia's video.

EXPERT SPEAKER

Do you agree with Lucia? How, do you think, does Lucia's job inform her answer?

2 VOCABULARY: Describing research

A 🔊 **2.28** PAIR WORK Look at the words in the box. Discuss their meanings. Use a dictionary or your phone to help you. Which are verbs? Nouns? Then listen and check the parts of speech. Were verbs or nouns used out of each pair in the interview in exercise 1A?

| analyze/analysis | assess/assessment | calculate/calculation | demonstrate/demonstration |
| examine/examination | identify/identification | survey/survey | |

B Now go to page 150. Do the vocabulary exercises for 10.2.

C PAIR WORK THINK CRITICALLY Look again at the customer's purchases in exercise 1A. What can you figure out, or guess, about this person? Think about: family situation, age, profession, financial situation, interests, likes, goals, and fears. Then compare your ideas with others in the class.

> We can **identify** the person's interests. They bought lipstick and expensive sunglasses so that **demonstrates** that they care about their appearance.

100

3 GRAMMAR: Causative verbs

A Read the sentences in the grammar box. Complete the rules with the options in the box. There is one option you do not need to use. Which verbs do we use to talk about things we do <u>not</u> want to happen?

> **Causative verbs**
>
> It **allows them to identify** your needs.
>
> … two different products to **prevent insects from biting** …

> **!** We use *let, make,* and *have* + base form of the verb when something or someone causes something to happen.
>
> *This list **lets** the store calculate how much the customer spent.*

base form of the verb	gerund	infinitive

1 After *allow, cause, enable*: Use an object + _____ .

2 After *keep, prevent, protect, stop*: Use an object + *from* + _____ .

B **Now go to page 138. Look at the grammar chart and do the grammar exercise for 10.2.**

C Complete the sentences about shopping habits with your own ideas. Then compare with a partner. Ask questions to find out more.

1 Shopping for new things makes me _____ .

2 Having a mall nearby helps me _____ .

3 Credit cards allow me _____ .

4 Nothing can stop me _____ .

5 Online shopping enables me _____ .

6 Having a budget prevents me _____ .

4 SPEAKING

A A new department store is opening near you. Write down some customer information about yourself. Explain what you want and need there. Use these headings:

1 Description (of me)   2 What I want/need to buy   3 What facilities I want/need to use

List three to five things under each heading.

B **PAIR WORK** Analyze your partner's profile. Then give your assessment of products and services that would be of interest to your partner. Say why.

> I've **examined** your profile and found you like eating out with friends. If the store had a restaurant, that would **allow you** and your friends **to eat** there.

> I like that idea. And I've **identified** you as someone interested in fashion. **To help you** find what you want, the store definitely needs to offer a variety of clothing styles.

10.3

A CAREFUL CHOICE

1 LISTENING

A   PAIR WORK   Imagine you need to order a cake for a party. What kind of things would you need to consider to make a good choice?

B   🔊 2.29   Listen to two friends deciding which company to order a cake from. Why do they want a cake? How many companies do they consider? How do they feel at the end?

C   🔊 2.29   LISTEN FOR CONTRASTING IDEAS   Listen again. List the strong points and weak points of each cake company and its products. Then predict which cake company you think they'll choose. Which one would you choose?

D   🔊 2.30   Listen to the rest of the conversation. Which cake company did they choose, and why?

E   PAIR WORK   THINK CRITICALLY   How can you tell if a company and its products are good when you're shopping online? For example, what can web design, photos, reviews, and the range of products for sale reveal?

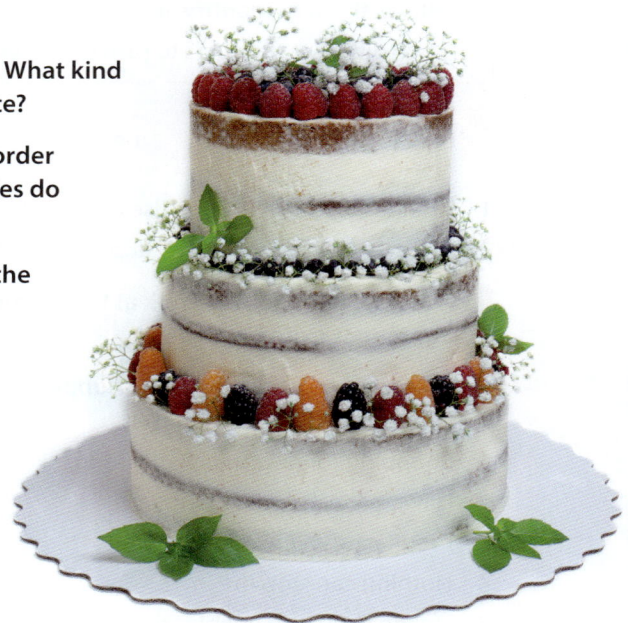

2 PRONUNCIATION: Quoting from a text

A   🔊 2.31   Listen to the speaker reading aloud from the cake website. Which parts are direct quotations? Add quotation marks " " around these parts. How are these pronounced differently?

The company profile says cakes for all occasions, designs for all themes and budgets, and skilled, professional cake decorating. That all sounds good.

It also says free personal advice – that's nice.

B   🔊 2.32   Look at the quoted section in the extract below. How would this be pronounced differently? Listen and check.

Madrona Cakes … "freshly baked, a variety of flavors, reasonable prices." And they also make cakes low in sugar, cakes with no egg, and dairy-free cakes.

C   PAIR WORK   Look back at the article on page 98. Choose a short extract to quote to your partner, like in exercises A and B above. Prepare your whole sentence (including the direct quotation from the article). Then say it to your partner. Can your partner identify which words came directly from the text?

3 SPEAKING SKILLS

A **PAIR WORK** Look at the expressions from the conversation in exercises 1A and 1C on page 102. Discuss the meaning of the underlined words. Use a dictionary or your phone to help you.

Give your impressions

1 I have a funny feeling (that) …
2 I get the impression (that) …
3 From what I can see, …
4 I have a hunch (that) …
5 Judging by the description, …
6 My gut feeling is (that) …
7 What strikes me (about …) is (that) …
8 As far as I can tell, …

B **PAIR WORK** Imagine you are in the following situations. Give your impressions.

1 You are standing in front of a new restaurant. You can see inside, and you can see the menu on the window. One of you thinks it looks good (clean, comfortable, good food). The other does not (crowded, noisy, not enough food choices).

Hmm, from what I can see, this restaurant looks …

> **INSIDER ENGLISH**
>
> *lose track of time* = forget when something is due or supposed to happen, often because of being busy with other things

2 You have to turn in a research and writing assignment on ancient pyramids. You lost track of time, and it's due tomorrow. One of you thinks you can finish in time (easy to find information, can divide the work, can stay up late). The other does not (takes time to research, no time to work together, have other homework).

About our essay, I have a funny feeling that I won't be able to … because …

4 PRONUNCIATION: Recognizing /eɪ/, /aɪ/, /ɔɪ/

A 🔊 **2.33** Underline the /eɪ/, /aɪ/, and /ɔɪ/ sounds. Listen and check your work. Then repeat.

1 What strikes me about this place is the choice of cakes.
2 I have a funny feeling that I may enjoy it.
3 Try one of our nice and tasty pies – you won't be disappointed!

B 🔊 **2.34** Circle the word that has a different diphthong.

1	straight	climb	fail		4	break	crayon	finally
2	voice	joy	ache		5	design	choice	voyage
3	weight	cycle	height					

C **PAIR WORK** Write down six of the words from exercise 4B. Take turns reading aloud one of the words from exercise 4B, saying the diphthong carefully. If you hear the word on your list from your partner, cross it out. The first student to cross out six words is the winner.

5 SPEAKING

A **PAIR WORK** You want to join a gym. Look at the online profiles of three gyms on page 158. Discuss the gyms, giving your impressions of each. Decide which one you'd each like to join and why. Then check with another pair and see if they had similar impressions and chose the same ones.

Well, judging by the description, gym 3 is modern and pretty large.

I agree, and as far as I can tell, it has good facilities. For example, …

A PROFESSIONAL PROFILE

1 READING

A Is it a good idea to have a profile on a social networking site for professionals? Why or why not? Read the article. Why does the author have a profile? Why does she decide she needs to improve it?

I recently graduated from college and am looking for a job. I joined a social network for professionals and wrote a fantastic profile for my page. I was sure that the first employer who read it would want to hire me.

KINSLEY GORDON

last updated six months ago

Contact me at 646-555-4302 or by email.

I am an individual with a unique personality, and I work very well with others. I recently graduated from New York University from the Gallatin School of Individualized Study. I put together my own program combining several areas of study. I hope to work for an English–Japanese bilingual company in the marketing department. In college, I had an internship at VTL-Wire, a large tech company. I also wrote poetry for a community magazine. Right now, I'm doing part-time freelance work, but I want to work full-time. Please contact me to find out how my skills could best work for your company.

No employers were responding, so I started reading articles about how to write a good profile. Mack Gelber, in his article called "8 Ways to Make Your Social Media Profile an Employer Magnet," had some really good advice. Here are some of his main points:

1 Have a complete and relevant profile

Make sure your profile contains your complete employment history and education, as well as any skills related to your job. Try to think through the eyes of an employer – no one wants to see a half-written profile.

2 Highlight skills and achievements that help employers

In your career history, be careful about the information you include. We don't need to know about how you organized the office softball team. Instead, try talking about specific goals you've met, and support your information with numbers. For example: "Sold $X while cutting costs by Y%."

3 Update your profile frequently

It's important to stay active on all social media sites. Start a new job? Post an update. Get a promotion? Update your title.

4 Keep your connections career-focused

Getting requests to connect from old roommates and people you don't remember from high school is only to be expected on social media, but you want to make sure the majority of the people you're connected to have similar career goals. This gives employers the impression that you're serious about your career.

5 Provide a clear link to your email address

Say an employer sees your profile and wants to get in touch with you about a potential job opportunity. Can they find your email address in a few seconds? Make sure it's linked somewhere that's clear and easy to see.

6 Have a professional-looking headshot

A good headshot is key to having a strong profile. That's not to say you need to wear formal office clothing (business casual is fine), but it pays to look engaged and put together.

Adapted from an article by Mack Gelber on the Monster website

B TAKE NOTES Read again. Take notes about each of the six points. Summarize each one with a phrase or two. Then share your notes with a partner. Were your ideas the same?

C THINK CRITICALLY According to Gelber's points, what problems does Kinsley's profile have? What do you think she could do to improve it?

2 WRITING

A | **THINK CRITICALLY** | Read Kinsley's new profile. What improvements did she make from her profile in exercise 1A on page 104?

KINSLEY GORDON
last updated yesterday

Marketing and more

I'm a recent graduate of New York University from the Gallatin School of Individualized Study who is dedicated to doing my best. I work very well on my own and with others. In order to focus on a marketing career, my field of study combined business, Japanese, and creative writing. I hope to work for an English–Japanese bilingual company in the marketing department. In college, I had an internship at VTL-Wire, a large tech company. My responsibilities included making online product demonstrations in English and Japanese, analyzing the comments people made on the demonstrations, and reporting people's impressions of the products to the company. I'm tech-savvy and learn new programs quickly. Although I'm currently doing part-time freelance work helping people design their websites, my ultimate goal is to work for a company full-time. I realize the benefits of starting small, especially at a company where there's the possibility of career progression. Please contact me to find out how my skills could best work for your company.

646-555-4302 • www.kinsleysays.com • kgordon@mailme.net • CONNECTIONS 225

REGISTER CHECK

Contractions are not normally used in formal writing. However, it's OK to use contractions on social media, like professional job sites.

Résumé, cover letter, etc.
I am tech-savvy and learn new programs quickly.

Social media site/profile
I'm tech-savvy and learn new programs quickly.

GLOSSARY
progression (*n*) when someone goes up to the next level or stage

B | **USE PROFESSIONAL LANGUAGE** | Read about three things to avoid when using professional language. Look at the examples, and then find good versions of each in Kinsley's profile in exercise 2A.

1. Don't use slang (= very informal language).

   not: I'm uber-excited to work for a company 24/7.

2. Avoid words like *kind of*, *probably*, and *maybe*. Use language that makes you sound confident.

   not: I'm kind of tech-savvy and probably can learn new programs pretty fast.

3. Don't be negative. Be positive and polite.

   not: I'm not sure I have the experience you're looking for, but contact me to see if my skills might work for your company.

WRITE IT

C | **PLAN** | You're going to create a professional profile on a social networking site. Tell your partner about the education, skills, and characteristics you have that make you a good candidate for future jobs. Then look at the profile in exercise 2A. What kind of information do you need to include at the beginning and end? How long should your profile be?

D | Write your professional profile. Be sure to use professional language.

E | **PAIR WORK** | Exchange profiles. Does your partner use professional language? Can you suggest any improvements?

TIME TO SPEAK
Attracting talent

LESSON OBJECTIVE
- develop a plan to improve a company website

Tech company

Hospital

Restaurant

Engineering company

A **PREPARE** In pairs, imagine you are experts who give advice to companies on how to make the career section of their website as attractive as possible to first-time employees. Choose a type of company from the pictures above or use your own idea.

B **DISCUSS** In pairs, brainstorm answers to this question: What do most first-time employees think about when choosing a company to work for? For example:

career progression
training opportunities

kinds of jobs available
workplace environment

products the company makes

C Compare your ideas with other pairs. Which areas do people think are most important?

D **DECIDE** In your original pairs, consider all the ideas you have. Decide which three areas are the most important to first-time employees of the company you chose in part A. Then decide how to present these areas on the company website in order to attract these employees. Use some of these options and your own ideas: photos, videos, interviews, reviews.

E **PRESENT** Tell the class what type of company you chose, present your ideas, and explain why first-time employees will like them.

F **AGREE** After the presentations, decide as a class which ideas will be most attractive to first-time employees. Then discuss which company you would like to work for.

To check your progress, go to page 156.

USEFUL PHRASES

DISCUSS
I get the impression that …
Judging by the people I know, …
Judging by what I've heard, …
As far as I can tell, …
My assessment is (that) …

PRESENT
This will allow first-time employees to …
This will help them …
This will enable them to …

UNIT OBJECTIVES
- talk about fake goods
- talk about untrue information
- express belief and disbelief
- write a persuasive essay
- share tips on solutions

REALLY?

11

START SPEAKING

A   Do you think this picture is real or fake? Why do you think so?

B   Can you think of some examples of fake photos you've seen? How easy or difficult is it to see that the photos are fakes?

C   When and why do some people choose to edit their photos? List the reasons. What kind of changes might they make to their photos? How do you feel about this? Answer the questions. For ideas, watch Bojan's video.

EXPERT SPEAKER

Do you agree with Bojan's opinion? Can you think of any other examples?

FAKE!

1 LANGUAGE IN CONTEXT

A Look at the picture of fake goods being destroyed. Do you think it's a waste? Read the newspaper article. What fake goods does the journalist mention?

THE HIGH PRICE OF CHEAP FAKES
By Emilia Flores

*Watches, purses, sneakers, jeans – **fake** consumer goods have become so common that the problems they cause are being forgotten.*

Hundreds of **counterfeit** soccer jerseys were recently discovered by the U.S. government while they were being shipped to Texas ahead of the World Cup. **Illegal** copies of clothes like these are often **imperfect** and even dangerous since they're not always made of safe materials, such as **fireproof** fabrics. Buying other kinds of counterfeit goods can be risky, too. Fake cosmetics often contain banned chemicals. Counterfeit electrical goods are often **second-rate** and can cause fires. And nobody is going to be helped by fake medicine; in fact, it can be **deadly**.

But not all fakes are so **inferior**. It's possible to buy copies of expensive watches, purses, and other top-quality products that look almost **genuine**. And when **sophisticated** counterfeits are offered cheaply, many people are willing to buy them, even though they know the items aren't **authentic** or **legal**. When the **original** products are being sold for over $1,000, it's easy to say that cheap copies are fair, since many of us couldn't afford to buy the real thing. But when we make this excuse, we forget that somebody's creative ideas have been stolen. We also fail to consider that the workers who produce fakes are normally paid very little and are often forced to work in dangerous conditions.

Unless we open our eyes to these realities, it's unlikely that counterfeiting will be stopped.

B Read the article again. According to the journalist, what problems do fake goods cause?

C PAIR WORK THINK CRITICALLY Which do you think is the most serious of these problems? Why? To what extent do you agree with the journalist's opinion?

2 VOCABULARY: Describing consumer goods

A ◀)) 2.35 PAIR WORK Look at the words from the article in exercise 1A in the box. Discuss their meaning. Use a dictionary or your phone to help you. Then listen and check your work.

FIND IT

authentic	counterfeit	deadly	fake	fireproof
genuine	illegal	imperfect	inferior	legal
original	second-rate	sophisticated		

B ▶ Now go to page 150. Do the vocabulary exercises for 11.1.

C PAIR WORK Have you ever seen or bought fake goods? What were they like? How can customers tell the difference between counterfeit and authentic goods?

3 GRAMMAR: Passive forms

A Read the sentences in the grammar box. Circle the correct options to complete the rules. Then add the correct passive form (a–f) to complete the rules (3–8).

> ### Passive forms
>
> Counterfeit soccer jerseys **were** recently **discovered** by the U.S. government while they **were being shipped** to Texas.
>
> They**'re** not always **made** of safe materials.
>
> Nobody **is going to be helped** by fake medicine.   It's unlikely that counterfeiting **will be stopped**.
>
> The original products **are being sold** for over $1,000.
>
> We forget that somebody's creative ideas **have been stolen**.

We use passive forms when we don't know, or it's not important, who [1]**did / received** the action. The person or thing [2]**doing / receiving** the action is more important, so it becomes the subject of the sentence.

a	simple past	**3**	The ___	passive: *am/is/are* + past participle.
b	past continuous	**4**	The ___	passive: *was/were* + past participle.
c	simple present	**5**	The ___	passive: *has/have been* + past participle.
d	future	**6**	The ___	passive: *will* + *be* + past participle <u>or</u> *am/is/are going to* + *be* + past participle.
e	present continuous	**7**	The ___	passive: *am/is/are* + *being* + past participle.
f	present perfect	**8**	The ___	passive: *was/were* + *being* + past participle.

B ▶ Now go to page 138. Look at the grammar chart and do the grammar exercise for 11.1.

C PAIR WORK Make sentences about counterfeit goods using these words, passive forms, and your own ideas. Check your accuracy. Then compare with another pair.

1 Fake sunglasses / sell / in my city

_____

2 In the future, / fake products / sell

_____

3 Not long ago, / buy / by teenagers

_____

4 Discover / by the police / recently

_____

> ✔ **ACCURACY** CHECK
>
> **Don't forget to use the auxiliary *be* in continuous tenses: correct form of *be* + *being* + past participle.**
>
> *Counterfeit soccer jerseys were discovered while they were shipping to Texas.* ✗
> *Counterfeit soccer jerseys were discovered while they were being shipped to Texas.* ✓

4 SPEAKING

A GROUP WORK Where are counterfeit goods usually sold? Why do people buy them? Discuss using the ideas below. Then compare your answers with the class.

Fake goods: accessories, clothes, cosmetics, electronic goods, shoes, etc.

Illegal copies: books, computer games, DVDs/Blu-rays, music, software, etc.

> Fake brand-name watches have been sold in our city's markets for years. These days, they're sometimes found in stores, too. They're usually second-rate, but people buy them because …

INTERNET TALES

1 VOCABULARY: Degrees of truth

FIND IT

A ◀)) **2.36** [PAIR WORK] **Look at the words expressions in the box. Describe them in other words. Use a dictionary or your phone to help you. Which are adjectives? Nouns or noun phrases? Then listen and check the parts of speech.**

accurate	biased	controversial	dishonest	exaggerated
false	hoax	inaccurate	misinformation	misleading
rumor	suspicious	trustworthy	urban legend	white lie

B ▸ **Now go to page 151. Do the vocabulary exercises for 11.2.**

2 LANGUAGE IN CONTEXT

A ◀)) **2.37** **Read and listen to a radio show about five possibly fake stories. What are they about? Then answer the host's last question with a partner.**

◀)) **2.37 Audio script**

Host Today's topic is **rumors**, **urban legends**, and other fake stuff on the internet. When I was ten, I told my parents the moon landing was filmed in a TV studio. They said that was a lie, but I replied, "No, it's true. I read it on the internet!" I didn't expect to be laughed at, but I was. I learned, as we all do, that you can't always trust the web. So, I asked my listeners for internet stories that might be **false**. Listen to a few. Here's Raúl from Doral, Florida.

Raúl I read that hundreds of deadly snakes escaped from a truck that crashed in our town. But I never heard anything more, so I guess the information was **exaggerated** or **inaccurate**. This kind of **misinformation** has to be stopped because in the end, all news becomes **suspicious**.

Host Nina from Denver, Colorado, said this.

Nina Recently I saw a photo of a purple watermelon on Snapchat. It was probably a **hoax**. People say **misleading** photos shouldn't be posted, but they usually don't do any harm.

Host Let's listen to Gabe from Portland, Oregon.

Gabe I read online that there are more trees on Earth than stars in the galaxy. That can't be **accurate**! All online articles need to be checked. But where do you check? Online?

Host And Britt called in, all the way from Windsor in Canada.

Britt A video of a human-looking robot walking down a street went viral. A few people thought robots were taking over the world! If you look closely, the video seems to be made on a computer. I don't think it's from a **trustworthy** site.

Host So, are these stories true or not? I'll tell you after the break.

GLOSSARY
the galaxy (*n*) a very large group of stars that contains our sun and the planets that go around it

B ◀)) **2.37** **Read and listen again. Which speakers explain why they think the information is false? What are their reasons?**

C ◀)) **2.38** **Listen to the end of the program. Were the stories true or not?**

D [GROUP WORK] [THINK CRITICALLY] **Do you think the internet spreads more truth or lies? Why? For ideas, watch Bojan's video. Can you think of some recent examples?**

EXPERT SPEAKER

Do you agree with Bojan? What do you think of his solution?

3 GRAMMAR: Passives with modals and modal-like expressions; passive infinitives

A   Read the sentences in the grammar box. Complete the rules about the passive with *be* or *to be*.

Passives with modals and modal-like expressions	Passive infinitives
Misleading photos **shouldn't be posted**. This kind of misinformation **has to be stopped**. All online articles **need to be checked**.	I **didn't expect to be laughed at**. The video **seems to be made** on a computer.

1   After modals, like *should* and *could*, use _____ + a past participle.

2   After modal-like expressions, like *have to*, *need to*, and *had better*, use _____ + a past participle.

3   After verbs like *expect*, *seem*, and *want*, use _____ + a past participle.

> **!** In the passive, the main verb is always in its past participle form, never the base form. So, for passives after modals and modal-like expressions, use *be* + past participle, not the base form. *Something **has to be done** to stop fake stories from spreading.*

B   Now go to page 139. Look at the grammar chart and do the grammar exercise for 11.2.

C   Complete the sentences with the correct passive form of the verbs in parentheses ( ) and your own ideas. Then compare with a partner. Do you agree with your partner's ideas?

1   If we … , we are _____ (not be likely / believe) by anyone.

2   I think controversial issues _____ (shouldn't / discuss) during …

3   Friends _____ (must / inform) when our social media photos are …

4   I _____ (hope / tell) the truth when I …

5   We _____ (could / trick) by reading … , so be careful.

6   I only _____ (want / tell) white lies if …

4 SPEAKING

A   **PAIR WORK**   What stories have you heard or read online that weren't true? You can look online for stories if you want. Did people believe them? Why? Did you believe them at first?

FIND IT

> I read that alligators live in the sewers in New York City. I think people believed the story because it gave a lot of **accurate** information about alligators. But the article had a lot of grammar mistakes and **seemed to be written** by a teenager, so I thought it was a **hoax** right away.

B   **GROUP WORK**   Share two of your stories with another pair.
Do you think stories like this need to be stopped?
Why or why not?

> Urban legends, like alligators in the sewers, **shouldn't be spread** because they make people panic.

<table>
<tr><td>11.3</td><td></td></tr>
</table>

11.3 BELIEVE IT OR NOT …

LESSON OBJECTIVE
- express belief and disbelief

---

1 LISTENING

A Do you often look at the night sky? What kind of things do you think of? What questions would you ask someone who's been in space?

B 🔊 **2.39** Listen to Damon and his friends talking about the NASA Parker Solar Probe. How many of them definitely believe the probe is going to the sun?

C 🔊 **2.39** **UNDERSTAND IMPORTANT DETAILS** Listen again. What arguments do the friends make for and against the story?

D 🔊 **2.40** Listen to part of a news program about the Parker Solar Probe. What's the significance of these numbers?

    a 6 million   **b** several million   **c** 1,400

E **THINK CRITICALLY** Who is more believable, Damon or Rose? Why? How can you normally tell if someone is telling the truth?

2 PRONUNCIATION: Listening for intonation on exclamations and imperatives

A 🔊 **2.41** Listen to the high falling intonation on exclamations and imperatives.

Yeah, right, Damon! ↘   Tell me another one! ↘

B 🔊 **2.42** Listen and mark the high falling intonation.

  1 The connection's worse than in outer space!   **4** Wow! That's hot!

  2 They're going to land at night!   **5** That's still hot!

  3 I'm telling you, it's true!

C Circle the correct option to complete the sentence.

There is a *high/low / fall/rise* intonation on exclamations and imperatives.

112

3 SPEAKING SKILLS

A Match the correct headings from the box to each column. Write headings in the correct places. Would high falling intonation occur in any of these expressions? If so, where?

> Belief   Disbelief   Some belief

Yeah, right!	Maybe there's some truth in it.	… , believe it or not.
Tell me another one.	It's/That's partly true.	I'm absolutely positive (that) …
I find that hard to believe.		
There's no truth in it/that.		

B **PAIR WORK** Take turns saying these rumors and expressing belief or disbelief about them.
1 By 2025, we'll be able to text just by thinking.
2 It won't be long before people will be settled on the moon.
3 In the next 20 years, there will be no ice in the Arctic.
4 Dinosaurs have been created in a lab somewhere, using DNA from fossils.
5 The number of people who own cars will soon decline, and car-sharing will be used instead.
6 Young people will increasingly work online from home, so they'll be able to live anywhere.

4 PRONUNCIATION: Saying /oʊ/ and /aʊ/

A 🔊 2.43 Listen to the difference between the /oʊ/ and /aʊ/ sounds.

/oʊ/	/aʊ/		/oʊ/	/aʊ/
no	now		tone	town
coach	couch		load	loud
known	noun			

B 🔊 2.44 Choose a suitable word with either an /oʊ/ or /aʊ/ sound to put in the conversation. Then listen to check your work.

A I don't believe a p_____ could g_____ s_____ far into space. H_____ a_____ you?

B It'd be difficult, but it's possible, th_____. Maybe not n_____ but in ten years or s_____ .

A Come on, there's z_____ chance! I d_____ k_____ much a_____ science, but that's impossible.

B There's n_____ reason why not. When it happens, I'll say, "I t_____ you s_____ !"

C **PAIR WORK** Read the conversation aloud, focusing on the /oʊ/ and /aʊ/ sounds.

5 SPEAKING

A **PAIR WORK** Create a role play of two people discussing a rumor, real or imaginary, about one of the topics in the box. Express belief or disbelief about the rumor. Practice your role play and then act it out for another pair. They express belief or disbelief about the rumor, as well.

> college/workplace   food/health   places in your city or country
> politics   sports/entertainment

I heard a **rumor that** final exams **are going to be canceled** and that students **will** only **be graded** on their coursework.

Yeah, I heard that, too, but **there's no truth in it**. It was a **false** story started by some students who wish it was true!

CONVINCE ME

1 READING

A **SUMMARIZE KEY POINTS** Have you ever trusted a review that turned out to be fake? Read the article. Why do companies want to stop fake reviews? What can we do to figure out if reviews are fake? Summarize each of the nine tips.

SPOT 'EM –

Fake product reviews
by Ken Evoy

Companies depend on hundreds of thousands of consumer reviews that point you to "the best of whatever." They work hard to minimize fake reviews because it's good business to prevent customer disappointment due to inaccurate information. There are honest reviews, of course, but you still need to check reviews yourself, whether you're buying a book, a hotel room, or a Ferrari. Here are some tips to help you.

1 Fight technology with technology

A good way to assess whether a review is computer-generated is to use a computer program. *Fakespot* is an online tool that helps you figure out which reviews are trustworthy and which are not. Simply paste a review's URL into Fakespot's search engine to get results. It may not always be totally accurate, but it's a good place to start.

2 Check the reviewer's profile

Most sites ask users to register before leaving a review. Click on the username to see past reviews. Most "real" people buy a wide range of products from large companies, so they'll have a wide range of reviews.

3 Compensation

Is this review paid? Did the reviewer receive the product in return for a review? If so, it's not necessarily fake – but it may be biased.

4 Review quality

Reviews that rely on individuals being paid small amounts of money to write as many as possible will be short and nonspecific. The goal is to put the item into the five-star category quickly by posting as many "excellent" reviews as possible. So the author needs to be able to copy and paste a large number in a short time. Look for phrases like "great product" or "wonderful service."

5 Lack of detail

Researchers found that some reviewers of hotel rooms did not talk about the specifics of the hotel at all. They couldn't – they had never been there. So they'd write instead about the *reason* they were there. "Spent a wonderful weekend here with the family" and "will always use this hotel for future business trips" are the kinds of things that show a hotel review might be fake.

6 Lack of experience

Similarly, if the reviewer has never had a product, the explanation of what's good and bad about it will be limited. If a review sounds more like a product manual than a real-life experience, it probably is.

7 Use of language

Some dishonest companies will provide templates for their "reviewers" to make it easier for quick copying and pasting. If you see the same or similar words and phrases in different reviews, be suspicious. Reviews with words like "best thing ever" and "worst thing ever" without any explanation are likely to be created from a template.

8 When haters start to love

A common form of fake review is for the reviewer to insist that they hated a product but were given one as a gift and they suddenly discovered it's the best thing since sliced bread. Also look for a lot of question marks and exclamation points. "Why didn't I buy this sooner??? I love it!!!!!!"

9 All or nothing

Fake reviews tend to be either one star or five stars. Make sure you check reviews at two, three, and four stars, too – real reviews tend to be more moderate.

B **GROUP WORK** **THINK CRITICALLY** Why do you think people write fake reviews? Which tips from the article have you used or might you try in the future to identify fake reviews? Can you think of more tips for identifying them?

INSIDER ENGLISH

Say *the best* or *greatest thing since sliced bread* to describe extremely useful and important things.

2 WRITING

A Read part of an essay. What's the author's position? What research and example are given?

Are product reviews useful or not?

Although many people don't trust product reviews, **I strongly believe that** they are useful. You can't trust advertisements to … However, you can trust honest reviewers to … It's very easy to read reviews before you buy to help you …

Reviews are valuable because they give you a genuine picture of … **Research shows that** 84 percent of people trust online reviewers as much as they trust their friends. This is because … **One time I** wanted to a buy a toaster, so I read several reviews on the product. I found out … This was helpful because … Mistakes can be avoided if you read reviews first.

While it's true that many reviews aren't authentic, it's easy to figure out whether they're fake or not. You can … You can also … Reviews must not be ignored because … If you read a large number of reviews for a product, it helps you … The benefits are more numerous than the problems.

In conclusion, **I feel that** reviews help us make better decisions. They give us a true idea … Many are … , and it's not difficult to … Read reviews to avoid bad purchases.

B **USE PERSUASIVE LANGUAGE** Read about how to write a persuasive essay. Add the bold expressions in the essay in exercise 2A to the examples of persuasive language below. Then, in pairs, think of ideas to complete the essay.

In a persuasive essay, your aim is to convince your reader to agree with your view. It usually has three or four paragraphs:

Introduction: State your position on the topic.

Body (one or two paragraphs): Support your position with facts and examples. You can also state the opposite position and say why it is not true.

Conclusion: Restate your position and main points. Give a strong concluding statement to make your reader agree with you.

Useful persuasive language:

Give your opinion: I firmly believe that … , _____ … , _____ …

Give facts: According to … , _____ …

Give personal examples: When I used/tried … , _____ …

Give the opposite position: Although some will say that … , _____ … , _____ …

WRITE IT

C **PLAN** You're going to write a persuasive essay. Work with a partner. Choose one of the options below, and discuss your ideas. Then plan the structure of your essay: What opening sentence are you going to use? What information are you going to include in each of the paragraphs listed in exercise 2B?

> Are   product reviews / restaurant reviews / movie reviews / app reviews / hotel reviews   useful or not?

D Write your persuasive essay. Make sure you use some persuasive language.

E **PAIR WORK** Exchange essays with another partner. Do you agree with the writer's position?

TIME TO SPEAK
Does it really work?

how to cure a cough

how to sleep better

how to keep mosquitos away

how to remove coffee stains

how to fix a wet phone

A **PREPARE** With a partner, look at things people searched for on the internet. Discuss examples of tips the searches might find. Talk about any you have tried and say how effective they were.

how to cure a cough	how to sleep better
how to keep mosquitos away	how to cool soda quickly
how to remove coffee stains	how to get in shape in a month
how to fix a wet phone	

B **RESEARCH** With your partner, think of a few other tips you have heard of or tried. You can choose two or three topics from the ideas in part A or use your phone to check for ideas online. The tips can be effective or ineffective.

FIND IT

C **DISCUSS** In groups, share your topics and tips. The others guess which ones are effective. If you have tried any of the tips, at the end of the discussion, say how effective they were. The group chooses two of the most interesting tips: an effective one and an ineffective one.

D **PRESENT** In your groups from part C, present your two tips to the class without mentioning the problems they solve. The class guesses what the problems are. Then each group reveals the answers.

E **DECIDE** As a class, discuss whether the tips you heard are effective or not and say whether you've tried any.

To check your progress, go to page 156.

USEFUL PHRASES

PREPARE
I've tried that before and …
… seems like a great tip.
… can't be true.
That just doesn't sound right.

DISCUSS
… , believe it or not.
I find that hard to believe.
It's partly true.
Maybe there's some truth in it.
Tell me another one!

PRESENT
According to … ,
The best way to … is …
In order to …
It turns out, if you …

GOT WHAT IT TAKES?

UNIT OBJECTIVES

- talk about talent
- discuss how to make life better
- describe your ambitions
- write a review of a performance
- give a presentation about yourself

START SPEAKING

A   What can you see in the picture? Why do you think the person chose to learn this skill?

B   What skills or characteristics do you think a person needs to have to be good at the activity in the picture?

C   In your opinion, what does it take to be highly successful – whatever you choose to do in life? For ideas, watch Wendy's video.

EXPERT SPEAKER

Are any of Wendy's ideas similar to yours?

PRACTICE MAKES PERFECT

1 LANGUAGE IN CONTEXT

A **PAIR WORK** Look at the picture. How long do you think it took the person to learn to do this? Talk about an activity you know about that takes a lot of practice to do well.

B Read the social media posts. What is the 10,000-hour rule? What talents and skills are mentioned?

Comments   ○ Profile   ○ Sign Out

Victor Gomez
I just read about the 10,000-hour rule: You have to practice something for 10,000 hours to become truly good at it. It made me wonder if anyone is really born **gifted** or if ability just comes from being **determined** and working really hard. Thoughts?

Rhonda Peters
Jimi Hendrix was one of the greatest guitarists in history, but he never took guitar lessons. So, if he wasn't a **trained** musician, then you figure he was just exceptionally **talented**. But it's not necessarily true that his natural **musical** ability was the only factor. When he got his first guitar at age 15, he practiced for hours and hours every day. So he didn't play especially well at first. It takes practice to become a **skilled** musician, no matter what natural talent you may have.

Kyle Manson
I'm studying engineering, and some of my classes are technically advanced, but I pick up the ideas fairly easily. Others are having real difficulty, even though I'm no smarter than they are and they work as hard as I do. Design classes are where I struggle. I'm reasonably **imaginative**, but I'm definitely a **technical**, **analytical** person, not **artistic** at all. I can make a diagram of a complicated structure like a bridge without much effort, but drawing never came particularly easily to me. So we're studying the same things, but we're each better in different classes. The only **logical** explanation is natural ability. That's my (analytical) conclusion!

C Read again. How do Rhonda and Kyle feel about practice versus being born with talent?

2 VOCABULARY: Skill and performance

A 🔊 **2.45** Look at the adjectives in the box used to describe talents and skills. Which of them are used in the posts in exercise 1B? Count the syllables in the words and guess where the main stress is. Discuss their meanings. Use a dictionary or your phone to help you. Then listen and check your work.

FIND IT

| analytical | artistic | athletic | competent | determined | gifted | imaginative |
| intellectual | logical | musical | skilled | talented | technical | trained |

B ▶ Now go to page 151. Do the vocabulary exercises for 12.1.

C **PAIR WORK** **THINK CRITICALLY** Do you think very successful people are born gifted, or is their talent due to practice? For ideas, watch Wendy's video.

EXPERT SPEAKER

Do you think Wendy is right? Can you think of other examples?

3 GRAMMAR: Adverbs with adjectives and adverbs

A Read the sentences in the grammar box. Answer the questions.

> ### Adverbs with adjectives and adverbs
>
> You have to practice something for 10,000 hours to become **truly good** at it.
>
> But it's not **necessarily true**.
>
> So he didn't play **especially well** at first.
>
> Drawing never came **particularly easily** to me.

1 What part of speech can you use with an adjective or an adverb to provide more detail about it? _____

2 Is it placed before or after the adjective or adverb it modifies? _____

B ▶ **Now go to page 139. Look at the grammar chart and do the grammar exercise for 12.1.**

C Write something about yourself that is true for each topic below. Use adverbs with adjectives or adverbs. Then work with a partner. Guess what your partner's sentence might be. Then compare your answers.

1 Cooking: _____

2 Technology: _____

3 Fixing things: _____

4 Money: _____

5 Decision-making: _____

_____

4 SPEAKING

A GROUP WORK Think about your experiences in these areas and discuss the questions. Did you ever (a) find it especially easy to become good at something because of natural talent, (b) find it particularly difficult or impossible to accomplish something even with practice, or (c) become good at something through practice even though it was difficult at first?

> art (painting, drawing, photography, etc.) athletic activities (soccer, yoga, running, etc.)
> education (math, language learning, computers, etc.) performance (singing, playing an instrument, dancing, etc.)

> I think I'm **exceptionally skilled** with technology. For example, **technical** issues with my computer are easy for me to understand and fix. But I've never been **artistically gifted**. I took an art class, but I couldn't even do a simple drawing of a bowl of fruit.

CHANGE THE WORLD

1 LANGUAGE IN CONTEXT

A ◀)) 2.46 **Imagine you have to give a short talk on how to make the world a better place. What would you talk about? Then read and listen to Pietro giving a talk at a conference. Circle the best title for his talk.**

a Big Ideas for a Better World

b A Better World for Everyone

c Think of Others before Yourself

"Things don't have to change the world to be important." –

Steve Jobs.

◀)) **2.46 Audio script**

Hello! Wow, thank you for that warm welcome. It really makes me smile! I actually smile a lot these days, but that wasn't always the case. In fact, meeting me used to **be a real downer**. I know this because a good friend told me so. She said seeing me would instantly **ruin her day** because I was always complaining about something. She told me that my negative attitude **was getting her down**. Well, that was a shock, but it **did me good** because it showed me that I needed to change.

I started doing small, simple things to **raise my spirits**. Listening to a great piece of music while getting dressed. Having a cup of coffee and a cookie in the afternoon, just because. Changing my desktop wallpaper to a beautiful work of art. Sticking an inspirational quote or a great piece of advice on the fridge so it was the first thing I saw every morning.

Then I used the same idea – small, simple things – to help **brighten up** other people's lives. Just simple acts of kindness, like cooking a meal for my mom, driving my elderly neighbor to her friend's place, or offering a few words of encouragement to my younger brother for something he was doing. A little bit of kindness can really **make someone's day** and **leave a lasting impression on** them and on you.

So here's my big idea for how to change the world – think small. By all of us doing small things, we all collectively make the world a better place.

B ◀)) 2.46 **Read and listen again. How does Pietro suggest making (a) yourself happy and (b) others happy? In your opinion, what's Pietro's best idea? Why?**

2 VOCABULARY: Describing emotional impact

A ◀)) 2.47 **PAIR WORK** **Look at the expressions in the box. Which describe a positive impact, a negative impact, or both? Use a dictionary or your phone to help you. Then listen and check your work.**

FIND IT

be a (real) downer	brighten up sth	capture sb's imagination
do sb good	get sb down	leave a lasting impression on sb
make sb's day	put sb's mind at rest	raise sb's spirits
ruin sb's day	stress sb out	take sb's mind off sth

B ▶ **Now go to page 152. Do the vocabulary exercises for 12.2.**

C **PAIR WORK** **THINK CRITICALLY** **Talk about examples of people's behavior that affect you negatively and positively.**

3 GRAMMAR: Making non-count nouns countable

A   Read the sentences in the grammar box. (Circle) the correct options to complete the rules.

> ### Making non-count nouns countable
>
> Listen to **a** great **piece of music** while getting dressed.
>
> Have **a cup of coffee** and **a cookie** in the afternoon.
>
> Change my desktop wallpaper to **a** beautiful **work of art**.
>
> Stick an inspirational quote or **a** great **piece of advice** on the fridge.
>
> **A little bit of kindness** can really make someone's day.

1   You can make non-count nouns countable by using expressions that describe specific **qualities or characteristics /
    quantities or amounts**.

2   **Sometimes you can / You can never** use the same noun (e.g., piece) with different categories of things.

B   ▶ Now go to page 140. Look at the grammar chart and do the grammar exercise for 12.2.

C   Complete the sentences with your own ideas. Check
    your accuracy. Then compare ideas with a partner.
    Are they similar?

> ✔ **ACCURACY** CHECK
>
> **When making non-count nouns countable,
> be sure the subject and verb agree.**
>
> *All of the ~~piece~~ of advice he gave were useful.* ✗
> *All of the pieces of advice he gave were useful.* ✓

1   One of my favorite pieces of _____ is

    _____ .

2   I think _____ is a really nice
    act of _____ .

3   I once got a very useful piece of _____ from a
    friend. It was: _____ .

4   I'd really like to get a bunch of _____ together for a game of _____ .

5   I never have enough articles of _____ ! I need some more _____ .

6   I sometimes go out for _____ to brighten up my day.

4   SPEAKING

A   [PAIR WORK] [THINK CRITICALLY] Think of more small things you can do to make the world a better place for
    yourself and others. Explain why they're good ideas. Make a list.

> Well, one way to **make someone's day** is to give them a gift for no reason.
> Maybe **a box of** Turkish delight or some flowers.

> Nice one! And if someone's stressed, you could suggest a day trip
> together to **take their mind off things** – or maybe **a game of** soccer.

B   [GROUP WORK] Share your ideas and reasons with another pair. Then choose the two best ideas that the other
    pair suggested.

Turkish delight

MAYBE ONE DAY ...

1 LISTENING

A **PAIR WORK** Daniel is interviewing to get into a theater program in college. What do you think the interviewer asks him about?

B 🔊 **2.48** Listen to the interview. What does the interviewer ask about? Were your guesses in exercise 1A correct?

C 🔊 **2.48** **LISTEN FOR CONTRASTING IDEAS** Listen again and match Daniel's optimistic ideas with his cautious ones.

1 My dream scenario is to play leading roles. ____

2 There's no guarantee I'll end up in Hollywood. ____

3 I may not succeed in playing any type of character. ____

4 It may not be easy to learn new things. ____

a But there's no harm in trying.

b But I realize things might not go as planned.

c But I'm determined to be open-minded and try everything.

d But I'm confident that I'll have some level of success.

D **PAIR WORK** **THINK CRITICALLY** How realistic do you think Daniel's ambitions are? What do you think of his attitude during the interview? Does he have the right attitude to be an actor? Explain.

2 PRONUNCIATION: Listening for sounds that change

A 🔊 **2.49** Listen to how the /d/ sound changes in connected speech.

Well, my dream scenario would be to play leading roles in movies. (/d/ → /b/)

Listen to examples of how other sounds change:

I think she had the best part in the film. (/t/ → /p/)

There were only seven people in the theater. (/n/ → /m/)

I met one guy who had been in Hollywood. (/n/ → /ŋ/)   (/d/ → /b/)

B 🔊 **2.50** Work in pairs. Mark the possible sound changes at the end of words. Listen and check.

1 I love that part where the son meets his real father.

2 They arrived before everyone came.

3 The movie had bad reviews on most websites.

4 It was an action movie set in Greece.

C Circle the correct options to complete the sentence.

In connected speech, words that *start / end* in /t/, /d/, and /n/ can change before words *starting / ending* in /p/, /b/, /m/, /k/, and /g/.

3 SPEAKING SKILLS

A 🔊 **2.48** Complete the expressions from the interview in exercise 1B on page 122 with the words in the box. Then decide which ones are used to (a) describe ambitions, (b) express optimism, or (c) express caution. Write *a*, *b*, or *c* next to each one. Will any of the sounds change in these expressions in connected speech? If so, which ones? Listen again to check.

certain	confident	determined	guarantee	harm	planned	reason	scenario	ultimate

Describe ambitions; express optimism and caution

1 My dream _____ would be to … _____
2 I realize things might not go as _____ . _____
3 There's no _____ (that) … _____
4 I'm _____ (that) … _____
5 My _____ goal is to … _____

6 There's no _____ in trying. _____
7 I can't say for _____ (that) … _____
8 I'm _____ to … _____
9 I see no _____ why I can't … _____

B **PAIR WORK** Choose one of the situations below and interview your partner about their ambitions. Use expressions from exercise 3A and your own ideas. Then choose a different situation and change roles.

attending a music school	attending law school	being on a reality TV show
getting an internship at a museum	working as an English teacher	volunteering at a hospital

4 PRONUNCIATION: Using syllable stress in words

A 🔊 **2.51** Listen to which syllable is stressed (a stressed syllable is said more loudly, longer, and at a higher pitch).

<u>ul</u>timate   guaran<u>tee</u>   sce<u>na</u>rio

B 🔊 **2.52** Which syllable is stressed in these words? Complete the chart. Listen, check, and repeat the words.

character	difficulties	encouragement	impression	interviewer	particular
performance	photograph	photography	positively	successful	technical

●●● **<u>com</u>petent**	●●● **de<u>ter</u>mined**	●●●● **<u>sat</u>isfying**	●●●● **ex<u>cep</u>tional**

C 🔊 **2.53** Complete the conversation with the word that matches the stress pattern. Listen and check your work. Practice the conversation with a partner.

I think Maria is such a ●●● *hard-working / positive* person. She's ●●●● *amazingly / wonderfully* talented.

Max is quite ●●● *creative / competent*, too. He did this ●●●● *incredible / complicated* work so well.

5 SPEAKING

A **PAIR WORK** Think of one or two of your ambitions – educational, personal, or professional. Then ask each other what you need to do to achieve the ambitions and how difficult it will be. Explain, expressing optimistic and cautious opinions.

> I'm **determined to** become an architect. My **ultimate goal is to** improve my city. I'll need a lot of training, but I'm **confident** I can manage it.

12.4 SUCCESS BEHIND THE SCENES

LESSON OBJECTIVE
■ write a review of a performance

1 READING

A Who helps make a concert successful in addition to the musicians? Read the article. What were Kevin's job responsibilities? What does he think was difficult about the job?

INSIDER ENGLISH

Say *by word of mouth* or *through word of mouth* when news, gossip, or other information is spread from person to person in conversation.

BACKSTAGE PASS

I loved life on the road when I was a guitar tech. Over the years, I traveled with many different bands – some small acts and some big stars. My job included unloading the equipment, setting it up on stage, tuning guitars, and making sure everything worked – pretty much getting things ready so the musicians could perform without problems in front of a bunch of excited fans.

When I was about eight years old, I saw the Rolling Stones perform on TV. I noticed that someone handed Keith Richards a guitar between songs, and I thought I'd like to do that one day. It left a lasting impression on me, but I didn't really think about the job again until I was 25. That's when a friend asked me to travel with his band as a guitar tech. I already knew a lot about music and guitars, but on the job, I really became technically skilled over time. People hired me by word of mouth, mostly musicians from headlining acts that we were touring with. I quickly had several jobs on my résumé – but it's really more of a see-and-be-seen business. You look at the people around you and see what jobs might be coming up. And you do your job exceptionally well every day – others see you work, know your skill set, and often ask you to work for them on future shows.

I enjoyed the pressure of live performances, but life on the road wasn't always easy. You take the good with the bad. Sometimes I slept in vans and sometimes on tour buses. When I stayed in hotels, they weren't necessarily nice, but with some of the more-famous musicians, we were in beautiful hotels, like the time I stayed on the Champs-Élysées in Paris. I worked in several different cities around the world, and dealing with the unknown

often made the job especially challenging. A lot of times I was working outside, and it could be very hot, really cold, or even raining. I also dealt with things like getting big trucks down tiny streets and getting huge equipment up narrow stairs or in small elevators. One time, in Malaga, Spain, the power went out in the entire city, and it messed up our schedule and computers, but the show went ahead as planned.

Any type of work in the music business is difficult. I've seen musicians on the way up, and I've seen them on the way down. It's tough to get to the top in my line of work, too, but the work is steadier once you're successful. And how do you stay at the top? Start with being on time. Then stay focused, and always remember you're not in the band. You're there to do a job – not to hang out with rock stars. I've seen a lot of techs make that mistake.

My last words of advice? I think there are three kinds of people in this world: (1) the kind that make things happen, (2) the kind that watch things happen, and (3) the kind that wonder what just happened. Be the kind of person that makes things happen. And remember, no matter what happens – the show must go on!

by Kevin Hurdman

GLOSSARY

unload (*v*) remove something from a vehicle
headlining act (*n*) the main performer or performers at an entertainment event
steadier (*adj*) happening in a more regular way than something else

B **UNDERSTAND CAUSE AND EFFECT** Read the article again. What is/was the result of these events?

1 Kevin got everything ready for the performance.
2 Kevin saw someone give Keith Richards a guitar on TV.
3 The power went out in Malaga before a concert.
4 You do your job exceptionally well.

C **PAIR WORK** **THINK CRITICALLY** In what other types of jobs is it helpful to "see and be seen"? What other advice does Kevin give that can be applied to different jobs?

124

A   Read the concert review from an online music magazine. What did the reviewer like? Did anything go wrong?

CONCERT REVIEW | ALEJANDRO SANZ

The Alejandro Sanz concert on Friday night was amazing. He's from Spain and tours all over the world. I was fortunate to see him in New York City at a sold-out show. He was the headlining act and sang exceptionally well. The band members were from Puerto Rico, the Dominican Republic, and the United States. The drummer was particularly good. They played mostly songs from his newest albums, but they also played some old favorites.

The show was a huge success due to the talented musicians, but it wasn't only their work that made it so special. The lighting and special effects were terrific, so the behind-the-scenes crew clearly did a great job, making sure everything ran smoothly and that there were no technical problems. And I loved the video clips on the giant screen at the back of the stage. It all helped to make the concert feel spectacular.

But the best part was when Sanz sang "Corazón Partío" and had the audience sing along. Everyone was disappointed when the show was over, and they shouted for more. As a result, Sanz performed an encore, which really made our day.

GLOSSARY

encore (*n*) an extra song or piece of music played at the end of a show because the audience shouts for it

B   **SHOW REASON AND RESULT**   Look at the sentences with words that show reasons and results. Find one more expression for each sentence from the review in exercise 2A.

The show was a huge success **because of /** [1] _____ the talented musicians.

They shouted for more. **Consequently / Therefore /** [2] _____ , Sanz performed an encore, which really made our day.

REGISTER CHECK

In conversation, *so* is often used instead of more formal expressions like *as a result*, *consequently*, and *therefore*. It's used to join two sentences.

Formal writing

*They shouted for more. **As a result**, Sanz performed an encore.*

Conversation

*We shouted for more, **so** Sanz performed an encore.*

WRITE IT

C   **PLAN**   You are going to write a review of a performance. With a partner, talk about a concert, play, or other performance you have seen. Discuss facts about the events and information about your experience: where and when it was; what you liked and didn't like about the performers, lighting, sound, and special effects. Then look at the concert review in exercise 2A. How will you organize the information you discussed?

D   Write your performance review. Remember to use expressions for showing reason and result.

E   **PAIR WORK**   Read your partner's review. Would you have liked the event? Why or why not?

TIME TO SPEAK
Me, in two minutes

A Choose three items that you always carry in your purse or bag. You can think about the apps on your phone that you never do without, if you like. Show them to your partner or group, or describe them. What do they show about you? (For example, your personality, hobbies or interests, or what you focus on each day.) Who has the most unusual items? Whose are the most revealing?

B Look at the mood board above. What objects and text can you identify? What does it tell you about the person who created the mood board? How does the person see themselves? What are their aspirations and dreams?

C **PREPARE** Now you're going to expand on how you described yourself in exercise A. Work with your partner to design a mood board for each of you. What objects and texts are on your boards? Why? To help you, look at the list of categories below and choose the ones that are relevant to you or use your own ideas.

current/past jobs	future plans/ambitions	childhood	family	friends
interests	personal ambitions	personality	challenges	skills

D Describe your mood board. What can your partner tell about you from the items you've chosen to include?

E Imagine you're going to talk about yourself for two minutes. Using your mood board, work alone to plan what you're going to say about yourself. Choose the best order to present your topics or areas of interest, and use examples to illustrate each topic.

F **DISCUSS** In groups, take turns talking about yourselves. Then say what aspects of each person's talk you liked (e.g., examples, topics, timing, body language / gestures, tone of voice). What lessons did you learn on how to talk about yourself in an interesting way?

G **AGREE** Share your ideas from part D with the class. Agree on a short list of tips on the most interesting way to talk about yourself (topics, sequence, etc.).

To check your progress, go to page 156.

USEFUL PHRASES

PREPARE

I'm determined to …

I'm fairly talented at …

I'm more analytical/artistic/…

My ultimate goal is to …

AGREE

You could try …

It might work well if you …

… could be very effective.

I've always had luck with …

REVIEW 4 (UNITS 10–12)

1 VOCABULARY

A **Complete the questions with the correct forms of the words in parentheses ( ). Sometimes, you do not need to change the word.**

1 These days, do children really need to learn to do _____ (calculate) without a calculator?

2 If you think an email is suspicious, how can you check that it's _____ (authentic)?

3 Are there many _____ (similar) between your native language and English?

4 Is there a _____ (like) between you and anyone famous?

5 Is asking people to fill out forms a good way to _____ (survey) customers?

6 In your country, are there any snakes or insects whose bites are _____ (dead)?

7 To be an _____ (art) person, do you need to be born with a natural talent?

8 Is it true that most jobs require people to be _____ (imagine) in some way?

9 If you do something that you didn't know was _____ (legal), should you be punished?

10 Is it good to change your _____ (look) completely sometimes?

B PAIR WORK **Discuss the questions in exercise 1A.**

2 GRAMMAR

A Circle **the correct option.**

1 Carrying your phone in your back pocket increases the risk *to break / of breaking* it.

2 When you apologize *to arrive / for arriving* late, you should always explain why you're late.

3 If I drink coffee in the evening, it prevents me *to sleep / from sleeping*.

4 People in my country learn English particularly *easy / easily* because it's similar to our language.

5 They should allow people *take / to take* phones into exams as long as they are put away.

6 Companies should let their employees *wear / to wear* what they want at work.

7 I've listened to my favorite piece *from / of* music at least 100 times.

8 Most *exceptional / exceptionally* gifted people discover their talent before they're 18.

9 It's always easy to find stuff online to help you *understand / understanding* difficult subjects.

10 I sometimes dream *to become / of becoming* famous.

11 I have one article *of / in* clothing that I wear much more often than any other.

12 Traffic jams cause me *arrive / to arrive* late more than any other problem.

B PAIR WORK **Do you agree or disagree with the sentences in exercise 2A? Discuss your views.**

3 VOCABULARY

A Circle the correct options.

| HOME | NEWS | **BLOG** | CONTACT US | ⊖ ⊡ ⊗ |

Regular readers of this blog will know that truth – or the lack of it – is one of my most frequent topics. I'm always complaining about things being posted online about other people, which are either totally [1]*accurate / inaccurate* or which are intended to be [2]*misleading / suspicious*. There's something about it that really [3]*gets me down / raises my spirits*. It's not so much that the actual information is [4]*false / trustworthy*. It's the fact that the people who post it are often deliberately being [5]*dishonest / exaggerated*. They're happy to [6]*make / ruin* someone's day (or week, or more) and don't seem to care. This kind of behavior came to mind recently after I saw several negative stories about celebrities, all of which were based not on facts, but on [7]*rumors / white lies*. In my view, the people who write this stuff are not [8]*biased / competent* journalists, and so I struggle to understand why there are so many of them. Is it true that the public enjoys reading this stuff? And if so, why? Do people have some kind of problem with [9]*features / individuals* who are famous because they're [10]*determined / gifted*?

_____

💬 5   ♡ 2   🔁 9

B **PAIR WORK** Say whether or not you agree with the views in the blog in exercise 3A. Discuss the questions at the end.

4 GRAMMAR

A **Complete the sentences with the correct form of *be*.**

1 All my work will _____ finished by the end of this week.

2 All my photos _____ stored on my phone.

3 I have some old stuff that needs _____ thrown out.

4 Most of the English words I know _____ learned in the classroom.

5 I always feel nervous when I'm _____ interviewed.

6 A lot of the things I say shouldn't _____ taken seriously.

7 I ordered something online, and it hasn't _____ delivered yet.

8 When I _____ delayed by traffic, I never get stressed about it.

9 Once, one of my online accounts _____ hacked.

10 Next weekend, all my time is going _____ spent relaxing.

11 I once saw a car that was _____ chased by the police.

12 I expect _____ invited to a party fairly soon.

B **PAIR WORK** Say which sentences from exercise 4A are true for you. For ones that are not, say a similar sentence that is true.

GRAMMAR REFERENCE AND PRACTICE

1.1 PRESENT HABITS (PAGE 3)

Present habits

Talk about present habits in different ways:

1   Simple present (sometimes with adverbs of frequency)

   *My friend **tells** me she **resists** change because she **usually likes** things the way they are.*

2   *Tend to* + the base form of a verb

   *I **tend to adapt** to new situations quickly.*

3   *Will* for events that happen often (present, <u>not</u> future)

   *I'll often **call** my parents when I want advice.*

4   Present continuous for a continuing activity that happens at the same time as another habit

   *I usually listen to music when I'**m cooking**.*

5   Present continuous for noticeable/unusual (often undesirable) habits; use *always* and *constantly* for emphasis.

   *I'**m always worrying** about how I'll cope with all of my work.*

A **Cross out the options that are <u>not</u> correct. Sometimes both options are correct.**

1   I usually forget all about the time when *I'm studying / I will study*.

2   *I'll often take / I tend to take* a shower in the morning unless I have to leave home early.

3   I *never listen / am constantly listening* when he complains about his job.

4   My friends *often tell / are always telling* me to stop working so hard.

5   How do you communicate with people when *you'll travel / you're traveling*?

6   *I'll usually think / I usually think* about a task for a few days before I start on it, unless it's urgent, of course.

1.2 PAST HABITS (PAGE 5)

Past habits

There are different ways to talk about habits, actions, and states that happened in the past but don't anymore:

1   *Used to* for past habits, repeated past actions, and states

   - *used to / didn't use to* + the base form of the verb
     *We **didn't use to make** video calls, but we do now.*

   - *never + used to* + the base form of the verb
     *They **never used to ride** their bikes to school.*

   - *use to*, not *used to*, with *didn't/did* in negative statements and questions
     ***Did** you **use to take** the bus?*

2   *Would* for past habits and repeated past actions, <u>not</u> for past states

   - *would ('d) / would not (wouldn't)* + the base form of verb

   - Use *would* only if it is clear when the action happened. Use *used to* if the time reference is not given.
     *We **would text** each other every night.*   <u>not</u> ~~I would have a big cell phone.~~

3   The simple past for past habits, repeated past actions, and past states (often with time expressions)
   *I **had** a big bedroom. I **went** to bed at 6:00 **every night**.*

4   The simple past for single completed actions in the past, <u>not</u> *used to* or *would*
   *I **watched** three shows **last night**.*   <u>not</u> ~~I'd watch three shows last night. / I used to watch three shows last night.~~

A **Change the simple past to *would* (*not*) when possible. When not possible, use (*not*) *used to*.**

When I was young, I ¹<u>didn't have</u> a TV in my room. My older brother ²<u>had</u> one in his. I ³<u>was</u> very jealous. But on the weekends, he ⁴<u>let</u> me watch his TV. We ⁵<u>watched</u> our favorite shows, but I usually ⁶<u>fell</u> asleep halfway through.

2.1 COMPARATIVE STRUCTURES (PAGE 13)

Comparative structures

1 *Fewer/less* + noun to show there is less of one thing than another
   - *fewer* + count nouns   *less* + non-count nouns

   The new project will require **fewer resources** and **less time**.

2 *Rather than* to show a preference for something
   - Compare nouns/pronouns
   - Use verbs to compare activities (base form of the verb or verb + *-ing*)
   - *To* can be used instead of *rather than* with *prefer* but not with other verbs

   I prefer ocean exploration **rather than space exploration**.

   I prefer to study the ocean **rather than learn/learning about** space.

   I **prefer** the ocean **to** deep space.

   I **want to study** Earth **rather than** Mars.   <u>not</u> ~~I want to study Earth to Mars.~~

3 Verb + *more/less* (as a pronoun)

   I **know less/more** about Venus **than** about Mars.

4 Adjective + (*not*) *enough* + infinitive to compare the degree of actual and required ability

   Technology is (**not**) **advanced enough to send** people to Mars.

5 A comparative + infinitive to compare actions

   It's **easier** to use a tablet **than** (to use) a laptop.

6 For many comparative structures, you do *not* need to repeat the first subject and verb.

   We're **less likely** to find life on the moon **than** (we are to find life) on Mars.

A   **Complete the sentences. Use constructions from the grammar box above.**

1   We haven't been lucky _____ to see a whale in the ocean.

2   Larry prefers sea animals _____ land animals.

3   We see _____ turtles on the beach than in the ocean. There are much more of them in the ocean.

4   Scientists know _____ about Venus than about Mars. Venus hasn't been explored as much.

5   Vicky wants to work with animals _____ people.

6   It's _____ difficult to memorize dates than it is to remember names.

2.2 SUPERLATIVE STRUCTURES; UNGRADABLE ADJECTIVES (PAGE 15)

Superlative structures

1 With quantities: Phrases such as *one of*, *two of*, and *some of* + superlative adjective + plural noun

   This country has **some of the highest** mountains in the world.

2 With *to*: Use a superlative + infinitive to show function or purpose.

   May is **the best** time **to hike** here.

3 *Least* is the opposite of *most* (the comparative form is *less*).

   This is surely **the least suitable** environment for anything **to live**.

4 With *that* clauses:
   - Use a superlative + a *that* clause.   - The use of *that* is optional.

   It's **the most fascinating** place (**that**) I've ever visited.

5 Ellipsis with *the*: Shows that one or more words have been left out to avoid repetition.

   I have three sisters. Susana is **the youngest** (sister).

Ungradable adjectives

1 Ungradable adjectives do not have different degrees and therefore don't usually have comparative or superlative forms.

*They were **furious** and **exhausted**.*

2 With most ungradable adjectives, we can use intensifiers such as *absolutely, completely, totally,* and *utterly*.

*The green parrots of Masaya Volcano are **totally amazing**.*

3 With other ungradable adjectives – for example, *male, female, married, single* – we don't use intensifiers.

*My first dog was **male**, but the second one was **female**.*

> **!** Gradable adjectives have degrees and can be used with adverbs, such as *very, a little,* and *really*, but **not** with intensifiers like *absolutely, completely,* etc.
>
> *Those animals are **very tough**.*
>
> **Note:** *Really* can be used with both gradable and ungradable adjectives.

A Circle the correct option.

1 I think your cat is very *male / cute*.

2 It seems like the worst place for birds *building / to build* their nests.

3 My friends were absolutely *furious / interesting*.

4 The weather is a little *cold / freezing* right now.

5 For many of us, snakes are probably the *less / least* lovable species.

6 The lion and the elephant are two *most / of the most* popular animals at the zoo.

3.1 RELATIVE PRONOUNS; REDUCED RELATIVE CLAUSES (PAGE 23)

Relative pronouns; reduced relative clauses

1 Relative pronouns are used to introduce relative clauses.

that/which = for things, *that/who* = for people, *where* = for places, *when* = for times, *whose* = to show possession

*My sister, **whose** children I often take care of, lives next door.*

*Today is the day **when** we decide it's time for a change.*

2 Subject relative clauses can be reduced by omitting the relative pronoun and the verb *be*. You can't reduce object relative clauses.

The following relative clauses are often reduced:

- with *be* + an adjective
- with *be* + past participle
- with noun phrases

*People **who are worried** about meeting strangers often get nervous at parties.* → *People **worried** about meeting strangers often get nervous at parties.*

*The bus **that is parked** in front of the office is the one we'll take to the conference.* → *The bus **parked** in front of the office is the one we'll take to the conference.*

*Steven, **who is a quick learner**, adapts easily to new situations.* → *Steven, **a quick learner**, adapts easily to new situations.*

A Cross out the words you can omit to reduce the relative clauses when possible. When not possible, write *X*.

1 The company whose logo is an apple is famous around the world.

2 Vincent van Gogh, who was an introvert, painted landscapes and self-portraits.

3 The book that was published anonymously sold millions of copies.

4 Psychology, which is normally a popular subject, is not her favorite.

5 This is the restaurant where my brother works.

6 People who are interested in others are often good conversationalists.

3.2 PRESENT PARTICIPLES (PAGE 25)

Present participles

Present participle = verb + -ing

1   To shorten sentences that describe two events happening at the same time, use the present participle of the second verb after a comma. Do not use *and*.

*I often work **and listen** to music.* → *I often work, **listening** to music.*

2   In reduced relative clauses, use the present participle. Do not use the relative pronoun and the verb *be*.

*Look at all those **lemons that are growing** on that tree.* → *Look at all those **lemons growing** on that tree.*

A   **Rewrite these sentences to shorten them or use reduced relative clauses.**

1   The mall is full of people who are shopping for the holidays.

_____

2   We're standing in line and waiting to check in for our flight.

_____

3   There are a lot of fans who are waiting outside the stadium.

_____

4   I love to stand on top of that hill and look down at the valley.

_____

5   In college, I saw a guy who was skateboarding down a hallway.

_____

6   The storm will affect people who live in the South.

_____

4.1 ADDING EMPHASIS: *so … that, such … that, even, only* (page 35)

Adding emphasis

1   *So* + adjective or adverb *(that)* … emphasizes the results or effects of something.
*It was **so funny (that)** I couldn't stop laughing.*

2   *Such (a/an)* + (adjective) noun *(that)* … also emphasizes the results or effects of something.
*She is **such a good friend (that)** everyone turns to her when they have a problem.*

3   *Even* before a word, phrase, or part of the sentence adds emphasis or signals that something is surprising.
***Even** the most confident person needs help sometimes.*

*He works long hours during the week and **even** works on Saturdays sometimes.*

*Building trust with people makes your life **even** happier.*

4   *Only* before a word, phrase, or part of the sentence adds emphasis.

■   *only* = "no one else" or "nothing else" than the people, things, amount, or activity mentioned
***Only** you can steer him away from making a big mistake.*

*Quitting your job will **only** hurt your career.*

A   **Complete the sentences with *so, such, even,* or *only*.**

1   It was _____ a big decision to move to Canada and start over again.

2   _____ a very intelligent person can do that job.

3   She is _____ ambitious that she has decided to work toward a PhD.

4   Everyone was on time, _____ Joseph, who is usually late for class.

5   It was time to leave, but they had _____ packed one of their suitcases.

6   He demonstrated _____ talent that they hired him immediately.

4.2 REFLEXIVE PRONOUNS; PRONOUNS WITH *OTHER/ANOTHER* (PAGE 37)

Reflexive pronouns

Use a reflexive pronoun:

1 when the subject and object of a sentence are the same
*I enjoyed **myself** at the party.*

2 directly after a noun or pronoun for greater emphasis
*The employees **themselves** decide what time they start and finish work.*

3 at the end of the clause for some emphasis
*You and your brother should be able to do the job **yourselves**.*

4 after *by* to mean "alone" or "without help"
*I can't lift this box **by myself**.*

> **!** ***You*** **has two reflexive pronouns: *yourself* (singular) and *yourselves* (plural).**

Pronouns with *other/another*

1 *the other* = the remaining member of a pair
*One of his shoes was blue, **the other**, brown.*

2 *another* = an additional member of a group
*I'd like to hire **another** assistant.*

3 *the others* = the remaining members of a group
*Six people in my class are from this city. **The others** are from different cities.*

4 *others* (without *the*) = not the members of the group already mentioned, but different ones
*Some people drink coffee. **Others** prefer tea.*

5 *each other* and *one another* = show that each person in a group does something to the others
*During exams, students are not allowed to help **each other** / **one another**.*

A **Complete the sentences with the correct reflexive pronouns or pronouns with *other/another*.**

1 We knew it was going to be a tough job, but we told _____ we could do it as a team.

2 Do you and Antonio need help moving your furniture, or can you do it _____ ?

3 I know you already have two roommates, but is there room in your apartment for _____ ?

4 Come on guys, work as a team! Help _____ !

5 My job involves a lot of teamwork, so I'm used to working with _____ .

6 I was fixing the ceiling light and almost fell. I had one foot on a chair and _____ on the table.

5.1 REAL CONDITIONALS (PAGE 45)

Real conditionals

1 Present: *if/when/whenever* + simple present + simple present in the main clause

   - to describe general facts or routines
   *I **feel** nervous **if/when/whenever** I **think** about flying.*

2 Future: *if/when/whenever* + simple present + *will / be going to* in the main clause

   - for possible future situations and their results
   ***If** you **try** the therapy, it **will make** you more confident.*
   (You may or may not try the therapy. But if you do, it will make you more confident.)

   ***When/Whenever** you **try** the therapy, it **will make** you more confident.*
   (You will try the therapy, and when you do, it will make you more confident.)

3 With modals and modal-like expressions: *if* clause + a modal in the main clause

   - to show how likely or necessary the result is
   ***Whenever** you're worried, you **have to** try not to panic.*

A Add the words in parentheses ( ) to the correct places in each sentence. Use a capital letter when necessary.

1 I arrive at the airport, I call you right away. (when, will)

2 Max anxious he sees a plane. (feels, whenever)

3 That app really helps people exercise, I buy it. (if, may)

4 I face my fear of heights I go over that bridge. (have to, whenever)

5 Everyone take off their shoes they want to enter that building. (must, if)

6 We take a trip to France your French improves. (can, when)

5.2 CONDITIONALS: alternatives to *if* (page 47)

Conditionals: alternatives to *if*

You can use real conditionals with expressions other than *if*, but they have different meanings:

1 *Even if*: Stresses that the condition doesn't matter. The condition may happen, but the result will be the same.
   Even if *video calls improve, talking in person is much nicer.*

2 *Only if, providing / provided (that), as/so long as, on condition that*: Show the result or effect will happen when a specific condition becomes true. No other condition will have this result.
   I'll lend you my phone, ***only if / provided / providing / as/so long as / on condition that*** *you promise to return it soon.*

3 *Unless*: Describes a possible negative condition in the present or future = "except if" or "if … not."
   We can't reach an agreement ***unless*** *you communicate more openly.*

A Circle the correct option.

1 I'm willing to try virtual office meetings *providing / unless* the technology is reliable.

2 *On condition that / Even if* we meet in person, we may not be able to reach an agreement.

3 We'll leave at 3:00 *provided / even if* everyone is ready.

4 You shouldn't study late *unless / only if* it's absolutely necessary.

5 *Even if / So long as* the company makes a profit, the boss is happy.

6 He should be able to get into that college *as long as / unless* he gets unexpectedly bad grades in high school.

6.1 NARRATIVE TENSES (PAGE 55)

Narrative tenses

1 Simple past for the main completed events and situations in a story.
   He ***became*** *famous when he* ***was*** *only 14.*

2 Past continuous (*was/were* + verb + *-ing*) for background activities in progress at the same time as the main event in the simple past.
   She ***translated*** *what the president* ***was saying***.

3 Past perfect (*had* + past participle) for an event that happened before another event in the simple past.
   All my friends ***went*** *to the concert, but I* ***'d forgotten*** *to buy a ticket.*

4 Past perfect continuous (*had* + *been* + verb + *-ing*) for an event that continued up to another event in the simple past. It shows the continuing nature of a past activity/situation leading up to a more recent past time.
   ■ It can show a reason.   ■ It can give background information.
   The band ***had been playing*** *all night, so they* ***were*** *very tired.*
   I ***had been dreaming*** *of being famous for years, and suddenly it* ***happened***.

A Complete the sentences with the verbs in parentheses ( ) in the correct tense.

We were exhausted when we ¹_____ (reach) the town. We ²_____ (travel) for days! There, we ³_____ (interview) several people about what they ⁴_____ (see). As we ⁵_____ (travel) back, we ⁶_____ (hear) that the story ⁷_____ (already / go) viral.

6.2 REPORTED SPEECH WITH MODAL VERBS (PAGE 57)

Reported speech with modal verbs

1 Some modals change when the reporting verb is in the past:

| *will – would* | *can – could* | *may – might* |

"**Will/Can** you **help** me?" → *Jen asked me if I'd / I could help her.*

2 Some modals don't change, even if the reporting verb is in the past: *might, could, should, must*

"What **could** they do about traffic?" → *He wondered what they **could** do about traffic.*

> ! Only change the tense of the main verb when the reporting verb is in the past tense.

A Complete the sentences.

1 "We won't study space next week." The teacher announced _____ .

2 "Everyone should study for the test. " The teacher feels _____ .

3 "We may not have time to see a movie. " Lisa explained _____ .

4 "Could the Tigers win the baseball game? " Joe asked me _____ .

5 "When will you finish the project? " My boss asked me _____ .

6 "I can play the piano well. " I said _____ .

7.1 GERUNDS AND INFINITIVES AFTER ADJECTIVES, NOUNS, AND PRONOUNS (PAGE 67)

Gerunds and infinitives after adjectives, nouns, and pronouns

Infinitives (*to* + verb)

1 Adjective + infinitive
It's boring and difficult to work at night.

2 Noun + infinitive – to show purpose
It was an interesting place to visit.

3 Pronoun + infinitive – to show purpose
I need something to eat.

Gerunds (verb + *-ing*)

1 Adjective + gerund
It was boring waiting in line for the roller coaster. But it was cool riding on it.

2 Fixed expression + gerund
e.g.: *be worth, have fun, spend/waste time*
I spend a lot of time traveling for my job.

A Circle the correct options. More than one answer may be possible.

I start work at 6:00 a.m. It's hard ¹*to get / getting* up so early, and I usually don't want to spend time ²*to make / making* breakfast, but I try to have something simple ³*to eat / eating*. At least I have no trouble ⁴*to get / getting* to work, as I don't waste time ⁵*to sit / sitting* in traffic jams. I think that's a big advantage ⁶*to have / having*.

> ! Some adjectives can be followed by either gerunds or infinitives, others - only gerunds or only infinitives.

7.2 INFINITIVES AFTER VERBS WITH AND WITHOUT OBJECTS (PAGE 69)

Infinitives after verbs with and without objects

1 Verb + infinitive   Common verbs: *agree, decide, hope, manage, plan, seem, tend*
They agreed not to climb the mountain without an instructor.

2 Verb + object + infinitive   Common verbs: *allow, convince, encourage, teach, tell, urge, warn*
He did not convince us to hire him.   (The object performs the action of the infinitive.)

3 Verb + (object) + infinitive   Common verbs: *ask, expect, need, promise, want, would like*
- No object – subject performs the action of the infinitive
- With object – object performs the action of the infinitive

I'd like to buy the lamp. (I'm buying it.)   *I'd like you to buy that lamp. (You're buying it.)*

> ! Use *not* before the infinitive to show the infinitive is negative. Use *not* before the main verb to show it is negative.

A **Which of these sentences are correct without an object? Add the object in parentheses ( ) where possible.**

1   I like to shop online. (you)
2   I'd like to move closer to my dad. (my sister)
3   Jack tends to forget his friends' birthdays. (them)
4   My parents advised to save money. (me)
5   You convinced to buy a new computer. (them)
6   They expect to get good grades. (her)

8.1   MODAL-LIKE EXPRESSIONS WITH *BE* (PAGE 77)

Modal-like expressions with *be*

1   *Be bound to / Be certain to / Be sure to* for things that are definitely going to happen
    *If you drop that glass, it's **bound to** / **certain to** / **sure to** break.*

2   *Be likely/unlikely to* for things that are probably (not) going to happen
    *There's a lot of traffic, so we're **likely to** be late.*

3   *Be supposed to* for things expected to happen (because they were arranged or sb is responsible for them)
    *My mom **was supposed to** pick me up at 3:30, but she didn't arrive until 4:00.*

4   *Be about to* for things that you're going to do soon or are going to happen soon
    *Quick, turn on the TV. The game **is about to** start.*

5   *Be required to* for things that we are made to do (e.g., because of rules)
    *Everyone who travels by plane **is required to** have a passport or some kind of photo ID.*

6   *Be forced to* for things that we are made to do, but don't want to
    *I missed the last bus, so I **was forced to** walk home.*

7   *Be allowed to / Be permitted to* for things that we have permission to do
    *They're **allowed to** / **permitted to** use their phones in school, but not in class.*

A   Circle the correct option.

1   The president just came into the room, so I think she's *about to / unlikely to* start her speech.
2   He hardly went to any classes, so he was *bound to / about to* do badly on the exam.
3   My coworker was off from work all week, so I was *sure to / forced to* do two jobs – mine and his.
4   We were *allowed to / required to* give our passport numbers when we checked into the hotel.
5   Only people who bought tickets online were *forced to / permitted to* go into the theater.
6   They're *about to / supposed to* announce the exam results in six weeks.

8.2   FUTURE FORMS (PAGE 79)

Future forms

1   Present continuous: for general future intentions and definite plans or arrangements *I'm **making** a film about college life.*
    *I'm **meeting** my friends tomorrow at 6:00 p.m.*

2   *Be going to*: for general future plans and intention and predictions about the future *I'm **going to make** a film about college life.*
    *It's **going to be** a big surprise for them.*

3   *Might, may,* or *could*: when you're not sure about the future
    *I **might start** my own business one day.*

4   *Will*: for predictions about the future and decisions made at the moment of speaking
    *It **will be** a big surprise for them.*
    *That looks difficult. I'll **help** you with it.*

5   *Will + be + verb + -ing* (the future continuous): for an action in progress at a future time and for plans and intentions
    *In a few years, I'll **be looking** for a job.*
    ***Will** you **be coming** to the meeting on Thursday?*

> **!** The future continuous and *be going to* can both express future plans and intentions. The future continuous is more formal.

A Complete the conversation with the verbs in parentheses ( ) in appropriate future forms.

A I'm not sure yet, but I ¹_____ (ask) Juan for help. Do you know if he ²_____ (come) out with us tonight?

B No. He ³_____ (not, leave) the office yet. He's so busy these days! He ⁴_____ (get) sick unless he takes it easy.

A No. I think he ⁵_____ (be) fine. His vacation starts next month, so soon he ⁶_____ (relax) on a beach somewhere.

9.1 UNREAL CONDITIONALS (PAGE 87)

> ### Unreal conditionals
>
> **Present and future**
>
> *if* clause: *could*, simple past, or past continuous (imagined situation)
>
> result clause: *would/could/might* + base form of a verb (predicted or possible result)
>
> *If Josh **was/were studying** at the library, I **could help** him with his homework.*
>
> *If we **got** / **could get** tickets to the concert, we **wouldn't watch** it on TV.*
>
> **Past**
>
> *if* clause: past perfect (something possible that did not happen)
>
> result clause: *would/could/may/might have* + past participle (imaginary past result that didn't happen)
>
> *I **could have been** an X-ray technician **if** I **had studied** medicine.*
>
> Or *would* + base form of a verb (imaginary present result)
>
> *I **would have** a nicer apartment **if** I **hadn't bought** a new car.*

A Complete the sentences with the correct form of the words in parentheses.

1 If Brenda was trying out for that play, she _____ (get) a good part.

2 I would take a dance class if I _____ (not hurt) my ankle.

3 I _____ (change) jobs if I could, but I can't right now.

4 If I had gotten to the restaurant later, I _____ (not see) my cousin.

5 If I had heard the news, I _____ (be) at your house right now.

6 If they _____ (work) fewer hours, they wouldn't be so tired.

9.2 WISHES AND REGRETS (PAGE 89)

> ### Wishes and regrets
>
> *I wish (that)* / *If only* express a wish for something to be different or feelings of regret.
>
> 1 For wishes about general situations in the present: *I wish* / *If only* + simple past
>   *I wish* / *If only I **knew** the answer to this question.*
>
> 2 For wishes about continuous situations in the present: *I wish* / *If only* + past continuous
>   *I wish* / *If only I **was/were sitting** at home and not in this traffic jam.*
>
> 3 For wishes about ability or possibility in the present: *I wish* / *If only* + could/couldn't
>   *I wish* / *If only I **could** find that book.*
>
> 4 For wishes about situations in the past: *I wish* / *If only* + past perfect
>   *I wish* / *If only I **had bought** tickets in advance.*
>
> **!** After *I wish* / *If only*, you can use *was* (informal) or *were* (more formal) with *I, he, she,* and *it*.

A Complete the conversation.

Jose Wow, it's hot on this bus! I wish it ¹_____ ten degrees cooler.

Ed If only we ²_____ buy some cold sodas.

Jose Yeah, this water's warm. I wish I ³_____ the bottle in the refrigerator last night.

Ed Right now, I wish I ⁴_____ in a refrigerator! If only the air conditioning ⁵_____ broken!

10.1 GERUNDS AFTER PREPOSITIONS (PAGE 99)

Gerunds after prepositions

1 Verb + preposition + gerund (e.g., *boast about, care about, insist on, plan on, result in, think of, worry about*)
  Josh **boasted about buying** a new car.
2 *be* + adjective + preposition + gerund (e.g., *be afraid of, be excited about, be guilty of, be interested in*)
  We **are guilty of spending** too much time on social media.
3 Noun + *of* + gerund (e.g., *benefits, cost, danger, fear, idea, importance, possibility, process, risk, way*)
  My **fear of flying** has stopped me from visiting you.

A Complete the sentences with the gerund form of the correct words.

develop	do	recycle	try	win	work

1 Mia often complains about _____ on the weekends.
2 What are the benefits of _____ plastic?
3 Larry isn't afraid of _____ unusual foods.
4 The soccer team succeeded in _____ every game this season.
5 I'm guilty of _____ the same thing instead of trying new things.
6 You need to concentrate on _____ your plan before you can start a business.

10.2 CAUSATIVE VERBS (PAGE 101)

Causative verbs

1 *Help/let/make/have* + object + base form of the verb	My parents **make me save** money for my future.
2 *Allow/cause/enable* + object + infinitive	Surveys **enable stores to estimate** sales.
3 *Keep/prevent/protect/stop* + object + *from* + gerund	Her advice **kept me from losing** my job.

A Complete the sentences with the words in parentheses ( ) in the correct form. Add *from* when necessary.
1 Customer feedback frequently _____ our products. (make, we, improve)
2 We tried to _____ too much money, but we failed. (prevent, he, spend)
3 Having my own home has _____ independent. (enable, I, be)
4 After a business trip, I usually _____ an extra day off. (let, my team, take)
5 My computer is broken, which has _____ any work done. (keep, I, get)
6 Worrying about his business _____ a lot of weight last year. (cause, he, lose)

11.1 PASSIVE FORMS (PAGE 109)

Passive forms

Passive and active sentences have similar meanings. But in the passive, the receiver of the action is more important than the doer and becomes the subject of the sentence. Add *by* + the agent if necessary.

1 Simple present passive: *am/is/are* + past participle	These products **are** usually **imported**.
2 Simple past passive: *was/were* + past participle	**Were** you **given** a refund?
3 Present perfect passive: *has/have been* + past participle	The order **has been canceled**.
4 Future passive: *am/is/are going to/will* + *be* + past participle	The goods **will be checked** before they're shipped.
5 Present continuous passive: *am/is/are* + *being* + past participle	Many goods **are being imported**.
6 Past continuous passive: *was/were* + *being* + past participle	The store **wasn't being used** until now.

A Rewrite the sentences in the passive form. Add *by* + the agent if it's important.

1 We won't solve the problem of counterfeit goods easily . _____
2 A man found illegal copies of movies and games in a garage. _____
3 They're going to debate the issue of fake goods on TV. _____
4 For a long time, people were selling fake goods openly in markets. _____
5 Recently, they've changed the laws on counterfeit goods. _____
6 The government is now watching traders more carefully. _____

11.2 PASSIVES WITH MODALS AND MODAL-LIKE EXPRESSIONS; PASSIVE INFINITIVES (PAGE 111)

> **Passives with modals and modal-like expressions; passive infinitives**
>
> 1 Passive with modals + *be* + past participle
>   - Common modals: *can, could, might, may, should, must*
>   **Should** the photos **be taken** in natural light?
> 2 Passive with modal-like expressions + (*to*) + *be* + past participle
>   - Common expressions: *have to, need to, had better, be likely to, be supposed to*
>   Rumors **had better not be spread** at this school.
>   Good journalists **don't need to be told** what to do.
> 3 Passive infinitives (verb + *to be* + past participle)
>   - Common verbs and expressions: *ask, be likely, expect, hope, refuse, seem*
>   The problem **isn't likely to be solved** soon.

> **!** For negative sentences, use *had better not* + *be* + past participle.

A Write sentences with passive forms.

1 the facts / must / check / by the editor / _____ .
2 the manager / ask / show / the sales figures / _____ .
3 people / might / harm / by that false story / _____ .
4 the rumor / couldn't / control / _____ .
5 the journalists / refuse / tell / what to write / _____ .
6 that photo of me / had better / removed / from your post / _____ .

12.1 ADVERBS WITH ADJECTIVES AND ADVERBS (PAGE 119)

> **Adverbs with adjectives and adverbs**
>
> **With adjectives**
> 1 Use an adverb before an adjective to provide more detail about it.
>   - Common adverbs: *especially, exceptionally, mainly, (not) necessarily, particularly, reasonably*
>   John is **especially skilled** at painting, while his brother is **mainly good** at drawing.
> 2 Use an adverb before an adjective to say what the adjective is related to.
>   - Common adverbs: *artistically, athletically, financially, musically, physically, scientifically, technically*
>   Sandra is **artistically talented** in many ways, but she's not **musically gifted** at all.
>
> **With adverbs**
> 3 Use an adverb before another adverb to provide more detail about it.
>   - Common adverbs: *especially, exceptionally, particularly, reasonably*
>   Some people are able to learn languages **particularly easily**. For example, my friend Paolo learned five languages **exceptionally fast**.

> **!** An adverb + an adjective describes a noun.
> <u>The concert</u> was **reasonably good**.
> An adverb + an adverb describes a verb.
> Sandra <u>paints</u> **exceptionally well** for a beginner.

A **Circle the correct option.**

1 My accountant always gives me financially *correct / correctly* information.

2 Is she exceptionally *good / well* at music?

3 Jorge finished the test especially *quick / quickly*.

4 Eve learns new computer programs particularly *easy / easily*.

5 I like all kinds of music, but I'm mainly *interested / interestingly* in classical music.

6 Natasha's house is full of artistically *beautiful / beautifully* objects.

12.2 MAKING NON-COUNT NOUNS COUNTABLE (PAGE 121)

Making non-count nouns countable

Make non-count nouns countable with expressions describing specific quantities or amounts. For example:

1 Abstract ideas
- a little bit of (kindness/luck/space/time)
  A little bit of kindness brightens up people's lives.
- a piece of (advice/information)
  This is a useful piece of information.
- a word of (advice/encouragement/sympathy/wisdom)
  He was full of words of wisdom and useful pieces of advice.

2 Activities and sports
- a game of (basketball/chess/soccer/tennis)
  We played a few games of basketball over the weekend.

3 Food
- a box of, a bunch of, a can of, a grain of, a loaf of, a package of, a piece/slice of, a pound of, a serving of
  I need a bunch of parsley and a packet of cereal.

> ! **A pound = about .45 kilograms**
> **A gallon = about 3.8 liters**
> **A quart = about .95 liters**

4 Liquids
- a bottle of, a cup of, a glass of, a drop of, a gallon of, a quart of
  At the café, we ordered two cups of coffee and a glass of juice.

5 Miscellaneous
- an act of (bravery/kindness)   *Helping me move was an act of kindness.*
- an article/item of (clothing)   *What is your favorite item of clothing?*
- a piece of (clothing/equipment/furniture/music/news)   *That's a fantastic piece of equipment!*
- a work of (art)   *This painting is my favorite work of art.*

A **Complete the sentences with the words in the box. Use the plural form when necessary.**

act	article	game	serving	word	work

1 His _____ of encouragement really raised my spirits.

2 She gave each person a _____ of ice cream.

3 I think that being able to change yourself is a real _____ of bravery.

4 I lost three _____ of chess with my brother, and it ruined my evening.

5 I don't think we need any more _____ of art in this room.

6 How many _____ of clothing can you fit in that tiny suitcase?

VOCABULARY PRACTICE

1.1 FACING CHALLENGES (PAGE 2)

A **Circle the correct option.**

1 I usually *welcome / resist* change – unless it's dangerous, of course!
2 Many people *accept / get a grip* that they have a limit to what they can do.
3 I've never *been capable of / been frightened of* learning new things. I love it!
4 When I'm really busy at work, I can't *cope with / underestimate* other things. I'm too tired.
5 My dad used to tell me, "You need to *welcome / adapt* in order to be successful."
6 I *tackle / can't take* all this work. It's too much!
7 When I'm stressed, I tell myself to *get a grip / be a step forward* and deal with things.
8 My good friends often help me *underestimate / get through* difficult times.
9 They say it's hard to *survive / be capable of* in this city, but I'm doing fine!

B **Complete each sentence with the correct word or phrase from the box.**

accept	adapt	can't take	capable of
frightened of	step forward	tackle	underestimate

1 I'm afraid I'm not _____ doing a sales manager's job. I don't have the skills.
2 We told the police what happened, but they wouldn't _____ our explanation.
3 You usually _____ well to big changes in your life.
4 Congratulations on your graduation! It's a _____ in your life, and a big one.
5 Don't _____ your ability to face challenges. You've always been good at dealing with new things.
6 She's moving to the country because she _____ the pressure of city life anymore.
7 I have to _____ some boring jobs around the house this weekend. They have to be done.
8 My mom says I was _____ other people when I was a child. Actually, I was just shy.

1.2 DESCRIBING ANNOYING THINGS (PAGE 4)

A **Cross out the word or phrase that does <u>not</u> work in each sentence.**

1 This app always crashes. It *is infuriating / is awkward / drives me crazy*.
2 My little sister asks a lot of questions. It *gets on my nerves / drives me crazy / is hard to operate*.
3 This remote control is *complex / time-consuming / tricky*. I can't figure out how to record a show.
4 Old laptops *were awkward / were clumsy / lost my patience* because they were too big and never fit in a bag.
5 This door is *a waste of time / infuriating / frustrating*. It always makes a loud noise when someone opens it.

B **Complete each sentence with the correct form of the words or phrases in the box.**

be a waste of time	be hard to operate	complex
get on sb's nerves	lose patience	time-consuming

1 These drones _____. The remote controls aren't easy to use at all.
2 Our internet connection really _____. I can't stream any movies.
3 Jackie _____ over little things – like when people ask her the same question more than once.
4 Painting our house is _____. We've been working for hours, and we've only done one room.
5 These directions are _____. I can't figure out how to put this table together.
6 Playing that game on your phone _____. You should be studying.

2.1 SPACE AND OCEAN EXPLORATION (PAGE 12)

A   **Complete each sentence with the correct word. There is one item you won't use.**

atmosphere	come across	investigation	launched	observe
resources	satellite	species	surface	

What's Mars like? The ¹_____ of Mars is very different from the air around Earth. For example, there's very little oxygen in it. From ²_____ images we can see that the ³_____ of Mars is covered with rocks and red dust, so Mars is often called the Red Planet. People haven't been to Mars, but they've ⁴_____ spacecraft to ⁵_____ and explore it. They haven't ⁶_____ any plant or animal ⁷_____ on the planet, but they've found ⁸_____ , like water and iron.

B   **Circle the correct option.**

Ocean ¹*exploration / atmosphere* is useful in many different ways. For example, scientists are making breakthroughs in medicine by ²*launching / observing* different ocean ³*species / investigation*. So it's important to ⁴*monitor / come across* the ocean waters to ⁵*preserve / use up* life there, not only for food ⁶*exploration / resources*, but also because we have so much more to learn from it.

2.2 THE NATURAL WORLD (PAGE 14)

A   **Circle the correct option.**

1   We climbed to the top of the *pond / volcano* to admire the view.
2   Ants and rats are excellent *sea life / survivors*.
3   How many animals are *endangered / adaptable* in your country?
4   What other *creatures / territory* can you find in this area?
5   The frog's natural *form of life / habitat* is in or around water.
6   There's a huge variety of *plant life / environment* in the Amazon rainforest.
7   Tigers are one of the most *poisonous / endangered* species on Earth.
8   Dinosaur bones give us clues to their *origins / animal life*.

B   **Complete each sentence with the correct word or phrase. Use each option only once.**

adaptable	animal life	forms of life	pond
survivors	sea life	territory	

1   Animals and birds try very hard to protect their _____ .
2   Foxes are good _____ in both the city and the countryside.
3   There are many more _____ on Earth than we know of.
4   Unfortunately, there isn't much _____ in this forest anymore.
5   There's something swimming on the surface of the _____ .
6   Ants might be small, but they are _____ creatures that can live in many environments.
7   Fish are one of the most common forms of _____ .

3.1 DESCRIBING PERSONALITY (PAGE 22)

A   **Match the words (1–5) with their definitions (a–e).**

1   show off ____   a   talk and do things with other people
2   speak up ____   b   try to get attention
3   extrovert ____   c   someone who is shy and quiet
4   interact ____   d   an energetic person who enjoys being with other people
5   introvert ____   e   to speak in a louder voice so that people can hear you

B **Circle the correct option.**

My sister and I often go out together. She likes meeting new people and ¹*enjoys the company of / shows off* strangers, but I prefer to hang out with people I know. She loves to ²*feel left out / socialize* in any environment, but I need to feel comfortable before I ³*interact / speak up* with people. When people invite us to their homes, she's ⁴*reserved / the life of the party*, and everyone loves her stories and jokes. I tend to ⁵*speak softly / speak up* and often ⁶*feel left out / attract attention* because I feel that no one wants to hear my stories. Sometimes, I think she ⁷*shows off / interacts*, but I guess that's not really true. I'm probably just a little jealous. The truth is, I never ⁸*am reserved / speak up*. If I did, everyone would probably listen to me, too. It's OK – if I find one person to talk to, I'm perfectly happy.

3.2 STRONG FEELINGS (PAGE 25)

A **Complete each sentence with the correct word. Sometimes there is more than one possible answer.**

bizarre	creepy	disgusting	fabulous	impressive	irritating
satisfying	stunning	tense	uneasy	weird	

1 My internet connection has been slow lately. It's really _____ .

2 We saw some strange species of insects in the forest. They were like aliens – really _____ .

3 Having worked so hard painting the apartment, it was extremely _____ to see the results.

4 I'll never eat in that restaurant again. The food was absolutely _____ !

5 I felt confident in the interview but not before it. Before it started, I was really _____ and couldn't relax.

6 This landscape is _____ ! Let's take some pictures before it gets dark.

7 I used to get scared going into that old house. It was such a(n) _____ place.

8 We had a wonderful time on the coast. It was a(n) _____ weekend.

B **Cross out the word that does not work in each sentence.**

1 From our hotel balcony, we could see the ocean. The view was *fabulous / uneasy / stunning*.

2 Cheryl thinks spiders are *creepy / disgusting / fabulous*, but she likes snakes.

3 I think it's *satisfying / weird / bizarre* that John can't stand the feel of plastic.

4 I always feel *tense / uneasy / irritating* when I have to speak in public.

5 Martin's new car is *tense / impressive / stunning*. I wish he'd let me drive it.

6 It was *an irritating / a tense / an impressive* situation, but we got through it.

4.1 PROFESSIONAL RELATIONSHIPS (PAGE 34)

A **Circle the correct option.**

1 I think they need to *build trust / demonstrate* before they start that project.

2 Can you tell me who *oversees / acts as* student registration?

3 I had a difficult time at first because I had no one to *take on / turn to*.

4 The adviser at my college *enabled me to / contributed* get my first job.

5 My mother *steered me away from / kept an eye on* a lot of trouble when I was a child.

6 We want you to *build a relationship / assist* the general manager as soon as you can.

B   Complete each paragraph with the correct words in the simple past.

act as	build trust	enable me to
keep an eye on	steer me away from	take on

My cousin Frederico [1]_____ my tutor when I was in college. He [2]_____ the responsibility of helping me study and prepare for exams. He [3]_____ all my work and [4]_____ making mistakes. We [5]_____ together, and I can honestly say that he [6]_____ graduate with good grades.

assist	build a relationship	contribute
demonstrate	oversee	turn to

Marina quickly [7]_____ with her students, and they [8]_____ her whenever they needed help. She [9]_____ them with their studies in every way and [10]_____ all their exam preparations. She [11]_____ useful suggestions and ideas at every staff meeting and always [12]_____ interest and enjoyment in her job as a teacher here. I'm sorry she's leaving, but I wish her all the best for the future.

4.2   ASSESSING IDEAS (PAGE 36)

A   Circle the correct option.

It can be hard to make decisions. It's not always easy to [1]*assess / draw* what the final [2]*aspects / consequences* might be. And even if it's possible to think [3]*out / through* everything in detail, ideas often have both good and bad [4]*aspects / strengths*. This sometimes forces us to [5]*be destructive / weigh the pros and cons*. Things get even more complicated if a decision has to be made as a team. Team members often point [6]*out / up* the problems with each other's ideas. This can cause problems. Success depends on the personal strengths and [7]*cons / weaknesses* of team members. Some people are good at expressing criticism in a positive, [8]*constructive / destructive* way. They are careful to [9]*draw / point* attention only to valid points. Others are not as careful. They can sound rude, and the results can be [10]*constructive / destructive* to team relationships.

B   Cross out the word or phrase that doesn't work in each sentence.

1   I think he was being too critical. A lot of his points were *destructive / valid / unreasonable*.

2   We need to *assess / think through / point out* this plan and decide if it will work.

3   I'm really concerned about the *aspects / consequences / weaknesses* of his proposal.

4   Can I just *draw attention to / weigh the pros and cons / point out* a possible problem?

5   The boss was pleased with my *unreasonable / valid / constructive* suggestions.

5.1   DEALING WITH EMOTIONS (PAGE 44)

A   Circle the correct option.

1   When planes land, I'm *scared to death / conscious of* an uneasy feeling among the passengers.

2   You need to *calm down / panic* and think clearly.

3   Do you think the therapist can *regain control / cure* my fear of spiders?

4   Right now, my *breathing technique / anxiety level* is low.

5   I was afraid to drive, but my mom helped me *be scared to death / overcome my fear*.

6   It's important to *be rational / be in control of* when faced with fear.

7   Do you think trying *therapy / an anxiety level* will help him?

B **Complete each sentence with the correct word or phrase from the box.**

| be in control of | be rational | breathing technique | cure |
| panic | regained control | was scared to death | |

1 After panicking for a few minutes, I _____ and started to relax.
2 Do you want to _____ your emotions when flying? If so, try our VR therapy.
3 The movie was so frightening. I _____ .
4 We're trying to _____ about the decision, but it will change our lives completely.
5 Try not to _____ about your driving test. Breathe deeply and relax.
6 She feels much better, but the medicine didn't completely _____ her cough.
7 You might feel more relaxed if you try this _____ .

5.2 WILLINGNESS AND UNWILLINGNESS (PAGE 46)

A Circle the correct options.

1 I'm *passionate / eager* to learn languages, but my friend has no *desire / intention* of learning another language.
2 My dad is *more than happy / reluctant* to help me study, but he is *against / eager* helping me write my essays.
3 Some of us are *dying / hesitating* to go camping, but others are *anxious / passionate* to stay at home and study for their exams.
4 It's great you're *prepared / unwilling* to meet us at the airport. We're *reluctant / dying* to see you again!

B **Complete each sentence with the correct phrase.**

| am prepared to | am unwilling to | are anxious to | have no intention of |
| hesitated to | is against | is passionate about | are reluctant to |

1 I saw he was in trouble, but I _____ help him. I didn't want to make the situation worse.
2 We _____ meet your new friends. We can hardly wait.
3 I hate flying and _____ getting on a plane ever again!
4 She _____ keeping fit. She runs ten kilometers every day.
5 Sorry, but I _____ work this weekend. I'm tired and need to rest.
6 My mother can repair anything. She _____ buying new things if she can fix the old ones.
7 They _____ leave their house because they're watching a soccer game on TV.
8 I _____ accept the job if the salary is good enough.

6.1 TALKING ABOUT FAME (PAGE 54)

A Circle the correct option.

Jason [1]*had a good reputation / got hits* as a music student in college. One of his performances
[2]*caught the media's attention / made an appearance*, and he soon [3]*heard of it / was getting a lot of publicity*.
He never intended to [4]*seek fame / praise himself*, but he enjoyed the attention. After that, he
[5]*raised awareness / made appearances* on several TV shows. I noticed he [6]*did the broadcast / made headlines*
almost every day, so I went to one of his concerts. Jason really [7]*raised my awareness of / caught my attention*
the power of music.

B **Cross out the expression that does not work in each sentence.**

1 The singer's videos *got a lot of publicity / got a lot of hits / made an appearance* in a short amount of time.
2 As a young artist, he *praised / caught everyone's attention / sought fame*.
3 Our band *did a broadcast / has heard of / made an appearance* online.
4 Famous people often have a need to make *headlines / appearances in public / a bad reputation*.
5 The teacher *raised awareness of / praised / made them entertaining* our creative videos.

6.2 REPORTING VERBS (PAGE 56)

A Match the words (1–12) with the definitions (a–l). Use a dictionary or your phone to help you.

1	announce ____	a	not be sure of something
2	argue ____	b	promise
3	boast ____	c	talk too proudly about something connected with you
4	claim ____	d	guess the size, value, amount, cost, etc., of something
5	confirm ____	e	tell people new information
6	deny ____	f	say something is true
7	estimate ____	g	give reasons to support or oppose an idea, action, etc.
8	have doubts about ____	h	suggest a plan or action
9	hope to ____	i	say something is not true
10	insist ____	j	want something to happen
11	propose ____	k	say something must be done
12	swear ____	l	to say that based on evidence something is true

B Circle the correct option.

1 My friends often *boast / hope to / swear* about their good grades.

2 When will you *insist / announce / claim* your plans to sell the company?

3 I was happy that the report *confirmed / estimated / denied* my numbers were correct.

4 I know that John was at a concert last night, but he *insists / denies / proposes* it.

5 Jenny *denied / had doubts about / swore* she told me about the party, but she hadn't.

7.1 POSITIVE EXPERIENCES (PAGE 67)

A Circle the correct options. Sometimes both are correct.

1 In my job, I have a positive effect on people. They *are of use / value* what I do.

2 I'm proud of the work I do. It *makes a contribution / is an honor* to work for this company.

3 My job is a lot of fun. I *take pleasure in / am a good influence on* my work.

4 It's good to make a contribution – to feel that what you do is *beneficial / worthwhile*.

5 When people are scared, it makes a difference if you *devote your life / reassure* them.

6 Janelle is an excellent nurse and *is a good influence on / devotes her life to* others.

7 When you do a job well, you generally *get satisfaction out of / reassure* it.

8 I want a job that has a positive effect on the world. I want to *make a contribution / make a difference*.

B Complete the sentences with these expressions. Sometimes more than one answer is correct.

devoted their lives to	get satisfaction out of	make a contribution	make a difference
reassure	take pleasure in	value	was beneficial
was of use	was worthwhile		

1 I enjoyed working on the construction of the new hospital. I felt it _____ for my city.

2 Thanks for your help. I always _____ the career advice you give me.

3 My sister and her husband have _____ helping others.

4 If we hire you, how can you help the company? How will you _____ ?

5 I often help people in trouble, and of course, I _____ that.

6 Don't worry. Let me _____ you everything will be fine.

7.2 MAKING PURCHASES (PAGE 68)

A   Complete the conversation with the correct words.

> be foolish   convinced me   look ridiculous   makes financial sense
> practical   purchase   regret a purchase

Marcy   I think we should ¹_____ these snowboards.

Jason   Yeah, the salesperson ²_____ it's cheaper than renting them.

Marcy   It really ³_____ . We snowboard a lot in the winter, so it's ⁴_____ .

Jason   But I'm not sure about these bright colors. I don't want to ⁵_____ in front of our friends.

Marcy   I think they're really cool, but I don't want you to ⁶_____ that was kind of expensive. Why don't we go home and look at some other options online?

Jason   Good idea. There's no reason to ⁷_____ and make a quick decision.

B   Circle the correct option.

1   Owning an environmentally friendly car has a lot of *appeal / sense*, and I *convince / encourage* you to consider getting one.

2   For me, buying new clothes *is not worth the money / looks ridiculous*. I get bored with them after a couple of weeks, and I always *regret the purchase / urge you to buy them*.

3   My sister *regrets / urged me* to a buy a laptop, but I think this tablet *has potential / is foolish*, too. It's cheaper and will do everything I need it to.

8.1 DESCRIBING NEATNESS AND MESSINESS (PAGE 76)

A   Circle the correct option. Sometimes both options are correct.

1   We've put the files in alphabetical order / folded the files so they can be found easily.

2   Someone has *arranged the towels / hung up the towels* neatly.

3   He left his papers *all over the place / tangled up*.

4   She carefully *lined up / threw* the books on the shelves.

5   My dad *hung up his tools / put his tools in a pile* on the wall of his garage.

6   I keep telling my kids to *throw in / put away* their clothes.

7   All the dishes *are organized / are disorganized* neatly in the cupboard.

8   Your computer cables are all *jumbled up / tangled up*.

B   Complete the paragraph with these expressions. Sometimes there's more than one correct answer.

> arranges   disorganized   fold   hangs up   jumbled up
> leaves … all over the place   lines up   organized   puts away
> tangled up   throws … on

Leo and Ed are roommates, but they have completely different habits. Leo is ¹_____ . He always
²_____ his clothes neatly in the closet, and he ³_____
his shoes side by side on the floor. But Ed is completely ⁴_____ . His clothes are always
⁵_____ , and he ⁶_____ them _____ .
He doesn't ⁷_____ them, but just ⁸_____ them _____ the floor.

8.2 TALKING ABOUT PROGRESS (PAGE 78)

A Circle the correct option.

1 My friend studied really hard, and *effectively / as expected*, she did well on her exams.

2 He does everything very quickly and *with ease / little by little*.

3 If you want to work on that project, you will have to do it *efficiently / on your own time*, not during work hours.

4 I researched the subject *thoroughly / smoothly*, but I still had trouble writing my essay.

5 It's a wonderful feeling to complete a project *successfully / steadily*.

6 I felt relaxed because I was allowed to work *with difficulty / at my own pace*.

B **Put the words in parentheses ( ) in the correct place in each sentence. There's sometimes more than one correct place.**

1 I have to do this because it's easy to make mistakes. (little by little)

2 We read the instructions but couldn't find the information we wanted. (thoroughly)

3 Just work on it, and don't worry about the schedule. (steadily)

4 How can we manage this project? (effectively)

5 If you want to complete this, that's fine with me. (on your own time)

6 It's amazing that you can work in this noisy office. (efficiently)

7 I completed the project, and I didn't enjoy it at all. (with difficulty)

8 Everything went, so we were all very pleased. (smoothly)

9.1 LUCK AND CHOICE (PAGE 86)

A **Complete the sentences with the correct expressions.**

be in the right place at the right time	chance encounter
deliberate decision	determination
fate	believe my luck
path	was fortunate

1 A(n) _____ with a famous singer set me on a _____ to study music.

2 Sara believes in _____ . She says it's the reason she met her boyfriend, but I just think she happened to _____ .

3 Joaquin made a _____ to study law. He'll need a lot of _____ to finish his degree.

4 I _____ to get the last two concert tickets. I can't _____ !

B Circle the correct options.

1 College was a *life-changing experience / fate* for me.

2 Laura got a *path / lucky break* when she was asked to appear on a reality TV cooking show.

3 Seeing my cousin at the mall was a *right place at the right time / coincidence*.

4 Gavin studied biology, but he *wound up / was fortunate* being a gym teacher.

5 She made a *chance encounter / deliberate decision* to cancel her trip when she heard about the storm.

9.2 COMMENTING ON MISTAKES (PAGE 89)

A   Circle the correct options.

1   Now I realize it was a bad *side / move*. It was a dumb *mistake / thing* to do.

2   My clothes were totally wrong for the party. I found myself in an *awkward / incompetent* situation, but I could see the *bad / funny* side of it.

3   I tripped over a bench because I wasn't *watching / learning* what I was doing. I don't text while walking now, but I learned that the *silly / hard* way.

4   Her dog bit me, which was *incompetent / unfortunate*. It *was my own fault / kicked myself* because I accidentally scared it.

5   It was a *hard / silly* mistake. And I made it because I was in too much of a *hurry / move*.

B   Complete the sentences with the expressions in the box.

dumb thing to do	incompetent at	kicked myself	learned that the hard way
found myself in an awkward situation	sees the funny side	too much of a hurry	unfortunate

1   Because I was quite _____ math, I decided not to become an engineer.

2   I couldn't remember the company director's name, so I _____ .

3   I left my phone outside. Phones don't like rain! I _____ .

4   I tried to carry six glasses. It was a _____ .

5   Out of everyone in the restaurant, I was the one hit by the flying tomato! I was so

_____ .

6   At the airport, I realized I'd forgotten my passport. I could have _____ !

7   Take your time. You're always in _____ .

8   He's a pretty positive guy. He usually _____ of things.

10.1 DESCRIBING CHARACTERISTICS (PAGE 98)

A   What are the sentences describing? Write the correct expression.

a look	a match	build	features	look-alikes

1   Tom is very tall and has a lot of muscles. _____

2   Mike and Joey aren't related, but people think they're brothers. _____

3   I love the clothes my Aunt Larisa wears, and she always has a trendy hairstyle. _____

4   Mario has dark eyes, a small nose, and a wide mouth. _____

5   Jim and Cara are great for each other. They have a lot in common and get along well. _____

B   Circle the correct options.

1   My brother and I have similar features and *likeness / characteristics*, but our interests are completely different.

2   You have to complete the form with your name, contact information, and *feature / gender*.

3   My dog Charlie is a *male / female*, and he's very shy.

4   The *features / similarities* between Isabel and her cousin make them seem more like sisters.

5   John is a very independent *individual / match*. He always does what he wants, even if it's not popular.

6   Lara has a medium *build / look*, while her sister is really tall and slim.

10.2 DESCRIBING RESEARCH (PAGE 100)

A **Circle the correct options.**

We did a ¹*survey / calculation* of our customers two months ago. One of the marketing staff then ²*analyzed / demonstrated* their profiles and ³*calculated / identified* ten customers who could become our special advisers. We want them to ⁴*examine / survey* our menu and give their ⁵*survey / assessment* of which dishes no longer interest people. In return for their help, we will give them cooking classes, including ⁶*demonstrations / analysis* and hands-on lessons. In addition, the manager has ⁷*examined / calculated* that we can afford to pay them $50 each for their time.

B **Complete the sentences with the correct words. Sometimes there's more than one correct answer.**

analyze	assessed	assessments	calculations
demonstrations	examined	identify	surveys

1 Would you please _____ this sales report and let me know if it's reliable?

2 I carefully _____ the printer, but I didn't see anything wrong with it.

3 We watched a couple of interesting _____ of how to interview new graduates.

4 I've _____ the information and am going to start writing my essay this afternoon.

5 We found out later that most of his _____ were wrong.

6 Unfortunately, the results of both customer _____ were unclear.

7 Can you _____ one or two employees who have the potential to be managers?

11.1 DESCRIBING CONSUMER GOODS (PAGE 108)

A **Complete the sentences with the correct words in the box. Sometimes there is more than one correct answer.**

authentic	counterfeit	deadly	fake	fireproof
genuine	inferior	legal	second-rate	sophisticated

1 Is this watch real or not? If it's a copy, it's a very _____ one.

2 Don't buy that phone. It's made of cheap, _____ materials, which won't last.

3 Your purse is _____ . It's definitely made by our company.

4 Is it _____ to copy designer clothing if you openly say it's not real?

5 One of the chemicals used in this hair dye is dangerous. In fact, it's _____ . Throw it away!

6 I got a(n) _____ $5 bill in my change yesterday. I took it to the bank, and they gave me a real one.

7 This blanket is made of _____ material and is very safe for your child's bed.

B **Circle the correct options.**

My friend says she doesn't mind if goods are ¹*counterfeit / sophisticated* as long as they're cheap. But it's an ²*inferior / illegal* trade, so that's why I prefer to buy ³*fake / genuine* goods. Besides, I don't like ⁴*second-rate / original* stuff.

I bought some ⁵*fireproof / inferior* gloves because I often have barbecues in the summer. But it turned out they weren't ⁶*a deadly / an authentic* product. The design was ⁷*imperfect / original* and had many problems. To me, this was a ⁸*fake / legal* issue because of the risk of injury, so I went to the police.

11.2 DEGREES OF TRUTH (PAGE 110)

A Complete the sentences with the expressions in the box. There is one you won't use.

controversial	dishonest	inaccurate	misinformation
suspicious	trustworthy	urban legend	white lie

1 I never believe what Joe tells me because he's _____.
2 I told Julie a _____ because I didn't want to hurt her feelings.
3 I don't believe the _____ about the clown statue that came to life.
4 Making clones of animals is a(n) _____ issue.
5 That news article is _____. Over 21 million people live in Mexico City, not 11 million.
6 I always post articles on social media from _____ sites because I want to inform people about the truth.
7 Donna's story is _____. I don't think she was in Los Angeles. I wonder where she *really* was!

B Cross out the word that doesn't work in each sentence.

1 Although the information is true, that article is *biased / inaccurate / controversial* because the author is friends with the person she interviewed.
2 Did you really think the story of a man owning a 200-pound cat was real? It was just *a hoax / a white lie / a rumor*.
3 Janice's story sounds *suspicious / exaggerated / trustworthy*. I don't think she really was lost for *15* hours!
4 That photo is *accurate / misleading / false*. Sharks can't live in lakes.
5 *Misinformation / Urban legends / Rumors* are entertaining as long as they don't harm anyone.

12.1 SKILL AND PERFORMANCE (PAGE 118)

A Circle the correct options.

My friend Tasha is [1]*talented / analytical* in many creative fields. She's very [2]*trained / artistic*, even though she's never taken an art class. She paints, draws, and is an excellent photographer. I like her paintings the best because they're so [3]*imaginative / determined*. She's also very [4]*athletic / musical* and is [5]*a skilled / an intellectual* piano player. Her father taught her how to play when she was three. Even though she's [6]*technical / gifted* in these creative areas and finds math difficult, she wants to be an engineer. She's [7]*determined / musical*, but I don't think it's a [8]*logical / competent* choice.

B Complete the sentences with the correct words.

analytical	athletic	competent	intellectual	technical	trained

1 Josh isn't a(n) _____ life coach, but he gives very good life advice.
2 Sarah likes her science classes because she has a very _____ mind.
3 You have to be a(n) _____ person to be able to run a marathon.
4 I need help with some _____ problems on my computer.
5 My accountant is very _____, but I prefer to keep track of my budget myself.
6 _____ games that require skill and knowledge make you smarter while you play them.

12.2 DESCRIBING EMOTIONAL IMPACT (PAGE 120)

A **Circle the correct options. Sometimes both are correct.**

1 I'm so happy! You've really *brightened up my day / made my day*.

2 I didn't like that movie. It *was a real downer / took my mind off my problems*.

3 His wonderful speech *stressed me out / left a lasting impression on me*.

4 Thanks so much! Your party *raised my spirits / got me down*.

5 The doctor was great. She *put my mind at rest / ruined my day*.

6 Seeing the new art sculptures in the park *did me good / captured my imagination*.

B **Cover exercise A. Complete the sentences with the verbs in the correct form.**

be	brighten	capture	do	get	leave	raise	ruin	stress	take

1 He says his work is _____ him out right now.

2 You need something to _____ your mind off your problems.

3 The things he said _____ a lasting impression on me.

4 It will _____ you good to get out of the house for a while.

5 Failing my exam yesterday _____ a real downer.

6 You can _____ up people's lives with just a smile.

7 The speaker's ideas really _____ our imagination last night.

8 This cloudy, rainy weather is _____ me down.

9 Going out to dinner and a movie should _____ your spirits.

10 That bad news _____ my day yesterday.

PROGRESS CHECK

Can you do these things? Check (✓) what you can do. Then write your answers in your notebook.

Now I can …

☐ talk about facing challenges.

☐ talk about present habits.

☐ describe annoying things.

☐ talk about past habits.

☐ discuss issues and agree strongly.

☐ write an opinion essay.

Prove it

Use four words to describe how someone you know deals with challenges.

Write three things you do every day using three different forms.

Think of a tech item you don't like. Use four words to say why.

Write five things you used to do ten years ago. Use three different forms.

Complete the conversation with words that are true for you.
A   As for _____ , I think _____ .
B   Overall, _____ .

Look at your formal essay from lesson 1.4. Find three ways to make it better.

Now I can …

☐ talk about exploration and research.

☐ use comparative structures.

☐ talk about life forms in different environments.

☐ use superlative structures and ungradable adjectives.

☐ exchange important information.

☐ write a description of an area.

Prove it

Complete the sentences.
1   I think travel to outer space _____ .
2   Exploring the ocean floor _____ .
3   We need to preserve _____ .

Compare living underwater in a submarine to living in outer space in a spacecraft. Use these words: *endangered, habitat, plant life, poisonous, territory.*

Write five "amazing facts" about the animal, plant, and sea life in your country.

Use superlative structures to describe the amazing facts you wrote above.

Someone wants to visit your country for the first time. Give them some important information to help plan the visit.

Look at your description from lesson 2.4. Find three ways to make it better.

Now I can …

☐ describe personality.

☐ use relative clauses.

☐ talk about things I love or hate.

☐ use present participles.

☐ make and respond to requests.

☐ write a personal statement for a job application.

Prove it

Describe two people you know. How are their personalities different?

Complete these sentences.
My [family member], whose _____ , *is* _____ .
Winter is a time when _____ .

Write about a sight, sound, or smell you love and one you hate. Say how they make you feel.

Complete the sentences with present participles and your own ideas.
I'm just sitting here, _____ .
Animals _____ *are* _____ .

Write a short conversation where one person makes a request and the other person refuses at first but finally agrees.

Look at your personal statement from lesson 3.4. Find three ways to make it better.

PROGRESS CHECK

Can you do these things? Check (✓) what you can do. Then write your answers in your notebook.

PROGRESS CHECK

UNIT 4

Now I can …

☐ talk about my support team in life.

☐ use *so*, *such*, *even*, and *only* to add emphasis.

☐ make decisions.

☐ use reflexive pronouns and pronouns with *other/another*.

☐ discuss advantages and disadvantages.

☐ write a summary.

Prove it

Write about two people you know and describe how they support you.

Write four sentences describing how easy, hard, or fun your daily life is. Don't forget to add emphasis.

Write three sentences about how you assess ideas. Use *weigh the pros and cons*, *constructive*, *point out*.

Write three sentences with examples of reflexive pronouns. Write one sentence with a form of *other* and one with *another*.

Write about the pros and cons of job sharing.

Look at your summary from lesson 4.4. Find three ways to make it better.

UNIT 5

Now I can …

☐ talk about dealing with emotions.

☐ use real conditionals.

☐ express willingness and unwillingness.

☐ use alternatives to *if* in conditionals.

☐ consider and contrast ideas.

☐ write an online comment with examples.

Prove it

Write sentences using each of these expressions once: *anxiety level*, *be scared to death*, *calm down*, *regain control*.

Complete the sentences with your own ideas.
If I decide to travel, I'll _____ .
I might _____ *if* _____ .

Complete the sentences.
I have no desire to _____ .
I'm dying to _____ .

Write four sentences about communicating with people. Use *as long as*, *unless*, *even if*, *only if*.

Write about the pros and cons of studying online.

Look at your comment from lesson 5.4. Find three ways to make it better.

UNIT 6

Now I can …

☐ talk about fame.

☐ use narrative tenses.

☐ use reporting verbs.

☐ use reported speech with modals.

☐ make assumptions.

☐ write an interesting story.

Prove it

Give definitions of these words: *broadcast*, *get hits*, *raise awareness*.

Look back over the last five years of your life. Describe how you came to be in your English class now from that point in your life. Use narrative tenses.

Which reporting verb means: Say something is not true? Say you plan to do something? Say you want someone to do something?

Change these sentences to reported speech.
Julian announced, "I'll be famous some day!"
A website claims, "The owner of Amazon is the richest man in the world."
My sister insisted, "We can sing well."

Imagine your friend took a vacation abroad. Write six assumptions about what their trip was like. Then write their reply to each one. Imagine some of your assumptions were totally correct, some were partly correct, and some were incorrect.

Look at your story from lesson 6.4. Find three ways to make it better.

PROGRESS CHECK

Can you do these things? Check (✓) what you can do. Then write your answers in your notebook.

Now I can ...	Prove it
☐ describe positive experiences.	Write three sentences about something you get satisfaction out of, something you take pleasure in doing, and something that you value.
☐ use gerunds and infinitives after adjectives, nouns, and pronouns.	Write three sentences about how you spend your free time, how you waste time, and how people often spend weekends in your town.
☐ talk about purchases.	Write two sentences about a practical purchase you've made and two sentences about a foolish purchase.
☐ use infinitives after verbs with and without objects.	Complete the sentence with your own ideas. *Last year, I persuaded* _____ .
☐ bargain for a purchase.	Write down two expressions each for (1) bargaining, (2) accepting an offer, (3) rejecting an offer.
☐ write a for-and-against essay.	Look at your essay from lesson 7.4. Find three ways to make it better.

Now I can ...	Prove it
☐ describe neatness and messiness.	Write four sentences using each of these expressions: *put sth in alphabetical order, arrange sth neatly, be jumbled up, put away.*
☐ use modal expressions with *be*.	Complete the sentences. *We're supposed to* _____ . *Don't worry. He's bound to* _____ .
☐ talk about progress.	Complete the sentences. *These days,* _____ *is going smoothly.* *I* _____ *with difficulty.*
☐ use future forms.	Write two predictions and two plans about your future.
☐ suggest and show interest in ideas.	Write your response to a suggestion to have a pool party this weekend. Then write another suggestion.
☐ write a complaint letter.	Look at your complaint letter from lesson 8.4. Find three ways to make it better.

Now I can ...	Prove it
☐ talk about luck and choice.	Complete the sentences: *I don't believe in* _____ . *Good things happened to me because of* _____ .
☐ use unreal conditionals.	Complete the sentence: *If I could* _____ , *I* _____ .
☐ comment on mistakes.	Complete the sentences to match the comment. *Recently, I* _____ . *That was a bad move.* *Yesterday, I* _____ . *I wasn't watching what I was doing.* *Once, I* _____ , *but luckily, I saw the funny side of it.*
☐ express wishes and regrets.	Complete the sentences about small things you regret. *I wish I could* _____ . *If only I* _____ . *I wish I hadn't* _____ .
☐ reassure someone about a problem.	Complete these expressions of reassurance. *It's no use* _____ . *What are you* _____ ?
☐ write an article with tips.	Look at your article from lesson 9.4. Find three ways to make it better.

PROGRESS CHECK

Can you do these things? Check (✓) what you can do. Then write your answers in your notebook.

PROGRESS CHECK

UNIT 10

Now I can ...	Prove it
☐ describe people's characteristics.	Write three sentences about the features, build, and look of a well-known person.
☐ use gerunds after prepositions.	Complete the sentence: *I believe in* _____ .
☐ describe research.	Describe some analysis you would like to do on the grocery shopping habits of your class. How would you go about the research and what would the research demonstrate?
☐ use complements of verbs describing cause and effect.	Write four sentences. Use each of these verbs once: *enable, keep from, let, protect from.*
☐ give my impressions.	Complete the sentences about what your friends are doing or thinking about. *I have a hunch that* _____ . *I get the impression that* _____ .
☐ write a professional profile.	Look at your professional profile from lesson 10.4. Find three ways to make it better.

UNIT 11

Now I can ...	Prove it
☐ describe consumer goods.	Write sentences with these words: *authentic, fireproof, illegal, second-rate.*
☐ use passive forms.	Complete the sentences with passive forms and your own ideas. *This fake watch was* _____ . *One day, goods will* _____ *by* _____ .
☐ talk about degrees of truth.	Write sentences with these words: *accurate, dishonest, exaggerated, hoax.*
☐ use passives with modals and modal-like expressions; use passive infinitives.	Complete the sentence: *Fake purses shouldn't* _____ *online.*
☐ express belief and disbelief.	Write two expressions each for expressing belief, some belief, and disbelief.
☐ write a persuasive essay.	Look at your persuasive essay from lesson 11.4. Find three ways to make it better.

UNIT 12

Now I can ...	Prove it
☐ talk about skill and performance.	Write three sentences. Use a pair of words in each sentence: *analytical/logical, athletic/trained, musical/artistic.*
☐ use adverbs with adjectives and adverbs.	Complete the sentences with an adjective or adverb and your own ideas. *I sing especially* _____ . *Soccer is an athletically* _____ *sport.*
☐ describe emotional impact.	Write four sentences. Use each of these expressions once: *get me down, leave a lasting impression on me, make my day, stress me out.*
☐ make non-count nouns countable.	Complete the sentences. *My teacher gave me two* _____ *advice.* *How many* _____ *clothing are you taking?* *Are you free for a(n)* _____ *basketball?* *Everyone needs a(n)* _____ *kindness.*
☐ describe my ambitions.	Complete the sentences with your own ideas. *I'm determined to* _____ . *I'm confident that* _____ . *But I can't say for sure that* _____ .
☐ write a review of a performance.	Look at your review from lesson 12.4. Find three ways to make it better.

156

PAIR WORK PRACTICE (STUDENT A)

1.3 EXERCISE 3C   STUDENT A

1 **Discuss smartphones with Student B. Give your opinions about the issues below.**

Issues:

- easy or difficult to set up?
- large enough screen?
- good camera?
- enough battery life?
- usefulness of pre-installed apps?

2 **Listen to Student B's opinion about laptops. Say if you agree strongly or give your own opinion on the issues.**

2.3 EXERCISE 3B   STUDENT A

1 **Student B will ask you for advice about buying a backpack. Use the information below to advise them.**

The backpack should:

1 be comfortable (very important)
2 be light
3 be the right size for you
4 have a waterproof cover
5 have a belt to go around your waist

2 **Then ask Student B for some advice about what kind of clothing to take on a skiing trip. Also ask about what kind of gloves to take. Your hands get cold easily, and you're worried about this.**

3.3 EXERCISE 3C   STUDENT A

1 **Ask Student B for a favor:**

Conversation 1

You want them to be your guest at a company party this weekend.

2 **Listen to Student B, and for each refusal, use these cues to respond:**

- the people are nice and very friendly
- there will be good food, games, and music
- bring nephew; some coworkers have kids; kid-friendly activities are planned; he'd love it

3 **Student B is going to ask you for a favor. Listen and use the cues below to respond.**

Conversation 2

- refuse; you don't really like dancing
- refuse again; you're too shy; you'd be embarrassed
- refuse again; it's probably too expensive
- accept in the end

4.3 EXERCISE 3B   STUDENT A

You're going to discuss open-plan offices (offices where all employees work in one big room). Tell your partner these advantages and disadvantages. Listen to their ideas.

Advantages:

- makes teamwork easier and increases creativity
- encourages people to work harder because they see others working

Disadvantages:

- is so noisy that it's difficult to work
- others can hear your work calls

5.3 EXERCISE 3C   STUDENT A

1 **Imagine you like swimming. Tell your partner about its good and bad sides. Say how certain you are.**

+ Being in water keeps you cool.
+ A swimsuit is usually pretty cheap.
+ It doesn't hurt your knees and ankles.

– Chlorine from the water is hard on your skin.
– You have to pay to use the pool.
– You can get an ear infection.

2 **Now listen to your partner. They will tell you about the good and bad sides of running.**

3 **Compare your sports.**

PAIR WORK PRACTICE

6.1 EXERCISE 4A STUDENT A

A **You're going to tell a story about becoming famous quickly. Read the story quickly. Then read it again and underline key points. Pay attention to verb tenses. Then tell your partner the story in your own words.**

K-Pop Rocks

South Korean band Monsta X started in 2015 and became instantly famous for their synchronized choreography and unique mix of hip-hop, pop, and electronic dance music. The band had formed when its members participated in a TV talent show. Their first U.S. performance was in Los Angeles in 2015, but it was their first studio album with the title song *Beautiful* that reached number one in the Billboard World Albums chart in March 2017. In April 2018 their Japanese single *Spotlight* received an official gold certification by the Recording Industry Association of Japan. Now almost everything they do goes viral; the fans want to know everything. Like, did you know that the band leader Shownu loves dancing, is a good swimmer, and can pick things up with his toes? And Wonho, the lead singer and dancer, has acrophobia (fear of heights).

B **Give your opinion of the stories.**

7.3 EXERCISE 5 STUDENT A

Conversation 1

Read the information. Then use these arguments while bargaining to get the best price from Student B.

Situation: You want to sell your mountain bike for $175 (your opening price can be higher).

- It's very strong and reliable.
- You've only used it for a few months. It has no damage.
- It's a popular model. Mountain bikers love it.
- You can throw in a lock for free.

Conversation 2

Situation: You want to buy a couch from Student B. Find out the price and bargain hard to get the best deal.

9.3 EXERCISE 3C STUDENT A

Conversation 1

You and Student B are close friends.

Problem: You forgot your eight-year-old nephew's birthday, and he's really upset. Tell your friend about it and ask for advice.

Conversation 2

You are a professor. Student B is your student.

Listen to Student B's problem and give advice. Reassure them, using expressions that are appropriate for your relationship.

10.3 EXERCISE 5A

Discuss the gyms, giving your impressions of each. Decide which one you'd each like to join, and why.

	Gym 1	Gym 2	Gym 3
Cost	Programs for all budgets	Student discounts	Pay by month or by year
Location	Two locations: uptown and downtown	Six convenient central locations	One convenient central location
Classes	50 classes a week: yoga, dance, swimming, diet and weight loss	Boxing, karate, judo, personal training	Fitness classes, 8 large studios, personal trainers, athletic training
Equipment	Weights, running machines	Weights, running, and cycling machines	modern equipment, wall/rope climbing
Social area	Wi-Fi, healthy snack bar	TVs, Wi-Fi, café and juice bar	Café, lounge, TVs, Wi-Fi
Pool	Large changing rooms	✗	Clean changing room, spa
Hours	Open daily 8:00 a.m. to 10:00 p.m.	Open 24/7	Open 6:00 a.m. to midnight

PAIR WORK PRACTICE (STUDENT B)

1.3 EXERCISE 3C   STUDENT B

1   **Listen to Student A's opinions about smartphones. Say if you agree strongly or give your own opinion on the issues.**

2   **Discuss laptops with Student A. Give your opinions about the issues below.**
    Issues:

- size OK?
- weight OK?

- fast enough?
- enough battery life?

- usefulness of pre-installed software?

2.3 EXERCISE 3B   STUDENT B

1   **You want to buy a new backpack. Ask Student A for some advice. Also ask about using the backpack in the rain. You're concerned that stuff inside it will get wet.**

2   **Then Student A will ask you for advice about what kind of clothing to take on a skiing trip. Use the information below to advise them.**
    Things you'll need:

1   a ski jacket (very important): thick, waterproof, strong
2   snow pants

3   ski goggles to protect your eyes (large sunglasses)
4   a warm hat

5   ski gloves: thick, waterproof, long enough to cover your wrists

3.3 EXERCISE 3C   STUDENT B

1   **Student A is going to ask you for a favor. Listen and use the cues below to respond.**
    Conversation 1

- refuse; you don't know anyone
- refuse again; you don't think you'd enjoy it

- refuse again; you might have to take care of your ten-year-old nephew that day
- accept in the end

2   **Ask Student A for a favor:**
    Conversation 2
    You want them to join the dancing class you teach (decide the kind of dancing).

3   **Listen to Student A, and for each refusal, use these cues to respond:**

- it's really fun; they will love it
- dancing will make them more confident and outgoing

- it's not expensive; you'll give a big discount

4.3 EXERCISE 3C   STUDENT B

You're going to discuss open-plan offices (offices where all employees work in one big room). Tell your partner these advantages and disadvantages. Listen to their ideas.

Advantages:

- can encourage introverted employees to interact
- can save the company money

Disadvantages:

- people tend to waste more time because it's easy to talk to others
- can cause stress, especially for employees used to having a personal office

PAIR WORK PRACTICE

5.3 EXERCISE 3   STUDENT B

1   Listen to your partner. They will tell you about the good and bad sides of swimming.

2   Now imagine you like running. Tell your partner about the good and bad sides of your sport. Say how certain you are.

+ It's a good way to get outdoors.

+ You don't have to pay to use sports facilities.

+ You can listen to music while you're running.

– In hot, cold, or wet weather, it's not much fun.

– Good running shoes can be expensive.

– It can be hard to find quiet routes without people and traffic.

3   Compare your sports.

6.1 EXERCISE 4A   STUDENT B

A   You're going to tell a story about becoming famous quickly. Read the story quickly. Then read it again and underline key points. Pay attention to verb tenses. Then tell your partner the story in your own words.

DIY Style

Wengie has been entertaining her friends for years, but she's only been a famous YouTuber for a short time. She was born in China and has lived in Australia since she was a child. She started writing one of Australia's top blogs, called the Wonderful World of Wengie, in 2011. She later started a YouTube channel that now has more than 11 million viewers. Her videos have gotten over 50 million hits. She gives tips on fashion and makes videos showing people how to make DIY (do-it-yourself) projects, such as colored pencils and holiday gifts. She had worked in a business office before she became a famous blogger and YouTuber. She gave up a well-paying job to follow her dream. Now she makes appearances around the world and is worth almost $2 million.

B   Give your opinion of the stories.

7.3 EXERCISE 5   STUDENT B

Conversation 1

Situation: You want to buy a mountain bike from Student A. Find out the price and bargain hard to get the best deal for yourself.

Conversation 2

Read the information. Then use these arguments while bargaining to get the best price from Student A.

Situation: You want to sell your large couch for $200 (your opening price can be higher).

■ It's in excellent condition, almost new.

■ It's large and seats three people comfortably.

■ It's a very stylish dark-gray color. The material is very strong.

■ You can throw in three pillows for free.

9.3 EXERCISE 3C   STUDENT B

Conversation 1

You and Student A are close friends.

Listen to Student A's problem and give advice. Reassure them, using expressions that are appropriate for your relationship.

Conversation 2

You are a student. Student A is your professor.

Problem: You have failed two tests recently. You are worried about the future of your studies. Tell your professor about it and ask for advice.

IRREGULAR VERBS

Base form	Simple past	Past participle
be	was/were	been
become	became	became
begin	began	begun
break	broke	broken
bring	brought	brought
build	built	built
buy	bought	bought
can	could	-
catch	caught	caught
choose	chose	chosen
come	came	come
cost	cost	cost
cut	cut	cut
do	did	done
draw	drew	drawn
drink	drank	drunk
drive	drove	driven
eat	ate	eaten
fall	fell	fallen
feel	felt	felt
find	found	found
fly	flew	flown
forget	forgot	forgotten
get	got	gotten
give	gave	given
go	went	gone
grow	grew	grown
have	had	had
hear	heard	heard
hit	hit	hit
keep	kept	kept
know	knew	known
leave	left	left
lend	lent	lent
lie	lay	lain

Base form	Simple past	Past participle
lose	lost	lost
make	made	made
mean	meant	meant
meet	met	met
pay	paid	paid
put	put	put
read	read	read
ride	rode	ridden
ring	rang	rung
run	ran	run
say	said	said
see	saw	seen
sell	sold	sold
send	sent	sent
show	showed	shown
sing	sang	sung
sit	sat	sat
sleep	slept	slept
speak	spoke	spoken
spend	spent	spent
stand	stood	stood
swim	swam	swum
take	took	taken
teach	taught	taught
tell	told	told
think	thought	thought
throw	threw	thrown
understand	understood	understood
wake	woke	woken
wear	wore	worn
win	won	won
write	wrote	written

This page is intentionally left blank

EVOLVE

VIDEO RESOURCE BOOK

J.L. Barksdale, Jennifer Farmer,
and Alex Paramour

5

CAMBRIDGE
UNIVERSITY PRESS

This page is intentionally left blank

CONTENTS

ACKNOWLEDGMENTS

The authors and publishers acknowledge the following sources of copyright material and are grateful for the permissions granted. While every effort has been made, it has not always been possible to identify the sources of all the material used, or to trace all copyright holders. If any omissions are brought to our notice, we will be happy to include the appropriate acknowledgments on reprinting and in the next update to the digital edition, as applicable.

Key: B = Below, BR = Below Right, CL = Center Left, CR = Center Right, T = Top, TL = Top Left, TR = Top Right.

Photograph

The following photographs are sourced from Getty Images:

Video Resource Book: p.1 (TL) Joseph Shields/Photographers Choice RF; p.1 (BL) Kameleon007/iStock/Getty Images Plus; p.1 (TC) KingWu/E+; p.1 (BC) Francisco Rama/EyeEm; p.1 (TR) Larysa Shcherbyna/iStock/Getty Images Plus; p.1 (BR) Tzido/iStock/Getty Images Plus; p.5 (T) Stocktrek Images; p.5 (B) Stocktrek Images; p.6 NASA/Handout/Getty Images News; p.9 (L) harpazo_hope/Moment Open; p.9 (R) Johner Images; p.13 (TL) Steve Debenport/E+; p.13 (TR) Erik Isakson; p.20 (L) PeopleImages/E+; p.20 (C) onurdongel/iStock/Getty Images Plus; p.20 (R) stanisluva/iStock/Getty Images Plus; p.28 Hero Images; p.32 Ariel Skelly/Digital Vision; p.33 (T) 10'000 Hours/DigitalVision; p.36 (L) Manuela/Cultura; p.36 (C) Tinpixels/iStock/Getty Images Plus; p.36 (R) skynesher/E+; p.37 (L) svetikd/E+; p.37 (C) Caiaimage/Chris Ryan; p.37 (R) Tempura/E+; p.41 (TL) mevans/E+; p.41 (TC) ipopba/iStock/Getty Images Plus; p.41 (TR) StarRForeman/iStock/Getty Images Plus; p.41 (BL) Regina Podolsky/EyeEm; p.41 (BC) Classen Rafael/EyeEm; p.41 (BR) Yagi Studio/DigitalVision; p.44 (L) Zinkevych/iStock/Getty Images Plus; p.44 (R) Andreas Mann/EyeEm; p.45 Jose Luis Pelaez Inc/DigitalVision; p.48 (L) AndreyPopov/iStock/Getty Images Plus; p.48 (CL) Sam Bloomberg-Rissman; p.48 (CR) Photographer is my life./Moment; p.48 (R) Dean Mitchell/E+; p.68 (B) fonikum/DigitalVision Vectors.

Video

Documentary videos by ITN Productions:

U1: With thanks to: Wall To Wall Media Ltd. and Screenocean; Getty Images; U2: With thanks to: NASA; ESA; Roscosmos; AP Archive; U3: With thanks to: TVF International; Getty Images; U4: With thanks to: TVF International; Getty Images; U5: With thanks to AP Archive; U6: With thanks to: AP Archive; Getty Images; U7: Licensed from Infobase; Clips and stills from TEACH used with permission from Participant Media, LLC; with thanks to: Getty Images; U8: Copyright Homemade/CMJ Productions II inc.; U9: © Twofour Broadcast Limited; U10: With thanks to: AP Archive; Getty Images; Bloomberg; U11: With thanks to AP Archive; U12: With thanks to AP Archive.

Expert speakers

Bojan Andric, Carolina Hakopian, Jacqueline Castañeda Nuñez, Lucia D'Anna, Odil Odilov, Wendy Sanchez-Vaynshteyn.

OUT OF OUR HANDS

BEFORE YOU WATCH

A   PAIR WORK   Look at each pair of pictures. Do you prefer the objects in picture A or B? Why? Which objects would you be more likely to actually buy, picture A or B? Why?

B   PAIR WORK   Match each idea to one or more products in exercise A. Explain your choices.

1   No two items are **identical**. _____

2   These are made by a **craftsperson** using traditional **production methods**. _____

3   They probably **mass-produce** these on an **assembly line**. _____

4   The design is very **innovative**. _____

5   I think just one person **assembled** this. _____

6   They have the same **functional attributes** but different designs. _____

7   It took a lot of **craftsmanship** and **man-hours** to make this. _____

C   PREDICT   Look at the picture from the video. What do you think will be discussed? Make a prediction.

WHILE YOU WATCH

A   **Watch the video. Was your prediction from exercise C on page 1 correct?**

B   **Put the facts in the order that they are mentioned in the video. Number the sentences 1–7.**

_____ Craftsmanship was replaced by mass-production, which reduced the cost of goods.

_____ Ford's cars were all identical, but other car companies gave consumers more choices.

_____ Craftspeople used to make all of the products people used in their daily lives.

_____ The first assembly line was used to build Ford cars.

_____ The motor industry started to produce cars in a variety of colors, materials, and shapes.

_____ The disadvantage of mass-production was that fewer people learned skills.

_____ Mass-production significantly reduced the time it took to assemble a car.

C   **Answer the questions based on the information in the video.**

1   How did consumers feel about the goods made by craftspeople before mass-production?

   _____

2   How did consumers feel when products made by craftspeople were replaced with mass-produced goods?

   _____

3   How did the changes at the Ford factory affect craftspeople?

   _____

4   How did people feel about mass-produced products that were all alike?

   _____

5   What has happened to car design since mass-production began?

   _____

D   **Complete the sentences with words from the video.**

1   In those days, people _____ that making anything was a
   _____ – _____ process.

2   Consumers _____ quickly and _____ these changes.

3   This idea was a huge _____ for the car industry …

4   It meant that factories like Ford's were _____ _____ producing cars in much less time.

5   Ford _____ the public's demand for options …

6   Suddenly at that point is when design was born because we had answered the _____
   _____ of moving the customer from point A to point B.

E   **What do the words in bold mean? (Circle) the best answers.**

1   Traditional, handmade products started to be replaced by less expensive, easier-to-make **versions**.

    a   completely different things   **b**   new kinds of the same things

2   After all, mass-production made things cheaper, but there was a **downside**.

    a   disadvantage   **b**   exception

3   We're going to take the skill away from **the majority of** people and we're going to invest it in a smaller group.

    a   most   **b**   a few

4   There were no skilled workers in his factories—instead they were filled with unskilled **laborers**.

    a   people who do physical work   **b**   people who design products

5   Instead of having one guy at a bench make a whole **transmission**, what if we have several guys at a bench …

    a   a machine in a factory   **b**   part of a car

6   Although Ford's production methods were efficient, he made one **crucial** mistake …

    a   extremely important   **b**   insignificant

F   **Watch the video. Summarize in your own words what the experts mean by the expressions in bold.**

1   Bob Casey, Historian at the Ford Museum, on **deskilling**:

2   J Mays, Global Head of Design at Ford Motors, on **when design was born**:

G   **Complete the concluding idea presented in the video.**

Although progress is usually a good thing for _____ , we shouldn't forget the importance of _____ and the value of _____ .

H   PAIR WORK   **Answer the questions with a partner.**

1   Is there any evidence in the video that progress is good for consumers? If so, what?

2   Is there any evidence in the video that design is important to consumers? If so, what?

3   Is there any evidence in the video that craftsmanship is important to consumers? If so, what?

AFTER YOU WATCH

A   PAIR WORK   Think of the products you have bought or would like to buy. Complete the chart. Compare your ideas with a partner.

Products that are mass-produced	Products with a great design	Products made by craftspeople

B   PAIR WORK   Think about how the products in the chart have changed in your lifetime. Complete the chart. Discuss your ideas with a partner.

Product	One change	Your feelings about the change
Phones		
Screens		
Beds		
Music software		

C   GROUP WORK   Read the quote from the video. Discuss the questions. Use the phrases below to express your opinions.

> "Progress is usually a *good* thing for consumers."

1   What progress have consumers seen over the last 20 years? Think about how and where we shop, choice of products, quality, design, and product safety.
2   Overall, do you agree or disagree with the statement?
- When it comes to …
- Looking at the big picture, I think …
- Generally speaking, …
- Overall …

D   GROUP WORK   Discuss the questions.
1   What products benefit from being identical?
2   Are you willing to pay more for products that are time-consuming to make? Why or why not? If so, which ones?
3   In some countries, consumers prefer goods that are not mass-produced. Is that true of your country? What types of products?
4   Do you personally know any skilled craftspeople? How do craftspeople run their businesses these days?
5   What changes would you like to see in the products of the future?

BEFORE YOU WATCH

A   **Look at the picture and read the text. Then match each bold word from the text with its definition.**

1 _____ : to travel in a circle around the sun, Earth, or another planet

2 _____ : the force that makes objects stay on the ground or fall to the ground

3 _____ : the fourth planet from the sun; also called "the Red Planet"

4 _____ : all the people in the world as a group

5 _____ : someone whose job is to travel into space

6 _____ : to move to and live in a place for a long time

Heading for the Stars

Science-fiction movies make life in space look pretty straightforward, don't they? You arrive at a space station in a pod. You awake from hyper-sleep and greet your fellow astronauts. Then you wander down to the dining hall for breakfast. Perhaps you stop by the gym for a workout or call your family via video link. Later that day, you and your coworkers might head out to a local planet to check on the colony of humans living there …

In real life, humans do not yet live on other planets. But did you know there have been space stations **orbiting** Earth since the 1970s? Just how close is **humankind** to being able to live in space? Take the quiz to find out how much you know.

True or false?

1	Modern space stations have air, so people can breathe without a space suit.	True / False
2	Modern space stations have **gravity**, so people can walk around.	True / False
3	Tourists can now go and stay in space hotels in Earth's orbit.	True / False
4	**Mars** is the most likely planet where humans will **settle**.	True / False
5	**Astronauts** have now visited the surface of the planet Mars.	True / False

B   PAIR WORK   Do the quiz in *Heading for the Stars*. Circle *True* or *False* for each statement.

C   PAIR WORK   **You will watch a video about the International Space Station. Look at the picture and answer the questions.**

1 Where do you think the International Space Station is?

_____

2 Why do you think it is called the *International* Space Station?

_____

3 How long do you think people stay on the Space Station? Why?

_____

D   PREDICT   **What do you think will you learn about the International Space Station from the video? Make a prediction. Check (✓) one main idea.**

a ☐ what daily life is like for astronauts on the International Space Station

b ☐ what the goals of the International Space Station project are

c ☐ what discoveries have been made on the International Space Station

WHILE YOU WATCH

A   Watch the video. Was your prediction in exercise D on page 5 correct?

B   Check (✓) the information that is mentioned in the video.

   ☐ 1 Scientists are studying human life in zero gravity on the ISS.

   ☐ 2 Scott Kelly will soon travel to Mars with some Russian cosmonauts.

   ☐ 3 Scientists have wanted to send people to Mars for a long time.

   ☐ 4 Scientists want to learn how to keep humans alive in space for longer periods of time.

C   Use your answers in exercise B to write a summary of the main purpose of the ISS project.

D   Complete the sentences with information from the video.

   1 The ISS was launched in _____ .

   2 Astronauts perform _____ on the ISS.

   3 ISS discoveries will let astronauts go _____ .

   4 The scientists have been studying _____ using rovers.

   5 Scott Kelly traveled to the ISS with two _____ .

   6 The journey from Earth to the ISS can be _____ for the astronauts.

   7 When he returned home to Texas, Scott Kelly received a _____ .

   8 What we learn about _____ on the ISS may allow everyday people to go to Mars one day.

E   PAIR WORK   Discuss the questions.

   1 What do you think *rovers* are?

   2 What do you think the difference is between an *astronaut* and a *cosmonaut*?

   3 What do you think makes the journey to the ISS *stressful*?

   4 What is meant by *a hero's welcome*, which Scott Kelly received when he returned to Earth?

F   **Put the words in order to complete the sentences from the video.**

1   The International Space Station is _____ .

(*of / achievements / one / greatest / humankind's*)

2   Their objective? To find out _____ astronauts to go farther into space than ever before.

(*allow / to / zero gravity / in / information about life / enough*)

3   It will be _____ he's ever done.

(*things / the / one / hardest / of*)

4   _____ , I think, is just missing the people, you know, your loved ones …

(*concern / my / greatest*)

5   I think _____ the space station as an orbiting vehicle that keeps humans alive in space for long periods of time.

(*most / is / the / experiment / important*)

6   I was lucky to spend _____ with _____ that are here today to greet me back on Earth.

(*incredible / people / some / an / year / incredible*)

G   **Match the pictures with the correct words in the box.**

flight control center	lift off	on their way
perform scientific experiments	successfully lands	zero gravity

International Space Station Flight Control Room
Johnson Space Center – Launch Day

H   PAIR WORK   Take turns describing what each picture shows in exercise G.

AFTER YOU WATCH

A | PAIR WORK | Discuss the questions.

1 How do you think Scott Kelly prepared to live on the ISS?

2 What do you think would be the most difficult thing about living in space for a year?

3 Do you think that Scott Kelly was able to communicate with his family while he was away? Why or why not?

B | PAIR WORK | Think about life on the ISS. How is it different from life on Earth? How might the astronauts adapt? Take notes in the chart about each topic.

	Differences from Earth	Astronauts' possible solutions/routines
Food	less variety of food more difficult to cook fewer fresh vegetables to eat not enough space to store food	eat less eat smaller meals with higher calories take vitamin tablets
Hygiene		
Sleep		
Exercise		
Communication with coworkers		
Communication with family and friends		

C | PAIR WORK | Role play the situation with a partner.

Student A

You are interviewing an astronaut (Student B) who has just returned from six months on the International Space Station. Ask questions to find out about their journey to and from space and their time on the ISS. Work together to prepare some questions before you start.

• Is there any danger of / a risk of … when you … ?

• How exactly do you … in space / in the ISS?

• What would you recommend doing if … ?

Student B

You are an astronaut who has just returned from six months on the International Space Station. Student A is a journalist. Help Student A prepare some questions to ask you. Then use your ideas from this lesson to provide information about your mission.

D | GROUP WORK | Discuss the questions.

1 In what way does Scott Kelly have to be "a tough cookie" to do his job?

2 Would you like to stay on the ISS for a year? Why or why not?

3 Why do you think traveling to Mars is the ultimate goal?

4 What goals do you think scientists will have once people reach Mars?

Documentary EVOLVE 5   Unit 2

BEFORE YOU WATCH

A   PAIR WORK   Look at the pictures and discuss the question.

Are the children, or the behaviors, shown in the pictures unusual to you? Explain your answer.

B   GROUP WORK   Discuss the questions.

1   Is the idea that boys and girls are different accepted or controversial where you live? How do you feel about that?

2   Do you think it's helpful or unhelpful for a culture to expect girls and boys to behave differently? Explain your answer.

C   Look at these expressions from the video. Do you think they are about *nature* (characteristics you are born with) or *nurture* (things you learn from the people around you)? Write them in the correct column of the chart.

biologically determined	biologically driven	differences at birth
interacting	limited by other people's expectations	shaped by the experiences we have
socializing	socially determined	socially driven
the way you are raised	treated differently	your biology
your genes	your make-up	your upbringing

Nature	Nurture

D   PREDICT   PAIR WORK   Do you think gender differences in behavior are because of nature or nurture? What do you think the video will say about this issue? Choose a prediction.

a   only nature   b   only nurture   c   both nature and nurture

WHILE YOU WATCH

A   **Watch the video. Was your prediction in exercise D on page 9 correct?**

B   **Use the words in the box to complete the paragraphs about the experiments shown in the pictures.**

accurate	estimate	pushed	slope	steeper	underestimated

Moms were asked to [1]_____ how well their babies could crawl down a [2]_____ .
While the mothers of boys were very [3]_____ about how well their babies could crawl, the mothers of
girls [4]_____ their abilities. "With a few exceptions, we found that these moms [5]_____
their boys to crawl at a slightly [6]_____ slope than the girls."

associated	fluffy	repeated	stir	trucks	went for

They give the chimpanzees some toys that are stereotypically [7]_____ with boys or with girls to see
which they prefer. "Surprisngly, the original experiment, which has been [8]_____ , did show that male
monkeys seem to prefer [9]_____ and female monkeys [10]_____ dolls." "The idea that
males, even among monkeys – even among chimpanzees – would prefer wheeled toys and females would prefer
stuffed animals … caused quite a [11]_____ when the studies came out."

   Documentary   **Photocopiable** © Cambridge University Press 2020   EVOLVE 5   Unit 3

C   **Check (✓) the sentences that are true. Correct the false statements.**

☐ 1   All the members of the public that Nathan Wallis speaks to believe that there are no differences between male and female brains.

☐ 2   It is difficult for scientists to discover whether nature or nurture is the main reason for gender differences in behavior.

☐ 3   Parents usually treat baby boys and baby girls the same way.

☐ 4   A study showed that mothers often underestimate how well their baby girls can crawl.

☐ 5   Another study showed no difference in the kinds of toys that male and female chimpanzees preferred.

☐ 6   Nathan Wallis's research makes him believe that we are shaped more by biology than by our experiences.

D   **Match the words and phrases in the box with the definitions.**

cause a stir	estimate	fluffy	go for sth	push sb to do sth	underestimate

1   to choose something: _____

2   to guess an amount, size, value, etc.: _____

3   to create a lot of interest or excitement: _____

4   soft like the wool of a sheep or the fur of a cat: _____

5   to try to make somebody else achieve something: _____

6   to think that someone is less strong or less effective than they really are: _____

E   PAIR WORK   **Answer the questions.**

1   What does the study with mothers and babies suggest about gender differences? Why?

2   What does the study with chimpanzees suggest about gender differences in human children? Why?

F   **Read the statements from the video. Match them to the experts. Write numbers.**

Nathan Mikaere-Wallis, neuroscientist: _____ _____

Dr. Annette Henderson, University of Auckland: _____ _____

Bart Ellenbroek, professor of neurology: _____ _____

1   "The idea that males … would prefer wheeled toys and females would prefer stuffed animals, that suggests it is more biologically determined rather than socially determined."

2   "I'm about to step into one of the most controversial areas in all of neuroscience."

3   "Some research suggests that at birth there are differences between males and females in terms of their brain structure."

4   "The problem is, is as soon as babies come out of the womb, they're treated differently, according to their gender."

5   "One of the biggest things confirmed for me: we really are shaped by the experiences we have and what we do throughout our lives."

G   PAIR WORK   **Discuss the quotes in exercise F. Is each statement an opinion or a fact? Do you agree with the opinions? Why or why not?**

AFTER YOU WATCH

A ⬛ PAIR WORK ⬛ **Discuss the questions.**

1 Were the results of either of the experiments in the video surprising to you? Explain why or why not.

2 In your experience, how are boys and girls treated differently by adults?

3 Do you think gender roles in your culture have changed since your parents' generation? If so, explain how.

B ⬛ GROUP WORK ⬛ **Read the topics in the chart. Write notes about how you think nature and nurture influence each one.**

	Nature	Nurture
Your physical strength		
Your intelligence		
How outgoing you are		
How hard you work		
Your skill at music or sports		

C ⬛ PAIR WORK ⬛ **Look at the list of topics in exercise B again. How could scientists determine whether nature or nurture influences those characteristics? Choose one topic and suggest experiments scientists could do. Take notes.**

D ⬛ PAIR WORK ⬛ **The topics in this lesson are considered** *controversial*. **Write questions to ask each other about four controversial topics. Take turns asking and answering the questions politely.**

Questions

1 Would you be willing to tell me _____?

2 Is there any chance you could tell me _____?

3 Do you think it would be possible for you to tell me _____?

4 I don't mean to be rude, but could you tell me _____?

Answers

• Sorry, but I wouldn't be comfortable telling you that.

• I don't mean to be rude, but can we discuss something else?

• Of course …

• I'd be happy to …

UNIT 4   THE FOREST GUARDS

BEFORE YOU WATCH

A   **PAIR WORK**   Look at the pictures. What kinds of teamwork are shown? What other types of teams do young people get involved with inside and outside of school?

B   **PAIR WORK**   Look at the words in the box. Which do you associate more with young people (*Y*)? Which do you associate more with adults (*A*)? Why?

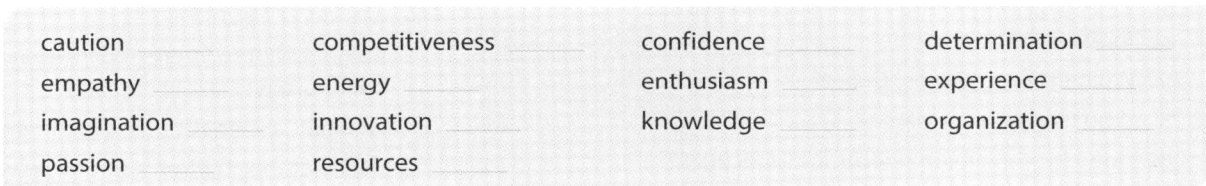

caution _____	competitiveness _____	confidence _____	determination _____
empathy _____	energy _____	enthusiasm _____	experience _____
imagination _____	innovation _____	knowledge _____	organization _____
passion _____	resources _____		

C   **PAIR WORK**   Read the statements about the participation of adults and young people in team activities. Score them from 1 (strongly agree) to 5 (strongly disagree). Compare scores with a partner and give reasons.

1   Youth teams do not need an adult to assist them in achieving something amazing. _____
2   With no adult to oversee things, there is nobody to act as a leader. _____
3   Team participants will lose focus if they are not steered in the right direction by adults. _____
4   Without adults to keep an eye on them, weaker or less confident teammates don't get the chance to contribute to the team. _____
5   Adults can enable young people to achieve things they could not achieve by themselves. _____

D   **PREDICT**   **PAIR WORK**   Look at the pictures from the video. What do you think this team of young people did together? Make a prediction.

WHILE YOU WATCH

A   **Watch the video. How accurate were your predictions in exercise D on page 13?**

B   Ⓒircle the correct words to complete the sentences about the team in the video.
   1   The team *entered / organized* a science tournament.
   2   They wanted to solve the problem of *forest fires / deforestation*.
   3   Their team *did not have / worked with* an adult coach.
   4   They designed a system called *Forest Guard / Fire Eye*.
   5   They won the *first / final* round of the tournament in Copenhagen.
   6   *LEGO® / An electronics company* helped the team build their system.

C   **Match the questions about the video with the correct answers.**

   1   What is the aim of the LEGO® League tournament? _____
   2   What type of challenge did the teams have to address for the tournament? _____
   3   What experience does the team have with forest fires? _____
   4   What exactly is Forest Guard? _____
   5   Who uses Forest Guard? _____
   6   How does the team feel about Heidi Buck? _____
   7   What has Heidi enjoyed about working with the children? _____
   8   After winning the tournament, where did the team demonstrate their idea? _____

   a   the public
   b   building trust with the children and seeing how they have matured
   c   climate problems in their communities
   d   She is very popular.
   e   to get children interested in science and technology
   f   at a global climate change conference
   g   Many of the children couldn't leave their homes for more than two weeks because of all the smoke from fires in the summer.
   h   an early wildfire detection system

D   **Complete each sentence with a word from the video.**

| broadcast | confidence | enables | implemented | overseeing |
| passionate | reality | teamwork | weaknesses | |

   1   The team felt _____ about the issue of forest fires.
   2   They _____ images of the forest to the internet.
   3   Forest Guard _____ the public to keep the forests safe.
   4   Heidi Buck was _____ the team as they developed their ideas.
   5   One of Alejandro's _____ used to be speaking in front of other people.
   6   Alejandro's _____ grew during the project.
   7   A remarkable idea and strong _____ helped the team win the tournament.
   8   A major electronics company helped them turn their ideas into _____ .
   9   Alejandro did not expect that their design would be _____ .

E   **PAIR WORK**   Read the quotes from the video. Who or what is each person talking about?

1   Aydan Pots: "… it was pretty big; it was about three miles I think." _____

2   Faith Oakes: "It uses solar-powered cameras mounted throughout the forest." _____

3   Aydan Pots: "Unlike other people, she doesn't side with anybody." _____

4   Heidi Buck: "When he first started, he wanted to be behind; he didn't want to talk; he didn't want to say anything." _____

5   Heidi Buck: "Even if someone asks a question and you know the answer, sometimes you have to learn to step back." _____

6   John Holdren: "It's a terrific way to get kids interested in science and technology and doing things that really matter." _____

7   Alejandro Vega: "It was really amazing." _____

F   **Write the captions under the correct pictures. Then number the pictures (1–6) in the order they happen in the video.**

Alejandro demonstrates confidence in his public speaking skills.

Team LEGO® Guard arrives in Copenhagen to compete in the LEGO® League competition.

The team sees their Forest Guard model at the Global Climate Change conference.

Kids from 56 countries participate in the First LEGO® League tournament.

The LEGO® Guard team does research in the field.

The team sees the first Forest Guard model.

G   **PAIR WORK**   **Look at the photos in exercise F. Imagine you are a team member and describe how you felt and what you learned during each stage of the project.**

1   researching and designing Forest Guard with Heidi Buck as your leader

2   competing with children from around the world in Copenhagen

3   exhibiting Forest Guard at an international climate change conference

4   working with a tech company to realize your design

AFTER YOU WATCH

A   PAIR WORK   Discuss the questions about the video.

1   Why do you think LEGO® wanted young people to get involved in this project?

2   How did the team need adults to assist in realizing their dreams?

3   Do you think competitions are the best way to get people to work as a team? Why or why not?

B   PAIR WORK   Explain the team's design. Then write your ideas about what they've created, why they created it, and how it works.

_____

_____

_____

_____

_____

_____

_____

_____

_____

_____

_____

_____

C   GROUP WORK   Evaluate the pros and cons of the team's design. Use the phrases below to express your ideas.

The main benefit is (that) …

Another plus is (that) …

It gives them the advantage of (-*ing* verb) …

One tricky issue is (that) …

A potential problem is (that) …

I'd be concerned (that) …

D   GROUP WORK   Discuss the questions.

1   If you could address one climate issue in your area, what would it be? Why?

2   Do you have any ideas about how you could address that issue? If so, what could you do?

3   Who would you want on your team and why?

4   Would you include young people on your team? Why or why not?

     EVOLVE 5   Unit 4

TECHNOLOGY: OBSTACLES AND OPPORTUNITIES

BEFORE YOU WATCH

A [PAIR WORK] What technology is used for these functions? Add more ideas to the mind maps.

a *CCTV cameras*

(improving security)

b *online shopping*

(making shopping more convenient)

c *hearing aids*

(assisting people with disabilities)

B [PAIR WORK] Look at your ideas from exercise A. Which types of technology have made the biggest difference to people's lives? How?

C Match the words and phrases to the definitions.

1 implant
2 3D printer
3 prosthetic limb
4 sensor
5 microchip
6 obstacle

a a very small object containing electronic circuits that can perform particular operations
b an object or device that is put into the body through a medical procedure
c something that blocks you so that it is difficult to go forward
d a device attached to a computer that makes solid objects from plastic
e an artificial arm or leg
f a device that detects and reacts to an aspect of the environment (e.g., light, heat, movement)

D [PREDICT] Look at the pictures from the video. What technological innovations do you think they show? Match them with the functions a–c in exercise A to make predictions about the video.

WHILE YOU WATCH

A   **Watch the video. Were your predictions in exercise D on page 17 correct? Complete the sentence starter below for each picture.**

The picture shows …

B   PAIR WORK   **Check (✓) the video's main message about the innovations it describes.**

☐ These innovations will be useful, providing that certain issues can be resolved.

☐ These innovations are likely to become very popular in the next few years.

☐ These innovations could do more harm than good.

C   **Check (✓) the statements that are true. Correct the false ones.**

☐ **1** At Epicenter in Sweden, all workers have to get a wrist implant.

☐ **2** The robot trucks are used to deliver food.

☐ **3** Local authorities are eager to introduce robot trucks into cities.

☐ **4** A wrist implant might contain information about how much time the wearer spends working.

☐ **5** Colby Viator finds it difficult to pick things up with his right hand.

☐ **6** 3D-printed limbs need to be replaced frequently because they break easily.

D **Answer the questions.**

1 Why does Sandra Haglof say the wrist implant will be a good thing for her?

_____

2 How do the robot trucks benefit customers?

_____

3 How do some pedestrians feel about the robot trucks?

_____

4 What does Ben Libberton want to know about the data collected by the wrist implants?

_____

5 Why is it expensive to provide children with prosthetic limbs?

_____

E **Complete the sentences with the correct forms of the pairs of verbs in the box. Decide whether the active or passive form is needed.**

benefit / use	continue / improve	let / drive down
mean / help	permit / use	use / navigate

1 It _____ sensors and cameras _____ the sidewalk.

2 The vehicle helps save money on deliveries, which means more people can _____ from _____ it.

3 It _____ us _____ the cost of delivery by 80 to 90 percent over time.

4 This means local authorities may not _____ them _____ at all.

5 Technology is _____ us. But in some areas, it comes with disadvantages.

6 Providing that new advances keep users in mind, technology can—and will— _____ _____ the lives of people in many different ways.

F PAIR WORK **Complete the chart with the ideas you can remember from the video.**

	Pros (+)	Cons (–)
Wrist implants		
Robot delivery trucks		
3D-printed limbs		

G PAIR WORK **What other pros and cons might each form of technology have for its users and for other people? Add your ideas to the chart.**

AFTER YOU WATCH

A **PAIR WORK** Complete each sentence with one or more of the options in the box. Then compare your opinions, giving reasons to support them.

wrist implants	robot delivery trucks	3D-printed limbs	none of the innovations

In my opinion, …

1 _____ will be widely used ten years from now.

2 _____ will be controversial.

3 _____ will change the lives of individuals.

4 _____ will change society as a whole.

B **PAIR WORK** Read this quote from the video. Then answer the questions.

> "Providing that new advances keep users in mind, technology can—and will—continue to improve the lives of people in many different ways."

1 How much do you agree with this statement?

2 How can developers "keep users in mind"? Do you think they are motivated to do so?

3 Should robot trucks be banned from public roads and sidewalks? Why or why not? Should any other forms of technology be banned or restricted by law?

4 Should governments, schools, and employers protect people from the effects of technology? If so, how might they do this?

C **GROUP WORK** Hold a debate about another form of technology. In a small group, choose one of the ideas below, or come up with your own idea.

Group A

You are eager to use the technology and believe it could benefit individuals and society.

Group B

You are against the technology and believe it could harm individuals and society.

fitness trackers · voice-activated virtual assistants · facial recognition technology

D **GROUP WORK** Recall the debates you had in exercise C. Can you think of a compromise that might relieve people's concerns about the technology? Use conditional forms in your group discussion.

I'd only be willing to use it if …

It could be useful providing that …

GLOSSARY

compromise (*n*) an agreement in an argument in which the people involved reduce their demands or change their opinion in order to agree

A MIRACLE ON THE HUDSON

BEFORE YOU WATCH

A   Think of some people who you consider to be heroes. They can be people you know, celebrities, public figures, or fictional characters. Make a list.

B   PAIR WORK   Compare your list with your partner's list. What do your heroes have in common? Together, complete the definition in your own words.

> **hero** *noun* /ˈhɪroʊ/
> a person who _____

C   Look at these words and phrases from the video. Check (✓) the ones you understand. Circle the ones you need help with and look up their meanings.

drown	flock of geese	freeze	glided	headlines
heroic	Hollywood producers	miracle	movie	pilot
rescued river	take-off			

D   PREDICT   The words in exercise C and the picture relate to an event that happened in 2009. Answer the questions with your predictions.

Captain Chesley "Sully" Sullenburger
Pilot

1   Do you know (or can you guess) the story that the words and picture relate to?

2   Who is Captain Sullenberger, and why is he considered to be a hero?

WHILE YOU WATCH

A   Watch the video. Were your predictions in exercise D on page 21 correct? What is the incident called? What is the pilot called?

B   PAIR WORK   Why is the incident known as the "Miracle on the Hudson"?

C   Number the events in order (1–10). Then watch again and check.

_____ The pilot glided the plane onto the Hudson River.

_____ The passengers waited on the wings of the plane.

_____ The story was made into a Hollywood movie.

_____ Both of the plane's engines failed.

_____ The plane took off from LaGuardia Airport.

_____ The pilot appeared on TV talk shows.

_____ A flock of geese flew into the plane.

_____ Boats came to rescue the passengers.

_____ The story made headlines around the world.

_____ The plane started going down fast.

D   Complete the sentences with information from the video.

1   The airplane was carrying _____ people in total.

2   While they were waiting for help, the passengers had to stand in water that was very cold and _____-deep.

3   When Linda Han looked out of the airplane window, she saw _____.

4   According to Captain Sullenberger, the first rescue boats arrived within _____ minutes.

5   The incident was later made into a movie called _____, starring Tom Hanks.

Photocopiable © Cambridge University Press 2020   EVOLVE 5   Unit 6

E   Complete the bold collocations (1–5) with nouns and match them to the definitions (a–e).

1   But that wasn't **the whole** _____ . _____
2   They were not **out of** _____ yet. _____
3   Sully … insisted that the result of the crash was **a team** _____ . _____
4   Soon Captain Sully was **in high** _____ . _____
5   The rescue was eventually turned into a fascinating movie … with actor Tom Hanks playing the **title** _____ . _____

a   main part
b   safe
c   a full explanation of what happened
d   wanted by a lot of people
e   thanks to the actions of a group of people

F   Complete what Tom Hanks says about Captain Sullenberger with the words in the box. Then explain the meaning of the bold phrases in your own words.

living   criterion   harm

"Well, you know, look, I think heroes are people who voluntarily put themselves in ¹_____ 's way. Uh … and I think by that … by that ²_____ , you could say anybody who flies an airplane for a ³_____ cheats death somehow."

G   Match the speech bubbles to the people in the box. Then rewrite the statements in reported speech using the reporting verbs you learned in Unit 6.

Captain Sullenberger   Hollywood producers   Linda Han   the narrator   Tom Hanks

1   _____   Anyone who voluntarily puts themselves in harm's way is a hero.

2   _____   We're going to make a movie about Captain Sullenberger.

3   _____   The plane was going down fast.

4   _____   I can't take all the credit for saving the passengers.

5   _____   The passengers will forever be linked to each other.

AFTER YOU WATCH

A   PAIR WORK   Based on the information in the video and your own assumptions, how do you think Captain Sullenberger felt about the incident afterward? How do you think the passengers felt?

He / They must have felt …

I suppose / assume they felt …

B   PAIR WORK   Do you agree that Captain Sullenberger is a hero for the reason that Tom Hanks gives? Why or why not? Is Captain Sullenberger a hero according to the definition you wrote in exercise B on page 21?

C   PAIR WORK   Role play the situation below. Then switch roles.

Student A

You're Linda Han or Captain Sullenberger and are going to be interviewed for a magazine. Think about how you felt at the time of the incident and afterward. Prepare to answer the interviewer's questions.

Student B

You're a magazine journalist and are going to interview Linda Han or Captain Sullenberger. Think of some interesting questions to ask about the "Miracle on the Hudson."

D   PAIR WORK   Why do you think Hollywood producers thought the "Miracle on the Hudson" would be a good subject for a movie? Would you like to see the movie? Why or why not?

E   PAIR WORK   Think of another movie or a TV series you have seen that was based on real people or events. Answer the questions.

1   What happened in the movie or series? Give a summary of the story using narrative tenses.

2   How accurately do you think it portrayed the people and events?

3   Did you know anything about the subject before you saw the movie? How did that affect your experience of watching it? Did the movie change your ideas in any way?

BEFORE YOU WATCH

A   PAIR WORK   Describe the best teacher you ever had. What made him or her a good teacher? Did he or she make a difference in your life? If so, how?

B   PAIR WORK   Read the text. How is it different from the education system in your country or other countries that you know about?

High School Education in the U.S.

In the U.S., there is no standard **nationwide** exam that students take at the age of 18. Instead, there are different types of courses that **high school** students can choose from according to their **educational goals**. Students who want to go on to study at **college** often take **honors classes** or an **Advanced Placement (AP) course**, both of which are more difficult than regular classes. At the end of an AP course, students take a challenging final exam. Students who **score highly** on this exam are more likely to get a place at college.

C   Match the definitions to the bold words in the text in exercise B.

1   a school for U.S. students ages 14–18   ....

2   two types of academically challenging classes   ....

3   a general word for a place of higher education   ....

4   a person's plans for further study or training   ....

5   get a good grade   ....

6   used throughout the country   ....

D   Read the introduction to the video. What does *underprivileged* mean?

This is Joel Laguna. He teaches Advanced Placement world history and English to a group of 43 underprivileged high school students who dream of going to college.

E   PREDICT   What do you think Joel Laguna will say are the rewards and challenges of teaching his students? Take notes in the chart.

Rewards	Challenges

WHILE YOU WATCH

A   Watch the video. Compare the ideas in the video with your predictions from exercise E on page 25. Add new ideas to the chart.

B   How would Joel describe his students? Check (✓) the best option.

☐ They're intelligent but not very ambitious.

☐ They're motivated but need to develop their writing skills.

☐ They're good at writing but not very interested in his subjects.

C   (Circle) the correct answers to the questions.

1   Why does Mixtle want to go to college?

a   to have new experiences   b   to achieve her career goals

2   How does Joel think he can make a difference in his students' lives?

a   by making them more confident   b   by giving them new skills

3   What do the students all say about Joel's classes?

a   They're fun.   b   They're challenging.

4   According to Joel, how do his students compare to many others in the U.S.?

a   Their level of academic achievement is lower.   b   They're more motivated.

5   How does Joel feel about his students in the days before the exam?

a   worried that they won't be ready   b   confident that they'll do very well

6   How many of Joel's students pass the exam?

a   more than 50 percent   b   around 30 percent

D   Complete the phrases in bold to have the same meaning as the phrases in parentheses. Use the words from the box. There are five extra words.

comes	cream	essay	goes	own
paid	paper	selves	took	top

1   It's clear they have potential and that's where Joel _____ **in**. (*has an important role*)

2   Do you get **the** _____ **of the crop** because you're AP world history? (*the best students*)

3   I feel a lot of my students are able to get the content, but then they're not able to explain that **on** _____ . (*in writing*)

4   Now the students **are on their** _____ . (*don't have anyone to help them*)

5   All that hard work and those sleepless nights _____ **off**. (*were worthwhile*)

E   Watch the video. Complete the sentences with adjectives and adverbs formed from the words in parentheses. Use the appropriate prefixes and suffixes.

1   Not passing the _____ final exam may decrease their chances of achieving their educational goal. (**challenge**)

2   Joel is determined to have one of the most demanding and _____ classes in the school. (**engage**)

3   _____ , as their final exam approaches, the students are not progressing as much as Joel would like. (**fortunate**)

4   They are _____ not where they need to be in terms of writing right now. (**definite**)

5   Despite the challenges, this _____ is an amazing achievement for Joel and his class. (**true**)

F   PAIR WORK   Read the quote. What do the words *huddle* and *warriors* mean? Watch the video for context, and then add the missing words.

"OK. ¹_____ or fail, do not ²_____ up. Is this clear? ... Huddle, huddle, huddle. I'm really ³_____ of you. I ⁴_____ you guys. Do amazing and remember: WE ARE WARRIORS!"

G   GROUP WORK   Look again at Joel's quote in exercise F. What techniques does he use to motivate his students before the exam? What else might teachers try to motivate their students? Which techniques do you think are the most effective?

AFTER YOU WATCH

A **PAIR WORK** To what extent do you think each of these factors determines academic success? How? Can you add any more ideas to the list?

career goals	classmates	emotions and attitudes	genes
languages	money	motivation	parents
past experiences	personality	school facilities	teachers

B **PAIR WORK** Circle your top three most important factors for academic success from exercise A. Then compare your ideas with your partner.

C What do you think it means to be a good teacher? Complete the sentence with your own ideas.

A good teacher is someone who …

D Read the opinion statements. For each statement, check (✓) whether you *strongly agree* (SA), *agree* (A), are *not sure* (NS), *disagree* (D), or *strongly disagree* (SD). Think of reasons and examples to support your opinions.

	SA	A	NS	D	SD
1 We should value teachers according to the difference they make in their students' lives, not according to exam results.					
2 Teachers who work in underprivileged areas should be paid more than teachers who work in wealthy districts.					
3 Universities and colleges should do more to encourage students from all backgrounds to apply.					
4 Exams are the best way to measure a student's abilities.					
5 High school students should be put into separate classes according to their level of ability.					
6 Academic ability can't be learned; people are either born with it or they aren't.					

E **GROUP WORK** Compare and explain your opinions with your group. Do you think your opinions have been shaped by your own educational experiences? Explain your answer.

UNIT 8 — AN ICONIC SIDE PROJECT

BEFORE YOU WATCH

A PAIR WORK Read the article and answer the questions.

Turning Dreams into Reality!

Many of us have a secret side project that we dream of accomplishing, whether it's a book we'd love to write, a band we'd love to form, or a house we'd love to build. Yet too few of us manage to transform our dreams into action. So how can you become one of the people who do? Here are our top tips:

- [ ] **A** Be ambitious. Think big!
- [ ] **B** Be realistic. Know how long it'll take.
- [ ] **C** Be determined. Don't worry about what other people think.
- [ ] **D** Be prepared. Make sure you'll have enough money to complete the project.
- [ ] **E** Be resourceful. Find creative solutions to problems.
- [ ] **F** Be knowledgeable. Make sure you have all the necessary skills and knowledge.
- [ ] **G** Be confident. Believe in yourself!

1 Do you have a side project that you would like to accomplish one day?

2 How useful do you think the advice in the article is?

3 What other tips can you add to the list?

B Match the words and phrases in the box to the definitions.

building permit (*n*) demolish (*v*) discard (*v*) expansive (*adj*)
construction (*n*) icon (*n*) redevelopment (*n*) scratch your head (*v*)

1 _____ : an official document allowing you to build something

2 _____ : the work of building something

3 _____ : the improvement of buildings that are in bad condition

4 _____ : covering a large area

5 _____ : a well-known person or item that is seen as a symbol of an idea, a way of life, etc.

6 _____ : throw away; get rid of

7 _____ : look puzzled; show that you don't understand something

8 _____ : destroy (a building)

C PREDICT PAIR WORK The words in exercise B all relate to an American couple's interesting side project. Can you guess what kind of project it is?

WHILE YOU WATCH

A   Watch the video. Was your prediction in exercise C on page 29 correct? What do you think about the Wings' project?

B   PAIR WORK   Check (✓) the pieces of advice in the article in exercise B on page 29 that the Wings followed.

C   Check (✓) whether the statements are true (*T*), false (*F*), or not mentioned (*NM*) in the video. Correct the false ones.

	T	F	NM
1 The Wings expected the castle to take about ten years to build.			
2 They finished the castle in the 1990s.			
3 It was difficult to get free building materials in the 1970s.			
4 Pete already had a lot of experience with construction work when he started building the castle.			
5 Over time, the Wings' friends and neighbors changed their minds about the castle project.			
6 Pete and Toni eventually made a lot of money from their project.			

D   **Who expresses each idea in the video? Write *T* (Toni), *P* (Pete), *V* (Vincent), or *M* (Margaret).**

1   The idea for the castle was inspired by the local scenery.   _____

2   We used building materials that other people had thrown away.   _____

3   Only 15 percent of the material used to build the castle was new.   _____

4   Pete seemed to have an instinct for construction work.   _____

5   I thought the project was very strange.   _____

6   Pete became a local celebrity.   _____

E   **Complete the phrasal verbs with the correct particles and prepositions.**

1   Little by little, the castle started to **come** _____ , thanks to Pete and Toni's hard work.

2   He'll start out sometimes, and I'll think, like, I don't know what he's doing now and it's really weird and I don't think this is going to **work** _____ .

3   He's at a point now where, you know, he's proven himself. He **won** people _____ .

4   But guests should be careful: they just might be inspired to start a side project of their own, which isn't a bad thing, as long as it's something they could **look** _____ and be proud of in the end.

F   PAIR WORK   **Match the definitions to the phrasal verbs in exercise E.**

1   a phrasal verb that means *to think about something that happened in the past* _____

2   a phrasal verb that means *to start to look complete* _____

3   an adjective that means *strange* or *bizarre* _____

4   a phrasal verb that means *to end in a satisfactory way* _____

5   an adverb phrase that means *gradually* _____

6   a phrasal verb that means *to convince someone that you're right* _____

AFTER YOU WATCH

A ☐ PAIR WORK ☐ Read the quote from the video. Do you think the Wings' attitude is irresponsible or inspiring? Why?

> "We had no money to do this. We just had lots of ideas and energy, and really, the thought that we could do it."

B ☐ PAIR WORK ☐ Read the statements. What is stopping these people from starting their side projects? Do you identify with any of these reasons? Do you think they're valid reasons not to start a project? How might the people overcome these obstacles?

1 I really want to try yoga, but I'm studying for a degree and don't have the energy to start anything new at the moment.

2 I dream of learning to play the guitar, but I've got a full-time job and two young children. I guess I need to accept that isn't possible right now.

3 I'd love to start a blog, but what if no one reads it? Or worse, what if people leave critical comments?

4 It's always been my ambition to run a marathon, but I'm unemployed at the moment, and gym membership is so expensive.

5 I have an interesting idea for a novel, but I can't seem to start writing it. I'm scared that it won't be as good in reality as it is in my head.

6 I've always wanted to learn Italian, but I got terrible grades in French at school. I just don't think I have any talent for languages.

C ☐ PAIR WORK ☐ Role play the situation below. Then switch roles.
Student A

Choose one of the people from exercise B. Explain your problem to your life coach, Student B, giving more information about your situation and how you feel.

Student B

You are Student A's life coach. What advice and practical suggestions can you offer?

D ☐ GROUP WORK ☐ Imagine that you and some classmates have decided to take on a building project together. Discuss the following points in your group:

- what the building will be used for
- what your building will look like (size, layout, style of architecture, decoration, etc.)
- where it will be located
- what materials and skills you will need
- what problems you might encounter and how you will solve them

E ☐ GROUP WORK ☐ Present your plans to the rest of the class. Prepare some questions to ask about other groups' projects.

Photocopiable © Cambridge University Press 2020

BEFORE YOU WATCH

A   **PAIR WORK**   **Look at the picture and answer the questions. What kinds of problems do you think the businesswoman has? Who do you think she could be calling? Why?**

B   **Read the text. Match the phrases in bold to the definitions.**

Back on the Road to Success

I've always been good at cooking, so I decided to operate my own food truck as soon as I left school. After two failed starts, I found myself in a really **financially awkward situation**. So instead of trying again, I made a **deliberate decision** to invest the money I had left in a business course. My time at college was a **life-changing experience**. It only took a year for me to understand the mistakes I had made and to **get me on the right path** again. Now things are going well for me, but I **learned the hard way** that it's important to get some basic understanding of how to **get your margin** in your industry before you open a business.

1 _____ : something that happens that strongly affects your future
2 _____ : to discover what you need to know through failure or by making mistakes
3 _____ : to make enough profit on a product or service to be successful in business
4 _____ : to cause a set of actions that lead to the correct result or a goal
5 _____ : a time when you have money problems
6 _____ : a planned choice

C   **Complete the sentences with the expressions in the box.**

call in	change direction	passed away	puts it into practice
set him on the path	thanks to his dedication	turned her life around	

1   It was great advice, and I'm sure things will improve as soon as he _____.
2   I can't believe how much happier she is now! She's completely _____.
3   Sadly, my brother _____ last year after a long illness.
4   The school had to _____ a psychologist for advice on what to do.
5   It was his experiences in the education system that _____ to becoming a politician.
6   She was once an accountant, but she decided to _____ and became an architect.
7   _____ and years of hard work, he is now able to make a profit in the restaurant business.

D   **PREDICT**   **Look at the picture and read the quote from the video. Make predictions to answer the questions.**

> "After finding himself in a financially awkward situation, Pratik has decided to call in the experts."

1   Who do you think Pratik is? _____
2   What kind of experts do you think he's calling in? _____
3   What do you think Pratik wants the experts to do? _____

WHILE YOU WATCH

A   Watch the video. Were your predictions in exercise D on page 33 correct?

B   Check (✓) the sentences that are true. Correct the false ones.

☐ 1   Pratik has always been in the restaurant business.

_____

☐ 2   Business used to be good at Pratik's restaurant.

_____

☐ 3   Alex and Oliver are running Pratik's restaurant for him.

_____

☐ 4   The price of Pratik's lamb dish was too expensive.

_____

☐ 5   The chef has written a new menu.

_____

☐ 6   The changes at the restaurant seem to have been a success.

_____

C   Answer the questions about the video.

1   When did Pratik decide to open a restaurant? _____

2   How soon did the business start to have problems? _____

3   Why is Alex and Oliver's advice important for Pratik and his family? _____

4   What are two aspects of the business Pratik needed to change? _____

5   How did Pratik feel before opening the restaurant for a busy night? _____

6   What positive feedback did the head chef get from the experts? _____

D   Complete excerpt from the video. Then choose the meaning of each phrase.

"We had a really good, sort of, two- or three-month period where I thought, do you know,
we're ¹_____ _____ _____ , we'll be fine.
And then ²_____ _____ _____ ."

1   ☐ The business was financially secure.   2   ☐ Customers suddenly stopped coming.

☐ The business had no chance of success.   ☐ The restaurant had customers but no money.

E   Watch the video. Who says each thing? Check (✓) the correct people.

	Pratik Master	The head chef	Oliver Peyton	Alex Polizzi
1 We'll start a restaurant!				
2 Business has been, er, poor to awful.				
3 The scary thing for me was the lamb.				
4 This menu, I haven't seen yet.				
5 We want tonight to go fantastic.				
6 I have to admit, I'm pleased.				

F   **Match what the speakers said (1–6) to the reason they said it (a–f).**

1   We'll start a restaurant! _____

2   Business has been, er, poor to awful. _____

3   The scary thing for me was the lamb. _____

4   To be honest, this menu, I haven't seen yet. _____

5   We want tonight to go fantastic. _____

6   I have to admit, I'm pleased. _____

a   asking his opinion.

b   explaining why he called in the experts

c   recalling conversations with his mother

d   discussing Pratik's progress

e   feeling surprised the dish was so cheap

f   explaining why he was nervous

G   **Complete each sentence with a word from the video.**

1   Pratik Master made the deliberate decision to change _____ and open his own restaurant.

2   "Five years ago my mom _____ away and we'd always said we'll start a restaurant."

3   Alex Polizzi is a hotel _____, checking rooms' quality and cleanliness.

4   Alex and Oliver need to help _____ the restaurant around.

5   "You should be selling this dish at around 34, 35 pounds, something in that variety to be getting your _____."

6   After lots of hard work putting the new ideas into _____, the first evening is a success.

7   Thanks to some good advice and his own _____, the restaurant is back on the right path.

H   [**PAIR WORK**]   **Number (1–5) the events from Pratik's life in the order they happened to him.**

_____ finding himself in a financially awkward situation

_____ learn things the hard way

_____ life-changing experience

_____ back on the right path

_____ deliberate decision

AFTER YOU WATCH

A PAIR WORK Complete the sentences with the correct forms of the verbs in parentheses. Do you agree with the ideas?

1 If Pratik's mother hadn't _____ (pass) away, he wouldn't _____ (start) the restaurant.

2 If Pratik had _____ (learn) about the restaurant business before he opened, he wouldn't _____ (need) the experts.

3 If Pratik had _____ (price) his menu correctly in the first place, he could _____ (make) a sensible margin.

4 If Pratik hadn't _____ (volunteer) to be on the show, he would _____ (have to) shut the restaurant down.

5 If Oliver Peyton hadn't _____ (tell) the chef about the new menu, nobody would have _____ (do) it and the evening would have _____ (be) a disaster.

B PAIR WORK Discuss the questions.

1 Why do you think Pratik started a business at the time he did?

2 What other kinds of changes do you think the experts recommended?

3 What's your opinion of Pratik as a business owner?

4 What do you think could help Pratik's business succeed in the long term?

C GROUP WORK Look at the pictures and read the captions. What could cause problems for businesses like these?

1
a food truck with no customers

2
a salesperson selling a health food or drink product with no sales

3
a web start-up marketing international food recipe boxes with no profit

D PAIR WORK Role play the following situation. Choose one of the small businesses in exercise C.

Student A

You are a small business owner. You are very worried about your failing business. You are going to consult an expert, Student B, about your business problems. You need to tell the story of your business.

How long have you been open?

What exactly do you sell?

What silly mistakes do you think you've made?

What bad luck do you think you've had?

Useful language:

If only I'd / I hadn't …

I wish I'd / I hadn't …

Student B

You are an expert business consultant. You need to help Student A with their struggling business, reassure them, and tell them how to improve the situation.

What advice can you give the business owner?

Useful language:

You're not the only one who's done that.

We all make mistakes.

That's the way it goes.

It's not that bad.

It could have been worse.

   EVOLVE 5 Unit 9

BEFORE YOU WATCH

A [PAIR WORK] Look at the pictures and answer the questions. Why do you think each person is taking a selfie? In what other situations do people often take selfies? What kinds of selfies do you take? Who do you share them with?

B [PAIR WORK] Read the text. Match the expressions in bold to their definitions.

How to Become a Social Media Influencer

You don't need to be a glamorous model or a business guru to become a social media influencer. Many influencers are ordinary people who have **used social media to their advantage** and **engaged** an audience of followers. You too can build an online **presence**. Start by tweeting and blogging about topics that interest you —and posting selfies and videos. You need to create a personal **vibe** to separate yourself from the pack. This kind of **self-promotion** helps to build a positive **image** so that others will strive to be like you. Success won't happen **overnight** though. When you have enough followers, you can **leverage** your online presence to earn a living. When you build your personal brand, companies will pay you to promote their products!

1 _____ : to use something you have, such as influence, to achieve something new or better
2 _____ : the act of advertising your own person
3 _____ : a quality that makes people notice or admire you, even when you are not speaking
4 _____ : the way that people think you are
5 _____ : to interest someone in something and keep them thinking about it
6 _____ : to use an online presence to help you succeed
7 _____ : (informal) the mood or character of something
8 _____ : suddenly and unexpectedly

C [PAIR WORK] Read the text again and discuss the meaning of these phrases. Do you try to do any of these things? How exactly?

1 build a positive image
2 separate yourself from the pack
3 leverage your online presence
4 build your personal brand

D [PREDICT] [PAIR WORK] What does it mean to *leave a trail*? What do you think a *digital trail* is? Predict how these will be described in the video.

WHILE YOU WATCH

A   **Was your prediction in exercise D on page 37 correct?**

B   **Number the ideas (1–6) in the order they happen in the video.**

_____ Selfies are a way for people to show they are special.

_____ It's important to manage your digital trail.

_____ Selfies are a useful tool for celebrities.

_____ A good online profile can help you get a job.

_____ Your digital trail can affect your daily life.

_____ Students should be aware of their digital trail.

C   **Complete the sentences with words or phrases from the video.**

1   Selfies are powerful tools that can help an individual become more _____.

2   Like celebrities, people who post selfies want to show how _____ their lives are.

3   An online presence isn't just about _____ and fame.

4   College _____ _____ decide who will study at their institution.

5   College applicants can also use social media to their _____.

6   Social media and _____ are also a factor when it comes to employment.

7   LinkedIn has become such a powerful tool that even well-known celebrities use it to build their _____ _____.

D   **Answer the questions about the video.**

1   Why is it important to manage your digital trail? _____
_____

2   What is a benefit of sharing information on social media? _____
_____

3   Why do people want to appear glamorous online? _____
_____

4   What are college admissions officers doing more these days? _____
_____

5   What do students need to be aware of about their digital trail? _____
_____

6   What does LinkedIn allow jobseekers to do?
_____
_____
_____
_____

7   What should you do before you post something
online? _____
_____
_____

Photocopiable © Cambridge University Press 2020   EVOLVE 5   Unit 10

E   **Match the people with the opinions they express in the video.**

1   Alyssa Lipsky _____

2   Murray Weissman _____

3   Martha Blevins Allman _____

4   Meghan Stauts _____

a   thinks social media profiles give her/him information that college applications don't
b   recommends that college applicants use social media to show their interest in colleges
c   believes people who take selfies want to show they are different from everybody else
d   believes selfies can help unknown people become famous

F   **Complete the quotes from the video. Use expressions in the box.**

fill in	interact	set up	wield

1   "Selfies _____ power."
2   "They want to _____ what separates me from the rest of the pack."
3   "Using social media gives admissions officers just another tool to _____ the blanks."
4   "_____ with that college that you want to go to on Instagram."

G   **Check (✓) the best summary of the ideas in the video.**

☐ 1   If you don't manage your digital trail, it can cause serious harm to your future.
☐ 2   Managing your digital trail allows you to control the way other people see you, and this is increasingly important to your future.
☐ 3   Selfies can improve your reputation as well as damage it, so make sure you manage your digital trail!

AFTER YOU WATCH

A   PAIR WORK   Read the quotes from the video. How do you feel about each use of online profiles? Why?

1   **People who post selfies**: "They want to set up what separates me from the rest of the pack … This is where I went; this is what I ate; this is where I'm going … and they want to set themselves apart."

2   **College admissions:** "Using social media gives colleges just another tool to fill in the blanks, to get a clearer picture of a student."

3   **College admissions:** "Interact with that college that you want to go to on Instagram. Comment on their pictures. If you go to visit a college, post a picture of your visit."

4   **A professional online profile:** "LinkedIn … helps me really create my vibe. It gives a visual to people: what I'm all about, what my brand is all about, and what I strive to be."

B   PAIR WORK   Some people have two social media profiles on the same platform. Why is this? How would you expect them to be different? Complete the chart.

Platform	Profile 1	Profile 2
LinkedIn		
Instagram		
Facebook		
Twitter		

C   **Complete the statements with your own ideas.**

1   Having two LinkedIn accounts can allow _____ .

2   Having two Instagram accounts can help _____ .

3   Having two Facebook accounts can prevent _____ .

4   Having two Twitter accounts can enable _____ .

D   GROUP WORK   Discuss the questions.

1   If you were a recruiter or an admissions officer and you could not find an individual's online profiles, what impression would you get of that person?

2   If you were a recruiter or an admissions officer, what kind of online presence would impress you the most? Think about applicants for these roles:

-   a program manager for an art gallery
-   a high school physics teacher
-   an MBA student
-   an international relations undergraduate

3   What would a recruiter or an admissions officer in an area of work that interests you be looking for in an online profile? How well does your own profile reflect that?

UNIT 11 — DISHONEST AND DANGEROUS

BEFORE YOU WATCH

A **PAIR WORK** Look at the pictures. Discuss the questions. What brands do you trust to be good quality for each type of product? Why? Which sellers would you trust to buy these products from?

motor vehicles

digital technology

formal wear

perfumes and cosmetics

medication and food supplements

sporting goods

B **Circle** the correct definition for each expression in bold.

1 Counterfeiting **comes at a high price** for criminals who are caught.

   a is very expensive   **b** causes unwelcome consequences

2 If you **have an appetite for a bargain**, online marketplaces are a great place to buy products.

   a want to get a good deal   **b** want to buy the latest things

3 Counterfeiters know what they do is illegal, but they keep making fake products **regardless**.

   a by mistake   **b** despite what they know

4 I thought my new cell phone was **the real deal,** but it was a fake!

   a a genuine product   **b** the cheapest product

5 **Authorities** want to know about anyone selling dangerous products.

   a shops and other businesses   **b** the police or government officials

6 When I exercised **vigorously,** my $200 shoes fell apart. I want my money back!

   a slowly and carefully   **b** hard and fast

C Complete the sentences with the correct words in the box.

> choking   electrocuted   hazard   lead   overheat

1 Leaving things on the stairs is a _____ – someone could get injured.

2 The ingredients arsenic and _____, which we now know to be poisonous, were commonly used in household paints.

3 Electrical devices are designed to stop working if they _____.

4 You need to be careful when you use electrical devices near water – you might get _____.

5 You can't give a toy with small parts to a baby – there's a risk of _____.

WHILE YOU WATCH

A **Put the topics in the order (1–5) they are mentioned in the video.**

a _____ examples of modern security measures

b _____ the reason people buy counterfeit goods

c _____ the danger of counterfeit goods

d _____ the advantage of knowing how to identify fakes

e _____ the difficulty of identifying counterfeit goods

B (Circle) **the correct words to complete the sentences from the video.**

1 They're part of a(n) *large / illegal* multibillion-dollar industry.

2 Counterfeit children's toys can be *risky / deadly*.

3 It's *impossible / hard* to believe people are willing to risk their health just to save money.

4 Until they can easily identify whether those goods are *genuine / real* or not, it will be very difficult for them to make that choice.

5 If counterfeiting is going to be stopped, it will need to be done using *simple / sophisticated* security.

6 Consumers who know what to look for can avoid wasting their money on a *cheap / fake* product.

C **Answer the questions.** (Circle) **all the correct answers based on the video.**

1 Who do counterfeit goods come at a high price for?

a the authorities   b well-known brands   c the consumer

2 What are some dangers of counterfeit children's toys?

a choking   b being electrocuted   c being burned

3 What's the most poisonous ingredient found in counterfeit cosmetics?

a arsenic   b lead   c cyanide

4 Who finds it difficult to spot a fake?

a consumers   b authorities   c store owners

D **Look at the pictures. Complete the summaries that describe what they show. Use all the words from each box.**

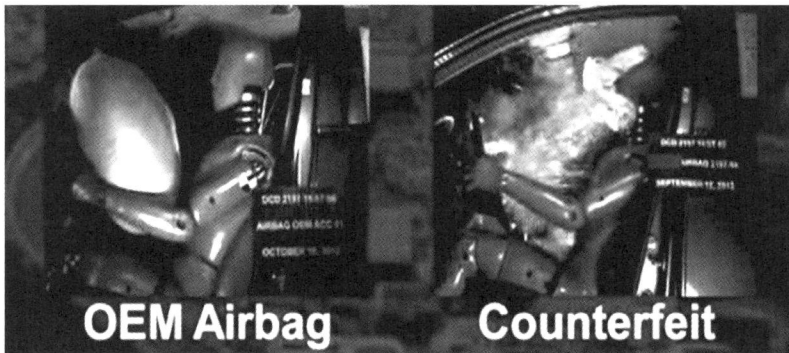

OEM Airbag   Counterfeit

| fitted | risks | imperfectly | inferior | legal | crucial |

Airbags are a ¹_____ part of car safety. It is a ²_____ requirement for all new cars to be ³_____ with both driver and passenger airbags. An ⁴_____ airbag, or one that has been fitted ⁵_____ , has very serious safety ⁶_____ .

| date | disappear | graphic | heat | ink | reappear |

Super Bowl tickets have two sophisticated kinds of security. On the front, there is a laser-cut ⁷_____ which you can see through – it's not printed on. Then, on the back, there is a(n) ⁸_____ in thermochromic ⁹_____ . If you apply ¹⁰_____ it will ¹¹_____ . Then it will ¹²_____ as it cools off.

E **Answer the questions. Use ideas and examples from the video.**

1 How do counterfeit goods "come at a high price" for the consumer?

_____

2 Which consumers buy counterfeit goods when they know they are counterfeit?

_____

3 In what way does "knowledge equal power" for Super Bowl ticketholders?

_____

AFTER YOU WATCH

A PAIR WORK **Discuss the questions with a partner.**

1 Who do you think buys and installs fake camshaft tensioners, airbags, and other car parts?

2 Do you think that counterfeiters will start to use the same technology as the genuine manufacturers of Super Bowl tickets? Why or why not?

3 How do counterfeit goods come at a high price for well-known brands?

4 How does the consumer's appetite for a bargain affect counterfeiters and the authorities?

B PAIR WORK **Discuss with a partner the consequences consumers could face if they bought counterfeit versions of these products.**

designer earrings

a designer wedding dress

a pair of brand-name sneakers

a music festival or sports ticket

perfume or aftershave

a hairdryer

an electric razor

a video game

C PAIR WORK **How could a consumer tell the difference between a real and a counterfeit version of each product in exercise A before buying them (1) in person and (2) online?**

D GROUP WORK **Role play the situation. Use the expressions below in your conversation.**

Student A	Student B	Student C
You are a customer at an outdoor market. You see a wonderful bargain – your favorite brand of _____ at less than half the normal price. Try to buy the product.	You are Student A's best friend. Your friend thinks they see a wonderful bargain at an outdoor market, but you think the product is counterfeit. Try to stop your friend from buying the product.	You are a vendor. You are selling *genuine/counterfeit* products of a well-known brand very cheaply. Try to convince your customers (Students A and B) that the products are genuine.

- I'm absolutely positive (that) …
- Yeah, right!

- Tell me another one.
- Believe it or not, …

BEFORE YOU WATCH

A   **Read the text. Answer the questions about the words in bold.**

Community Spirit

Disasters often bring out the best in our communities. When **word spreads** of a horrific tragedy, it's not long before members of the public arrive to offer shelter, set up **soup kitchens**, and try to help people in distress. The level of community spirit we see at these times is **phenomenal**, especially in contrast to the daily experience of many people. In a world where a close relationship with a colleague is more likely than one with a neighbor, vulnerable individuals can **feel they don't belong**. **Asylum seekers**, seniors, and the homeless often have to rely on public services and volunteers just to survive.

We need to see that community spirit now. With **upcoming** cutbacks to funding of services, we need more **outstanding** individuals to get involved with their communities and help **raise the spirits** of those in need. If you're considering volunteering, it can be a great way to **take your mind off** your problems and have the real reward of **making somebody else's day**.

1   What happens when **word spreads**? _____
2   What is provided at a **soup kitchen**? _____
3   What is a synonym for **phenomenal**? _____
4   What words do you associate with **feeling like you don't belong**? _____
5   What is another word commonly used to describe **asylum seekers**? _____
6   If a change is **upcoming**, when will it happen? _____
7   How does someone's mood change when you **raise their spirits**? _____
8   Does **outstanding** mean *special* or *helpful*? _____
9   If you **take your mind off** something, does it make you more or less worried? _____
10   If you **make someone's day**, how do they feel? _____

B   PAIR WORK   **Do you think the text in exercise A is true about the community you live in? What is similar? What is different?**

C   PAIR WORK   **What do you think are some challenges these four groups face?**

• asylum seekers   • children in hospitals   • the elderly   • the homeless

D   PREDICT   **Look at the list below. The video depicts each thing being used to help one of the groups in exercise C. Match to make a prediction.**

1   Nutritious meals: _____
2   Tutus: _____
3   Free bicycles: _____
4   Outings: _____

WHILE YOU WATCH

A   **Watch the video. Were your predictions in exercise D on page 45 correct? Who does each project help?**

1   Salvation Army Community Center: _____

3   The Bike Project: _____

2   Tutu Tuesday: _____

4   Cycling Without Age: _____

B   **Read the excerpts. Complete the sentences with words used in the video.**

1   Sometimes, it really doesn't take much to _____ _____ someone else's day.

2   Jeff Ansorge is the _____ _____ at a Salvation Army Community Center, which provides support to homeless people and others who can't always afford a healthy meal.

3   Meanwhile, a hospital in Florida _____ people's _____ in another way.

4   It all started when a hospital employee wanted to _____ a young patient's _____ _____ her upcoming operation.

5   In Europe, a few imaginative people are using bicycles to _____ _____ .

6   In Copenhagen, Denmark, another group is also using bicycles to _____ _____ .

C   **Answer the questions about the video.**

1   How are Jeff Ansorge's meals special?

a   They have more nutritional value.

b   There are vegetarian options.

c   They are cheap to buy.

2   How did others get involved in Tutu Tuesday?

a   The patients asked the staff members to wear tutus.

b   The staff members brought in a lot of tutus.

c   People in the hospital talked about it.

3   When did Jem Stein start the Bike Project?

a   when he had a spare bike to give away

b   when his bike broke and he couldn't travel anywhere

c   when he noticed the difference a bike made to a refugee

4   What is the difference between Cycling Without Age's outings and typical outings for seniors?

a   The seniors can decide where they go.

b   The seniors can be involved with local people.

c   The seniors can enjoy the company of other seniors.

Documentary

EVOLVE 5   Unit 12

D Complete the excerpt from the video with the words in the box.

back	cut	grains	kitchen	nutritional
phenomenal	proteins	sent	soup	value

"What I try and bring is ¹_____ ²_____. You know, making sure that they're getting their vegetables and the fruits and their ³_____ and appropriate ⁴_____ and trying to ⁵_____ ⁶_____ the fats and the sugars through desserts, I cut those out."

"It is not your old-fashioned ⁷_____ ⁸_____ where you get a bowl of soup and a piece of bread and ⁹_____ on your way. He makes ¹⁰_____ meals that you would pay quite a bit of money to go to a restaurant and have."

E Read the quotes from the video. What is each person talking about? Match the answers.

1 "On a scale of one to ten, I give him an eight-and-a-half!" _____
2 "She was so nervous, and she was scared." _____
3 "It's definitely not what you expected to see." _____
4 "It makes you feel you are alive." _____
5 "Feeling that you belong is so important." _____

a the feeling of owning a bicycle
b the meals at the community center
c the tutus in the hospital
d the benefits of Cycling Without Age
e the patient that Tutu Tuesday began with

F Take notes on how people describe the response to three of the projects from the video.

Tutu Tuesday: _____
_____
_____

The Bike Project: _____
_____
_____

Cycling Without Age: _____
_____
_____

AFTER YOU WATCH

A PAIR WORK Discuss the questions with a partner.

1 Which of the projects in the video would be helpful to the greatest number of people in your community?

2 How could you adapt the ideas in these projects to help a slightly different group of people?

- Jeff Ansorge's nutritious meals
- Tutu Tuesdays
- The Bike Project
- Cycling Without Age

- housebound elderly people
- adult patients
- refugees living in rural communities
- patients who have recently left the hospital

B GROUP WORK Look at the community projects. Choose one or your own idea. Use the phrases in the box to explain how the project works.

brighten up	capture your imagination	do you good
get you down	leave a lasting impression on	make your day
put your mind at rest	raise your spirits	stress you out

The Community Fridge

Gives low-income families access to fresh food for their family

Reading Together

Enables parents with literacy issues to learn to read with their children

Wear Me Out

Gives underprivileged teens clothing choices

Cut Out for Success

Helps homeless people look their best

C PAIR WORK Role play a conversation with another student about your project.

Student A

You want to spread the word about your community project so that more people will get involved. Use your ideas in exercise B to explain to a journalist, Student B, how your project will brighten people's days. You're very optimistic that it's a great program.

Useful language:

I'm certain/confident that …

Our ultimate goal is to …

There's no harm in trying.

I'm determined to …

Student B

You're a journalist. You'll be writing a news article to help promote Student A's project. But you need to be sure it's a safe program. Ask questions and get all the details about the project you can.

Useful language:

There's no guarantee (that) …

You can't say for certain (that) …

Our expert speakers are highly proficient non-native speakers of English living and working in the New York City area.

Scan the QR codes below to listen to their stories.

Wendy Sanchez-Vaynshteyn
from Bolivia
Data scientist

Bojan Andric
from Serbia
Interpreter

Carolina Hakopian
from Brazil
Dentist

Jacqueline Castañeda Nuñez
from Mexico
Urbanist

Lucia D'Anna
from Italy
Lead promotion specialist

Odil Odilov
from Tajikistan
Finance assistant

A STEP FORWARD

Meet Jacqueline
Occupation: Urbanist
Country of origin: Mexico

Are inventions always good for humanity?

WHILE YOU WATCH

A (Circle) the correct answers to complete the sentences.

1 According to Jacqueline, the _____ has had a positive effect on people.

   a automobile
   b bicycle
   c computer

2 In her opinion, this invention _____

   a helps people get around more quickly.
   b helps people communicate better.
   c is inexpensive.

3 Jacqueline believes that _____ have had a negative impact on society.

   a automobiles
   b computers
   c weapons

4 The reasons she gives include _____

   a they can ruin lives.
   b people don't always use them correctly.
   c people can be injured by them.

B (Circle) the word in each pair that Jacqueline uses to talk about positive and negative effects.

1 beneficial / useful
2 to assist / to help
3 environmentally friendly / sustainable
4 incorrect / wrong
5 to injure / to hurt
6 to destroy / to damage

AFTER YOU WATCH

A What do you think about Jacqueline's answers? Do you agree with her opinions? Why or why not?

B [PAIR WORK] The list below is the top ten inventions that have changed the world, according to Carla Hayden, Librarian of Congress in the U.S. Do you agree with the list? What do you think is missing? How have these inventions had a positive (or negative) effect on people? Discuss with a partner.

printing press	automobile
light bulb	clock
airplane	telephone
personal computer	refrigeration
vaccines	camera

C What inventions from the past 15 to 20 years have changed the way you live or work? How?

More about Jacqueline
Likes: Music videos

WHAT DO YOU THINK?

Is nostalgia a positive or a negative feeling?

WHILE YOU WATCH

A Check (✓) the sentences that are true. Correct the false ones.

☐ 1 Jacqueline feels nostalgic about her childhood because she had fewer responsibilities then.

☐ 2 The downsides of being an adult include having to pay monthly expenses.

☐ 3 While growing up, Jacqueline enjoyed watching movies and musicals on TV.

☐ 4 She used to spend hours watching TV in the morning before school.

☐ 5 As a 15-year-old, she especially liked watching music videos by popular musicians.

B Answer the questions based on the information in the video.
1 What object from her childhood does Jacqueline miss?
2 What did she find "really cool" about that object at the time?
3 What do people use now instead of that object?
4 What were the advantages of the object that she misses?
5 What are the disadvantages of the objects that have replaced it?

AFTER YOU WATCH

A Do you feel nostalgic for your childhood? What was better back then? How is your life better now?

B If you traveled back in time to relive one week of your childhood, what week would you choose and why? What would you experience during that week? Would you be tempted to do anything differently?

C [PAIR WORK] Compare what you used to do for entertainment as a child to what you do now. Are the differences due to changes in technology, changes in your tastes, or both? Explain.

- I used to …
- I never used to …
- Back then I would …
- Now I often …
- I tend to …
- Nowadays I'm always …

Meet Odil

Occupation: Finance assistant

Country of origin: Tajikistan

WHAT DO YOU THINK?

Can a big-city person have a relationship to nature and wildlife?

WHILE YOU WATCH

A   (Circle) the correct answers to complete the sentences.

1   Odil likes spending time in nature because _____
   a   he likes to go hunting.
   b   he finds the city too noisy.
   c   it is so different than being in the city.

2   According to Odil, cutting down forests and _____ have a negative effect on wild animals.
   a   using the land for farming
   b   constructing new buildings
   c   building highways

3   When he lived in London, he found it _____ to see foxes living so closely to people in the city.
   a   frightening
   b   surprising
   c   unsurprising

4   For him, seeing foxes in the city showed that _____
   a   wild animals and humans can still live together.
   b   hunters have forced wild animals from their natural habitat.
   c   wild animals have benefited from the destruction of their habitat.

B   **Answer the questions based on the information in the video.**

1   What three benefits of human activity in nature does Odil mention? Connect the verbs and noun phrases for the answers.
   a   doing   new places
   b   discovering   our understanding of science
   c   improving   new research

2   In his opinion, what are the drawbacks of human activity with respect to nature?

3   Why does he think doing things that negatively affect wildlife and the natural world is sometimes justified?

AFTER YOU WATCH

A   Have you ever had a close encounter with a wild animal? Where was it, what happened, and how did it make you feel?

B   PAIR WORK   Most scientists agree that human beings have made a major impact on the planet. With a partner, brainstorm a list of the ways humans have affected normal earth processes over the past 100–200 years.

C   Should human needs and interests be put before those of wildlife? Imagine that there are plans where you live to build a housing development for people with low income on land that is currently used as a wildlife refuge. Would you be for or against the project? Why?

UNIT 2

DEEP OCEAN OR DEEP SPACE?

More about Odil
Interesting fact: Lived in London

WHILE YOU WATCH

A Check (✓) the sentences that are true. Correct the false ones.

☐ 1 Odil believes that ocean exploration is very important.

☐ 2 Two-thirds of the planet consists of oceans and there is still a lot we haven't explored yet.

☐ 3 He feels it is less important to explore space because we already know so much about it.

☐ 4 According to Odil, people tend to explore places that are easy to get to.

☐ 5 Places that are hard to get to are more dangerous and riskier to explore.

B **According to Odil, what are the top three areas for research and exploration that can help the planet? Check (✓) the areas he mentions.**

☐ oceans   ☐ Antarctica   ☐ Africa
☐ deserts   ☐ medicine   ☐ microenvironments
☐ biology   ☐ space   ☐ rain forests

AFTER YOU WATCH

A **PAIR WORK** What are the most extreme places you have been? Compare with a partner. Are your experiences similar? Say why you went there and what you learned.

> The highest mountain I have climbed was …

> The coldest place I have ever been was in …

> The most desolate place I have seen was …

B **GROUP WORK** Do you agree with Odil's opinion about the three most important areas of research and exploration that would help the planet? Explain.

C **PAIR WORK** Imagine a committee has to decide on a single research or exploration project that will get funding for the next ten years. Come up with a project to present to the committee. Be specific about the scope of the project and the results you hope it will achieve. Prepare a 30-second pitch for the class.

Meet Wendy
Occupation: Data scientist
Country of origin: Bolivia

WHAT DO YOU THINK?

What do our feelings say about our
personality or character?

WHILE YOU WATCH

A **Circle** the four words Wendy uses to describe riding on a roller coaster.

| anxious | drop | exhilarating | fall | fear | fly | risk | scary | speed | thrill |

B **Circle** the correct answers to complete the sentences.

1 Wendy feels that extreme situations _____
   a help people understand their own character.
   b show people's true nature.
   c give people the chance to express themselves.

2 The best situations for revealing one's character are those that require _____
   a optimism and determination.
   b hard work and patience.
   c endurance and grit.

3 At the beginning of the marathon, Wendy felt _____
   a tired.
   b unwell.
   c excited.

4 During the race, she realized she was _____
   a going too slowly.
   b stronger than she had thought.
   c not going to reach the finish line.

C **Which words does Wendy use to express the following ideas?**

1 courage and determination: g_____
2 the ability to keep doing something even though it is difficult: e_____
3 a feeling of responsibility to follow through or complete something difficult: c_____
4 being able to accept or deal with problems without getting angry or worried: p_____

AFTER YOU WATCH

A Have you ever done something really challenging like a marathon? If so, what was it like and what did you learn about yourself in the process? If not, is this something you would like to do? Explain.

B **PAIR WORK** How do the situations below reveal what people are really like? Can you think of other situations or life events that might reveal the truth about our personality or character?

- assembling furniture
- dealing with serious illness
- playing a board game

"To find a man's true character, play golf with him."

– P. G. Wodehouse, British author

More about Wendy

Likes: Running marathons

WHAT DO YOU THINK?

What different feelings do you usually have in an average day?

WHILE YOU WATCH

A Write the things Wendy mentions in the correct categories.

being with family
getting served the wrong food
people in the way when she is in a hurry

eating meals with friends
not knowing what's going to happen
taking her sick child to the ER

getting a massage
walking her dog

Things she loves	Things that irritate her
Things that make her feel fabulous	**Things that make her feel tense**

AFTER YOU WATCH

A Are Wendy's answers to the four questions true for you? How would you fill in the chart above?

B PAIR WORK Think about the previous year of your life. Finish these sentences or write similar sentences of your own. Compare your answers with a partner.

1 The thing I most loved doing over the past year was _____.

2 One of the most fabulous things I remember was _____.

3 Something irritating that happened was _____.

4 A situation that made me very tense involved a person who _____.

C The quotes below give advice about dealing with situations that are irritating or frustrating. Do you think they are good advice? Why or why not? Do you have a similar quote or saying that you think about when you feel tense?

> "Don't sweat the small stuff ... and it is all small stuff."
> – Dr. Richard Carlson (best-selling author)

> "Don't worry, be happy."
> – Meher Baba (Indian mystic) and Bobby McFerrin (musician)

> "Don't make a mountain out of a molehill."
> – English idiom

Meet Lucia
Occupation: Lead promotion specialist
Country of origin: Italy

WHILE YOU WATCH

A   Check (✓) the sentences that are true. Correct the false ones.

☐   **1** Lucia works on a small team with six people.

☐   **2** The team members all work in the area of marketing.

☐   **3** Lucia's team members are supportive and share the same objectives.

☐   **4** Lucia's team is very good at meeting deadlines.

☐   **5** One of the disadvantages of teamwork is that everyone is working on different aspects of a project and it makes things less efficient.

☐   **6** Lucia says it can be a disadvantage if teammates are incompatible and work at different speeds.

B   **Read the quotes from the video. What do the words in italics mean? Choose the correct answers.**

1 "I like that we work through the same *common objectives*." _____

2 "Sometimes we *struggle* a little bit *with* deadlines." _____

3 "We have to keep in mind different time zones to organize meetings and to *collaborate* with these people." _____

4 "Sometimes … other team members are not *compatible*." _____

5 "A project can be stuck because different timings are not *in sync*." _____

a well suited
b lined up together
c have a hard time with
d shared goals
e work together

AFTER YOU WATCH

A   Think of a time you worked on a team. What was the experience like? Did you work effectively with the other members? What challenges did you face?

B   What do you think Lucia is like to work with? Would you like to have someone like her on your team? Explain.

C   GROUP WORK Teams count on the different roles and skills of individuals to work effectively. If your group had to work as a team, how would you contribute to the team's success? Discuss with your classmates.

IT TAKES A TEAM

More about Lucia
Personality: Good listener and someone who can keep a secret

WHILE YOU WATCH

A **Circle the correct words or phrases to complete the sentences.**

1 Lucia's role on her team involves promoting events and also helping authors with *advertising / logistics*.

2 She gets support from two team members who help with *presentation / administrative* tasks.

3 She once had to organize a business trip to *Europe / Asia* for a group of *eight / ten* people.

4 Booking the flights was complicated because people were traveling *to different cities abroad / from different states in the U.S.*

5 A red-eye is an overnight flight where people have *very little / a lot of* time to catch up on sleep.

6 Lucia received *positive / negative* feedback from her boss about her work, and it made her feel *helpful / nervous*.

7 Her *friends and family / coworkers* appreciate that she listens well and *always / never* tells their secrets.

B **Answer the questions based on the information in the video.**

1 What emotions did Lucia experience while and after organizing the trip? What caused those feelings?

2 What do you think Lucia learned from her experience as a decision-maker?

3 How is Lucia known in her family? How is she different from the rest her family?

AFTER YOU WATCH

A **How would *you* have handled organizing the trip Lucia describes? What would you have done well? What would have been the most challenging part for you?**

B **Do you have a system for organizing tasks and keeping schedules? How important to you are tools such as to-do lists, calendars, spreadsheets, and collaboration software?**

C **PAIR WORK** **In some situations it is better to make decisions on your own, but other times it might be better to involve the people affected by your decisions. What are the advantages and disadvantages of each approach? Brainstorm ideas with a partner.**

> *The advantage of making decisions on your own is (that) …*

> *A potential problem with involving other people is (that) …*

> *The upside/downside is (that) …*

> *Another plus/potential problem is (that) …*

THE HUMAN FACTOR

Meet Carolina
Occupation: Dentist
Country of origin: Brazil

WHAT DO YOU THINK?

What makes a machine or device "intelligent"?

WHILE YOU WATCH

A   Circle the correct answer based on the information in the video.

1   Carolina mentions using an intelligent _____

     a refrigerator.   **b** vacuum cleaner.   **c** microwave oven.

2   She is really looking forward to using _____

     a driverless cars.   **b** 3D printers.   **c** drones.

3   According to Carolina, robots are better than humans at _____

     a making decisions.   **b** doing tasks that need to be repeated.   **c** teaching.

4   She implies that humans are better than robots at doing tasks that require _____

     a precision.   **b** accuracy.   **c** creativity.

B   **In Carolina's profession of dentistry, which of the tasks below would she say only humans can do? Check (✓) the boxes.**

☐ **a** Analyze the results of a patient's medical examination.

☐ **b** Consider a patient's emotional state.

☐ **c** Decide on the proper treatment.

☐ **d** Analyze X-rays.

☐ **e** List possible diagnoses.

☐ **f** Take the patient's entire situation into consideration.

C   **Answer the questions based on the information in the video.**

1   How will driverless cars change our lives? _____

2   Who will they benefit? _____

3   What tasks or skills require what Carolina calls the "human component"? _____

4   What factors need to be taken into consideration when making diagnoses? _____

AFTER YOU WATCH

A   Would you rather be diagnosed by an intelligent machine or a human being? Why?

B   Have you ever used intelligent machines or smart devices? If so, how have they made your life easier? Is there anything that they don't do as well as you?

C   PAIR WORK   What new intelligent appliance or machine would you like to see on the market? How would it change the way you work or live your life? Work with a partner to write a description.

More about Carolina
Interesting fact: Would like a driverless car

WHAT DO YOU THINK?

Will virtual reality be more useful for health professionals or their patients?

WHILE YOU WATCH

A (Circle) the correct answers to complete the sentences based on the information in the video.

1 Carolina hasn't tried virtual reality yet _____

   a and isn't sure she wants to.

   b but wants to try it one day.

   c and wants to do more research about it.

2 She has a lot of friends who _____

   a use VR regularly in their jobs.

   b have tried it.

   c have it on their bucket lists.

3 These friends said that _____

   a they think it will soon be very popular.

   b it was somewhat disappointing.

   c they enjoyed it a lot.

B **What words did Carolina use?** (Circle) **the correct options.**

1 Using VR is on Carolina's *to-do list / bucket list.*

2 She thinks VR can make the patient's experience more *comfortable / convenient.*

3 She thinks it would be *amazing / surprising* if VR could be used to help reduce stress.

4 For training purposes, using VR to practice doing surgeries would involve less *risk / pain.*

AFTER YOU WATCH

A **PAIR WORK** **How do you feel about going to the dentist? Do you think VR goggles could help improve your experience there? How? Discuss your answers with a partner.**

> Whenever I go to the dentist, I ...

> If VR is available next time I go to the dentist, I'll ...

> As long as ...

> I think it might help but only if ...

B **PAIR WORK** **Do you think virtual training can ever be as effective as practicing on real patients? With a partner, brainstorm advantages and disadvantages of each approach.**

EXPECT THE UNEXPECTED

Meet Bojan
Occupation: Interpreter
Country of origin: Serbia

WHILE YOU WATCH

A (Circle) the correct options to complete the sentences based on the information in the video.

1 Bojan travels a lot and *likes to plan ahead / enjoys dealing with the unexpected*.

2 He relies on *a planner / time slots* to keep to his plan.

3 Bojan talks about *saying something unexpected / getting an unexpected reaction* while speaking Dutch.

4 When he lived in the Netherlands, he *hadn't yet learned to speak Dutch well / quickly became fluent in Dutch*.

5 He couldn't find an item he needed in a *drugstore / bookstore,* so he asked the sales clerk a question.

6 She *frowned / smiled* when she heard he had trouble expressing himself in her language.

7 The clerk's *mother / mother-in-law* couldn't speak Dutch either despite having lived there longer than Bojan.

B **PAIR WORK** Can you tell Bojan's stories in your own words? Put the events of each story in the correct order (1–7). Then tell the stories in the past.

The airport lounge			The store in the Hague		
_____	a	doesn't speak to the celebrity	_____	a	approaches a sales clerk
__1__	b	traveling home to New York	_____	b	speaks English
_____	c	learns who the celebrity is	__1__	c	lives in the Hague
_____	d	waits in a lounge in Amsterdam	_____	d	gets an unexpected response
_____	e	is in London on a layover	_____	e	can't find an item he wants
_____	f	sees a celebrity	_____	f	goes shopping
_____	g	talks to a man from the lounge	_____	g	tries to speak Dutch

AFTER YOU WATCH

A **PAIR WORK** Have you or someone you know ever had an unexpected encounter with a celebrity? Describe what happened. How does the experience compare to what happened to Bojan in the airport lounge?

> I was once _____ , when I _____ .

> I hadn't _____ until _____ .

> I first _____ , and then I _____ .

> While I was _____ , …

B Do you like surprises, or are you more like Bojan, who thinks that "anything unexpected tends to ruin the plan"? How prepared are you for the unexpected?

More about Bojan

Likes: Traveling

WHAT DO YOU THINK?

Is fame a good thing or a bad thing?

WHILE YOU WATCH

A   Circle the correct answer, or answers, based on the information from the video.

1   If Bojan woke up one morning and saw his name in the headlines, he would be _____
   - a   shocked.
   - b   surprised.
   - c   happy.

2   If his name was in the headlines because of something negative, he would _____
   - a   take time to think about what to do.
   - b   contact a lawyer immediately.
   - c   try to reach family members to warn them.

3   He could imagine appearing on a game show, where he would _____
   - a   need to have a wide range of knowledge.
   - b   answer questions.
   - c   win money.

4   He thinks he would enjoy being on the game show _____
   - a   if he did well.
   - b   even if he did poorly.
   - c   for a short amount of time.

5   He would not like to be famous because he _____
   - a   doesn't have the right personality.
   - b   would have to be careful about what he does.
   - c   prefers his privacy.

6   He feels celebrities have a harder time nowadays because of _____
   - a   the lack of privacy.
   - b   the media and paparazzi.
   - c   social media.

B   **Answer the questions in your own words.**

1   How often is Bojan online and what does he do there? _____

2   Why does he think social media has made it harder to be famous? _____

3   What does he say is a "nightmare"? Why? _____

C   **What words does Bojan use to express these ideas?**

1   to communicate (with a person): "I would _____ and find a lawyer"

2   understood in the wrong way: "any little thing they do can be _____"

3   in a way that other people can see: "what context they're showing up _____ in"

AFTER YOU WATCH

A   **Would you want to be famous? Why or why not? If you became famous, what changes would you make to the way you live?**

B   **Some people are described to be "famous for being famous." What does that mean? Do you think people who get their fame on social media fall into this category? Why or why not?**

C   **Does being famous require a certain personality type? Is it a consequence of having certain talents and skills? Explain your answers.**

Meet Odil
Occupation: Finance assistant
Country of origin: Tajikistan

WHAT DO YOU THINK?

How do you determine the value of an object?

WHILE YOU WATCH

A   Check (✓) the sentences that are true. Correct the false ones.

☐ **1** Odil owns a very expensive painting that was given to him by a friend.

☐ **2** A painting was given to Odil when he was visiting the country he grew up in.

☐ **3** Odil has always placed a high value on things that cost a lot.

☐ **4** As he grew older, things like kindness and charity became more valuable to him.

☐ **5** More than anything else, he values things that remind him of his home country.

B   Circle the correct answer or answers based on the information in the video.

1 Why is the painting Odil talks about so important to him?

  a It has monetary value.
  b It has sentimental value because of who gave it to him.
  c It reminds him of the place he came from.

2 How have Odil's views about what is valuable changed since he was younger?

  a He used to value acts of kindness, but now he values expensive possessions.
  b He used to value expensive things, but now he thinks positive human qualities are more valuable.
  c He used to think where you lived and what you drove were important, but now he thinks what you do and how you act carry more value.

3 How does Odil define "worth"?

  a how important something is to him personally
  b how important something is to society
  c how much money something costs or can be sold for

AFTER YOU WATCH

A   PAIR WORK   What objects do you own that have sentimental rather than monetary value? Describe them to a partner. Why do they mean so much to you?

B   In 2018, a 72-year-old man with serious health problems saved his 1929 classic car as he escaped from a deadly wildfire in Paradise, California. He said he didn't want his "baby" to be destroyed in the fire. If you had to flee your home very quickly, what would you take with you and why?

WORTHY HELPERS

More about Odil

Likes: Visiting friends and family

WHAT DO YOU THINK?

Is it better to give help or get help?

WHILE YOU WATCH

A **Choose the correct options to complete the sentences based on the information in the video.**

1 Odil *often / sometimes* has to assist his coworkers with their work problems.

2 The coworkers come to Odil with *personal finance / work-related* issues.

3 He *enjoys / doesn't enjoy* helping his coworkers and *avoids assisting / assists* them whenever he can.

B **Write whether the statements are *true* (T), *false* (F), or *not mentioned* (NM) in the video. Correct the false ones.**

☐ 1 Odil recently traveled by boat with his grandmother to his home country.

☐ 2 She is disabled and has trouble walking.

☐ 3 She usually uses a wheelchair to get around.

☐ 4 Odil was worried that his mother would have trouble getting on the plane.

☐ 5 The assistant pushed his mother to the gate, and Odil helped her get on the plane.

☐ 6 The assistant did a good job and everything went smoothly.

☐ 7 Odil was relieved that his mother was able to travel.

☐ 8 Odil sent an email to the airline thanking them for their help.

C **According to Odil, what qualities does a good helper need to have? Check (✓) the qualities he mentions.**

☐ endurance   ☐ enthusiasm   ☐ friendliness

☐ interest in people   ☐ kindness   ☐ passion

☐ patience   ☐ positivity   ☐ strength

AFTER YOU WATCH

A **Do you agree with Odil's assessment of what makes a good helper? If so, why are the qualities he mentions important for helping people? If you have other opinions, explain what qualities you think make a good helper.**

B **PAIR WORK** It is often said that helping benefits both the people receiving the help and the person giving it. How do you think people benefit from giving somebody a helping hand?

SMALL THINGS MATTER

Meet Jacqueline
Occupation: Urbanist
Country of origin: Mexico

WHAT DO YOU THINK?

What does the appearance of a workspace or home say about a person?

WHILE YOU WATCH

A What personal items are on Jacqueline's fridge? Why did she choose them? Check (✓) the boxes.

Personal items	Why she chose them
☐ pictures of family	☐ feel happy
☐ cartoons	☐ look pretty
☐ pictures of pets	☐ remember
☐ drawings	☐ cool
☐ pictures of coworkers	☐ useful
☐ magnets from Mexico	☐ reminds
☐ pictures of her and her partner	☐ beautiful

B Answer the questions based on the information in the video.

1 What objects in Jacqueline's workspace make her feel grounded? Why do you think that is?

_____

2 Why do you think it's important to Jacqueline to write down her thoughts and feelings?

_____

3 Why does she like to keep pictures on her fridge? How do they make her feel?

_____

4 What does Jacqueline's choice of pictures tell you about her?

_____

AFTER YOU WATCH

A How do your workspace and fridge compare to Jacqueline's? What would the appearance of these personal spaces tell someone about you as a person?

B Read the quote below by American author and podcaster Gretchen Rubin. Is it true for you? Do you think the appearance of a workspace reflects a person's state of mind and potential for achievement?

> "For most people, an orderly environment helps them feel more energetic, more creative, and more cheerful. This isn't true for everyone, but it's true for most people."

C **PAIR WORK** Imagine you are starting a new job and have the chance to design your ideal workspace. What kind of desk will you have? How will you decorate your workspace? Tell a partner.

First of all, I'll _____ .

I won't _____ , but I'm definitely going to _____ .

I might _____ .

UNIT 8

SIDE PROJECTS

More about Jacqueline
Interesting fact: Works from home

WHAT DO YOU THINK?

For what reasons do people have side projects?

WHILE YOU WATCH

A Circle the correct answer, or answers, based on the information in the video.

1 As a side project, Jacqueline does farming _____
   a in a community garden.
   b on the roof of her apartment building.
   c in her backyard.

2 Working toward a certificate in urban agriculture _____
   a is the reason she decided to start her side project.
   b helped her understand what it means to be a farmer.
   c was a difficult decision to make.

3 Farming makes her feel _____
   a lucky.   b grounded.   c calm.

4 She enjoys farming because _____
   a it gives her peace.   b she makes extra money.   c she likes having contact with plants.

B **Combine words from each list to make phrases that Jacqueline uses in the video. Complete the sentences.**

empower	have	nutritious	access	agriculture	food
sow	urban		people	seeds	

1 One day Jacqueline decided to _____ on her roof.
2 She then went on to study _____ .
3 She wants people to _____ to healthy and _____
   _____ .
4 She also wants to _____ to produce their own food.

AFTER YOU WATCH

A What do you think of Jacqueline's side project? Would you do what she does? Why or why not?

B GROUP WORK You are on a small team competing to get financial support for a side project. Choose a project and list the steps each team member will take to get started. What do you hope to achieve? Prepare a 30-second pitch.

We plan to …   We hope to …   We will start by …   In two years, we will …

C Pitch your plans to the rest of the class. Then take a class vote on which plan should get funding.

THINGS HAPPEN

Meet Carolina
Occupation: Dentist
Country of origin: Brazil

WHILE YOU WATCH

A   Answer the questions with the people in the box. Some words are used more than once.

> Alexander   Carolina   Carolina's cousin   Carolina's family

Who ...

a   organized a trip? _____

b   touched a statue of Juliet? _____

c   made fun of Carolina? _____

d   is a lawyer? _____

e   found a new home? _____

f   has a beautiful smile? _____

B   (Circle) the correct answers to complete the sentences.

1   Alexander _____
   a   moved to New York with Carolina.
   b   is friends with Carolina's cousin.
   c   has family in Brazil.

2   Carolina and her family _____
   a   stayed overnight in Verona.
   b   spent a day in Verona.
   c   traveled from New York to Italy.

3   Carolina _____
   a   likes to plan.
   b   likes to take life as it comes.
   c   doesn't believe in chance.

C   Answer the questions based on the information in the video.

1   What does the story about the statue of Juliet say? _____

2   What *amazing thing* changed Carolina's life? _____

3   Why does Carolina like to leave room for the unexpected? _____

4   According to Carolina, what three qualities make a person more open to new possibilities?
   _____

AFTER YOU WATCH

A   **PAIR WORK**   What if Carolina never met Alexander in Verona? Make up a different chance encounter that changed the course of her life. Then share your story with a partner.

B   **PAIR WORK**   Beatles bandmates John Lennon and Paul McCartney met at a Liverpool club. Apple cofounders Steve Jobs and Steve Wozniak were introduced by a mutual friend. What other chance encounters changed the course of history?

C   Think of and share a chance encounter that changed *your* life. How would your life be different now without that encounter?

WHY DID I DO IT?

More about Carolina
Likes: Soccer

WHAT DO YOU THINK?

What is the difference between *remembering* and *regretting*?

WHILE YOU WATCH

A Circle the correct words to complete the sentences based on the information in the video.
Carolina …

1 likes watching *football / soccer / volleyball*.

2 made her husband give away a *chair / desk / table*.

3 ordered *books / groceries / clothing* online.

4 took a *bus / taxi cab / train* back to her apartment.

5 watched a documentary about *minimalism / consumerism / globalism*.

B Carolina tells a story about seeing the funny side of things. Put the steps in the correct order. Then retell the story as a paraphrase.

_____ **a** arrived at new address with groceries

_____ **b** gave the online service her old address

_____ **c** ordered groceries online

_____ **d** laughed about the angry cab driver

___1___ **e** moved to a new address

_____ **f** picked up groceries at the old address

_____ **g** put groceries in a cab

_____ **h** was told groceries had been delivered to old address

AFTER YOU WATCH

A **PAIR WORK** Think of a time that something went wrong, but you were able to laugh about it later. Describe what happened to a partner.

B What is a life lesson you learned recently? How did it change your actions? Was it a hard lesson to learn?

C Studies show that over the long term, people tend to regret their *inactions* (things they didn't do) rather than their *actions*. What might you regret not having done in 20 years? What can you do about it now?

I regret not having _____ .

I wish I had _____ .

If I had(n't) _____ , …

Meet Lucia
Occupation: Lead promotion specialist
Country of origin: Italy

WHAT DO YOU THINK?

What do social media profile pictures tell people about you?

WHILE YOU WATCH

A   (Circle) the correct answers based on the information in the video.

1   Lucia's profile picture _____
   a   was taken less than a year ago.
   b   shows her with her son in her arms.
   c   shows her baby smiling at the camera.

2   She changes her profile picture _____
   a   every week.
   b   often.
   c   sometimes.

3   When Lucia changes her profile picture on Facebook, she uses _____
   a   amusing images.
   b   landscapes showing places she'd like to go.
   c   pictures of her pets.

4   If she posts on Facebook, she wants a picture that shows her _____
   a   looking professional.
   b   laughing with her friends.
   c   having a good time with her family.

5   She wants her profile pictures for LinkedIn to show that she is _____
   a   neat and attractive.
   b   a hard worker who likes to have fun.
   c   serious and professional.

B   **What does Lucia say about the ways people change their appearance to make an impression? Choose the correct option to complete the sentences.**

1   In job interviews, people often wear clothing that is *casual, but tidy / formal and neat*.

2   People dress this way because they want to look *friendly / professional*.

3   On a date, people pay more attention to how *attractive / interesting* they look.

4   Women might wear more *expensive / sophisticated* makeup, for example, and men will make sure they are *clean-shaven / well-dressed*.

AFTER YOU WATCH

A   PAIR WORK   **What impression does Lucia's current Facebook profile picture give about who she is? Would it be appropriate for her to use the same picture on other social media sites? Explain.**

B   PAIR WORK   **Some people use a default profile picture image on social media sites, like the ones below. What impression does an impersonal picture give to people who view your profile?**

C   GROUP WORK   **In some countries, job applicants are expected to put their photo of themselves on their résumé. Do you think a person's physical appearance should matter when applying for a job? How could that affect who gets invited to a job interview?**

YOU, THE CUSTOMER

More about Lucia

Likes: Sharing funny pictures

WHAT DO YOU THINK?

Who benefits when companies collect data from their customers?

WHILE YOU WATCH

A **Which sentence best summarizes how Lucia feels about companies collecting their customers' data?**

1 It's a waste of time for both companies and customers.

2 It's useful for companies but can be risky for people who share their information.

3 It's a good idea because it helps both companies and their customers.

B **Match the words Lucia uses in the video to the definitions.**

audience	demographics	secure	target	transparent

1 to focus on or aim at: _____

2 straightforward and open: _____

3 data about people in specific geographical areas or groups: _____

4 safe and protected from misuse: _____

5 the group of people a marketing company wants to reach: _____

AFTER YOU WATCH

A **Do you agree with Lucia's positive take on companies collecting data for marketing purposes? How do you think her job in the field of marketing might influence her views as a customer? Explain your answers.**

B **PAIR WORK** **Companies are also known to track actual and potential customers using in-store Wi-Fi or GPS tracking. What do you think businesses can learn from information gathered this way?**

> In-store Wi-Fi allows stores to …

> GPS tracking enables …

C **PAIR WORK** **What other ways do companies collect data about our shopping habits? How can customers make sure our data is secure?**

> If you're concerned about what companies know about you, you can …

> We can try to protect our data by …

Meet Bojan
Occupation: Interpreter
Country of origin: Serbia

Do photographs show how people really look?

WHILE YOU WATCH

A   **Correct these false sentences about Bojan's opinions to make them true.**

1   If something seems wrong about a picture online, you can't tell for sure if it has been altered.

2   In the example about the magazine, editing was done to make the women look slimmer and have better hair.

3   People who want to present themselves in the best light might go too far by going to the gym or applying makeup.

4   When photos are altered in fashion magazines, it is usually the subjects who ask for it.

5   It is important for photos to show you at your best, no matter how much editing you need to do.

6   Fashion magazines present standards of fashion and beauty that are easy for the average person to achieve.

B   **Answer the questions based on the information in the video.**

1   Why is it easier to see whether a photo on social media has been edited than one in print?

2   In the example Bojan mentions of a magazine photo, what was the problem with it?

3   Why does Bojan think people sometimes edit their photos?

4   According to Bojan, how do fashion magazines set exaggerated standards for people's appearance?

AFTER YOU WATCH

A   What do you do to present yourself in a good light in pictures on social media? Do you think some photo editing is acceptable? In what circumstances?

B   GROUP WORK The German fashion magazine *Brigitte* once experimented with featuring ordinary people instead of models. It started using models again a few years later after receiving complaints from both the fashion industry and from many readers. What do you think each group complained about? How would *you* have reacted, and why?

More about Bojan
Interesting fact: Bought his first computer in the 1990s

WHAT DO YOU THINK?

Can you remember life before the internet?

WHILE YOU WATCH

A Circle the correct answer or answers based on the information in the video.

1 What does Bojan do online?

   a banking
   b plays games
   c shops
   d orders take out
   e plays the stock market
   f communicates with friends
   g finds people to date
   h watches TV shows or movies

2 What does he say about his first computer?

   a He got it in 1994.
   b The connection to the internet wasn't reliable.
   c It took a long time to get online.
   d You could download a photo in an instant.

3 Back then, what was the internet mainly used for?

   a banking
   b shopping
   c getting information
   d communicating with people

4 What advantage did life have back in the early days of the internet?

   a You didn't have to leave your home as much.
   b You had more opportunities to talk to people face to face.
   c You didn't have to waste time on trivial tasks.
   d You could do lots of different tasks quickly.

B Answer the questions according the information in the video.

1 According to Bojan, what are the advantages and disadvantages of the internet?

2 What does Bojan think influences how we see and react to things, including news stories?

3 What example does he give of the internet being used for harmful purposes? And for good purposes?

AFTER YOU WATCH

A PAIR WORK Imagine you had to live offline (without the internet), for the rest of your life. What would you miss? What would be better about your life?

B When you read a surprising or disturbing news story online, do you ever check other sources to see how they portray the same story? Why or why not?

C GROUP WORK Your group has been tasked with finding a way to "fix" the internet. How can you prevent lies and harmful ideas from being spread? Brainstorm. Prepare to present your plan to the class.

Meet Wendy
Occupation: Data scientist
Country of origin: Bolivia

WHAT DO YOU THINK?

What is a role model?

WHILE YOU WATCH

A   (Circle) the correct answer or answers to the questions.

   1   Which statements about Wendy's mother are true?

     a   She was someone Wendy respected and looked up to.

     b   She was born to a poor family in the United States.

     c   She was able to make the best of even the most difficult situation.

   2   According to Wendy, what can help you be successful in life?

     a   being very patient

     b   knowing who you are and what is happening around you

     c   being honest about what you are striving for

   3   What does success look like to her personally?

     a   having few financial or health concerns

     b   making her mother happy

     c   being able to enjoy every day

B   **Answer the questions.**

   1   Why does Wendy see her mother as a role model?

   2   What does she think helps people make the right decisions to achieve success?

   3   How does her personal definition of success involve her family?

AFTER YOU WATCH

A   **Do you have a role model? If so, which of that person's qualities do you want to copy? If not, what qualities would your ideal role model have?**

B   PAIR WORK   **How do you define success? Who is someone you consider successful? (It could be yourself.) What did this person have to do to achieve success?**

C   **"Where there's a will, there's a way." What does this saying mean? Is it always true? Why or why not?**

More about Wendy
Interesting fact: Her family moved to the U.S.

WHAT DO YOU THINK?

What is the difference between talent and skill?

WHILE YOU WATCH

A   Check (✓) whether the sentences are *true* (T), *false* (F), or *not mentioned* (NM) in the video. Correct the false ones.

		T	F	NM
1	People become successful thanks to a combination of talent and hard work.			
2	If someone has a lot of talent, they don't need to work hard.			
3	People can succeed even if they start off with very little talent.			
4	A person's success also depends on their mentor or coach.			
5	Steve Jobs did very well at school, which is why he was so successful.			

B   What does Wendy think a great sportsperson needs in order to be successful? Check (✓) the qualities she mentions.

☐ be athletic
☐ be capable of learning from a coach
☐ enjoy competing with others
☐ work well on a team

☐ be the best at everything in their sport
☐ be talented at their sport
☐ work hard

C   According to Wendy, what do the following people need to be great? Complete the text with words in the box.

classical and modern art	community	express themselves visually	stockholders
team members	the world economy	world events and laws	

Politicians need knowledge of ¹_____ and the ability to communicate with the ²_____ they represent. Business people need knowledge of ³_____ and the ability to communicate with ⁴_____ and ⁵_____. Artists need talent to ⁶_____ and knowledge of ⁷_____.

AFTER YOU WATCH

A   ☐ PAIR WORK ☐ Do you agree with Wendy about what makes a good sportsperson, politician, business person, or artist? Why or why not?

B   Think of something you do very well. How much of your success is due to natural talent and how much to practice and hard work?

C   According to Scottish novelist and poet Sir Walter Scott, "For success, attitude is equally as important as ability." Do you agree? Why or why not?

This page is intentionally left blank

EVOLVE

WORKBOOK

Carolyn Clarke Flores and Michele Lewis

5

CAMBRIDGE
UNIVERSITY PRESS

This page is intentionally left blank

CONTENTS

1.1 LIFE CHANGES

1 VOCABULARY: Facing challenges

A **Complete the sentences with the words in the box.**

accept	adapt	resist	survive	tackle	~~underestimate~~	welcome

1 Law school students often _____underestimate_____ the amount of homework they will get. It is usually more than they expected.

2 Marisol finally decided to _____ graduate school. She plans to start next year.

3 She didn't take the job because she couldn't _____ the low salary.

4 When Daniel moved from Boston to Phoenix, it took him a few months to _____ to the hot climate.

5 I did not think I would _____ my first year as a doctor because it was so difficult. Luckily, kind coworkers helped me get through it.

6 If you _____ making changes in your life, you won't grow or have new experiences.

7 My boss told me I was _____ to participate in the meeting.

B **Match the challenges with the correct solution.**

1 You can't take crowds. _e_   a Study in Mexico.

2 You're capable of managing people. ___   b Use a good map.

3 You underestimated the amount of time you needed. ___   c Don't go to graduate school.

4 You're frightened of getting lost. ___   d Look for training opportunities.

5 You got through medical school. ___   e Don't move to a big city.

6 You want to take a step forward in your career. ___   f You expect to earn a good salary.

7 You can't get a grip on Spanish. ___   g You'll be a good boss.

8 You can't cope with studying for a higher degree. ___   h Schedule more time for the task.

2 GRAMMAR: Present habits

A **Circle the correct answer to complete each sentence.**

1 Ivan ___ friends easily. He'll meet a lot of new people when he moves.

   a tends to making

   (b) tends to make

   c is making

2 When I'm looking for a new job, ___ to as many companies as possible.

   a I'm applying

   b I applied

   c I apply

    3 I ____ trying to learn new skills. I think that's the key to success.
       a am constantly
       b tend to
       c constantly
    4 When I take a difficult class, I ____ my professor for help at least once a week.
       a am asking
       b always asking
       c ask
    5 I ____ for different ways to stay healthy. Yesterday, I went to a new exercise class.
       a always look
       b always looking
       c am always look
    6 When ____ bored with my classes, I think about changing my major.
       a feel
       b I'm feeling
       c I'm feel

B **Complete the sentences using the correct form of the verbs in parentheses.**
    1 I'm always _____ wondering _____ what my life will be like when I _____ retire _____ . (wonder, retire)
    2 When she's _____ stressed, she usually _____ her friend Stephan for
       support. (feel, call)
    3 He tends to _____ more after he _____ a new exercise routine. (eat, start)
    4 I often _____ about changing my career to something completely different. (think)
    5 He's always _____ his friends that they should travel if they ever _____
       the chance. (tell, get)
    6 I tend to _____ very excited for people when they _____ they're getting
       married. (get, announce)
    7 He's always _____ for new opportunities to make money and will _____
       all of his friends to support him. (look, ask)

3 GRAMMAR AND VOCABULARY

A **Complete the sentences so that they are true for you.**
    1 I tend to resist _____ trying new kinds of food _____ .
    2 I usually underestimate _____ .
    3 I'm feeling encouraged by _____ .
    4 I survive difficult times by _____ .
    5 I'm always adapting to _____ .
    6 I tend to accept _____ .

B **Write three more sentences with information that is true
   for you. Use *tend to*, *will*, and the present continuous.**

   _____
   _____
   _____
   _____

3

MEMORY LANE

1 VOCABULARY: Describing annoying things

A **Choose the correct words or phrases to complete each sentence.**

1 I always feel _____ when I give a presentation. I don't like to speak in public.

   (a) awkward   b frustrating

2 I study Arabic and I think the grammar is _____ . I don't fully understand it yet.

   a a waste of time   b complex

3 It takes time to find a new job, so don't _____ . Just take a break, and then try again.

   a lose patience   b get on your nerves

4 Can you please stop whistling? It's starting to _____ .

   a drive you crazy   b get on my nerves

5 To me, nothing is more _____ than when coworkers are late for a meeting.

   a time-consuming   b infuriating

6 I used to think school was _____ . When I got older, I realized how valuable it had been.

   a a waste of time   b clumsy

7 The early days of the internet were _____ because it took a long time to connect to websites, and then the connection was frequently lost.

   a frustrating   b hard to operate

8 Writing a research paper is so _____ . I wish I could write more quickly.

   a tricky   b time-consuming

9 I remember my first cell phone. It was _____ until I learned how it worked. Then, it was very easy.

   a time-consuming   b hard to operate

10 Understanding modern technology can be _____ , especially for people from older generations who didn't grow up with it.

   a tricky   b hard to operate

2 GRAMMAR: Past habits

A **Correct the mistakes in each sentence. There may be more than one way to correct each mistake.**

1 When I got sick, my grandmother would ~~made~~ *make* me chicken soup.

2 Before texting, we don't use to be in touch with our friends so often.

3 I would ate soup every day until I felt better.

4 I used to love go to the video store to rent movies.

5 My parents didn't used to let me watch a lot of television.

6 We used to played cards and board games instead.

7 I never use to like playing video games.

8 I am used to read books on rainy days.

B **Change the sentences to show past habits. Use** *(not/never) used to* **or** *would (not)*. **There may be more than one answer.**

1 They exchanged gifts on the holidays.

    They would exchange gifts on the holidays.

2 She cuts her daughter's hair.

3 He took a lot of photographs.

4 We don't play video games.

5 I picked them up from school.

6 You never study for your exams.

3 GRAMMAR AND VOCABULARY

A **Imagine you grew up in a time without the inventions in the box below. Write sentences about your past habits before these inventions. Use** *(not/never) used to*, **or** *would (not)* **and the vocabulary from exercise 1A.**

cars	electricity	eye glasses	internet	~~smartphones~~	washing machines

1   *It used to be frustrating to travel to new cities before smartphones were invented*

    because I would often get lost.

2

3

4

5

6

1 LISTENING

A 🔊 **1.01** Listen to the conversation and (circle) the correct answer.

1 According to Professor Silva, what is confusing for the students?

   a how they survived without smartphones in the past

   b the different rules on smartphones in class

   c why they have to have discussions with each other in class

2 What does Professor Novak think about smartphones in class?

   a She uses them too much.

   b They're useful in a lot of ways.

   c They shouldn't be allowed.

3 By the end of the conversation, both professors:

   a lose their patience.

   b disagree with each other.

   c agree that cell phones can help students.

2 CRITICAL THINKING

A **THINK CRITICALLY** What are the advantages and disadvantages of using a smartphone in a language class? How could it help you with reading, pronunciation, and listening?

_____

_____

_____

_____

_____

3 SPEAKING

A   **Put the conversation in order.**

___ **A**   Yeah, standing in line for tickets and popcorn was part of the excitement. Generally speaking, movies aren't as much fun now. Sure, you can watch from home, but you have to watch it alone or with only a few friends. It was better watching a great movie with a big crowd of people.

___ **B**   Count me in! As for *Star Wars*, I have a costume for almost every character. I'll be there.

_1_ **A**   It's so easy to watch movies nowadays, but I really miss going to the theater.

___ **A**   When it comes to wearing costumes, I usually have a costume party every time a new *Star Wars* movie comes out. You should come next time. It'll be a lot of fun.

___ **B**   That is so true! Remember when the first *Harry Potter* movie came out? There were so many people there. Everyone wore costumes of their favorite characters. It was like a big party.

___ **B**   I couldn't agree more. I miss it, too. Overall, watching movies is easy nowadays, but it's also boring. I used to love standing in line to get tickets, buy popcorn …

B   **Choose one of the topics. Write a conversation between two people. Use phrases for discussing issues and agreeing strongly.**

> 1   People are healthier now than they used to be.
> 2   We used to communicate with each other more frequently.
> 3   Classroom teaching has improved because of technology.
> 4   Social media is a waste of time.

A   _____

B   _____

A   _____

B   _____

A   _____

B   _____

1 READING

A IDENTIFY MAIN IDEAS **What types of activities could tourists do on a farm? Make a list and then read the text to check your answers.**

●●● ‹›

TAKING TOURISM
BACK TO ITS ROOTS

Home   News   About

These days, it often seems like computers do everything for us. But even with all the progress that technology has made, there is comfort in the traditional ways of life. That's why agritourism is on the rise and should continue to be promoted.

Agritourism refers to activities for tourists that take place on a farm or a ranch. There are two main goals of agritourism: to provide meaningful experiences for tourists and to help the farm industry stay alive. The farming economy has suffered. The cost of farm equipment has increased and younger generations don't want to cope with the difficult life of farming, so there is no one to carry on the work.

However, agritourism, which is a branch of eco-tourism, is now a fast-growing part of the travel and tourism economy, and is helping the farm industry improve.

Perhaps you've taken part in this style of tourism without knowing it. Many experiences count as agritourism, such as

touring a ranch or visiting a vineyard. Maybe you've visited a farm and collected fresh eggs, or learned to perform some of the many farming tasks that must be tackled on a daily basis.

Because there is agritourism around the world, many opportunities are available. Tourists can spend the weekend at a farm in the California mountains where they learn how to milk a cow and make cheese, but they can also take tea plantation tours in Taiwan, gather figs at a fig farm in Spain, and enjoy many other experiences where they can be close to nature.

Overall, ranches and farms welcome agritourism. One American study found that in the state of Virginia alone, agritourism supported more than 20,000 jobs and generated $840 million in income. It has been a big step forward in keeping the farming industry alive.

B IDENTIFY SPECIFIC INFORMATION **Read the article again. Then answer the questions.**

1 How do tourists benefit from agritourism? _____

2 How does the farm industry benefit from agritourism? _____

3 Why has the farming economy suffered in recent years? _____

4 What states and countries are mentioned where tourists can experience agritourism? _____

5 How did agritourism benefit the state of Virginia? _____

C IDENTIFY SPECIFIC INFORMATION **Read the article again. Find three agritourism activities a tourist may experience.**

2 CRITICAL THINKING

A THINK CRITICALLY **Why do you think the agritourism industry has become so successful? Would you be interested in an agritourism experience? Why or why not?**

3 WRITING

A The extracts are from an opinion essay about tourism. They are the beginning of each of the four paragraphs. Decide which paragraph each extract belongs in: first, second, third, or fourth.

1 Another problem is the impact of tourists on the environment. For example, one beach in Thailand is so popular that tourists create more garbage than the island can cope with. As a result, a lot of plastic, cans, and other damaging items end up in the ocean.

Paragraph: _____

2 Tourists around the world tend to visit the same places again and again. Everyone wants to see Times Square in New York City or the Grand Palace in Bangkok. However, I think visiting these popular destinations should be discouraged. Too many tourists in one place causes a lot of problems.

Paragraph: _____

3 Of course, it's understandable that tourists want to see popular places because they are interesting. However, it's time to think more about the problems that welcoming too many tourists can cause.

Paragraph: _____

4 The first reason tourists should consider non-popular destinations is because of overcrowding.

Paragraph: _____

B Complete the chart below with the advantages and disadvantages of tourism in a popular destination. Then write a paragraph about whether you agree or disagree that too much tourism can have a negative effect. Use *the first* and *the second,* or *first, next,* and *then* to organize your ideas.

Advantages	Disadvantages

CHECK AND REVIEW

Read the statements. Can you do these things?

UNIT 1	Mark the boxes. ☑ I can do it. ? I am not sure.		If you are not sure, go back to these pages in the Student's Book.
		I can ...	
VOCABULARY	☐	describe dealing with change.	page 2
	☐	describing annoying things.	page 4
GRAMMAR	☐	use the simple present and the present continuous to describe past habits.	page 3
	☐	express annoyance.	page 5
LISTENING AND SPEAKING SKILLS	☐	listen for opinions.	page 6
	☐	use expressions for discussing views on issues.	page 7
READING AND WRITING SKILLS	☐	identify main ideas and specific information.	page 8
	☐	organize information in an opinion essay.	page 9

2.1   DEEP OCEAN OR DEEP SPACE?

1   VOCABULARY: Space and ocean exploration

A   **(Circle) the correct word to complete the sentences.**

1   Some companies think they will be able to *launch* / *monitor* tourists into space within the next few years.

2   The researchers want to *use up* / *preserve* the natural beauty of the ocean.

3   Some experts are worried that humans will *use up* / *come across* the Earth's supply of oil one day.

4   I bought a telescope so I can *preserve* / *observe* the stars at night.

5   The equipment used to *monitor* / *come across* the ocean floor is very expensive.

6   Underwater vehicles are often used for ocean *exploration* / *atmosphere*.

7   Sometimes, *resources* / *satellites* are used to predict the weather.

8   Scientists are continuing their *resources* / *investigation* into why the rocket exploded upon take-off.

9   Too much pollution can create a dirty and unpleasant *atmosphere* / *species*.

10   The ocean contains many useful *resources* / *investigations*, such as salt, sand, copper, and oil.

11   Many *species* / *satellites* that live in the ocean are still being studied by scientists.

12   The tourists didn't *launched* / *come across* any rare type of fish on their boat trip.

13   I love to float on the *atmosphere* / *surface* of the water. It's so relaxing.

2 GRAMMAR: Comparative structures

A Circle the correct word to complete each sentence.

1 I prefer learning about recently discovered plants in the ocean rather than _____ for new types of fish.

   a to search   (b) searching

2 The idea of creatures living on Mars isn't realistic enough _____ searching for them.

   a to continue   b continuing

3 It is less important to find new species _____ it is to save the ones we already know about.

   a then   b than

4 In the future, there will be more jobs in ocean research than _____ space exploration.

   a in   b will be

5 I usually learn more about animals from going to museums _____ I do from watching movies.

   a than   b then

6 There is more water on the surface of the earth _____ land.

   a than   b than is

B Correct the mistake in each sentence.

1 She teaches ~~less~~ *fewer* lessons on space than she does on the ocean.

2 It seems like there is less money available for space exploration then for ocean exploration.

3 Traveling to Mars isn't safe enough justifying sending humans there yet.

4 It's much simpler to explore the ocean then to explore space.

5 The final exam on the stars and the planets was difficult than the English exam.

6 I prefer watching movies about space exploration rather than read about it.

3 GRAMMAR AND VOCABULARY

A Answer the questions with complete sentences. Explain your answers.

1 Which is more important: observing the effects of space on humans or finding life on other planets?

2 Should scientists focus more on preserving the ocean's environment than on discovering new species?

3 Is the International Space Station useful enough to spend government resources on?

4 Should more researchers be exploring the earth's oceans?

2.2 EXTREME LIFE

1 VOCABULARY: The natural world

A **Cross out the word that is different in meaning.**

1 territory   area   ~~border~~
2 sea life   sand   fish
3 plant life   creature   tree
4 origin   creation   destination
5 habitat   environment   pond
6 adaptable   fixed   flexible
7 pond   habitat   lake
8 animal life   volcano   frog

B **Circle the correct word to complete each sentence.**

1 Camels can live for months in the desert without drinking water. They are _____ .
   a plant life   b endangered   **c survivors**

2 The villagers did not hear the noise from the _____ , but they saw smoke rising in the sky.
   a animal life   b volcano   c environment

3 Scientists are trying to identify the new _____ they discovered in the river.
   a territory   b origin   c form of life

4 Cutting down trees in a forest can harm an animal's natural _____ .
   a environment   b creature   c pond

5 Some berries in the forest are _____ . They can make you very sick.
   a poisonous   b plant life   c adaptable

6 The Asian elephant is one of the most famous _____ animals. There are fewer than 50,000 of them left on the planet.
   a poisonous   b endangered   c adaptable

7 Mosquitos are my least favorite _____ . They usually head straight for me even if other people are around.
   a habitats   b origins   c creatures

2 GRAMMAR: Superlative structures; ungradable adjectives

A Complete each sentence with a phrase in the box.

absolutely freezing	completely terrifying	least amount
~~least poisonous~~	most dangerous animals	smallest bird

1 The _____ least poisonous _____ snake is called the rat snake. Its bite may hurt, but it isn't deadly.

2 The _____ that scientists have found is called the bee hummingbird.

3 Greenland is one of the coldest places on Earth. It is _____ , especially in the winter.

4 Crocodiles are one of the _____ in the world. They kill hundreds of people each year.

5 An active volcano is a/an _____ thing to see.

6 The _____ of sleep a typical adult needs to stay healthy is around six to seven hours per night.

B Complete the sentences with phrases from the box and your own ideas.

absolutely awful	most / least adaptable	most / least colorful	most / least dangerous	most / least enjoyable
most / least interesting	most / least pleasant	most / least unique	most / least unlikely	

1 The _____ fish in the ocean is the _____ .

2 Places with a lot of sun are the _____ places to live.

3 _____ are one of the _____ insects on Earth.

4 _____ are one of the _____ animals to see in their natural habitat.

5 The _____ animal in the world is the _____ .

6 The _____ threat to endangered animals is _____ .

3 GRAMMAR AND VOCABULARY

A Complete the sentences about three of the life forms in the box. Use vocabulary from exercises 1A and 1B, superlative structures, and ungradable adjectives.

cockroaches	great white shark	kangaroos
king cobra	~~octopus~~	

1 The octopus is the strangest and most beautiful form of sea life.

2 _____

3 _____

4 _____

1 LISTENING

A 🔊 **2.01** What activities are the people in the photos doing? What is the same about the two activities? What is different? Listen to the conversation and check your answers.

B 🔊 **2.01** **LISTEN FOR DETAILS** Listen to the conversation again. Complete the sentences with the correct number.

1 As a beginner, Felix will most likely dive in about _____ meter(s) of water.

2 A scuba diving oxygen tank lasts for _____ hour(s).

3 There are _____ steps to getting certified for scuba diving.

4 Felix will have to complete _____ dive(s) as part of his certification process.

2 CRITICAL THINKING

A **THINK CRITICALLY** How do you think scuba diving could be beneficial to the environment? How could it be dangerous to the environment?

_____

_____

_____

3 SPEAKING

A **Underline the expressions that ask for or provide specific information in each of the sentences below. Then match the questions to the answers.**

1 What exactly do you mean by saying tigers are endangered? _____
2 Is there any danger of the earth being overpopulated someday? _____
3 Would you recommend living in a desert climate? _____
4 Will tourists travel to space someday? _____
5 Is there a risk of injury when scuba diving? _____

a Maybe. One thing to keep in mind is the lack of rain.
b No. First and foremost, it will be too expensive.
c A small one, but it's generally a safe activity.
d There is a risk they will no longer exist someday.
e Yes, some experts say it will happen by the year 2050.

B **Read the situation below. Write three questions and then give three pieces of information. Remember to use phrases for exchanging information.**

Think of a city you've never been to but would like to go to. Imagine you are planning a trip to that city. You have a friend who recently went there, and you want to ask your friend for information. Write three questions you want to ask.

1 _____
2 _____
3 _____

Now, imagine your friend wants to visit a city you know. What three pieces of information would you give to your friend?

1 _____
2 _____
3 _____

1 READING

A **Look at the picture. Why do people like to watch survival reality shows? Read the article from an entertainment blog. Does it mention your ideas?**

Home   Shows   About

ONLY THE STRONG SURVIVE—And Get Paid For It

Why do we watch television shows where people are obviously uncomfortable? For about the last ten years, shows based on surviving in extreme environments have become very popular. In fact, there are currently more than 50 survival reality shows on television around the world.

These shows usually follow a basic structure. A group of strangers is dropped off in a remote location with limited, or no, supplies. They have to find food, water, and a safe place to sleep each night. Every week, the people on the show vote to remove one member of the group. The last remaining survivor usually wins money and prizes, sometimes up to $1 million.

Sometimes, there are only two people rather than a large group. They are allowed to select one tool, such as a sharp knife or something to help start a fire. They then have three weeks to walk to a new location, where food, water, and a ride home will be waiting for them. This becomes a lesson in working as a team and being patient under extreme circumstances.

Locations for survival reality shows are usually extreme; for example, the jungles of Micronesia, where the average annual rainfall is 100 to 200 inches (2540–5080 mm). The temperatures often reach over 100°F (38° C). One thing to keep in mind in these tropical climates is insects. People usually wake up with enormous mosquito bites, which add to other physical problems such as hunger and thirst.

Perhaps we watch these programs because we want to see how far people can push themselves, or we want to watch others have adventures that we'll never experience. Maybe we want to see them succeed, or maybe we're hoping they'll fail. Whatever the reason, it looks like people will be watching survival reality shows for a long time!

B **UNDERSTAND NUMERICAL WORDS AND PHRASES** **Read the article again. Read the statements. Then write *T* (true) or *F* (false).**

1 There are approximately 50 survival reality shows on television. ⎯⎯⎯

2 Contestants often win more than $1 million. ⎯⎯⎯

3 It usually rains up to 100 inches per year in Micronesia. ⎯⎯⎯

4 Temperatures might be higher than 100°F some days. ⎯⎯⎯

2 CRITICAL THINKING

A **THINK CRITICALLY** **Read the article again. What kind of information do the numbers in the text give?**

⎯⎯⎯

⎯⎯⎯

⎯⎯⎯

3 WRITING

A **USE NUMERICAL WORDS AND PHRASES** Think of a city or town that you would like to visit. Answer the questions about the place you chose. You will need to look up some information online.

1 What is the population?

2 What is the average yearly rainfall?

3 What is the average yearly snowfall?

4 Describe the range of temperatures.

5 Describe the environment.

B Write a paragraph that describes the place you chose in exercise 3A. Use numerical words and phrases, and noun + -*like*. Explain why you would like to visit and what makes it interesting.

CHECK AND REVIEW

Read the statements. Can you do these things?

UNIT 2	Mark the boxes. ☑ I can do it. ? I am not sure. I can …	If you are not sure, go back to these pages in the Student's Book.
VOCABULARY	☐ describe space and ocean exploration. ☐ talk about life forms in the natural world.	page 12 page 14
GRAMMAR	☐ use comparative structures. ☐ use superlative structures and ungradable adjectives.	page 13 page 15
LISTENING AND SPEAKING SKILLS	☐ listen for details. ☐ use expressions to exchange information.	page 16 page 17
READING AND WRITING SKILLS	☐ understand numerical words and phrases. ☐ write a description of an area.	page 18 page 19

3.1   POWER IN QUIET

1   VOCABULARY: Describing personality

A   **Complete each conversation with a phrase in the box.**

attract attention	enjoy the company of	speak softly
speak up	the life of the party	

1   **A**   Anna tells great stories about her world travels. People are always fascinated by them.

    B   Yeah, she sure is _____ .

2   **A**   Why are you sitting in the back of the classroom?

    B   I didn't do my homework, so I don't want to _____ to myself.

3   **A**   Can I come to the library with you to study?

    B   Sure, but we'll have to _____ so we don't disturb people.

4   **A**   Do you spend time with your co-workers outside of work?

    B   Sure. I really _____ my coworkers. They've become my friends.

5   **A**   You have creative ideas. You should _____ more in meetings.

    B   Thanks! That's good advice. I'll try to say more from now on.

B   **Circle the correct word to complete each sentence.**

1   Robert wasn't invited to the movies, so he *felt left out* / *was an introvert*.

2   Each time you *show off* / *interact with* a native speaker, your English will improve.

3   Even if you're *an extrovert* / *an introvert*, it's important to spend time with friends to avoid being alone too often.

4   Whenever we go to a party, Jorge loves to *show off* / *interact with* his dance moves.

5   If I leave my cell phone at home, I'm more likely to *socialize* / *be reserved*. That way, I meet a lot of new people.

6   At school, Jun chats with his friends a lot. It's obvious he *feels left out* / *is an extrovert*.

2   GRAMMAR: Relative pronouns; reduced relative clauses

A   **Combine the sentences to make one sentence.**

1   Wednesday is one day of the week. I have time to go to my exercise class.

    Wednesday is one day of the week when I have time to go to my exercise class.

2   You can read the book. I bought the book yesterday.

    _____

3   She brought her dog on vacation with her. Her dog's name is Duke.

    _____

4   Valentina invited 50 people to her party. Valentina loves celebrating her birthday with her friends.

    _____

5   I ate lunch at a restaurant. The restaurant was voted the best restaurant in the city.

    _____

B **Circle the correct word to complete each sentence.**

1 My favorite time of year is summer vacation, _____ to a lot of parties.
   a when invited   b which I get invited   **c** when I get invited

2 Some introverts prefer to live in small cities, _____ than large cities.
   a that are less crowded   b which are less crowded   c less crowded

3 My best friend grew up in a small town _____ Friendship.
   a where is called   b which calling   c called

4 People _____ social media often say they enjoy making new friends online.
   a who use   b use   c when they use

5 The speaker, _____ is about the effects of social media, gave an interesting presentation.
   a whose research   b which research   c who research

6 There are many studies _____ being alone too often is bad for a person's health.
   a say   b that say   c that saying

3 GRAMMAR AND VOCABULARY

A **Complete each sentence with a word in the box. You may use a word more than once. Then write a sentence that is true for you using the same relative clause structure.**

called	that	where	~~which~~	who	whose

1 a I like to show off my musical skills, ___which___ often makes me the life of the party.
   b I like to _show off my cooking skills, which makes me popular with my friends_ .

2 a I'm a person _____ enjoys the company of strangers.
   b I'm a person _____ .

3 a Being an introvert is a trait _____ should get more respect.
   b Being an introvert _____ .

4 a In class, _____ I'm more reserved, I don't speak up very often.
   b In class, _____ .

5 a Socializing regularly is an activity _____ I value.
   b Socializing _____ .

6 a I'm someone _____ friends are mostly extroverts.
   b I'm someone _____ .

7 a All of my classmates liked the information session _____ "How to succeed in college."
   b All of my classmates _____ .

B **Write a description of a person you know well. Use relative clauses and words to describe his or her personality.**

_____
_____
_____
_____
_____
_____
_____
_____
_____
_____

3.2 THINGS AND EMOTIONS

1 VOCABULARY: Strong feelings

A **Put the words in the correct places in the chart. You will use one word twice.**

~~bizarre~~	creepy	disgusting	~~fabulous~~	impressive	irritating
satisfying	stunning	tense	uneasy	weird	

Positive	Negative
fabulous	bizarre

B **Circle the correct words to complete the sentences.**

1 Overall, my semester was *stunning / satisfying*. I liked my professors and I learned a lot.

2 Animals tend to feel *disgusting / uneasy* before natural disasters, such as earthquakes.

3 Almost everyone agrees that her book is *fabulous / irritating*. It has won many awards.

4 The floor of the restaurant is *weird / disgusting*. There is food and dirt everywhere.

5 Therese feels *tense / fabulous* driving at night because she can't see very well.

6 Do you think my dress is *weird / uneasy*? I made it myself.

7 Those people in the theater were *impressive / irritating*. They talked throughout the entire movie.

8 I used to think broccoli was *creepy / gross,* but now it's one of my favorite vegetables.

9 The man's behavior was *bizarre / satisfying*, so no one wanted to sit next to him.

10 There is a *stunning / creepy* view of the city on top of that building.

11 Anthony gave a/an *weird / impressive* speech, which encouraged people to donate money.

12 I love stories about ghosts, even though I find them *satisfying / creepy*.

2 GRAMMAR: Present participles

A **Match the sentence halves.**

1. As a manager working at a large corporation, ___c___
2. Some people like to take the bus, _____
3. Today, I'm spending time with my childhood friends, _____
4. Abraham loves to sit on his porch alone, _____
5. The people _____
6. This weekend I'm relaxing, _____
7. The sight of someone _____

a. talking about the old days.
b. eating makes me hungry.
c. Lara works a lot of hours.
d. catching up on things I don't have time to do during the week.
e. using the time to read or study.
f. drinking coffee and enjoying the peace.
g. earning the most money donate generously.

B **Complete the sentences with the correct form of the verbs in parentheses.**

1. I get annoyed by ___sitting___ (sit) in traffic, ___waiting___ (wait) for the cars to move.
2. The plane _____ (arrive) from Paris was early, which _____ (make) everyone happy.
3. We _____ (try) the new restaurant, _____ (expect) an excellent meal.
4. As someone _____ (work) in the movie industry, I _____ (watch) a lot of films.
5. The sight of the car _____ (drive) quickly toward me was frightening.
6. She loved _____ (attend) the concert, _____ (listen) to her favorite singer.

3 GRAMMAR AND VOCABULARY

A **Complete the sentences so that they are true for you.**

1. As a child living in _____ , I thought _____ was fabulous.
2. As a student studying English, I think _____ is satisfying.
3. It's impressive to dance while _____ .
4. Animals eating _____ is disgusting.
5. The sound of people _____ is irritating.

B **Complete the sentences. Use present participles.**

1. _____ makes me uneasy.
2. _____ is stunning.
3. _____ looks bizarre.
4. _____ smells weird.
5. _____ sounds creepy.
6. _____ makes me tense.

1 LISTENING

A 🔊 **3.01** **LISTEN FOR INFERENCE** Listen to the conversations. Then answer the questions.

Conversation 1

1 What does Sam say to show that he's uneasy about taking the personality test?

2 What is the likely relationship between Yulia and Sam?

Conversation 2

3 Do you think Gabrielle has experience in the business world? Why or why not?

4 Do you think Gabrielle is an introvert or an extrovert? Explain your answer.

B 🔊 **3.01** Listen to the conversation again. Then answer the questions.

Conversation 1

1 Why does Sam think he might not be able to help Yulia?

2 What does Yulia say that makes Sam feel better about taking the test?

Conversation 2

3 What does Fernanda say to show she supports Gabrielle's idea to be a health coach?

4 Does Fernanda agree to give Gabrielle money for her business? What does she say?

2 CRITICAL THINKING

A **THINK CRITICALLY** What do you think a personality test might reveal about a person? What do you think a personality test might say about you? Would you feel comfortable sharing the results with strangers?

3 SPEAKING

A Answer the requests with phrases from the box and your own ideas. More than one answer may be correct. Use each phrase at least once.

I don't know how much I'd be able to …	I don't mean to be rude, but …
I'd be happy to help you out.	Sorry but I wouldn't be comfortable …
~~Yes, I can probably manage that.~~	

1 **A** Is there any chance you could give me a ride to work tomorrow?

 B _Yes, I can probably manage that._ I'll pick you up at 8 a.m.

2 **A** Do you think it would be possible for me to see your notes from class?

 B _____ didn't you take your own notes in class today?

3 **A** Would you be willing to lend me some money?

 B _____ How much do you need?

4 **A** Is there any chance you could teach me the new software program?

 B _____ I don't really know how the new software works.

5 **A** Do you think it would be possible for me to borrow your car?

 B _____ lending you my car. I'm usually the only one who drives it.

6 **A** I found a new apartment. Would you be willing to help me move?

 B _____ When is your moving date?

B Complete the conversations with phrases from the box in exercise 3A.

1 **Boss** Is there any chance you could work late tonight?

 Employee _____

 _____

2 **Roommate A** Do you think it would be possible for my friend Jack to move in with us?

 Roommate B _____

 _____

3 **Classmate A** Would you be willing to explain the teacher's lecture to me? I didn't understand most of it.

 Classmate B _____

 _____

THE RIGHT JOB FOR ME

1 READING

A Read the job names in the article. Name one thing a person who works each of the jobs might typically do. Then read the article and check your answers.

Get Out of Your Comfort Zone at Work

For some people, a typical work day includes sitting at a desk, taking phone calls, and tapping away at a computer. However, there are plenty of more unusual careers for people who want something a little different. Would you like to interact with poisonous snakes, study emoji icons, or eat ice cream all day and get paid for it? Read about three unique jobs and see if they are right for you.

EMOJI TRANSLATOR

Emojis have become so effective in communicating emotions that international corporations now use them to connect with clients. But just as human body language varies across cultures, so do expressions and gestures communicated by emojis. For example, the thumbs-up sign may be positive in the United States, but it is insulting in Russia. Companies are now hiring emoji translators who report on how emojis can cause problems in different cultures.

ICE CREAM TASTER

John Harrison starts his work day at 7:30 a.m. when his taste buds are at their sharpest. He then samples around 20 ice cream flavors, which he analyzes for taste and smell. It's not as easy as it sounds, though. Harrison's formal job title is "flavorologist." People who would like to have this dream-like career should have experience in food science, product development, and maybe even chemistry. They must have an excellent sense of taste, and they may also be responsible for inventing new ice cream flavors.

SNAKE MILKER

Are you uneasy around snakes? Then this job definitely isn't for you. A snake milker extracts poisonous venom from snakes, which is then used to develop treatments for medical conditions. Someone holding this job must be comfortable caring for snakes, making sure they are not harmed in the process. Snake milkers usually have degrees in animal biology, and they may work in research labs, universities, and zoos.

B IDENTIFY AUDIENCE Read the article again. Then answer the questions.

1 Who is the audience for the text?

a high school students

b people who like their jobs

c people looking for a career change

C How do you think most readers would feel about each job?

1 emoji translator _____

2 ice cream taster _____

3 snake milker _____

2 CRITICAL THINKING

A THINK CRITICALLY Would you like to work at any of the jobs mentioned in the article? Why or why not? Is there another unusual job you'd like to have?

_____

_____

_____

A Think of *five* words or phrases that describe your personality and give a specific example that illustrates each word or phrase.

B Look online for a job you would be interested in applying for. Think about skills you have that are relevant for the job.

C Write a personal statement for the job you chose in exercise 3B. It should highlight your skills and personality, explaining why they would make you suitable for the job. Use *in order to* in your answer.

CHECK AND REVIEW

Read the statements. Can you do these things?

UNIT 3	Mark the boxes. ✔ I can do it. ? I am not sure. I can …		If you are not sure, go back to these pages in the Student's Book.
VOCABULARY	☐ describe personality types.		page 22
	☐ express things I like and don't like.		page 24
GRAMMAR	☐ use relative clauses to add description to sentences.		page 23
	☐ use present participles to describe two events happening at the same time.		page 25
LISTENING AND SPEAKING SKILLS	☐ listen for inference.		page 26
	☐ role play making and responding to requests.		page 27
READING AND WRITING SKILLS	☐ identify audience for a text.		page 28
	☐ write a personal statement.		page 29

1 VOCABULARY: Professional relationships

A Circle the correct definition of the word in bold.

1 As a restaurant owner, I **oversee** every aspect of the business.
   a watch to make certain something is done correctly
   b ask someone for help or advice

2 Role models, such as famous writers or athletes, often **contribute** to a person's success in life.
   a accept responsibility for
   b give something

3 I couldn't decide which jobs I wanted to apply for, so I **turned to** a career counselor for help.
   a asked someone for help or advice
   b helped someone

4 Frances received a large grant to **assist** her in her research.
   a show or prove that something is true
   b help

5 In order to get the job, Ruth had to **demonstrate** that she could work well on a team.
   a watch to make certain something is done correctly
   b show or prove that something is true

B Complete the paragraph with the words in the box.

acts as	build a relationship	build trust
enables us to	~~keep an eye on~~	steer everyone away from

I come from a family with three kids. My sister Annie is the youngest. She's only seven, so we all have to
¹ _____keep an eye on_____ her. Monica is the oldest, which means she often ² _____
our boss, even when our parents are around! I'm in the middle, so it's my job to ³ _____
arguing with each other. Our parents often tell us how important siblings are because we
⁴ _____ with each one of them, and those relationships will be our models throughout
our lives. They also tell us it's important to ⁵ _____ with each other. That
⁶ _____ always have people in our lives to rely on.

2 GRAMMAR: Adding emphasis: *so ... that, such ... that, even, only*

A Complete the sentences with *even* or *only*.

1 I _____ need a little more money to buy the car of my dreams.

2 She can speak four languages, _____ Mandarin, which I find really difficult.

3 I'm so busy I don't _____ have time to cook.

4 I _____ trust one person and that's my best friend.

5 The company is growing so fast that their _____ focus is to hire more people.

B **Choose the correct words or phrases to complete each sentence.**

1 It was _____ movie that I left before it was over.

   a so scary   **(b)** such a scary

2 She was _____ that she fell asleep on the subway.

   a so much tired   **b** so tired

3 Rita _____ has a month to go before she finishes law school.

   a only   **b** even

4 Hyun has _____ homework that he has to stay up all night to finish it.

   a so much   **b** such

5 I'm _____ that I don't think I'll ever eat again!

   a so full   **b** such full

6 The snow was so heavy that I couldn't _____ see where the road was.

   a only   **b** even

7 Francis is _____ intelligent that he was accepted to all the best colleges.

   a so   **b** such

3 GRAMMAR AND VOCABULARY

A **Use the information to write new sentences. Use the words in parentheses to add emphasis.**

1 Adam's teacher keeps an eye on him at all times. (so … that)

   Adam is so lazy in class that his teacher keeps an eye on him at all times.

2 Vera was a good temporary department manager. (such … that)

3 My friends steer me away from bad decisions. (only)

4 That woman contributes money to the school every year. (so … that)

5 Mariah has very little money. She cannot pay the rent. (even)

6 I've built a strong relationship with my sister. (such … that)

7 It was difficult to demonstrate the new computer system. (so … that)

8 I oversee one small department of employees. (only)

4.2 DESTRUCTIVE TEAMS

1 VOCABULARY: Assessing ideas

A **Cross out the word that is different in meaning.**

1	valid	~~illegal~~	acceptable
2	destructive	productive	harmful
3	weakness	imperfection	advantage
4	aspect	part	whole
5	point out	hide	tell
6	assess	study	ignore
7	constructive	negative	useful

B **Complete the sentences with the words and phrases in the box.**

consequence	draw attention to
strength	~~think through~~
unreasonable	weigh the pros and cons

1 Lucas needs to _____think through_____ his job offer. The job would require him to move across the country, so it's a big decision.

2 When making a major decision, it's necessary to _____ . There are good and bad points to everything.

3 Being decisive is usually considered a/an _____ in the business world.

4 It is _____ to ask people to work more than five days per week.

5 In my presentation, I plan to _____ the problem of unemployment in our city. I want to make sure the audience is aware of it.

6 As a/an _____ of missing the final exam, Haewon failed the class.

28

2 GRAMMAR: Reflexive pronouns; pronouns with *other/another*

A **Circle the correct form of *other/another*.**

1 I got to the restaurant before everyone else. *The others / The other* hadn't arrived yet.

2 Every successful relationship requires respecting *one another / the other*.

3 Our team is too small to get the job done. We need *other / another* person.

4 I have two sisters. One is a lawyer and *the other / another* is a judge.

5 When the *other / others* arrive, we'll begin the meeting.

B **Complete the sentences with a reflexive pronoun.**

1 Before you say yes, ask _____yourself_____ if you really want to take on another project.

2 He enjoys going to the movies by _____ .

3 Our team won the championship. We should be proud of _____ .

4 The computer will shut _____ down in one hour.

5 She finally bought _____ a new car.

6 Are you and Dana going to leave _____ enough time to finish the project?

7 Before looking for a new job, he asked _____ what his strengths and weaknesses were.

3 GRAMMAR AND VOCABULARY

A **Answer the questions with information so that is true for you. Use complete sentences. Use reflexive pronouns, pronouns with *other/another*, and vocabulary from exercises 1A and 1B.**

1 When are the opinions of others more valid than your own opinions?

_____

2 How can spending too much time by yourself have negative consequences?

_____

3 Has another person ever told you that you were being unreasonable?

_____

4 When was the last time you had to really think something through?

_____

TWO PEOPLE, ONE JOB

1 LISTENING

A ◄)) **4.01** **LISTEN FOR ATTITUDE** Listen and answer the questions.

1 What attitude does Katrina have?

   a helpful   **b** happy   **c** negative

2 What attitude do the audience members have?

   a angry   **b** positive   **c** concerned

3 How certain is Katrina that her company retreat will be successful?

   a very certain   **b** partly certain   **c** not very certain

4 How does Katrina respond to the audience's questions?

   a with doubt   **b** with reassurance   **c** with impatience

B ◄)) **4.01** Listen again. Circle the correct answer.

1 Katrina's company offers:

   a one-day retreats   **b** seven-day retreats   **c** a variety of retreats

2 Katrina points out that employees on retreats might worry about:

   a being bored   **b** their schedule   **c** their clients

3 According to Katrina, the benefits of retreats include:

   a playing games   **b** building trust   **c** missing work

4 Katrina helps with:

   a scheduling   **b** looking after other clients   **c** having fun

2 CRITICAL THINKING

A **THINK CRITICALLY** Make a list of the advantages and disadvantages of a company retreat. What are some games or activities that would help build relationships at a company retreat?

3 SPEAKING

A **Put the conversation in order.**

_____ **A** Oh, no. I'd be concerned that I would get lost if I traveled by myself.

_____ **B** That's right, Angela. I'm leaving in a few weeks. I'll be gone for six months.

_____ **B** Well, the upside is that it makes you independent. If you get lost, you just figure it out on your own.

_____ **A** Aren't you worried about being lonely? Or bored?

_____ **A** That's true. I guess I have some unreasonable fears. I'm so worried about everything that I doubt I would have a good time. Well, have fun!

___1___ **A** Hi, Adrian. I heard you were planning to take a trip to South America by yourself.

_____ **B** No, not at all. The main benefit of traveling alone is that it's easy to build relationships with other travelers. Have you ever traveled alone?

B **Write a dialogue in which you try to convince your boss to let you do one of the following: take a year off to study a language abroad, work from home, or give you a raise. Use expressions for discussing advantages and disadvantages.**

You _____

Your boss _____

You _____

Your boss _____

You _____

Your boss _____

4.4 THE ME TEAM

1 READING

A Think of three benefits that playing team sports might have for children. Then read the article and check your ideas.

Sports for Life

Team sports have the potential to play a vital role in a child's life. Of course, there are the health benefits that exercise brings. An active child is overall a happier, healthier child. Another plus is that sports expose children to the value of working on a team. They learn to solve problems better, and they build relationships with others. This aspect of team sports is important later in life, too, when they're ready to enter the workforce.

You might say that the downside of team sports is the possibility of losing. In fact, losing contributes to important life skills, too. Everyone loves to celebrate when their team wins. But imagine if your child's team has practiced and worked hard and is confident they're going to win the next game, but they end up losing. That would be a real disappointment, wouldn't it?

But that loss demonstrates to your child that a person can work hard at something and still not succeed. Children learn to keep trying and not to give up. They keep hoping for a more successful outcome. After all, losing isn't a weakness; it's an opportunity for improvement. It also teaches children to share their disappointment with their teammates, so they don't have to take on those negative feelings all by themselves.

Parents often worry about the downside of team sports. They argue that sports can take up a lot of time that their child could spend on academics. However, athletes actually do better in school. Because games like soccer, baseball, and football have specific and complicated rules, memorization and repeated practice are required. These are skills that carry over into learning a language, for example when you weigh the pros and cons, it's obvious that team sports are the clear winner.

B **UNDERSTAND AUTHOR'S ATTITUDE** Read the article again. Then answer the questions.

1 What is the author's attitude toward team sports?

   a encouraging   **b** pessimistic   **c** undecided

2 Find three reasons to support your answer to Question 1.

   1 _____

   2 _____

   3 _____

C Read the article again. Answer the questions.

1 What are three benefits of team sports that the author gives? _____

_____

2 What does losing teach children? _____

_____

3 How do team sports help a child's academic performance? _____

_____

2 CRITICAL THINKING

A **THINK CRITICALLY** Do you think that the benefits of children playing team sports outweigh the challenges? Why or why not?

_____

_____

3 WRITING

A **Read the summary. Cross out the sentences that don't belong. Why don't the sentences belong in the summary?**

I recently read a book about a young man who grew up in the South of the United States. It was a true story. The author wrote about growing up in poverty and how it was a difficult life for him and his family. It also affected his performance in school. His grades suffered, and he almost dropped out of high school. I am glad his teachers helped him stay in school. He must have had good teachers who cared about him. The author finally graduated from high school and went on to college. While in college, he took a part-time job and was able to buy a car. When he graduated from college, he had excellent grades and he decided to go to law school. I don't know if I could ever finish law school because it sounds very difficult. After law school, he got a job and made enough money to help support his family. He felt very proud of the accomplishments he made in his life, even though it was a hard life at first.

B **SUMMARIZE MAIN POINTS** **Write a summary of the article on page 32. Decide if it's more appropriate to use *state* or *say* when you report the author's words.**

_____

_____

_____

_____

_____

_____

_____

_____

CHECK AND REVIEW

Read the statements. Can you do these things?

UNIT 4	Mark the boxes. ☑ I can do it. ? I am not sure. I can ...	If you are not sure, go back to these pages in the Student's Book.
VOCABULARY	☐ describe supportive people.	page 34
	☐ use words and phrases to assess ideas.	page 36
GRAMMAR	☐ use expressions that add emphasis.	page 35
	☐ use reflexive pronouns and forms of *other/another*.	page 37
LISTENING AND SPEAKING SKILLS	☐ listen for a speaker's attitude.	page 38
	☐ discuss advantages and disadvantages.	page 39
READING AND WRITING SKILLS	☐ understand an author's attitude.	page 40
	☐ summarize main points.	page 41

5.1   IMITATING REALITY

1   VOCABULARY: Dealing with emotions

A   **Complete the sentences with the words and phrases in the box.**

| anxiety level | are rational | breathing technique | cure | ~~overcome a fear~~ | try a therapy |

1   When you _____*overcome a fear*_____, you are no longer afraid of something.
2   When you _____ an illness, you make it better.
3   When your _____ is high, you feel nervous and upset.
4   When you _____, you can think about and explain things clearly.
5   When you are using a(n) _____, you might count your breaths.
6   When you _____, you should talk to an expert.

B   Circle **the words or phrases to complete the sentences.**

1   When you *panic /* (*calm down*) you feel more relaxed.
2   You might *cure an illness / panic* when you take a test.
3   If you are *scared to death / conscious* of taking risks, you probably won't start a business.
4   If you *try a therapy / regain control*, you have power.
5   When you *overcome a fear / are conscious* of something, you are aware of it.
6   Usually, people *are in control / regain control* of their actions.

2   GRAMMAR: Real conditionals

A   **Match the sentence halves.**

1   If you want to do yoga at home,   _c_   a   if he spends too much time online.
2   When patients need medical advice at home, _____   b   I can't sleep at night.
3   My anxiety level becomes very high   _____   c   you could watch some videos.
4   I might take away my son's tablet   _____   d   when I breathe deeply a few times.
5   If you want to meet tomorrow,   _____   e   I may see a therapist.
6   I usually regain control of my emotions   _____   f   some doctors will talk to them on Skype.
7   Whenever I see a scary movie,   _____   g   whenever I see a snake.
8   If I can't get over my fear of spiders,   _____   h   you'll have to come to my office.

B   **Check (✓) the correct sentences. Correct the incorrect sentences.**

1   If you're scared to death of something, listening to music might help you calm down.   ☑

2   If I ~~will~~ decide to try a new therapy, I'll ask you to recommend a therapist.   ☐
    If I decide to try a new therapy, I'll ask you to recommend a therapist.

3   I use a breathing technique when my anxiety level was too high.   ☐

4   When ever I panic about something, I imagine I am at the beach relaxing.   ☐

5   If I can overcome my fear of crowded places, when I will go to the concert.   ☐

6   When you will calm down maybe you'll be more rational.   ☐

7   I might try to run a marathon if I can regain control of my health.   ☐

8   Whenever I used my meditation app, I am more in control of my thoughts.   ☐

9   When you're conscious of the source of your fear, it's easier to overcome it.   ☐

10 Whenever I can cure my fear of heights, I may climb Mount Everest.   ☐

3   GRAMMAR AND VOCABULARY

A   **Read the situations below and give three suggestions for each one. Use real conditionals and the words in the boxes.**

1   Your friend dreams of going hiking in the jungles of Indonesia. However, your friend is terrified of snakes, and Indonesia is home to many poisonous snakes.

~~be scared to death~~	calm down	overcome a fear

a   If you are scared to death, try to think of something positive instead.
b   _____
c   _____

2   Your friend tells you that every time he goes to a party, he feels anxious. He is nervous meeting new people.

be conscious of	be in control of	breathing technique

a   _____
b   _____
c   _____

3   Your classmate is very intelligent, but she freezes every time she takes a test. She ends up getting a low grade.

anxiety level	panic	try a therapy

a   _____
b   _____
c   _____

5.2 THE END OF THE OFFICE?

1 VOCABULARY: Willingness and unwillingness

A (Circle) the correct words to complete the sentences.

1 Alexandra _____ work at home because she doesn't think she would get a lot of work done.

   a   is eager to   (b) is reluctant to

2 Morgan _____ be his own boss. He likes making his own schedule and not having to explain his actions to anyone.

   a   is more than happy to   b   has no desire to

3 I _____ communicate with coworkers via text message because I don't want to share my cell phone number.

   a   am unwilling to   b   have no intention of

4 Alisha doesn't like to wake up early. She _____ change her work schedule.

   a   hesitates to   b   is dying to

5 If an employee _____ driving to work every day, he or she might look for a job that involves working from home.

   a   is passionate about   b   is against

6 When starting your own business at home, you have to _____ separate your work time from your leisure time, so that you don't work too much.

   a   be prepared to   b   be anxious to

2 GRAMMAR: Conditionals: alternatives to *if*

A (Circle) the correct words or phrases to complete the sentences.

1 We can have our meeting via video call (*as long as*)/ *unless* the internet connection is strong.

2 My boss said I can work at home *even if* / *providing* I come into the office once a month.

3 A company is successful *only if* / *even if* the employees are happy and productive.

4 I won't work from home *unless* / *providing that* I move to a bigger house.

5 I don't mind working in an office *even if* / *provided that* I can set my own schedule.

6 I love working at home and wouldn't go back to an office, *so long as* / *even if* you paid me more money.

7 I will invest in your business, but *only if* / *unless* you give me a percentage of your profits.

8 You can take a long vacation *unless* / *so long as* you finish your work before you go.

B   Complete the conversation in a job interview between the interviewer (A) and the candidate (B). Use the correct form of the phrases in parentheses.

1   A   _____Are_____ you _____eager to_____ work here? (be eager to)

2   B   Yes. I _____ the work your company does. I want to work here even if I have to start at an entry level position. (be passionate about)

3   A   _____ you _____ socialize outside of work, provided that it's an event that helps build relationships with your coworkers? (be willing to)

4   B   Sure, I _____ , so long as I don't have to stay out too late. (be more than happy to)

    A   Do you plan to continue your training in this field? For example, do you have any intention of getting a master's degree?

5   B   Well, I _____ say yes to that because school is very expensive. I'd like to continue my training, but only if there was financial assistance. (hesitate to)

6   A   If you work here, you will share an office with several of your coworkers. _____ you _____ that? (be against)

    B   That's fine with me. I don't mind sharing an office.

    A   Great! Are you ready to start work immediately?

7   B   Yes, I _____ start tomorrow as long as you want to hire me. (be prepared to)

3 GRAMMAR AND VOCABULARY

A   Complete the sentences with your own ideas.

1   I'm reluctant to go back to school even if   _my job pays for it_

_____ .

2   I'm eager to travel to foreign countries so long as _____

_____ .

3   I hesitate to find a new job unless _____

_____ .

4   I'm more than happy to help you with your problem, providing _____

_____ .

5   I have no desire to go to the gym unless _____

_____ .

6   I'm anxious to learn how to drive even if _____

_____ .

5.3 STOP BLAMING GAMING

1 LISTENING

A 🔊 **5.01** **LISTEN FOR SPEAKER'S DEGREE OF CERTAINTY** Listen to the podcast about banning technology in the home. Is the speaker certain or uncertain about his or her ideas? Listen to the language describing these ideas and check (✓)the ones that sound confident.

☐ 1 **Ingrid** So yes, spending too much time online can lead to problems in a child's emotional development.

☐ 2 **Ingrid** Parents simply need to be conscious of how much time is spent online.

☐ 3 **Host** Their home is absolutely free of modern technology.

☐ 4 **Leon** You can bet those parents have inside knowledge about how companies make sure that kids want to use devices all the time.

☐ 5 **Leon** But who knows how long that calmness lasts?

B 🔊 **5.01** **Listen to the podcast again. Then answer the questions.**

1 Why did Leon ban technology in his home?

2 What is 27% more likely to happen when teenagers use social media too often?

3 Why did Leon say the parents have "inside knowledge?" What is their "inside knowledge?"

4 What alternative does Ingrid suggest to a total technology ban?

5 How does Leon feel about a "no-tech" week?

2 CRITICAL THINKING

A **THINK CRITICALLY** Whose view about banning technology in the home do you agree with the most? Why?

3 SPEAKING

A Complete the conversation with the expressions in the box. More than one answer may be correct.

at the same time	I don't have a clue	I guarantee that	it's a well-known fact
on the contrary	that said	Who knows	you can bet that

Thomas I'm going on a complete digital detox. I'm not going to use anything internet-based for 30 days.
¹ _I guarantee that_ I'll be more focused afterwards.

Ivan Well, ² _____ that too much screen time before bed negatively affects a person's sleep, so you'll also be more rested.

Thomas Exactly. And I'll have more free time. ³ _____? Maybe I'll learn a language or a musical instrument.

Ivan ⁴ _____, you might have *too* much free time. How do you plan to stay in touch with people?

Thomas ⁵ _____. I guess writing letters is a thing of the past.
⁶ _____, it might be a good way to connect with people more deeply.

Ivan ⁷ _____ it'll be tough at times.
⁸ _____, I don't think I could ever do it, and I respect you for trying.

B Write a contrasting answer to each statement. Use the expressions from exercise 3A.

1 When teenagers use social media too often, their risk of depression increases.
At the same time, it can be a good way to help shy kids interact with others.

2 People would be much happier if they didn't have to drive to their offices every day.

3 If people work at home, they may become lonely.

4 I guarantee that kids will complain if they can't use technology for one week.

5 I don't have a clue how you can work in the technology industry and not use technology.

5.4 WHAT LANGUAGE BARRIER?

1 READING

A Read the article. <u>Underline</u> the formal and informal connecting expressions. As an article on a blog, should it be more formal?

⊗ ▣ ⊖

CULTURAL ETIQUETTE IN THE DIGITAL AGE

When we think of language barriers while traveling, one of the first images that we often think of is a lost traveler, gesturing wildly to a confused local person.

The lost traveler doesn't know the local language, nor does he or she understand that gestures can be culture-based, too. In the last decade or so, another barrier to being understood in a new culture has appeared—cell phone etiquette.

OK, imagine this situation. An American man is on the subway in Japan when his cell phone rings. He answers and has a brief conversation. He keeps his voice low, but he still senses that people are annoyed. Later, he learns that it's actually rude to talk on a cell phone in public places in Japan. There's not much he can do to correct his previous poor behavior, so the next time he rides the subway, he simply switches his phone to silent.

Cell phone use can cause problems in the same way a misunderstood word or gesture can. And in the same way, knowing the correct action depends on which culture you're dealing with.

Trying to catch up on phone calls during lunch? If you're eating, you'll be considered rude if the person on the other end is from the United Kingdom. Therefore, save your UK calls for after lunch.

With regards to answering calls in public places, it's acceptable in the United States; however, it's rude if you're in the middle of a face-to-face conversation. In China, on the other hand, you may be in for a surprise if your in-person conversation is interrupted when your friend takes a call from another person.

It's easy to create cultural barriers. That said, the best way to avoid them is to educate yourself whenever dealing with cultures different from your own.

GLOSSARY

etiquette (n) the set of rules or customs that control accepted behavior in particular social groups or social situations
gesture (n) the movement of the hands, arms, or head to express an idea or feeling

B **UNDERSTAND PROBLEMS AND SOLUTIONS** Read the article again. How did the person on the subway in Japan correct his error?

_____

_____

C Read the article again. ⃝Circle the correct answer.

1 When it comes to cell phones:
  a etiquette is similar in most countries.
  b something rude in one culture may be acceptable in another.
  c it's alright to follow the culture you are from, no matter which country you're in.

2 The writer uses the example of the lost traveler to show that:
  a everyone should speak a foreign language.
  b everyone gets lost when they travel.
  c not knowing language and etiquette can cause problems.

3 What effect does the phrase, "OK, imagine this" have?
  a It asks the reader to picture a situation.
  b It asks the reader to agree with a situation.
  c It asks the reader to think of another example.

2 CRITICAL THINKING

A   What is your opinion of using cell phones in a public place? In what situations do you think this is acceptable or not acceptable?

_____

_____

_____

3 WRITING

A   Read the statements. <u>Underline</u> the organizing and connecting expressions. Then write *O* if it's an opinion and *F* if it's a fact.

1   With regards to cell phones, children in the United States get their first one around age ten, on average. ____

2   That said, speaking loudly on a cell phone in public is rude. ____

3   So yes, cell phone etiquette varies from country to country. ____

4   As for the increased use of cell phones, Finland was the first country to have more cell phones than landlines. ____

5   OK, cell phones are a necessary part of life. ____

B   STATE OPINION AND GIVE EXAMPLES   Write a paragraph about the use of cell phones in public. Give examples of times when it could be a problem, and how that problem could be solved. Use organizing and connecting expressions when possible.

_____

_____

_____

_____

_____

_____

CHECK AND REVIEW

Read the statements. Can you do these things?

UNIT 5	Mark the boxes. ✔ I can do it. ? I am not sure.	If you are not sure, go back to these pages in the Student's Book.
	I can …	
VOCABULARY	☐ use phrases to discuss emotions.	page 44
	☐ use phrases to explain willingness and unwillingness.	page 46
GRAMMAR	☐ use real conditionals for general facts and possible future situations.	page 45
	☐ use conditionals with alternatives to *if*.	page 47
LISTENING AND SPEAKING SKILLS	☐ listen for phrases that express degrees of certainty.	page 48
	☐ use expressions to discuss and contrast ideas.	page 49
READING AND WRITING SKILLS	☐ understand problems and solutions.	page 50
	☐ state an opinion.	page 51

6.1   GOING VIRAL

1   VOCABULARY: Talking about fame

A   **Match the sentences.**

1   There are a lot of negative comments about him on gossip websites.   _d_

2   He works hard to tell people about problems in our society.   a   He makes headlines.

3   His name is on the front page of the newspaper today.   b   It gets hits.

4   He will go to the party for a few minutes, but then he has to leave.   c   He raises awareness.

5   He can sing and dance, and he plays the piano.   d   He has a bad reputation.

6   Tens of thousands of people watch his video every week.   e   He makes concerts entertaining.

       f   He will make an appearance.

B   **Circle the correct words to complete the sentences.**

1   They asked Colin to *make headlines / do the broadcast* since he was the only person with television experience.

2   You *have never heard of / raise awareness of* someone if you don't know the person's name.

3   You should do something kind if you want to *make an appearance / catch somebody's attention*.

4   In his speech, he plans to *get hits / praise his mother* for helping him succeed.

5   You might *have a good reputation / get publicity* if you do something terrible.

6   She never intended to *seek fame / praise somebody*; however, everyone in the world knows her name.

2 GRAMMAR: Narrative tenses

A Circle the correct words to complete the sentence.

1 He hadn't _____ for attention when he planned his cross-country bike ride.

   a been looking   **b** been looked   **c** looks

2 As the man _____ the young girl, several people were recording it on their cell phones.

   a rescuing   **b** rescued   **c** had rescued

3 She made her students laugh while she _____ her class.

   a is teaching   **b** taught   **c** had taught

4 She had been an actor for ten years before people _____ recognizing her.

   a had started   **b** start   **c** started

5 She had been taking care of animals for a long time before her story _____ in the news.

   a appearing   **b** appeared   **c** had been appearing

6 People were already talking about her voice as she _____ the song.

   a finishes   **b** finishing   **c** finished

B **Underline** the event in each sentence that happens first. If the events happen at the same time, write *S* on the line.

1 When Kiley was growing up, she didn't play any sports. _____

2 In high school, she was trying to get in shape, and she started playing on a basketball team. _____

3 She had been playing for about six months before someone wrote an article about her in a magazine. _____

4 Kylie helped her team win game after game, even though she had only been trying to get in shape. _____

5 Kylie hadn't planned on becoming famous before the article appeared in the magazine. _____

6 From then on, during her athletic career, she encouraged other young girls to play sports, too. _____

3 GRAMMAR AND VOCABULARY

A **Respond to *three* of the statements with information so that is true for you. Use the past continuous, past perfect, or past perfect continuous.**

1 Describe a situation where you or someone you know got a lot of hits on social media.

   My friend had been putting pictures of her food on social media for about a year when she started to get a lot of hits.

2 Describe a time you or someone you know made headlines.

3 Describe how you caught your parents' attention when you were a child.

4 Describe a time when someone unexpected made an appearance at a big party or event.

5 Describe a situation in which you raised awareness of a social issue.

6.2 NOT AGAIN!

1 VOCABULARY: Reporting verbs

A Circle the correct definitions.

1 confirm
   a to say that something is true
   b to say that something is strange

2 hope to
   a to want something to happen
   b to say that something is true

3 announce
   a to talk with too much pride about what you have done
   b to tell a group of people about something

4 swear
   a to say that you are sure something is true
   b to pretend you don't know something

B Cross out the word or phrase that is different in meaning.

1	propose	suggest	~~remove~~
2	estimate	deceive	guess
3	have doubts about	be uncertain	be certain
4	insist	say firmly	forget
5	deny	accept	oppose

2 GRAMMAR: Reported speech with modal verbs

A Check (✓) the correct sentences. Correct the incorrect sentences. Sentences should be in the past tense.

1 I argued that we will need another month to complete the project. ☐
   I argued that we would need another month to complete the project.

2 They explained that they might not come to the ceremony. ☐

3 They confirmed that they won't refund my money. ☐

4 We told everyone that they should come to our house early. ☐

5 He said he had doubts that he can show up on time. ☐

B Rewrite the second line in each conversation as reported speech. Use a variety of reporting verbs.

1 **Guest** Do you have any rooms available tonight?
   Hotel employee No, sorry. We won't have a room free until tomorrow.
   The hotel employee claimed they wouldn't have a room free until tomorrow.

2 **Customer** I forgot my wallet, so I'm afraid I can't pay the bill.
   Waiter That's OK. You can come back tomorrow and pay.

3 **Mikhail** The subway isn't running. I don't know how I'm going to get to work.
   Judi I might be able to help you.

44

3 GRAMMAR AND VOCABULARY

A **Rewrite the sentences in reported speech using the subject and verb in parentheses. Supply a subject for the sentences if necessary.**

1 "The new smartphones will go on sale next week." (the company / announce)

   The company announced that the new smartphones would go on sale next week.

2 "We will arrive in Los Angeles on time." (pilot / claim)

3 "The meeting will start at 9:00 a.m." (my boss / confirm)

4 "I could do a better job if I were given the chance." (the young man / argue)

5 "The bus will not be late." (the driver / insist)

6 "I can make the best chocolate cake in the world." (the chef / boast)

B **Imagine you just moved into a new apartment. When you moved in, you found that the landlord had not done what he promised. Look at the conversation you had with the landlord and the problems below. Report the conversation to a friend. Use reporting verbs from the word box.**

claim	confirm	estimate	explain
insist	say	swear	tell

You Hmm, I don't think I like the bright green walls.

Landlord Oh, that's no problem. I can paint them white before you move in.

You OK. And are the neighbors upstairs noisy?

Landlord Oh, no. They're very quiet. You won't even know they're there!

You Great, but I don't see a refrigerator in the kitchen.

Landlord It's getting repaired and will be here soon. If it takes too long, I might just buy a new one.

You Sounds good. And what about the backyard? Can I use it whenever I want to?

Landlord Sure, it's all yours. You could even have parties and invite your friends.

Problems:

• He didn't paint the walls.

• The neighbors are very noisy.

• There's no refrigerator in the kitchen.

• The backyard is now full of old furniture.

   First, the landlord claimed he could paint the walls before I moved in.

SOMETHING IN THE WATER

1 LISTENING

A **Listen to a conversation between Evelyn and Luisa. How do they know each other?**

a they're neighbors

b they're mother and daughter

c they're close friends

B 🔊 **6.01** UNDERSTAND MEANING FROM CONTEXT **Listen to the conversation again. Guess the meaning of the words below. What clues helped you to work out their meaning?**

1 biscotti

guess: _____

clues: _____

2 dunking

guess: _____

clues: _____

3 love seat

guess: _____

clues: _____

4 brick and mortar

guess: _____

clues: _____

2 CRITICAL THINKING

A THINK CRITICALLY **What makes a good neighbor? Is Evelyn a good neighbor for coming to Luisa's house? Why or why not?**

_____

_____

_____

3 SPEAKING

A   **Put the conversation in order.**

_____ **Ben** You must have been hungry.

_____ **Ben** I assume they cancelled the party, and everyone went home.

_____ **Jun** The server brought our food on a tray, but because it was dark, he tripped and all of it went flying across the dining room. We waited another half an hour for new meals.

_____ **Ben** Uh-oh. What?

__1__ **Ben** How was the anniversary party last night?

_____ **Ben** I suppose you fed everyone and saved the party.

_____ **Jun** Not at all. We lit candles, and someone used their smartphone to play music. But then something terrible happened.

_____ **Jun** To an extent, but you know I always have snacks hidden in my bag.

_____ **Jun** It was interesting. Because of the big storm, the power went out. It was totally dark inside the restaurant.

B   **Write a short conversation for each situation below.**

1   You went to the airport to catch a flight for a business trip. You arrived on time for your flight, but when you went to check in, you realized you were at the wrong airport. You tell your coworker about it the next day.

You _____

Your coworker _____

You _____

Your coworker _____

You _____

Your coworker _____

You _____

Your coworker _____

2   You were working on a research paper when your computer crashed. You went to the school library to use one of the computers there, but it was closed. Your paper was due the next morning. You tell your classmate about it the next day.

You _____

Your classmate _____

You _____

Your classmate _____

You _____

Your classmate _____

You _____

Your classmate _____

GETTING IT WRONG

1 READING

A **Read the headline and the first paragraph of the story. What dream do you think came true for the writer? Read the story to check your answer.**

The dream that came true was: _____

_____

HOME   ABOUT   BLOG   CONTACT US   ⊖ ⊡ ⊗

A DREAM COME TRUE

It was my first time in New York City. I was with my best friend, and we wanted to see everything—Times Square, the Statue of Liberty …oh, and best of all, we had tickets to a Broadway musical. Neither of us had seen a live musical before, and we couldn't have been more excited. Years ago in high school, I was in the theater club, and I always dreamed of being a star.

On the evening of the performance, we had dinner near our hotel and then got on the subway. We had estimated that the subway ride to Broadway would take about 15 minutes. Thirty minutes later, we still weren't there.

When we finally arrived, we stood on the street looking around, and it certainly looked different from what I had imagined. First of all, I didn't see any tourists. Second, no theaters. I asked a woman for help. She told us that we were, indeed, at the Broadway subway station. Still confused, I showed her my ticket to the play. That's when it hit her.

We had taken the wrong subway to the wrong station and traveled to an entirely different area of New York City. There were no Broadway musicals anywhere near this Broadway station.

We thanked her and got into a taxi. I had heard that the theater didn't admit people if they were late, and I was panicking. When we hit traffic, the taxi driver insisted we'd get there faster if we got out and walked. He explained the best route and we jumped out and ran the rest of the way.

We arrived 20 minutes late, but they let us in. When we walked in, everyone in the audience turned to look at us.

I guess my dream of being the star of a Broadway show finally came true!

B **UNDERSTAND IRONY** **Read the story. Then answer the questions.**

1 How did the writer realize she had made a mistake?

_____

2 What is ironic about the subway station they went to?

_____

3 What is ironic about the writer's final sentence?

_____

C **Read the story again. Then answer the questions.**

1 In high school, the writer:
   a went to New York City.
   b wanted to be a star.
   c met her best friend.

2 When they got off the subway, the writer assumed:
   a there would be more tourists.
   b they were late for the play.
   c they would be in Times Square.

3 The writer panicked because:
   a the woman gave them the wrong information.
   b the driver told them to get out of the taxi.
   c they might not be let in to the theater.

2 CRITICAL THINKING

A **THINK CRITICALLY** What do you think the writer and her friend did when the audience turned to look at them? What do you think the audience thought about them?

---

3 WRITING

A **MAKE A STORY INTERESTING** Read the story again. Underline examples of each of the points below.

1 A variety of narrative verb tenses in the past.

2 Linking and organizing expressions.

3 Different kinds of sentences: conditionals (*if*), relative clauses (*who, which*), time clauses (*when, after*), *There was/were*, reported speech, etc.

4 Reporting verbs other than *say*.

5 Two long sentences and two short sentences.

B Write a story about one of the situations below. Use all of the writing points in exercise 3A to make your story interesting.

1 Imagine that you and your friend got lost on a desert island for one week. Explain how you ate, where you slept, and how you found your way to safety. Describe some of the things you and your friend said during the week you were lost.

2 Tell a story about a time when you went to a large social event. Describe what people wore, ate, and talked about.

CHECK AND REVIEW

Read the statements. Can you do these things?

UNIT 6	Mark the boxes. ✔ I can do it. [?] I am not sure. I can …	If you are not sure, go back to these pages in the Student's Book.
VOCABULARY	☐ use expressions to talk about fame. ☐ use a variety of reporting verbs.	page 54 page 56
GRAMMAR	☐ use narrative tenses to tell a story. ☐ use reported speech with the correct form of modals.	page 55 page 57
LISTENING AND SPEAKING SKILLS	☐ guess the meaning of unfamiliar words from context. ☐ use expressions to make, contradict, and clarify. assumptions	page 58 page 59
READING AND WRITING SKILLS	☐ identify and understand irony. ☐ make a story interesting with a variety of grammar techniques.	page 60 page 61

7.1 WORTHY HELPERS

1 VOCABULARY: Positive experiences

A **Complete the sentences with the words in the box.**

beneficial	contribution	devote	~~difference~~	honor	influence
pleasure	reassure	satisfaction	use	value	worthwhile

1 I started a recycling program at school because I wanted to make a _____ difference _____ .
2 The kid next door is a good _____ on Kevin.
3 Some people _____ their lives to serving their family, friends, and neighbors.
4 I needed my mother to _____ me that everything would be fine once I started college.
5 It was an _____ to have someone like him speak to the students.
6 Maybe his advice will be of _____ to you when you're older.
7 Many people take _____ in helping others.
8 She made an important _____ to today's meeting.
9 I _____ his friendship more than I could ever say.
10 She feels that teaching is a _____ career.
11 I get more _____ out of cooking than I do out of eating.
12 Drinking a lot of water is _____ for our health.

2 GRAMMAR: Gerunds and infinitives after adjectives, nouns, and pronouns

A **Match the sentence halves.**

1	It's unusual	_f_	a	to help us with the repairs in this house.
2	Latin is an interesting language	___	b	starting a new subject in school.
3	Simon often wastes time	___	c	being alone in a big noisy crowd.
4	She has places	___	d	to help him with his homework.
5	Valeria always feels nervous	___	e	to learn.
6	We need someone	___	f	to see them at this type of restaurant.
7	Samuel asked someone in class	___	g	to visit this summer.
8	It can be scary	___	h	watching TV.

B   Complete each sentence with the gerund or infinitive form of the verb in parentheses ( ).

1   I spent a lot of time _____trying_____ different sushi restaurants while I was in Japan. (try)

2   We had _____ about whether to buy their house or not. (think)

3   Sometimes it's hard _____ the only boy in the classroom. (be)

4   We needed someone _____ us a ride to the train station. (give)

5   I felt nervous _____ for the airplane to take off. (wait)

6   It's not unusual _____ more than you have. (want)

7   My car needs _____ fixed before I can drive it back home. (be)

8   There are sites that are interesting _____ in this ancient city. (visit)

3   GRAMMAR AND VOCABULARY

A   Circle the correct verb to complete the sentences. Then add another sentence using the cues in parentheses.

1   A   I spent time *to see* / *seeing* my sick grandmother this weekend. (make a difference)

     B   *I think it really made a difference* _____.

2   A   I think I need a teacher *to talk* / *talking* about my future goals. (reassure)

     B   _____ .

3   A   I didn't waste my time *explaining* / *to explain* it to them. (value)

     B   _____ .

4   A   It's common *testing* / *to test* a product first before putting it on the market. (beneficial)

     B   _____ .

5   A   They always have volunteers *to help* / *helping* them during a crisis. (devote their life to)

     B   _____ .

6   A   The charity always needs more people *to support* / *supporting* them. One way to do this is to give money. (make a contribution)

     B   _____ .

B   Use a gerund or infinitive to complete the sentences so that they are true for you.

1   I take great pleasure in _____ .

2   It's been beneficial _____ .

3   There's a lot of use in _____ .

4   I think it's worthwhile _____ .

5   I get a lot of satisfaction out of _____ .

7.2 BUYER'S REGRET

1 VOCABULARY: Making purchases

A **Circle** the correct meaning for each sentence.

1 I was silly to buy the expensive boots because I already have a closet full of them.

   a I regret the purchase.

   b I think the boots look ridiculous.

2 Our parents always help us to feel confident about doing things we don't think we can do.

   a Our parents convince us to do things.

   b Our parents encourage us to do things.

3 Mia has a lot of useful ideas that can help us solve these problems.

   a Mia's ideas are foolish.

   b Mia's ideas are practical.

4 My husband doesn't want me to buy the car because it is not a good value for the price.

   a He thinks the car is not worth the money.

   b He thinks the car does not have potential.

5 I hope the seminar will persuade you to sign up for French classes.

   a I hope the seminar will convince you.

   b I hope the seminar is practical.

6 Don't buy the cheapest shoes. They are not such good value.

   a I encouraged her to buy the cheapest shoes.

   b I urged her not to buy the cheapest shoes.

B **Complete the sentences with the words and phrases in the box.**

have appeal	have potential	look ridiculous
~~make financial sense~~	regretted the purchase	urged

1 It might _____make financial sense_____ to buy this when it's on sale.

2 We should take these costumes off before leaving the party, so we don't _____ walking home.

3 Several lawyers strongly _____ the parents to take further legal action.

4 These regions _____ for economic development.

5 The commercials _____ which will attract a lot of people to their website.

6 Javier bought an expensive table. After he paid the delivery fee, he _____ .

C **THINK CRITICALLY** **What are some things that people may regret buying? Why might they regret their purchases?**

_____

_____

_____

52

GRAMMAR: Infinitives after verbs with and without objects

A **Put the words in the correct order to make sentences.**

1 wanted / some of the repairs / she / to help / him / pay for / her

    She wanted him to help her pay for some of the repairs.

2 encouraged / she / for my business / to buy / a new computer / me

    _____

3 on time / needed / Alejandra / the project / to finish

    _____

4 online / she / to buy / likes / clothes

    _____

5 to come / always / my parents / urged / on time / home / us

    _____

6 want / tomorrow morning / the children / to sleep in

    _____

7 to / decided / so / he / to talk / a doctor / was sick / my brother

    _____

8 to travel / at night / she / not / alone / us / warned

    _____

3 GRAMMAR AND VOCABULARY

A Circle the correct infinitive and then write a phrase from exercises 1A and 1B to complete the conversation. **Watch your verb tense.**

1 A My friend encouraged me *to wear* / *wear* an animal dress to the party.
    B Oh, no. You must have _____ looked ridiculous _____ .

2 A We plan *waiting* / *to wait* on buying a house until the prices go down.
    B Good idea. It _____ .

3 A My boss is very upset because I forgot *to tell* / *telling* him I was going on vacation today.
    B No wonder he's mad. That _____ .

4 A I tend *wearing* / *to wear* comfortable shoes over fashionable ones.
    B So, do I. I think it _____ .

5 A I'm sad *to see* / *seeing* that it sold. I was hoping to buy it.
    B Don't worry. It was _____ .

6 A We decided *getting* / *to get* a new front door before we sell the house.
    B That's a good idea. It will certainly _____ .

1 LISTENING

A 🔊 **7.01** **Listen to the conversation. Then write *T* (true) or *F* (false) next to the statements.**

1 Jorge doesn't want to accept Stella's first offer. _____

2 Stella thinks the rug is too expensive. _____

3 Stella doesn't buy the rug. _____

B 🔊 **7.01** **UNDERSTAND PERSUASIVE TECHNIQUES** **Listen to the conversation again. Check (✓) the techniques each person uses to get the best deal.**

Stella says she loves the color of the rug ☐

says she only has $250 to buy the rug ☐

says the rug is too small ☐

says the rug is not worth that much ☐

says she's bought many rugs at street markets before ☐

tells Jorge she'll look around for another rug ☐

Jorge points out that many customers get a lot of satisfaction out of the rugs he sells ☐

tells Stella he made the rug himself ☐

refuses to give stuff for free ☐

reassures Stella that $250 is a good price for the rug ☐

says someone else will buy the rug if Stella doesn't ☐

says he'll clean the stain on the rug for Stella ☐

2 CRITICAL THINKING

A **THINK CRITICALLY** **Why do some people feel nervous about buying things at a street market? What are some advantages and disadvantages of buying things at a street market instead of a store?**

_____

_____

_____

3 SPEAKING

A   Complete the conversations with the phrases in the box. You can use the phrases more than once. Then decide which conversation accepts an offer, and which rejects an offer.

> a little on the high side
> go any lower
> how much are you asking for it
> the best I can do
> sounds fair enough
> would you be willing to accept
>
> don't think it's worth that much
> got a deal
> I can't accept that
> throw in some stuff for free
> sorry, but no deal

---

1   **A**   I love this chair. So, ¹ _how much are you asking for it_ ?

 B   I'm selling it for $100.

 A   Oh, really? Hmmm. That's ² _____ . Can you ³ _____ ?

 B   I can give it to you for $75.

 A   ⁴ _____ $60 for it?

 B   ⁵ _____ .

 A   Oh, that's too bad. I guess I'll have to shop somewhere else.

---

2   **A**   Is this the car you're selling? So,¹ _____ ?

 B   I would like $5,000 for it.

 A   I'm sorry, but ² _____ .

 B   I'll ³ _____ .

 A   Like what?

 B   A tank of gas and new windshield wipers.

 A   I'm sorry, but I ⁴ _____ .

 B   OK, $4,200 is ⁵ _____ .

 A   That ⁶ _____ .

B   Read the situation. Write a conversation that accepts an offer or refuses an offer between the buyer and the seller.

Situation: Mario is on vacation at a beach resort. He is approached by a woman selling necklaces for $45 each. He really wants to buy one for his girlfriend, but he only wants to spend $30.

 A   ¹ _____

 B   ² _____

 A   ³ _____

 B   ⁴ _____

 A   ⁵ _____

 B   ⁶ _____

7.4   MONEY'S WORTH

1   READING

A   IDENTIFY MAIN POINTS   **Read the article. Check (✓) the best summary.**

a   Spending money on yourself can increase happiness.   _____

b   Spending money on others can increase happiness.   _____

c   People who are wealthy should spend money on others.   _____

SPENDING ON OTHERS COULD MAKE A DIFFERENCE IN YOUR LIFE

There's a Chinese saying that goes something like this: "If you want happiness for a day, do something for yourself. If you want happiness for a lifetime, do something for others." Many researchers believe these words of wisdom when it comes to how you spend money, once your basic needs are met, of course.

In related studies, researchers Elizabeth Dunn and Michael Norton noted in their book *Happy Money: The Science of Happier Spending* (2013) that people who spend their money on others seem to get more satisfaction than those who spend their money on themselves. Spending on those you care about, or even strangers, can boost overall happiness levels. But they do point out that happiness comes from spending money on others because you want to, not from spending it out of guilt or obligation.

In another study, the World Happiness Report (2019) revealed that there is a high level of unhappiness among Americans. It was reported that this could be due to people not spending enough of their money on others. Spending money on charities, or making donations, could make people happier. Just ask someone like Bill Gates. According to many, this billionaire is happy devoting his time and money to others. It's been said that he gets more pleasure in spending most of his billions on charities and scientific research than on personal luxuries.

The good news is you don't have to be wealthy to spend money on others. Buying someone a coffee, making a small contribution to a charity, or giving a few dollars to a homeless person could be worthwhile as it helps us communicate and connect with people. That warm, happy feeling you get every time you spend on others rather than on yourself might make a big difference to your level of happiness and overall well-being.

B   IDENTIFY SUPPORTING DETAILS   **Read the article again. Answer the questions.**

1   According to the article, what kind of spending makes people happier?

2   What do researchers Elizabeth Dunn and Michael Norton say about how to spend on others?

3   Why might many Americans be unhappy?

4   As mentioned in the article, what are some ways that we can spend money on others to make ourselves happier?

2   CRITICAL THINKING

A   THINK CRITICALLY   **Besides personal happiness, think of other reasons why spending money on others could be positive in someone's life. In what ways do you spend money on yourself? What about on others? How do you feel when you spend money on others?**

WRITING

A Read part of an essay. What two arguments are given? What is the author's own opinion?

Can Money Buy Happiness?

Recently, there have been a number of articles about what makes people happy. Many authors argue that having enough money to buy the necessary things in life can be enough for people to be happy, while others believe that those things might not be enough.

Let's consider some arguments in favor of how having enough money for the basic things in life can make people happy. To begin with, happiness can be achieved if we have money to pay for shelter, food, and clothing. When people are able to buy these things, they don't have to worry about their families or themselves. One thing for sure is that money can give us a sense of … . For example, money can … . Furthermore, money can help us feel healthy. For instance, … . Overall, these things in life can certainly help us feel happy.

On the other hand, having only enough money for the basic things in life might not always bring happiness. For some people, happiness comes from having things that make them more comfortable. For instance, having money beyond what we need might make certain people feel … . In addition, some people are happy having things such as … . These things can make their life seem more valuable. However, if people don't have things in life such as … , then what good is having money?

Money might not always buy happiness. It's my opinion that money can't always buy the things that truly are important to the quality of our lives. We can't buy our health or our friends … .

B Read the essay again. Write ideas that could complete the essay.

CHECK AND REVIEW

Read the statements. Can you do these things?

UNIT 7	Mark the boxes. ✔ I can do it. [?] I am not sure. I can …	If you are not sure, go back to these pages in the Student's Book.
VOCABULARY	☐ describe positive experiences. ☐ talk about making purchases.	page 67 page 68
GRAMMAR	☐ use gerunds and infinitives after adjectives, nouns, and pronouns. ☐ use infinitives after verbs with and without objects.	page 67 page 69
LISTENING AND SPEAKING SKILLS	☐ understand persuasive techniques. ☐ use arguments to accept and reject an offer.	page 70 page 71
READING AND WRITING SKILLS	☐ identify main ideas and supporting details. ☐ write a for-and-against essay.	page 72 page 73

SMALL THINGS MATTER

ANNOYING LITTLE THINGS

1 **VOCABULARY: Describing neatness and messiness**

A **Complete the sentences with the phrases in the box.**

arrange them neatly	disorganized	fold sth	hang sth up
jumbled up	leave things all over the place	line up	organized
put away	put sth in alphabetical order	~~put sth in a pile~~	
tangled up	throw something in/on		

1 When you _____ *put sth in a pile* _____ , you position objects one on top of the other.

2 When you _____ , especially paper or cloth, you bend it so that it takes up less room.

3 When you _____ shoes, you put them in a neat row.

4 When a cord is twisted in an untidy mass, it is _____ .

5 When toys are mixed together untidily, they are _____ .

6 When you _____ dishes, you put them where they are usually kept.

7 When you _____ , you place it on a hanger or a hook.

8 When you _____ , you arrange it in the same order as the letters of the alphabet.

9 When you put something quickly and carelessly on a chair, you _____ it.

10 When you plan things carefully and keep things tidy, you are _____ .

11 When you put a group of objects in careful order, you _____ .

12 When you are not good at planning or organizing things, you are _____ .

13 When you _____ , they are spread out in a large area in a disorganized way.

2 **GRAMMAR: Modal-like expressions with *be***

A **Rewrite the sentences using the expressions in parentheses ().**

1 He is certain to be late because he cannot find his keys. (bound to)

   He is bound to be late because he cannot find his keys.

2 He's going to meet his friends at the train station. (about to)

   _____

3 The train is expected to leave at 4:10 p.m. (supposed to)

   _____

4 His friends are certain to be mad if he misses the train. (sure to)

   _____

5 When he got there, he was made to go to another platform. (forced to)

   _____

B Read the complaints that Tanya and Marco have about each other. (Circle) the correct modal to complete the sentences.

> It annoys me when I'm late for work. We are ¹*about to* /*supposed to* be at the train station at 8:00 a.m., but Tanya can never find her coat or shoes in the mornings. Since I don't want to be late again, I'm ²*bound to* / *forced to* put everything near the front door after she goes to bed at night. It annoys me that when I get home her things are ³*sure to* / *about to* be left all over the place again.

> He should talk! When we are ⁴*about to* / *sure to* leave in the morning, Marco always wants to wash the dishes first. We can never get to the train station on time. Sometimes, he's too organized. It really annoys me when I get home because he's ⁵*supposed to* /*bound to* be cleaning and putting my things away.

C **THINK CRITICALLY** Read the complaints again. Do you think it's reasonable for Tanya and Marco to be annoyed with each other? Give reasons why.

_____
_____
_____

D Complete the sentences so that they are true for you.

1 This week, I am due to _____ .

2 I was about to _____ , but

_____ .

3 The weather is sure to be _____ tomorrow.

4 When I was young, my parents forced me to _____ .

5 When I'm older, I'm bound to be _____ .

3 GRAMMAR AND VOCABULARY

A Write sentences with your own ideas using the word prompts.

1 forced to / leave things all over the place

   When I was young, my mother was forced to pick up the toys we left all over the place .

2 bound to / throw on

   _____ .

3 supposed to / put away

   _____ .

4 sure to / put in alphabetical order

   _____ .

5 about to / tangled up

   _____ .

8.2 SIDE PROJECTS

1 VOCABULARY: Talking about progress

A Circle the correct meaning of each vocabulary word or phrase.

1	as expected	did not happen as predicted	(happened as predicted)
2	with ease	without problems	with problems
3	smoothly	easily	with difficulty
4	efficiently	slowly and badly	quickly and well
5	little by little	slowly and gradually	quickly and rapidly
6	with difficulty	without problems	with problems
7	in my own time	when I am not working	when I am working
8	steadily	rapidly	gradually
9	successfully	achieving good results	achieving bad results
10	thoroughly	quickly	completely
11	at my own pace	at a speed comfortable to you	to do something slowly
12	effectively	with no results	with good results

B Complete the sentences with words or phrases from exercise 1A.

1 We can't repair our house all at once, so we'll have to repair it ___little by little___ .

2 _____ , he was late again for the meeting. He's always late.

3 If all goes _____ , we should arrive by nine o'clock.

4 I _____ enjoyed the performance tonight.

5 The medicine works more _____ if you take a hot drink after it.

6 Jorge finally finished his essay, but _____ .

7 She wasn't in any pain and won the 400-meter race _____ .

8 I like to make and sell wooden chairs _____ in the evenings and at weekends.

9 They are so organized. They run their business very _____ .

10 A number of patients have been treated _____ with the new drug.

11 Food prices have risen _____ over the years.

12 I studied English _____ at home. It was slower than taking classes, but less expensive.

2 GRAMMAR: Future forms

A **Underline** the verb phrase in each sentence that shows the future.

1 Eventually, <u>we'll be living</u> in our newly built home.

2 I don't think she's going to attend the event.

3 Sooner or later, she might want to go back to her home country.

4 In a few years, we'll be buying a new car.

5 This book won't fill you with joy, but it will give you some inspiration.

6 If my business doesn't run efficiently, I might hire more people.

7 I'm not going to her party unless she invites me herself.

8 This side project of mine is going to allow me to make some extra money.

B **Correct the mistake in each sentence.**

1 Next month, we're going ~~moving~~ to another area in the city.   *to move*

2 She'll be return from her trip very soon. _____

3 Eating too much candy won't be killing you, but it will hurt your teeth. _____

4 When you get there, you go to take the bus to their house. _____

5 Next week, we're going to be travel in Europe. _____

6 By the summer, they won't be make any more money from these hats. _____

7 I guess you will be feel tired after working in the sun all day. _____

8 This presentation is going take a long time, so let's get comfortable. _____

3 GRAMMAR AND VOCABULARY

A **Create sentences in the future form with your own ideas.**

1 as expected / technology in the future

   As expected, technology in the future will be changing all the time .

2 successfully / a side project

   _____ .

3 efficiently and effectively / my business

   _____ .

4 little by little / my future plans

   _____ .

5 in my own time / learn a new language

   _____ .

6 smoothly / getting more customers

   _____ .

B **THINK CRITICALLY** What are the pros of turning a side project into a business? What might be the cons?

_____

_____

_____

_____

_____

_____

THE LITTLE TOUCHES

1 LISTENING

A 🔊 **8.01** **Listen to the conversation between two siblings, Sarah and Leo. Check (✓) the "little touches" they are planning for their grandma's birthday.**

Bake her a cake ☐

Order pink balloons ☐

Order food from her favorite Greek restaurant ☐

Buy fancy napkins ☐

Have a fun theme ☐

Get a karaoke machine ☐

Play her favorite songs ☐

Tell people to dress like they did in the 50s ☐

B 🔊 **8.01** **RECOGNIZE EMPHASIS** **Listen to the conversation again and <u>underline</u> the words which are emphasized. Write C for the words that show a contrasting idea.**

1 I think we need to do something <u>really</u> special. ....

2 Hmmm, I'm not sure she would like that. ....

3 That's such a terrific idea! ....

4 Of course, I bet everyone will love that! ....

5 My house is such a mess. ....

6 How about we throw the surprise party in your apartment? ....

7 What a fabulous idea! ....

8 She likes the new Greek restaurant. ....

9 Grandma will be so happy. ....

10 Don't worry. It will. ....

11 That's such an awesome idea! ....

2 CRITICAL THINKING

A **THINK CRITICALLY** **How might choosing a theme for a party or an event help make planning it easier? How might having a theme make it difficult to plan?**

3 SPEAKING

A   (Circle) the correct words to complete the conversations.

1 **A** What should we do for Sandra's retirement party? She's worked here for almost 20 years!

   B Going out for lunch always ¹(*goes* / *went*) over well for retirement parties.

   A Hmmm, I don't think that's a good way to ²(*have* / *approach*) it. One ³(*thing* / *way*) we could do is have it catered.

   B I ⁴(*know* / *bet*) everyone will love that!

2 **A** What should we do for Dunia's graduation? She's worked so hard to become a lawyer.

   B It never ¹(*hurts* / *goes*) to give her money.

   A Hmmm. Or another ²(*idea* / *thing*) we could do is take her on a vacation.

   B That's always ³(*good* / *worth*) considering.

3 **A** What should we do for John's birthday? He'll be turning 12 years old!

   B One ¹(*approach* / *thing*) we could do is take him to a movie.

   A Hmmm, I don't think that's a good way to ²(*consider* / *approach*) it. Having a party always ³(*goes* / *went*) over well.

   B That's such an awesome ⁴(*idea* / *approach*)!

B   Choose an idea for an event from the list below. Write a conversation between you and a friend who is helping you plan the event.

- A dinner party to congratulate your husband on his big job promotion
- A going away party for your friends who are taking a trip around the world
- A New Year's Eve party
- A housewarming party to celebrate moving into your new house

A _____

B _____

A _____

B _____

A SMILE GOES A LONG WAY

1 READING

A **IDENTIFY WRITER'S PURPOSE** Read the article. What's its purpose? Check (✓) the best statement.

a To tell readers to be calm when they are in traffic. _____

b To advise readers why they shouldn't worry and complain about the small stuff. _____

c To warn readers that feeling stressed can weaken the immune system. _____

HOW DO YOU DEAL WITH THE LITTLE THINGS IN LIFE?

Are you one of those people who complain and worry about the small stuff? Well, don't. Scientists have recently discovered that people who worry and complain about the little annoyances in life may be putting their health at risk.

While there are some people who get through the small stuff—heavy traffic, miserable weather, or canceled dinner plans—with ease, there are those who react with anger or frustration. When these little challenges or difficulties arise, emotions are bound to rise, too. Our bodies react, but not in a good way.

Recent studies show that negative emotions can flood the bloodstream with stress hormones. These hormones are released into the body when it interprets danger or threat. When they do, it can decrease our energy levels, increase heart rate and blood pressure, and in some instances, slow down digestion and reproduction organs. If that's not enough, stress hormones can make the immune system weak, which can cause other illnesses in the body.

What can we do? Well, practice being calm. Meditate, find deep breathing exercises, or concentrate on happy, positive thoughts when things don't go smoothly. Visualize the road becoming free of traffic or that rainy day bringing sunshine. Calming the mind and imagining things will work out can improve our health, both physically and mentally.

It takes practice to be calm. But we need to train our brain to deal with strong emotions when something annoys or frustrates us. So, the next time something small irritates you, learn from it and take control of your reaction. Know that worrying over the little stuff will not only ruin your day, but will be sure to affect your health, too.

B Read the article again. What specific examples of why we shouldn't complain about the small stuff does the writer mention? What advice does the writer suggest?

2 CRITICAL THINKING

A **THINK CRITICALLY** What situations might make people worry and complain about the "big stuff"? Think of three examples. Why might they worry about these things?

_____

_____

_____

3 WRITING

A Read the complaint email. <u>Underline</u> the problem and how Mira would like the company to solve it.

Reply Forward

To: Ms. Suzanne Castillo
From: Mira Kim

Dear Ms. Castillo,

I recently bought a $450 printer from your company. I made the purchase on December 17 and the receipt number is 294738. It was a present for my husband who needed a high-quality laser printer for his new business. However, this product is definitely not high-quality. When the printer was delivered, the box was damaged and the paper tray was broken. Also, the glass is scratched, so any copies that we make have lines on them. Finally, the printer is very slow. This is unacceptable and I would like a replacement printer.

I have attached a copy of my receipt to this email. I would like your company to collect the broken printer from my house and deliver a new one as soon as possible. I look forward to hearing from you in the next week.

Sincerely,

Mira Kim

B Read the email again. Choose an idea below and write a more polite email that describes the problem and how you would like the company to solve it. Use expressions like *I find*, *I feel*, *I believe*, or *I think* if you can.

> The couch you ordered is wobbly and uncomfortable.
>
> Your car is still making a loud noise after it was repaired by a mechanic.
>
> The hotel room was small and dirty.

CHECK AND REVIEW

Read the statements. Can you do these things?

UNIT 8	Mark the boxes. ☑ I can do it. ? I am not sure.		If you are not sure, go back to these pages in the Student's Book.
	I can …		
VOCABULARY	☐	talk about neatness and messiness.	page 76
	☐	talk about progress.	page 78
GRAMMAR	☐	use modal-like expressions with *be*.	page 77
	☐	use future forms.	page 79
LISTENING AND SPEAKING SKILLS	☐	recognize emphasis.	page 80
	☐	suggest and show interest in ideas.	page 81
READING AND WRITING SKILLS	☐	identify the writer's purpose.	page 82
	☐	write a complaint letter.	page 83

1 VOCABULARY: Luck and choice

A **Circle the correct word or phrase in each sentence.**

1 Finding work was difficult for Greg, but he finally got a *lucky break* / *chance encounter* with this company.

2 Samuel was *in the right place at the right time* / *wound up* because he found a good parking spot.

3 Little did I know that she would *wind up* / *not believe my luck* as my next manager.

4 She was *deliberate decision* / *fortunate* to be cheerful at work.

5 Is it just a *coincidence* / *chance encounter* that the person who ran the contest won first prize?

6 Mariana went through a *life-changing experience* / *lucky break* when she survived the accident.

7 You can't help but admire her *fortunate* / *determination* to reach her goal.

8 We made a *lucky break* / *deliberate decision* to spend less money on things we don't need.

9 The *path* / *fate* to success is not without difficulty.

10 They believed that *fate* / *deliberate decision* brought them together.

11 I couldn't *be fortunate* / *believe my luck* when I saw I had won the prize.

12 He didn't expect to meet his wife through a *coincidence* / *chance encounter* at a café.

B **Imagine you are in these situations. What might you think? Complete the sentences with words from exercise 1A.**

1 You met a movie star in the elevator on your way down to the lobby.

   I was in the _____right_____ place at the right time.

2 You found someone to help you sell your car.

   It was very _____ I had him to help me.

3 You saw an old friend getting on the same plane as you.

   It was a _____ that we were on the same plane.

4 You got a job with that big company right after you graduated.

   It was a _____ that I got this great job so quickly.

5 You missed the bus so you wouldn't have to go to the meeting.

   I made a _____ decision to miss the bus.

6 You studied the lines for weeks to get the acting part.

   I had a lot of _____ to get this part.

GRAMMAR: Unreal conditionals

A   **Put the words in the correct order to make sentences.**

1   would've shopped / I / expensive / if / somewhere else / expensive / knew / I / it was going to be

   If I knew it was going to be expensive, I would've shopped somewhere else .

2   study / would've failed the exam / if / I / hadn't helped me / I / he

   _____ .

   _____ .

3   would help / if / could / I / you / I

   _____ .

   _____ .

4   the Great Wall of China / I / if / anywhere in the world / could go / go see / I'd

   _____ .

   _____ .

5   all the cake / she'd / if / could reach the table / eat / our dog

   _____ .

   _____ .

6   Tamara might've gotten the job / if / hadn't been late / she

   _____ .

   _____ .

B   **Circle the correct words to complete the sentences.**

1   If I'd known you were allergic to nuts, I _____ an apple pie.

   a   would make   **(b)**   would've made

2   If I hadn't _____ him when I did, I might not have become a dentist.

   a   have met   **b**   met

3   If you _____ a good friend, you'd help him with his exam.

   a   were   **b**   are

4   If Clara _____ busy, she might not have missed the call.

   a   weren't   **b**   hadn't been

5   I _____ figured this out if I hadn't read the instructions.

   a   couldn't   **b**   couldn't have

6   If the book had more action, I _____ be interested in reading it.

   a   would   **b**   will

3   **GRAMMAR AND VOCABULARY**

A   **Use your own ideas to complete the unreal conditional sentences.**

1   I was fortunate. If I hadn't had met her, I _____ _wouldn't have gone travelling_ _____ .

2   Fate is what brought those two together. If she _____ ,
   she might not have _____ .

3   If she _____ , she'd be on a much better path then
   the one she's on now.

4   If I _____ , I'd have more determination to finish
   this project.

5   It was a coincidence. If Andres _____ , he wouldn't
   _____ .

9.2 WHY DID I DO IT?

1 VOCABULARY: Commenting on mistakes

A **Find words in the word search.**

h	a	r	d	b	c	h	j	u	i	b
u	a	b	z	k	j	l	c	o	n	a
r	c	u	f	l	w	b	m	p	c	w
r	v	d	k	i	a	s	n	k	o	k
y	e	j	y	t	t	i	m	i	m	w
d	u	m	b	s	c	l	d	c	p	a
h	f	o	g	e	h	l	o	k	e	r
i	w	v	w	q	r	y	t	p	t	d
x	g	e	h	f	a	u	l	t	e	q
f	u	n	n	y	w	c	u	s	n	r
u	n	f	o	r	t	u	n	a	t	e

awkward	dumb
fault	funny side
hard	hurry
incompetent	kick yourself
move	~~silly~~
unfortunate	watch

B **Complete the sentences with words from exercise 1A.**

1 She showed little thought and judgment when she did that. It was a/an _____silly_____ mistake.

2 You are going to spill the milk if you don't _____ what you're doing.

3 Slow down. You're in too much of a/an _____ and you might make a mistake.

4 She found herself in a/an _____ situation when she forgot his name.

5 It's your own _____ that you lost your phone.

6 Lucky for me, he saw the _____ side of my error.

7 I learned the _____ way that going to school and working at the same time is challenging.

8 You know you'll _____ yourself if you forget to do it, so just do it now!

9 It was a bad _____ on my part for getting involved.

10 I know you need the money, but I think selling your favorite watch is a/an _____ thing to do.

11 She described him as being totally _____ at his job. He wasn't able to do the simplest task.

12 It was _____ that it rained during their game.

2 GRAMMAR: Wishes and regrets

A   (Circle) the correct words or phrases to complete the sentences. Then write if the sentences express present or past wishes.

1   If only I *could* / *can* play the piano!   <u>present</u>

2   I wish I *taught* / *was teaching* in that other school again.   _____

3   I wish she *attends* / *had attended* the meeting.   _____

4   If only they *have* / *had* been more careful.   _____

5   I wish you *could* / *can* see the movie with us.   _____

6   If only someone *had taught* / *was teaching* me this when I was younger.   _____

7   I wish I *talked* / *had talked* to her yesterday.   _____

8   I wish I *was going* / *can go* on vacation with them.   _____

B   Complete the sentences with the correct form of the verbs in the box.

go	grow	have	know	leave	perform	stop	~~study~~

1   I wish that I wasn't   <u>studying</u>   art history.

2   If only someone had _____ her from getting up on the stage and embarrassing herself.

3   I wish I had _____ a little sister when I was growing up.

4   Tomas wishes he could _____ vegetables in his garden, but it is too small.

5   If only I _____ how to use a computer, I'd be doing a different job.

6   If only he _____ the house earlier, he wouldn't be stuck in a traffic jam.

7   I wish I could _____ on vacation with you next week, but I'm busy.

8   Amelia wishes she was _____ in the school play this year.

3 GRAMMAR AND VOCABULARY

A   For each conversation, comment on mistakes using the phrase in parentheses. Then finish each response with a wish or regret.

1   A   I made a big mistake yesterday when I quit my job.

    B   _____<u>That was a bad move</u>_____ . (be a bad move)

    A   You're right. I wish I _____<u>hadn't quit my job</u>_____ .

2   A   I need to rush, or I'll be in trouble for being late.

    B   _____ . (be your own fault)

    A   You're right. If only my boss _____ .

3   A   I think I'm going to demand a big pay raise.

    B   _____ . (be a dumb thing to do)

    A   You're right. I wish I _____ .

4   A   I couldn't find my train ticket, so I had to buy another one.

    B   _____ . (be unfortunate)

    A   I know. If only I _____ .

5   A   He needs more training. He cannot do what I ask him to do.

    B   _____ . (be incompetent)

    A   You're right. I wish he _____ .

6   A   It was difficult starting my own business because I didn't get any help.

    B   I bet _____ . (learn sth the hard way)

    A   You're right. If only I _____ .

9.3 MY MISTAKE

1 LISTENING

A 🔊 **9.01** **Listen to the conversation. Then write T (true) or F (false) next to the statements.**

1 Henry has an audition today. ___F___

2 Carmen made a lot of silly mistakes. _____

3 Laura Medford was in a different room. _____

4 Carmen tells Henry to leave his phone at home or in his car. _____

5 Laura Medford showed up at the office. _____

6 Henry didn't notice Laura Medford at the coffee shop. _____

7 Laura Medford spilled coffee all over the front of Henry's expensive pants. _____

8 Henry was told to come and do the audition again. _____

B 🔊 **9.01** **IDENTIFY FEELINGS** **Listen to the conversation again. Circle the word that best describes Henry's feelings.**

1 When Henry said his lines in front of his favorite actress, he felt …

   a cheerful   **b** confused   **c** calm

2 When his phone rang in the middle of the audition, he was …

   a amused   **b** sad   **c** annoyed

3 When Henry saw Laura Medford at the coffee shop, he was …

   a surprised   **b** calm   **c** angry

4 When Laura spilled coffee all over his expensive shirt, Henry was …

   a confused   **b** annoyed   **c** calm

5 When he was told to come and do the audition again, he felt …

   a cheerful   **b** annoyed   **c** amused

2 CRITICAL THINKING

A **THINK CRITICALLY** **Why do you think it would be hard for some people to accept their mistakes? Think of how they might feel or what they might fear.**

_____

_____

_____

_____

_____

3 SPEAKING

A **Circle the correct word to complete the expressions of reassurances.**

1 **A** Look at my hair. It's a mess!
   B It's not that *good / bad*.

2 **A** I think I left my wallet on the table at the café.
   B We all make *mistakes / errors*.

3 **A** I didn't get the promotion I was expecting at work.
   B That's the way it *went / goes*.

4 **A** I'm upset that I broke my arm in the car accident last weekend.
   B It could have been *worse / better*.

5 **A** The vase broke when I accidentally dropped it.
   B You're not the only one who's *done / did* that.

6 **A** I'm so embarrassed that I forgot her birthday.
   B Don't worry. No one is *good / perfect*.

7 **A** If I don't find a job soon, I'll have to move out of this apartment.
   B It'll turn out all *wrong / right*.

8 **A** Well, it's done now. I can't go back and re-write the test.
   B You're right. There's no use in *crying / laughing* over spilled milk.

9 **A** I don't think they're going to call me back for a second interview.
   B What are you worrying *for / over*? It will be fine.

B **For each situation write an expression of reassurance and then give advice.**

1 **A** Oh, no. I got a terrible haircut!
   B It's not that bad. It'll grow out soon.

2 **A** I lost one of the books I borrowed from my friend.
   B _____

3 **A** I feel so bad. I won't be able to make it to her party this weekend.
   B _____

4 **A** I failed my driving test.
   B _____

5 **A** I couldn't get tickets to the big concert this weekend.
   B _____

6 **A** I'm sorry, but I got the schedule all wrong. I think we missed the train.
   B _____

9.4 GOOD CONVERSATIONS

1 READING

A **MAKE PREDICTIONS** Read the title of the article. What do you think the writer means by "conversation flow"? Then read the article. Was your prediction correct?

HOME   NEWS   BLOG   SIGN IN

THE SECRET OF CONVERSATION FLOW

What makes conversations so special? Well, they all have something called *conversation flow*. Conversation flow happens when conversation is comfortable, effortless, and smooth. It's the way conversations are supposed to work.

Sometimes, conversation flow seems to happen automatically. You and your conversation partner get along and the conversation feels very friendly and natural. That's great when it happens, but what do you do when the conversation doesn't flow?

That's where the ideas of invitation and inspiration come in. An invitation is when you say something that lets your conversation partner clearly know it's her turn to speak. And when your partner says something to you that makes you want to speak, that's known as inspiration. Invitation and inspiration are the key ingredients of smooth, comfortable conversation. These conversational strategies keep the conversation flowing. Learn how to use them and you will have conversations free of awkward pauses and fake small talk.

> **Here's how it works:**
> Let's say that you and your friend Steve are chatting as you work.
> You ask, "How was your weekend?"
> Steve replies, "Oh, it was great. How was yours?"
> You reply, "It was fine."
> Steve says nothing and goes back to work.

What happened? Well, you didn't give Steve a clear invitation or a strong inspiration. Without either of those things, he didn't know what to say next (and perhaps was unsure if it was his turn to speak). So, he didn't respond. The conversation failed.

Without an invitation or an inspiration, your partner might not know what to say or whether to respond. That's why you want to make sure to offer invitations and inspirations to your partner in order to have a conversation flow.

B Read the article again. How do invitation and inspiration keep a conversation flowing? What is an example of an invitation you could give Steve to keep the conversation going?

2 CRITICAL THINKING

A **THINK CRITICALLY** Do you know anyone who is good at conversation? What kind of things do they talk about, and what conversational strategies do they use?

WRITING

A   Read the article. Summarize the tips it gives. What is the easiest tip to do in the article? What about the hardest?

HOW TO START A CONVERSATION WITH THREE BODY LANGUAGE TIPS 🔍

BODY LANGUAGE TIPS

Using body language to help you start a conversation can lead to great conversation. You do not have to say much because just a look or a movement can be beneficial.

The following shows the main points of body language you should be aware of when you want to start a conversation.

EYE USE:
We can learn all about a person through their eyes. Your eyes can say many things and sometimes you may be unaware of what your eyes are saying. Be careful not to let your eyes say you are bored and are not listening.

BODY MOVES:
The way you move your hands, arms, feet, and head can say many things. Crossing your arms, tapping your foot rapidly, or putting your hands on your hips can all say things that might seem negative. Always be aware of what your body is saying.

FACIAL EXPRESSIONS:
Smiling can say more than words so be aware of your facial expressions at all times. You may frown and be unaware of it. Facial expressions can often be misunderstood if you give someone a serious look. They may think you do not like them.

Just make sure you are using the rest of your body to speak as well, and your facial expressions should come across clearly. Your eyes, body, and face can carry on a whole conversation for you.

B   Read the article again. Think of tips or go online for ideas about how to end a conversation. Write an article that gives at least three tips. Include a title, headings for each tip, and advice / explanations under each heading. Remember to use parallel structure in lists.

_____

_____

_____

_____

CHECK AND REVIEW

Read the statements. Can you do these things?

UNIT 9	Mark the boxes. ✔ I can do it. ? I am not sure. I can ...	If you are not sure, go back to these pages in the Student's Book.
VOCABULARY	☐ use expressions for luck and choice. ☐ talk about mistakes.	page 86 page 89
GRAMMAR	☐ use unreal conditionals. ☐ describe wishes and regrets.	page 87 page 89
LISTENING AND SPEAKING SKILLS	☐ reassure someone about a problem. ☐ use expressions of reassurance correctly.	page 90 page 91
READING AND WRITING SKILLS	☐ make predictions. ☐ write an article giving tips.	page 92 page 93

10.1 ARE WE UNIQUE?

1 VOCABULARY: Describing characteristics

A **Complete the sentences with the words in the box.**

build	characteristic	feature
female	gender	individual
likeness	look	look-alike
male	~~match~~	similarity

1 He was a perfect _____match_____ to Luisa's outgoing personality.

2 A big nose is a typical _____ in her family.

3 They have the same _____ . Their hair is very similar and so are their clothes.

4 It's more important to be a/an _____ than to copy everyone else.

5 Does this test show the _____ of the baby?

6 Her favorite _____ has always been her thick and curly hair.

7 I can see the _____ between you and your father.

8 She was voted the best _____ country singer in the world.

9 She has a slim _____ just like her mother.

10 Jorge is a twenty-five-year old _____ with dark hair and blue eyes.

11 When I look at you, there's a definite family _____ around the eyes.

12 She's a Marilyn Monroe _____ with her blond hair and pretty smile.

B **Answer the questions with your own information.**

1 What kind of look did you have when you were younger?

_____

2 What are some of your family's characteristics?

_____

3 Have you ever been told you're a look-alike for someone famous? If so, who?

_____

4 What is your favorite feature? What is your least favorite?

_____

C **THINK CRITICALLY** **What are some common reasons people change their facial features to avoid looking older? Do you think this is a good idea? Why or why not?**

_____

_____

_____

_____

2 GRAMMAR: Gerunds after prepositions

A Complete the sentences with the correct form of the verbs in the box. Then <u>underline</u> the verb and the preposition.

~~build~~	exercise	go	have
pay	understand	wear	win

1 We plan on _____building_____ a new addition at the back of our house.
2 I often wonder about the possibility of _____ back to school.
3 She was concerned about _____ surgery next week.
4 Antonio and his wife did not like the idea of _____ the extra fee.
5 He's always succeeded in _____ games of chess.
6 Have you thought about _____ a watch? You're always losing track of time.
7 What are the benefits of _____ daily?
8 The experiment resulted in _____ more about the cancer drug.

B Rewrite the sentences by putting the verbs in parentheses in the correct place.

1 He succeeded in more about his team. (learn)
   He succeeded in learning more about his team.

2 What are the risks of eights cups of coffee a day? (drink)
   _____

3 We really like the idea of him to visit us this summer. (come)
   _____

4 Martha and her husband were concerned about home in the heavy rain. (drive)
   _____

5 Christopher wondered about the possibility of a long vacation. (take)
   _____

6 We plan on this project by the end of the week. (finish)
   _____

3 GRAMMAR AND VOCABULARY

A Complete the sentences with a gerund and your own ideas.

1 I never plan on _____ my facial features because _____ .
2 I sometimes think about _____ my look so I can _____ .
3 The risks of _____ to change your build are _____ .
4 The idea of _____ a look-alike somewhere in the world is _____ .
5 Some benefits of _____ a female might be _____ .

YOU, THE CUSTOMER

1 VOCABULARY: Describing research

A **Complete the sentences with one of the word pairs from the box. Write *N* (noun) or *V* (verb) to show how each word is used in the sentence.**

analyze/analysis	assess/assessment	calculate/calculation	demonstrate/demonstration
~~examine/examination~~	identify/identification	survey/survey	

1 a They need to _____*examine*_____ the chemical content in the metal.   V

    b Once the data is collected, there will be a/an _____*examination*_____ of it.   N

2 a Let me give you a/an _____ on how this works.

    b He wanted to _____ to her how it works.

3 a They had to show their _____ before entering the building.

    b The research will be used to _____ training needs.

4 a They collect the data and _____ the store profits.

    b If their _____ is wrong, they have to collect new data.

5 a It's too early to _____ if the product will be successful.

    b Her _____ of the production cost was completely inaccurate.

6 a A recent _____ showed that teenagers prefer to shop online.

    b The researchers had to _____ two age groups for their report.

7 a Simon's team had to _____ ways to re-route heavy traffic.

    b This part of the project still needs a complete _____ .

2 GRAMMAR: Causative verbs

A **Complete the sentences with the correct form of the verb in parentheses.**

1 Working at night allows him _____to go_____ (go) to school during the day.

2 The school lets parents _____ (know) if their child needs help.

3 You need to protect your identity from _____ (be) stolen online.

4 Computerization should enable them _____ (reduce) staffing costs.

5 If you wait here, we will have someone _____ (collect) it for you.

6 A system failure can cause everyone _____ (panic).

7 It's important to keep this information from _____ (reach) your senior staff.

8 Our manager sometimes makes us _____ (stay) late on the weekends.

9 Unfortunately, her sprained ankle prevents her from _____ (drive).

10 They put up barriers on the highway to stop cars from _____ (enter).

B **Check (✓) the correct sentences. Correct the incorrect sentences.**

1 Online shopping allows people ~~having~~ more time to themselves.   (to have)   ☐

2 Security guards prevent people from stealing items from the store.   ✓

3 Having a good marketing strategy causes people wanting to buy more.   ☐

4 Something must be done to stop them from arguing.   ☐

5 Is this something they make all employees doing after their training?   ☐

6 The new procedure has everyone to sign in first before their shift.   ☐

7 The phone app lets you to know how much you have spent in the store.   ☐

8 Georgina's shoes enabled her walking comfortably around the mall.   ☐

3 GRAMMAR AND VOCABULARY

A **Circle the correct word and then complete the sentences with your own ideas.**

1 When people (calculate) / calculation their yearly budgets, it keeps _them from spending too much money_ .

2 Analyzing / analysis shopping trends allows _____ .

3 Using fake identify / identification can prevent _____ .

4 Demonstrate / demonstrating a new product on TV lets _____ .

5 Industry surveys / survey enables _____ .

6 Assess / assessing a product and its reviews makes _____ .

7 The examine / examination of people selling their products online has stopped some _____ .

1 LISTENING

A 🔊 10.01 **Listen to Anton talk about two jobs. What are they? How does he feel about them?**

B 🔊 10.01 **LISTEN FOR CONTRASTING IDEAS** **Listen to the conversation again. Are Anton's ideas about the research company (R) or the sales company (S)? Which job does he like most? Which job would you choose?**

1 Everyone looked happy there.   S
2 The work is similar to my current job.   _____
3 I'll be able to walk to work.   _____
4 I can make good money.   _____
5 I'd be responsible for a lot of the research.   _____
6 I'd use my sales skills.   _____
7 The pay isn't great.   _____
8 It'll be long hours.   _____
9 I'll learn more.   _____

2 CRITICAL THINKING

A **THINK CRITICALLY** **How can you tell by looking at a company online that it would be a good place to work? Think of three important things that you would look for.**

_____
_____
_____
_____
_____

3 SPEAKING

A **Complete the phrases with a word in the box.**

far	funny	gut	hunch
~~impression~~	judging	see	strikes

1 **A** You look happy today.

   B I get the _____impression_____ that everything went well at the meeting last night.

2 **A** Sandra still hasn't shown up to work.

   B I have a _____ feeling that she might not come in at all.

3 **A** Michael doesn't seem himself lately.

   B I have a _____ that he's going to quit soon.

4 **A** She left a big mess in the kitchen this morning.

   B _____ by appearance, she must've been in a rush.

5 **A** Their house is so big!

   B What _____ me about their house is that even though it's big, it still feels cozy.

6 **A** It's dark and there are no cars parked outside.

   B As _____ as I can tell, the restaurant is closed.

7 **A** She looks good in that dress.

   B From what I can _____, she's on a new diet.

8 **A** The technology company is doing very well.

   B My _____ feeling is that more people will apply to work here.

B **Look at the photos. Give your impressions about the two places. Use some of the expressions from exercise 3A.**

1   Restaurant 1

1 _____

 Restaurant 2

2 _____

2   Beach 1

1 _____

 Beach 2

2 _____

3   Workplace 1

1 _____

 Workplace 2

2 _____

A PROFESSIONAL PROFILE

1 READING

A How can a company make more money with a professional profile? Read the article. Were your ideas the same as those in the article?

⊗ ▣ ⊖

WRITE A COMPANY PROFILE THAT WINS BUSINESS

An attractive company profile is a great way to get potential customers to buy from you. Here are a few tips that will help you write the perfect profile.

1 Think about what customers want to know and adjust your content accordingly

Content is often based on what the company thinks their potential clients want to know. Before you prepare your document, you need to understand exactly what your potential clients would want to know about you.

2 Gather feedback

If you don't have a company profile, talk to the clients you already have, your friends, or your family. Ask them what questions they have about your products or services and try to provide the answers when you create the profile.

3 Update your current profile

If you already have a company profile, ask a few clients for their honest feedback on it. Think about the questions you are most frequently asked by your customers. These questions point to issues you'll need to address when you update your profile.

4 Use images

A lot of companies don't use images in their company profile, and this is a missed opportunity. If you're including information on the business owner and staff members, put photos next to their profiles. This helps to build a connection between the company and the client. You may also consider including a photo of your building or office.

5 Strengthen your brand

A company profile can be used to outline and reinforce what your business is about and establish your identity in the marketplace. Don't forget to use your logo and company colors. This will ensure that your customers will always know who you are. It also makes your profile look more professional.

B **TAKE NOTES** Read the article again. Take notes about each of the five points. Then summarize each point with a sentence.

2 CRITICAL THINKING

A **THINK CRITICALLY** Imagine you're a small business owner. If you want to win more business, what questions would you ask your customers?

_____

_____

_____

3 WRITING

A Read an excerpt from a company profile. <u>Underline</u> the language that is too informal. Is there any language that is considered too formal?

👤 COMPANY PROFILE

Write Design is a self-publishing company for the young and old, and everyone in between! Write Design makes it super easy for you to design, publish, and promote your book. You can probably sell a lot of the professional-quality printed books and eBooks that we will make for you.

WD was founded by Liza Demetria in 2012. She is an author herself. She is working with a team of designers and media experts who share a passion for helping people bring their stories to life. Write Design authors have created a ton of books using their collection of book-making tools. A new book is created almost every minute! They are based in New York with offices in London …

B **USE PROFESSIONAL LANGUAGE** Write a better version of the company profile in exercise A using more professional language. Add more details using ideas from the box or some of your own.

- She has over 10 years of publishing experience.
- She has worked for one of the biggest publishing companies in the world.
- She started writing at the age of five and learned from her grandmother who wrote a bestseller.
- She knows how tough the publishing industry is.
- Millions of Write Designs books have been sold on Amazon.
- Books are her business.

CHECK AND REVIEW

Read the statements. Can you do these things?

UNIT 10	Mark the boxes. ☑ I can do it. ？ I am not sure. I can …	If you are not sure, go back to these pages in the Student's Book.
VOCABULARY	☐ people's characteristics. ☐ customer research.	page 98 page 100
GRAMMAR	☐ use gerunds after prepositions. ☐ use complements of verbs describing cause and effect.	page 99 page 101
LISTENING AND SPEAKING SKILLS	☐ listen for contrasting ideas. ☐ give your impressions.	page 102 page 103
READING AND WRITING SKILLS	☐ take notes. ☐ write a professional profile.	page 104 page 105

11.1   FAKE!

---

1   **VOCABULARY: Describing consumer goods**

A   (Circle) the correct meaning of each vocabulary word.

1   fake
   a   an object that is made to look real or valuable   **b**   an object that is real or valuable

2   genuine
   a   real, exactly what it appears to be   **b**   not real, not what it appears to be

3   imperfect
   a   in perfect condition   **b**   damaged, has problems

4   authentic
   a   real, true, or what people say it is   **b**   not real, false, not what people say it is

5   legal
   a   not allowed by the law   **b**   allowed by the law

6   deadly
   a   likely to cause death   **b**   unlikely to cause death

7   fireproof
   a   able to be damaged by fire   **b**   unable to be damaged by fire

8   illegal
   a   allowed by the law   **b**   not allowed by the law

9   sophisticated
   a   made in a complicated way   **b**   made in an uncomplicated way

10   counterfeit
   a   made to look like the real thing   **b**   made to look better than the real thing

11   original
   a   related to a first or real product   **b**   related to copies of a real product

12   second-rate
   a   cheaply made   **b**   well made

13   inferior
   a   not as good as something else   **b**   just as good as something else

2 GRAMMAR: Passive forms

A **Underline the passive form in each sentence.**

1 These watches <u>are not always made</u> of quality material.

2 It's unlikely that the company will be stopped from producing these cheap products.

3 Two pink handbags were sold in the store last week.

4 Counterfeit watches were discovered while they were being sold on the streets.

5 Nothing is going to be sold by the athletic company this year.

6 The original painting was created by Sergio.

B **Rewrite the sentences using the correct form of the verbs in parentheses.**

1 The shoes _____*are made*_____ by a small, Italian company. (make)

2 Our house _____ by a professional company next year. (renovate)

3 The little dog _____ in her oversized handbag. No one saw it. (carry)

4 Instructions _____ to you in the next few days. (sent)

5 The operation was a success. All the counterfeit money _____ by the police. (collect)

6 Illegal copies of the movies _____ by many of the stores. (sell)

7 The store is closing. Everything _____ at half price.(sell)

8 The problem is that second-rate items _____ to last long. (not design)

3 GRAMMAR AND VOCABULARY

A **Complete the sentences with your own ideas. Use passive forms.**

1 The genuine leather shoes _____*were being sold at a much higher price*_____ .

2 Delicious food _____ at the authentic Italian restaurant.

3 Deadly chemicals _____ to make the jeans.

4 Sophisticated counterfeits _____ all over the internet.

5 It's unlikely that imperfect t-shirts _____ at the music festival.

6 Illegal copies of the artist's drawings _____ .

7 A waterproof and fireproof product _____ .

8 The fake gold necklaces _____ .

11.2 INTERNET TALES

1 VOCABULARY: Degrees of truth

A Circle the correct words to complete the sentences.

1 If you don't tell the truth, you're being *dishonest* / *honest*.
2 When you tell a lie to stop someone from being hurt, you tell a *suspicious* / *white* lie.
3 If people believe stories about something that actually never happened, then they fell for a *hoax* / *misinformation*.
4 A story or statement that's not true but is often repeated, and believed by many to be true, is an urban *legend* / *fact*.
5 When something is not completely correct, it is *accurate* / *inaccurate*.
6 When something is not real, it is *false* / *biased*.
7 If people feel that they can trust you, they call you *controversial* / *trustworthy*.
8 When you make something seem more important than it really is, it has been *exaggerated* / *misleading*.
9 You're *misleading* / *suspicious* when something doesn't seem right.
10 When a story could be true but might be invented, it is a *rumor* / *white lie*.
11 Something is *controversial* / *misinformation* when it causes disagreement and discussion.
12 If you like or dislike a person based on personal opinions, you are *suspicious* / *biased*.
13 It's *misinformation* / *controversial* when information is wrong or intended to deceive.
14 If a reporter uses a photo that suggests something that is not true, then the photo is *inaccurate* / *misleading*.
15 When something is exact and correct, it's *exaggerated* / *accurate*.

2 GRAMMAR: Passives with modals and modal-like expressions; passive infinitives

A Complete the sentences with *be* or *to be*.

1 Misleading stories shouldn't _____*be*_____ discussed on the news.
2 This new smartphone seems _____ the best thing since sliced bread.
3 That type of news has _____ stopped from reaching the students.
4 This story is a hoax and shouldn't _____ believed.
5 She didn't expect _____ given an award for her news stories.
6 This report needs _____ done by this afternoon.
7 That type of work couldn't _____ done by one person.
8 I didn't want _____ thought of as a dishonest person, so I told the truth.

84

B   **Complete the sentences with a modal or modal-like expression from the box. Use the correct verb tense.**

could	expect	have	must
~~need~~	seem	should	want

1   All news stories _____*need*_____ to be checked.

2   They didn't _____ their story to spread as quickly as it did.

3   All the information _____ be collected and recorded first.

4   You _____ better listen to him or you'll be fired from your job.

5   We _____ be given directions for how to use this machine. It's complicated.

6   This _____ to be an important issue these days.

7   Future problems _____ be avoided if you address these issues now.

8   Jenna didn't _____ to be part of our team anymore.

C   **THINK CRITICALLY**   **What do you think spreads faster: facts or lies? Give reasons why.**

_____

_____

_____

_____

_____

3   GRAMMAR AND VOCABULARY

A   **Write a sentence using the prompts and a word in the box. Use the passive forms with modals or modal-like expressions.**

~~accurate~~	false	hoax	misleading	rumor	trustworthy

1   only / information / report / news channel
    Only accurate information should be reported on a news channel.

2   story / tell / reporters

    _____

3   publish / stop / magazines

    _____

4   stories / research / source

    _____

5   information / check / report

    _____

6   dangerous / avoid / penalty

    _____

BELIEVE IT OR NOT ...

1 LISTENING

A 🔊 **11.01** **UNDERSTAND IMPORTANT DETAILS** **Listen to Chris and Adam talk about a possible hoax. Check (✓) the points people make to argue that the moon landing was fake.**

1 The American flag was waving, but there's no atmosphere on the moon. ☐

2 There isn't a big hole where the jet engine lifted off the moon. ☐

3 The moon reflects light from the sun. ☐

4 There were suspicious shadows and other light sources. ☐

5 Stars in the background cannot be seen when photographs were taken. ☐

6 The flag hangs completely limp in space when he steps away from it. ☐

7 The moon's atmosphere wouldn't have changed. ☐

B 🔊 **11.01** **Listen to the conversation again. Complete the sentences with a number from the box.**

21	billions	hundred	seven	ten	thirty

1 I heard that _____ percent of Americans now believe that the United States never went to the moon.

2 People talked about the American flag that was planted on the moon on July _____ , 1969.

3 The moon's atmosphere is something like _____ trillion times less dense than Earth's atmosphere.

4 There are _____ of stars in space.

5 The moon reflects about _____ percent of the light from the sun.

6 Over a _____ trustworthy scientists showed that this point, as well as the other points, were easily proven false.

2 CRITICAL THINKING

A **THINK CRITICALLY** **Which are more believable – the arguments for or against the moon landing? Give reasons why.**

_____

_____

_____

3 SPEAKING

A (Circle) the correct word and then write *B* (Belief), *S* (Some belief), or *D* (Disbelief) beside each expression.

1 **A** By 2030, everyone will be able to scan using their eyes.

   B There's no (truth) / *right* in that.   D

2 **A** I love to watch scary movies.

   B Really? I've never watched one in my entire life, *believe* / *like* it or not. _____

3 **A** Did you hear the story about the woman with three heads?

   B You're so funny! *Tell* / *don't tell* me another one. _____

4 **A** Eating only green vegetables can actually reverse the signs of aging.

   B Hmmm. I find that *easy* / *hard* to believe. _____

5 **A** So, that computer virus they warned us about was a hoax?

   B Yes, I'm absolutely *positive* / *right* it was. _____

6 **A** Did you hear about the new drug that can cure all diseases?

   B Yeah, *wrong* / *right*! _____

7 **A** She takes the subway to work every day because it's fast.

   B That's partly *true* / *false*. But she also doesn't like the bus. _____

8 **A** This story says that he lost his fortune because he was careless.

   B There's probably some *truth* / *belief* in that. _____

B **Express belief or disbelief about the rumors using the expressions from exercise 3A.**

1 Did you hear the rumor about <u>spaghetti</u> growing on <u>trees</u>?

   I did. There's no truth to it. Spaghetti is not a fruit or a nut.

2 Did you hear the rumor about an asteroid destroying Earth next year?

3 Do you think that dogs will really be able to talk one day?

4 I heard a rumor that people might soon be able to live to 150.

5 Drones are being used to find people lost at sea, believe it or not.

6 Someone said that by 2030, there won't be any clean water left in the world.

1 READING

A **Read the article about diamonds. How are "fake" diamonds different from "real" diamonds? How are they the same?**

REAL FAKE DIAMONDS

For centuries, diamonds have been a symbol of wealth, status, and love. They are the subject of legends, fairy tales, and Hollywood movies. We value diamonds for their beauty, of course, but mostly because they are rare and their number is finite.

The diamond in a ring today was formed millions of years ago. Deep inside the earth, under conditions of extreme heat and pressure, carbon was pressed and cooked into the hardest of minerals. Powerful eruptions – bigger than any current volcano could produce – brought them to the surface. The conditions necessary to create diamonds no longer exist naturally, but they can be simulated in a lab. Instead of millions of years, man-made diamonds can be created in about a month.

Chemically, man-made diamonds are exactly the same as natural diamonds: They are 100% carbon, formed by high heat and immense pressure. They look identical, too. Even professional jewelers have a hard time telling them apart. In fact, the only real difference is history. For some people, however, history matters. A natural diamond has flaws that make it imperfect but also unique. Man-made diamonds are "too perfect."

Man-made diamonds have advantages over natural ones, beyond their lower price (usually about 30% less). They are not politically controversial, like the so-called "blood diamonds" of the past. Best of all, man-made diamonds can be made to order. If you want a stone of a particular size and with a slight pink color, you don't have to search the world for it. Just tell the manufacturer when you place your order. In a few weeks, you'll have your own personalized real fake diamond.

B **UNDERSTAND WORDS IN CONTEXT** **Read the article again. Then <u>underline</u> the correct definitions of the words.**

1 beyond: *more than just / related to*

2 finite: *limited / unlimited*

3 flaw: *big difference / error or imperfection*

4 mineral: *a type of stone, like marble or coal / an element, like carbon or oxygen*

5 pressure: *space / force*

6 simulate: *to prove the accuracy of / to copy or recreate*

2 CRITICAL THINKING

A **THINK CRITICALLY** **Would you say that man-made diamonds are fake diamonds? Why or why not? Imagine you wanted to buy a piece of diamond jewelry today. Would you choose natural or man-made diamonds? Why? Give at least three reasons to explain your preference.**

3 WRITING

A Read the review about a face product. Does it sound fake? Would you want to try it? Why or why not? Underline the language used to persuade.

```
•••  ◁▷                                                    ⚲ ⌂
```

| HOME • ABOUT • NEWS • **BLOG** • CONTACT | SIGN IN |

Jessica M ★ ★ ★ ★ ★

Although some might say that MIRACLE FACE CREAM, a new anti-aging wrinkle cream on the market, doesn't work, I've tried it and I look younger!

This miracle cream can take years off your face in just three days. When I used it the first day, I could already see the difference. It erased all my lines and wrinkles. It's like an instant facelift. The special formula will make your skin look brighter and smoother, and if you have dark spots, they'll be completely gone, too.

Who needs plastic surgery when you have this cream? And the best thing about this cream is that you only need a small amount to cover your entire face. It's the best thing since sliced bread!

I firmly believe that this cream will be a success because it works. It's not cheap, but it's really worth it! And according to the company who makes it, they have a few celebrities who support it, too. I feel if the word gets out about this magic cream, you won't be able to order it anytime soon.

I hope you get the same amazing results that I've had with MIRACLE FACE CREAM!

Jessica

👍 Like   💬 Comment

B **USE PERSUASIVE LANGUAGE** Read the review again. Choose a product below and write a review with a strong opening sentence that gives the opposite opinion first. Use persuasive language.

hair thickener	nail polish	shampoo for dry hair
shaving cream	sunglasses	toothpaste whitener

CHECK AND REVIEW

Read the statements. Can you do these things?

UNIT 11	Mark the boxes. ☑ I can do it. ? I am not sure. I can …	If you are not sure, go back to these pages in the Student's Book.
VOCABULARY	☐ describe fake goods. ☐ talk about untrue information.	page 108 page 110
GRAMMAR	☐ use passive forms. ☐ use passive with modals and modal-like expressions, and passive infinitives.	page 109 page 111
LISTENING AND SPEAKING SKILLS	☐ listen for specific information. ☐ express belief and disbelief.	page 112 page 113
READING AND WRITING SKILLS	☐ work out meaning from context. ☐ write a persuasive essay.	page 114 page 115

12.1 PRACTICE MAKES PERFECT

1 VOCABULARY: Skill and performance

A Complete the sentences with the words in the box.

analytical	artistic	athletic	competent	~~determined~~
gifted	imaginative	intellectual	logical	musical
skilled	talented	technical	trained	

1 Sebastian was _____determined_____ to finish his medical degree to become a doctor.

2 I like romantic or funny movies, nothing too _____. I don't want to think too hard.

3 He's very _____ in the arts and will likely be famous one day.

4 Her _____ abilities show in every soccer game.

5 If I had any _____ ability, I'd make a painting for this wall.

6 It was the _____ thing to do in order to save time and money.

7 Luciana is not a/an _____ musician. She has just begun to play the guitar.

8 He hasn't shown himself to be very _____ at his job.

9 You have a/an _____ mind, so writing a story will be easy for you.

10 He has always been naturally _____, even from an early age.

11 She wasn't _____ properly to do this type of job.

12 I wish I could sing, but I have no _____ ability at all.

13 You need to have _____ and _____ skills if you want to be an engineer.

2 GRAMMAR: Adverbs with adjectives and adverbs

A Underline the adverb that provides more detail about the adjective or adverb in the sentence. Circle the modified word and identify it as *Adj.* (Adjective) or *Adv.* (Adverb) next to each sentence.

1 She became <u>amazingly</u> (quick) at solving math problems.   Adj

2 Some children are exceptionally bright. _____

3 I think she is really funny. _____

4 He picked up the baby extremely gently. _____

5 It'll sell especially well just by word of mouth. _____

6 Learning a new language never came particularly easily to me. _____

7 Can I be brutally honest with you? _____

8 Henry did a fairly good job on his English test. _____

B **Add more detail to each sentence by adding the adverb in parentheses.**

1 I thought she looked beautiful when she walked down the aisle. (amazingly)

   I thought she looked amazingly beautiful when she walked down the aisle.

2 But it's not true. (necessarily)

3 It's supposed to be cloudy tomorrow. (partly)

4 I'm excited about going backstage after the concert. (especially)

5 They weren't interested in buying the house, but they said they'd think about it. (particularly)

6 There was enough food in the cupboards. (barely)

7 There's plenty of food leftover after dinner. (always)

8 He walked quickly down the street. (rather)

3 GRAMMAR AND VOCABULARY

A **Write sentences using your own ideas and the word prompts.**

1 exceptionally / athletic

   She's exceptionally athletic when it comes to sports .

2 amazingly / intellectual

   .

3 especially / logical

   .

4 hardly / trained

   .

5 extremely / gifted

   .

6 particularly / musical

   .

B **Complete the sentences so that they are true for you. Use an adverb to modify the adjectives.**

1 I think I'm skilled at _____ .

2 I don't think I'm imaginative when it comes to _____ .

3 I'm competent at _____ .

4 When I was younger, I was talented at _____ .

5 I'm determined to _____ .

CHANGE THE WORLD

1 VOCABULARY: Describing emotional impact

A **Circle the correct word(s) in each sentence.**

1 He tried to ⟨raise her spirits⟩ / *ruin her day* by taking her out to a fancy restaurant.

2 All this extra work is going to *make my day* / *stress me out*.

3 I need to *take my mind off of this matter* / *raise somebody's spirits* for a while and just relax.

4 Taking a vacation right now might *make your day* / *do you good*.

5 The books he writes *capture the imagination of children* / *are a real downer* all over the world.

6 He *brightens up* / *gets down* just thinking about his boring job.

7 She *ruined my day* / *put my mind at rest* when she walked away without apologizing.

8 The memory of this vacation will *do me good* / *leave a lasting impression on me*.

9 Finding $10 on the bus today really *took my mind off* / *brightened up* my day.

10 Rainy days can *stress me out* / *be a real downer*. They make everything look so gray.

11 It *captured her imagination* / *made her day* when her best friend called.

12 Once you know the reason, you can relax and *brighten up* / *put your mind at rest*.

B **Complete the sentences using phrases from exercise 1A. More than one answer can be correct for some sentences.**

1 When my friend is down, I _____brighten up_____ her day with some chocolate ice cream.

2 Traffic in the morning can really _____ when I'm trying to get to work on time.

3 Taking the afternoon off to enjoy the sunny weather might _____ .

4 Seeing him cry can _____ for me.

5 Knowing Adam was safe at home _____ .

6 Her incredible story has _____ .

7 I need to leave the office for a while and _____ work.

8 The flowers he sent _____ .

2 GRAMMAR: Making non-count nouns countable

A **Complete the sentences with an expression in the box.**

a bunch of	a cup of	a piece of	a slice of	piece of	work of

1 Do you want to have _____a cup of_____ tea before you go?

2 She had _____ lemon pie for dessert.

3 This sculpture is a real _____ art.

4 I listened to a wonderful _____ music when I was at her house.

5 She bought _____ stuff at the store.

6 My professor gave me _____ advice about my future goals.

B Correct the mistake(s) in each sentence. Then <u>underline</u> the expression that makes the non-count noun countable.

1 Everyone should show <u>a little bits of</u> kindness to their neighbors.

2 I heard a great pieces of advice on the radio today.

3 I had a slice of cake and two cup of coffee for lunch today.

4 There was a bunches of newspaper on the table.

5 Ariana and her friends played a games of cards at the party.

6 Would you like a slices of cheese on your hamburger?

7 Can I have two piece of bread with my dinner?

3 GRAMMAR AND VOCABULARY

A Write sentences using your own ideas and the word prompts. Make the non-count nouns countable.

1 coffee / brighten up sth

   He brightened up my day when he bought me a cup of coffee .

2 music / capture sb's imagination

   _____ .

3 kindness / make sb's day

   _____ .

4 advice / raise sb's spirits

   _____ .

5 chess / take sb's mind off sth

   _____ .

6 art / leave a lasting impression on sb

   _____ .

7 cake / do sb good

   _____ .

B **THINK CRITICALLY** In your opinion, what are some things we could do to make someone's day positive? What are some things that might make someone's day negative?

MAYBE ONE DAY …

1 LISTENING

A 🔊 **12.01** **Listen to the conversation. Match each statement.**

1	Work	_d_	**a** can teach you how to write.
2	Develop	____	**b** the love of it.
3	There are many websites that	____	**c** technical skills.
4	There are a lot of workshops	____	**d** hard.
5	Write for	____	**e** you'll be successful at it.
6	Enjoy it and	____	**f** you can take.

B 🔊 **12.01** **LISTEN FOR CONTRASTING IDEAS** **Listen to the conversation again. Are the ideas optimistic or cautious? Write _O_ or _C_ next to each one.**

1 I can't say for certain that all these imaginative stories in my head will turn into books. _C_

2 But I'm confident that one day it'll happen. ____

3 I saw no reason why I couldn't. ____

4 There was no guarantee that it would happen. ____

5 There's no harm in trying to learn how to write. ____

6 Well, things might not go as planned. ____

2 CRITICAL THINKING

A **THINK CRITICALLY** **Do you think Valeria has the right attitude to become a famous author? Why or why not?**

_____

_____

_____

3 SPEAKING

A Complete the expressions with a word from the box. Then put them in the correct columns.

| certain | confident | guarantee | harm | planned | ~~reason~~ |

1 I see no _____reason_____ why (I can't).
2 I can't say for _____ .
3 I will do this. I'm _____ that …
4 I realize that things might not go as _____ .
5 There's no _____ in trying.
6 There's no _____ that …

Expressing optimism	Expressing caution
I see no reason why (I can't.)	

B For each situation, complete responses to express both optimism and caution. Use expressions from 3A.

1 Can you help me move some boxes this weekend?

   A _I see no reason why I can't. I'm not working_ .

   B _I can't say for certain, but I might be working_ .

2 I'd love to travel there one day.

   A _____ .

   B _____ .

3 My dream scenario would be to have my own business.

   A _____ .

   B _____ .

4 Can we try to get tickets to the game on Saturday?

   A _____ .

   B _____ .

5 My ultimate goal next year is to become a music teacher at this school.

   A _____ .

   B _____ .

95

SUCCESS BEHIND THE SCENES

1 READING

A   **Do you think working as an actress is fun and exciting? Read the article. Was your prediction correct? What was the day like for the actress?**

Life as an actress

By Mariel van White

Yesterday, I had the opportunity to spend the day with an amazingly talented actress, Ashley Stone. And from what I experienced, being an actress not only takes a lot of skill, but determination and patience, too.

As soon as she arrived to work, at 6.00 a.m., she got checked for hair, makeup, and wardrobe. These things need to be perfect when the camera is rolling. After that, she checked in with the assistant director to make sure there hadn't been any changes to her lines. There had—and it seems there are script changes most days—so she had to memorize them before she was called in front of the cameras.

When Ashley got to the set, the director and crew were busy setting up the scene with special lights and checking camera angles. She stood around waiting, and waiting … and then, when it was time to step in front of the cameras, someone had to adjust her makeup while the wardrobe assistant checked her outfit, again!

After an *exceptionally* long time, she got to say her lines. But right in the middle of them, the director shouted "Cut!" Something wasn't perfect. It was a missing light. There are little problems like this all the time on a movie set. Ashley just had to go back to her trailer to practice her lines again. When all the actors were called back to the set, the scene was shot before another break, this time for lunch. After lunch, Ashley and the other actors spent the rest of the day shooting scenes and rehearsing for the next day. Finally, but not until 10.00 p.m., someone called it a wrap—time for everyone to go home.

Fun? It certainly didn't seem like it. There was a lot of standing around. You need to be extremely focused and patient. That's part of what acting is all about. But Ashley told me it's worth it in the end because when the film is released, millions of people around the world will see her work on the big screen.

B   **UNDERSTAND CAUSE AND EFFECT** **Read again. What is/was the result of each of these events?**

1   The actress arrived to work.
2   The assistant director changed the lines.
3   There was a missing light.
4   Actors were called back to the set.
5   Someone called it a wrap.
6   The film is released.

2 CRITICAL THINKING

A   **THINK CRITICALLY** **Make a list of some other jobs that might seem exciting and fascinating, like an actor's. Choose one and think about what the reality of the job might be like.**

3 WRITING

A Read Amelia's review of a movie. Did she like it? Why or why not? <u>Underline</u> words that show reasons or results.

To: Christian
From: Amelia
Subject: Favorite Movies

Hi Christian,

I just got back from seeing the sequel to *After the Attack*. I know the first one was one of your favorite movies. But this one was really bad, so don't waste your time!

The special effects were done exceptionally well, but the dialogue and plot were too simple. It felt like it was made for kids, so I got bored halfway through. The acting was OK, but because of the unknown actors, I wasn't connecting to anyone. There was some beautiful scenery which was as impressive as the special effects, but nothing like the first movie. The scenes were too long and drawn out; consequently, I fell into a deep sleep.

Anyway, I thought I'd save you some money!

Can't wait to see you this weekend!

Amelia

B **SHOW REASON AND RESULT** Think about a movie you liked or didn't like. Write a review of it using words such as *so*, *therefore*, *as a result*, and *consequently*.

CHECK AND REVIEW

Read the statements. Can you do these things?

UNIT 12	Mark the boxes. ✔ I can do it. ? I am not sure. I can …	If you are not sure, go back to these pages in the Student's Book.
VOCABULARY	☐ talk about talents and skills. ☐ describe how to make life better.	page 118 page 120
GRAMMAR	☐ use adverbs with adjectives and adverbs. ☐ make non-count nouns countable.	page 119 page 121
LISTENING AND SPEAKING SKILLS	☐ describe your ambitions. ☐ express optimistic and cautious opinions.	page 122 page 123
READING AND WRITING SKILLS	☐ understand cause and effect. ☐ write a review of a performance.	page 124 page 125

EXTRA ACTIVITIES

1.5 TIME TO SPEAK A step forward

A   Talk to someone you know who is a generation or more older than you (parent, grandparent, teacher, etc.).
     Try to speak in English, if possible. Take notes in English. Use the questions below to help you.

- Ask how life was different in the past compared to the present.
- Ask about any new technology he or she witnessed, the type of clothes he or
  she wore, the different kinds of entertainment, what school was like, and so on.

B   During your next class, discuss your results with a classmate.

2.5 TIME TO SPEAK Natural limits

A   Search online for outdoor adventure travel companies. Look at a few different websites and identify an outdoor
     adventure you are interested in. Write down at least three questions you have about your selected trip and
     research the answers.

B   Tell a classmate about your activity. Did you have the same questions? How are your activities similar?

3.5 TIME TO SPEAK The way I am

A   Interview someone who has an interesting job. Interview the person in English, if possible. Take notes. Use the
     prompts below to help you.

- Ask the person to describe the job.
- Then ask what qualities a person should have in order to do the job well.

B   During your next class, share your findings with a classmate.

4.5 TIME TO SPEAK It takes a team

A   Think of or research a list of jobs you could do from home. Write the advantages and disadvantages of working
     from home.

Jobs you can do from home	Advantages	Disadvantages

B   Present your ideas in your next class. Compare your ideas with other students.

5.5 TIME TO SPEAK The human factor

A   Create a survey about cell phone behavior. Think of four or five questions to ask. Give the survey to your family and friends. Use the example questions below to help you.

> **Example survey questions**
> - Do you think it's OK to eat while you're talking on your cell phone?
> - What annoys you the most about other people's cell phone behavior?
> - Do you use your cell phone when you're in a restaurant? Why or why not?

B   Bring the results to your next class and share them with your classmates. Who had the most interesting survey questions and responses?

6.5 TIME TO SPEAK Expect the unexpected

A   Prepare to tell a story about one of the topics below. Make some notes. Practice telling your story by saying it out loud. You can also record yourself and listen to your story to see if you want to make any changes.

> **Topics:**
> - the worst haircut I ever received
> - the first/last day at my job or at school
> - a time when I miscommunicated with someone

B   Tell your story to a friend, family member, or classmate. Ask them if they have a story about a similar topic.

7.5 TIME TO SPEAK Negotiate for a price

A   Look for three to five items in your home that you no longer want. Answer the questions below for each item.

> - What makes the item worth selling?
> - What would be the highest price you would want to get for it?
> - What would be the lowest price you would sell it for?

B   Take your list of items to your next class. Bring photos of the items if you can. Negotiate and bargain for a price for other items in the classroom and for the items you are selling.

8.5 TIME TO SPEAK Make a podcast on ways to reduce stress

A   Think of the last time you were really stressed. Make notes. Use the questions below to help you.

> - What were you stressed about?
> - What action or actions did you take to reduce the stress?
> - Was this action simple and effective?

B   Share what happened and what you did in your next class.

EXTRA ACTIVITIES

9.5 TIME TO SPEAK Talk about key events in your life

A   **Think of important or interesting things you've done or experienced in the past five years. Use the questions below to help you.**

> - What have I done or experienced?
> - What have I been doing in my free time?
> - Do I have any regrets?
> - Have my relationships been good or bad?
> - Where have I traveled/worked?

B   **Share your list and then listen to a partner's list. Make positive comments about good things you hear and reassuring comments about not-so-good things.**

10.5 TIME TO SPEAK Attracting talent

A   **Go online and find three companies where experienced and talented employees would want to work. Use the questions below to help you.**

> - Who are they?
> - What do they do?
> - Why would employees like to work for them?
> - What makes their websites attractive?

B   **Create a presentation about your companies and bring it to your next class. What company would your class like to work for the most? What about the least? Ask the class to give you reasons.**

11.5 TIME TO SPEAK Does it really work?

A   **Think of a tip that you might follow when you are sick with a cold or flu. Use the questions below to help you.**

> - What is the tip?
> - Where did you find it?
> - What do you have to do?
> - How effective is it?

B   **In your next class, present your tip to the class. As a class, choose the tips you believe will be the most effective.**

12.5 TIME TO SPEAK Me, in two minutes

A   **Go online and research someone famous with a special talent. Use the questions below to help you.**

> - What skills does/did the person have?
> - Was the person born gifted or trained?
> - What has the person done?

B   **In your next class, pretend you are this person. Describe your talents and abilities for about two minutes to the class. The class then asks questions to find out who you are.**

The authors and publishers acknowledge the following sources of copyright material and are grateful for the permissions granted. While every effort has been made, it has not always been possible to identify the sources of all the material used, or to trace all copyright holders. If any omissions are brought to our notice, we will be happy to include the appropriate acknowledgments on reprinting & in the next update to the digital edition, as applicable.

Key: U = Unit.

Text

U9: Daniel Wendler for the adapted text from 'The Secret Of Conversation Flow', https://www.improveyoursocialskills.com/conversation/conversation-flow. Copyright © Daniel Wendler. Reproduced with kind permission. **U10:** The Professional Writer for the adapted text from 'How to write a Company Profile that wins business' by LYNDALL. Copyright © The Professional Writer. Reproduced with kind permission of Lyndall Guinery-Smith.

Photographs
The following photographs are sourced from Getty Images.

U1: Absodels/ABSODELS/Getty Images Plus; Alistair Berg/DigitalVision; Cavan Images/Cavan; Chris Tobin/DigitalVision; Steve Debenport/E+; Hemant Mehta; Schon & Probst/Picture Press/Getty Images Plus; **U2:** Stocktrek Images; Monty Rakusen/Cultura; Rohit Singh/EyeEm; Photography by Thy Bun/Moment Open; Stuart Westmorland/Corbis Documentary/Getty Images Plus; shalamov/iStock/Getty Images Plus; A. Martin UW Photography/Moment; Rob Janné/500px Prime; Westend61; **U3:** Dougal Waters/DigitalVision; Carlina Teteris/Moment; Caiaimage/Lukas Olek; -goldy-/iStock/Getty Images Plus; monkeybusinessimages/iStock/Getty Images Plus; Tomas Rodriguez/Corbis; Tom Kelley Archive/Retrofile RF; **U4:** Maskot; LightFieldStudios/iStock/Getty Images Plus; shapecharge/E+; Caiaimage/Paul Bradbury; Hoxton/Tom Merton; skynesher/E+; portishead1/E+; Hero Images/DigitalVision; **U5:** GSPictures/E+; Westend61; Compassionate Eye Foundation/Dan Kenyon/DigitalVision; Hero Images; Sasha Bell/Moment; Caiaimage/Paul Bradbury; **U6:** Jupiterimages/Stockbyte; oberschneider/RooM; Fancy/Veer/Corbis; Westend61; Hero Images; Hero Images; David Oliver/Taxi/Getty Images Plus; Fresh photos from all over the worls/Moment; **U7:** Westend61; LenaSkor/iStock/Getty Images Plus; blue jean images; Anfisa Kameneva/EyeEm; claudio.arnese/E+; Maskot; Tim Robberts/Taxi/Getty Images Plus; **U8:** Kathleen Finlay/Image Source; Westend61; skynesher/E+; FangXiaNuo/E+; WHL; **U9:** sturti/E+; Neustockimages/E+; Deagreez/iStock/Getty Images Plus; Maskot; bernardbodo/iStock/Getty Images Plus; **U10:** Eugenio Marongiu/Cultura; Hero Images; PeopleImages/E+; F.J. Jiménez/Moment; MangoStar_Studio/iStock/Getty Images Plus; mustafagull/E+; Petardj/iStock/Getty Images Plus; John Harper/Moment; levente bodo/Moment; pixelfit/E+; skynesher/E+; gradyreese/E+; **U11:** JAY DIRECTO/AFP; mustafagull/E+; Strauss/Curtis; Mihajlo Maricic/EyeEm; World Perspectives/Photographer's Choice/Getty Images Plus; Photographer is my life/Moment; mevans/E+; **U12:** andresr/E+; Michael Blann/DigitalVision; Hinterhaus Productions/Taxi/Getty Images Plus; Chaiyaporn Baokaew/Moment; Westend61; Paolo Sartori; Yurdakul/E+.

Front cover photography by Hans Neleman/The Image Bank/Getty Images Plus/Getty Images.

Typeset by emc design ltd.

Audio
Audio production by CityVox, New York.

URL
The publisher has used its best endeavors to ensure that the URLs for external websites referred to in this book are correct and active at the time of going to press. However, the publisher has no responsibility for the websites and can make no guarantee that a site will remain live or that the content is or will remain appropriate.

Corpus
Development of this publication has made use of the Cambridge English Corpus (CEC). The CEC is a multi-billion word collection of contemporary spoken and written English. It includes British English, American English, and other varieties. It also includes the Cambridge Learner Corpus, the world's biggest collection of learner writing, developed in collaboration with Cambridge Assessment. Cambridge University Press uses the CEC to provide evidence about language use that helps to produce better language teaching materials. Our Evolve authors study the Corpus to see how English is really used, and to identify typical learner mistakes. This information informs the authors' selection of vocabulary, grammar items and Student's Book Corpus features such as the Accuracy Check, Register Check, and Insider English.